BEYOND PROGRESS

BEYOND PROGRESS

AN INTERPRETIVE

ODYSSEY TO THE

FUTURE

Hugh De Santis

The University of Chicago Press
CHICAGO & LONDON

Hugh De Santis is professor of international security affairs at the National War College in Washington, D.C. He is the author of *The Diplomacy of Silence: The American Foreign Service, the Soviet Union, and the Cold War, 1933–1947,* also published by the University of Chicago Press.

The University of Chicago Press, Chicago 60637
The University of Chicago Press, Ltd., London
© 1996 by The University of Chicago
All rights reserved. Published 1996
Printed in the United States of America
05 04 03 02 01 00 99 98 97 96   54321

ISBN (cloth): 0-226-14295-7
ISBN (paper): 0-226-14296-5

Library of Congress Cataloging-in-Publication Data

De Santis, Hugh.
    Beyond progress : an interpretive odyssey to the future / Hugh De Santis.
       p.   cm.
    Includes index.
    ISBN 0-226-14295-7 (alk. paper).—ISBN 0-226-14296-5 (pbk.) :
    1. World politics—1989– .   2. Social change.   I. Title.
    D860.D47   1996
    909.82′9—dc20   95-37971
                                                                   CIP

For Alexander George

"It is perfectly true . . . that life must be understood backwards. But . . . it must be lived forwards."

Kierkegaard

CONTENTS

This book was conceived in 1988, conceptualized in 1990, and written and revised in 1993–94. It originated in the turbulence of social and political change the world experienced at the end of the 1980s and in the search for its meaning. It seemed to me that the much-acclaimed attempts to account for global change reduced complex phenomena to simplistic formulas presented with an air of religious certainty. I refer to the "endism" popularized by Paul Kennedy's theory of great-power ascendancy and decline, Francis Fukuyama's end-of-history thesis, and, in the same spirit, the spate of books and articles declaring the dawn of a Pacific century that were inspired in part by Ezra Vogel's decade-earlier paean to Japan Inc. Even more disturbing was the rapturous public response, particularly in the United States, to these eschatological utterances, the power of which seemed to have dispossessed entire societies of critical thought. It was in this milieu, and in a decidedly agnostic frame of mind, that I grew interested in the vagaries of change and set out on a journey through time and space that has taken me from the recesses of the past into the void of the future.

To be sure, every age is an age of change. But not all change is the same. The cataclysmic change that precludes the effective operation of social structures and processes and destroys long-held convictions about the world in which we live will have a greater effect on humanity than will the gentle, containable ripples of change that lie between such historic disjunctions. Knowing the difference between what I have referred to as "evolutionary" versus "epochal" or "historic" change does not imply that one is removed from the flow of time and events—suspended above the fray, as it were. Quite the contrary, knowledge, particularly synoptic knowledge, derives from one's self-conscious immersion in the wave of change, or from one's "lived-experience." This fusion of subject and object is what sociologists refer to as "participation-observation." It is the empathic understanding of the whole being that underlies psychotherapy, the artistic distance of the painter and the poet.

In the journey that follows, I have tried to accomplish three objectives. The most important of these was to challenge the superficial and the facile and the intellectual conformity they produce. In the first instance, this is a book about the complexity of life and the eternal human struggle to impute meaning to a world that is both limited and contingent. In addition, I have sought to describe the manifold trends that are slowly and inconspicuously transforming old patterns of social behavior and incipiently stimulating people everywhere to impart new meaning to the change they are helping to create. My third aim was to conceptualize change, that is, to create an intellectual framework that would give coherence to the disparate but mutually reinforcing trends I have defined. Conceptualizing change has more than abstract value. For policy makers, understanding the international milieu in which one is operating must precede the evaluation of alternative courses of action.

Despite some suggestive concluding observations about the changing nature of the structures and processes of international relations in the dawning future, however, this book is not a policy primer. It does not prescribe a set of initiatives that, if implemented, will facilitate an effective, orderly transition from the modern to the postmodern world. Indeed, it makes no attempt to predict the future. This book is, rather, an interpretive discourse on the creative tension between social structures and processes, on the one hand, and belief systems or ideologies, on the other. It views change holistically rather than as the sum of its parts. It searches for the generalizations that underlie the particular, the potential, and the unique. It focuses on trends and patterns of human development rather than on empirically deduced elements of social continuity and discontinuity.

Nor is this book a historical treatise. It does not pretend to break new ground on some unexplored aspect of the human record. It is neither a comprehensive accounting of historical change in all its human and cultural variation nor a detailed investigation of the transformative processes of the past. Because it is a synthesis of a huge span of time, it unavoidably pays short shrift to discrete periods or events or peoples or classes in the evolution of humanity, as historians who have devoted their lives to particular areas of research will readily acknowledge. Indeed, it relies on the expertise of recognized authorities in their fields rather than primary sources. It should be added that this book betrays a Western bias that reflects both the increased westernization of world affairs after the sixteenth century and my own cultural orientation.

Finally, this book does not aim to establish a normative framework for responding to the emerging future, and the use of the term "mutualism" should not be so interpreted. In contrast to the array of literature that is engaged in the search of ways to create a functional utopia, this study self-consciously avoids any attempt to interpret the future in accord with "universal" values or "oughtness." What I present is neither an optimistic nor pessimistic agenda for the future, but a possibilistic approach to socially transforming change. Cultural, philosophical, and religious differences aside, humanity may develop certain shared norms of behavior. But such norms will necessarily derive from the competitive interests of peoples, not from a moral calling.

In short, *Beyond Progress* is a speculative inquiry, but one that is informed by the complexity of social and historical change. It explores the interaction between social process and ideas, on the one hand, and between subsystems of the larger international system and the world as an integrated community, on the other. Rather than concentrate on a particular unit of analysis, this study takes into account political, social, cultural, economic, ethnic, and religious factors.

The intellectual foundation of the argumentation is a hybrid of phenomenology, specifically the phenomenology of existence, cognitive dissonance theory, and the epistemology of Michael Polanyi. It is my belief, as these pages will show, that there is no immanent truth guiding humanity through history. Nor is there a scientific model that will operationally predict the future in linear progression from the present. The future is an interpretation of reality. It is what we imagine it to be in the context of our awareness of the possibilities and limitations of the objective world and our awareness of ourselves participating in the world. The epoch of mutualism that is examined in these pages is one interpretation of the future. It may be faulty, biased, or simply inaccurate. It may turn out that humanity is not in the formative stages of mutualism after all.

Conceptually, this book is divided into three parts, each of which comprises three chapters. Part 1 (chapters 1–3) examines the ideology of "endism" generated by the writings of Ezra Vogel, Paul Kennedy, and Francis Fukuyama and its special fascination for Americans. Chapter 1 is a *mise-en-scène;* it is a critical assessment of the concepts of the Pacific Century, great-power decline, and the end of history. This chapter is intended to establish the contemporary relevance for the journey that follows, particularly for the trend analysis in chapter 7 and the alternative postmodern future of mutualism that is the primary focus of the book. Chapter 2 analyzes the intense reaction to "endism" in the United States in the context of America's cultural experience and its unique interpretation of historical change. These chapters provide grist for the conceptualization of historical change in chapter 3 and for the ensuing periodization of human history. The themes articulated in part 1 prepare the ground for the discussion of mutualism in part 3.

Part 2 (chapters 4–6) offers an interpretation of the two great epochs of human history preceding the watershed that we presently face and of the dialectics of change that eventually led to their collapse as social and ideological frameworks for the future. Chapter 4 addresses the preoccupation of civilization from antiquity through the millennium after Christ with the maintenance of order in a mysterious, unpredictable, and predatory world. It introduces the theme of social inclusivism/exclusivism, which provides a backdrop to the discussion of modernity that follows in the next chapter. Chapter 5 explores the rise of individualism and science and the consolidation of political and economic activity in an increasingly Eurocentric world order that is morally and intellectually legitimized by a belief in human progress. Chapter 6 elaborates on the divergence between the ideology of progress and the social and economic realities of everyday life introduced in chapter 5. It analyzes the evolution of anti-Western westernization and its excesses as well as the conditions that have eroded the social and intellectual foundations of unlimited progress.

These chapters provide a necessary introduction to part 3 and also intellectually reinforce the case I am making for historical change. In order to assert that the world community is undergoing a process of socially transforming change, it is logically incumbent on me to answer the question, change from what? The chapter on modernity and progress lays out the institutional and intellectual trends that differentiate the recent past from the emerging future. To strengthen my argument for epochal change, which is what this book is about, it is equally important to show that the epoch of progress is not merely a contrivance used to make an a priori case for mutualism; hence, the need for chapter 4.

Furthermore, the chapters in Part 2 animate the abstract discussion in chapter 3 about real and perceived change. We are constantly making the future; in so doing, we necessarily rewrite the past. What these brief historical excursions attempt to demonstrate is that successive generations never understand the past in the same way as those who lived it because the circumstances of their lives and what is meaningful to them is different. It is when our lives cannot be reconciled with the past, and when we are therefore severed from the future, that we face the watershed of epochal change.

Part 3 (chapters 7–9) projects the present and the past (Parts 1 and

2) into the future. It elaborates on trends driving international affairs, explores the emergence of the epoch of mutualism, and reflects on the indeterminacy of human choice as we plunge into the unknown. Chapter 7 identifies five discrete but mutually reinforcing trends that are transforming the world and thus the conduct of international relations: technological diffusion, ecological erosion, migratory flux, political decentralization, and economic consolidation. Collectively these trends, which we are simultaneously shaping and being shaped by, are giving rise to a future that will impel the human community to establish new social orientations and beliefs to redress the anxiety of change.

Chapter 8 develops the social and intellectual framework of mutualism as one option for redefining relations between peoples and states in the context of shared risks and rewards. This chapter explores nascent signs that the world is becoming an interrelated network of relations in which self-interest and the need for affiliation are likely to become consonant with the common good. It further suggests that regionalism may be the operative structure of international relations in the future. As chapter 9 points out, whether mutualism or the emergence of new competing power blocs or global anarchy defines the future will depend on which choices the human community makes. The future is neither historically predetermined nor the product of a scientifically derived computer model. It is what we make it.

THIS PROJECT was a daunting undertaking from start to finish, and it could not have been completed without the emotional support of friends and colleagues. Words fail adequately to express my heartfelt gratitude to Deborah Wustner De Santis for finding the strength and love to see me through the rigors of research and writing. Dr. Richard Sutton, Bruce Nardulli, Bowman Miller, Robert Manning, Yve Laudy, and Robert Hansen revived sagging spirits at critical moments in my journey.

Intellectual assistance came from many quarters and in different ways, from friends and associates in the United States and abroad, from scholars as well as practitioners. It would be impossible to list the countless people who challenged assumptions, corrected misconceptions, and otherwise helped me to refine my thinking on the ideas that are expressed in this book. However, several people deserve to be singled out for their generosity and support. Larry Fabian, currently at the Council on Foreign Relations but at Carnegie Endowment for International Peace when this book was conceived, provided critical advice during the conceptualization of the project. James Rosenau, formerly of the University of

Southern California and now at George Washington University, provided help in the preparation of the research design. Carl Builder and Dr. Thomas Lincoln of the RAND Corporation helped me to develop the framework of analysis. Robert Lieber, chair of the Department of Government at Georgetown University, made it possible for me to use the facilities at Lauinger Library.

My greatest debt is to those friends and colleagues who read and commented on the manuscript in its entirety and who helped to improve it. I am deeply grateful to Alexander George for his early encouragement of the idea for the book, his substantive criticism of the manuscript, and his support in helping this project see the light of day. I also wish to express my gratitude to Frank Ninkovich for his critical historical mind, his openness to new ideas and methods of analysis, and his inexhaustible supply of source materials. Thanks are also due to Eric Willenz for his philosophical insights, his vast knowledge of international affairs, and his judicious advice on all manner of intellectual inquiry. I further want to thank Paul Gallis for his keen editorial eye and for imparting his erudite knowledge of antiquity and the Middle Ages to an amateur medievalist.

Despite the generous assistance I have received, I alone bear responsibility for whatever errors and inconsistencies lurk in these pages. I am hopeful, however, that such flaws will not detract from the concept that underlies this book, the value of which does not lie in its rightness or wrongness or its analytical prescience, but in its appeal to escape the conformity of mind that inhibits us from risking the possible.

The New Ideology

In 1979, in the lingering afterglow of the American bicentenary, a new book by a Harvard professor somberly announced that the United States was about to be overtaken by Japan as the world's preeminent economic power. A decade or more earlier, when General Motors and IBM were the international standards for automotive and technological excellence and the dollar ruled the world's markets, such a funereal message would have been ridiculed. By the beginning of the 1980s, however, such shimmering symbols of American global dominance had lost their luster, much as the American public had lost confidence in the nation's economic resiliency.

THESES

America Eclipsed

Ezra Vogel's *Japan as Number One* was more than a eulogy to Japan's post–World War II economic miracle.[1] It was also a primer for post-industrial America. As suggested by the subtitle, "Lessons for America," the book extolled Japan as a model of social engineering. With its communitarian spirit, informed citizenry, and efficiency in production, Japan was portrayed as an enviable contrast to the industrial sclerosis, political gridlock, and urban decay that formed the mosaic of America in the post-Watergate–Vietnam era.

The popular image of Japan as the new economic superpower hardened in the early 1980s. This was partly the result of the recession in the United States and President Ronald Reagan's restrictive monetary policies, which increased domestic interest rates and inflated the dollar in foreign exchange markets. But it also reflected the growing view that the

economic future lay in the Pacific, with Japan and the dynamic economies of East and Southeast Asia.

The statistics were incontestable. By the end of the 1980s, Japan was
running a trade surplus in manufactured products with every country in
the world. It had supplanted the United States as the world's creditor,
and it had become the leading dispenser of foreign aid. As a result of
ballooning current-account surpluses, Japanese capital poured into the
United States at a furious pace. Suddenly rich Japanese were everywhere,
caught up in a seemingly indiscriminate and, as far as one could tell,
insatiable buying frenzy that included the purchase of such cultural landmarks as Radio City Music Hall, Rockefeller Center, Columbia Pictures,
and the Pebble Beach golf course. The Pacific Century had arrived.[2]

The economic explosion in Japan and in the Asia–Pacific region as
a whole proved more than a little unsettling to Americans. The fright-
ening perception that the United States was for sale or, worse, on sale
unleashed a spate of books and articles that vilified Japan for being an
economic predator. The publication of *The Japan That Can Say No,* a
shrill, nationalistic polemic that predicted Japan's economic eclipse of
the United States, did not help to moderate anti-Japanese sentiment.
"The calendar clearly indicates that we are moving toward the end of a
century," co-author Shintaro Ishihara ominously predicted, and with it
is coming the end of the modern era as developed by white Westerners.
History," he triumphantly pronounced, "is entering a period of new
genesis."[3] Worse still was the flood of U.S.–Japanese trade disputes over
automobiles, steel, and semiconductors that impassioned American critics attributed to Tokyo's nefarious trading practices.

The stereotype of Japan as an unfair, even conspiratorial, economic
competitor has provoked different reactions in the United States. Some
analysts urge the adoption of an industrial policy to promote and, where
necessary, subsidize American exports and protect domestic markets,
more or less simulating Japan's practice of managed trade. Cultures,
however, are not fungible. Unlike Japan, where the symbiosis between
government and industry is a historical survival of that country's feudal
past, government-business relations in the United States tend to be
adversarial.[4]

Others prefer to rationalize the disparities between the economies of
the two countries. Among the more imaginative rationalizations is Zbigniew Brzezinski's proposal for a mutually cooptative military-economic
joint venture, whereby the Japanese would supply capital and technological expertise to the United States in exchange for America's continu-

ing security commitment and unfettered access to its markets. Such a relationship, Brzezinski reckons, could be transformed into an organic partnership that he calls "Amerippon,"[5] although who the Amerippon-ians would be is anyone's guess.

A third way of dealing with Japan's economic might is to direct one's anger at the perceived guilty party. "Japan bashing" takes many forms, most of which are verbal assaults on Japan's restrictive trading practices and its refusal to assume more extensive military responsibilities than its U.S.-drafted constitution permits. It sometimes manifests itself in violent acts, however, as was the case in 1988, when four congressmen who ostensibly were outraged by Toshiba's sale of militarily transferable tech-nology to the Soviet Union publicly sledge-hammered products manu-factured by the company on the Capitol lawn.

America-in-Decline

Still another response to the impending Pacific Century is to accede to the painful reality that the United States is a nation in decline. This was the message that catapulted British historian Paul Kennedy's otherwise dry disquisition of *The Rise and Fall of the Great Powers* onto the best-seller list in 1988. Although it was a popular seller in Japan and Europe, and mandatory reading among reformers in the rickety Soviet Union, the book enjoyed its greatest success in the United States. Kennedy's thesis validated the pervasive pessimism that had emerged in cultural counter-point to the indefatigable frontier optimism of Ronald Reagan's "Morn-ing in America" campaign.[6]

According to Kennedy, the rise and fall of states, like the growth and decay of other organisms, was governed by the laws of nature. The history of the past 500 years revealed an immutable causal relationship between a nation's economic and productive capabilities and its growth and decline as a military power. Whereas a country's ability to expand militarily and exercise international power depends on the accretion of national wealth, its propensity to devote increasing sums to maintain its global security commitments ultimately weakens its economic po-sition and hastens its decline. Such an unhappy fate now awaited the United States, which also had fallen victim to the affliction of "imperial overstretch."

The coincidence of this historical dirge with Japanese economic ex-pansionism seemed to have a clarifying effect on the economic muddle in which the United States found itself at the end of the Reagan years. Kennedy's sacerdotal pronouncement of last rites on a fading power elicited a sigh of relief from a large segment of the American public that had become increasingly disaffected from the government's efforts to restore the nation's vitality. Kennedy supplied corporate executives, journalists, and academics with a formulaic explanation for America's mounting trade and payments deficits. How else to explain the decrease in the American savings rate, which fell from about 7 percent in the period from 1950 to 1980 to between 2 and 3 percent by the beginning of the 1980s? Or the rise in consumer debt? Or the secular decline in American productivity since the 1970s? If recent productivity trends continued, warned the Houston-based American Productivity and Quality Center, Japan, France, Italy, and South Korea would all surpass the United States in overall productivity by the beginning of the next century.[7]

Notwithstanding the economic boom that followed the 1981–82 recession, structural defects in the economy, the national propensity to consume virtually every penny of the national income, and the growing foreign ownership of American businesses and property led to the widespread view that the United States was no longer master of its own economic destiny. President George Bush's decision in the summer of 1990 to reverse his famous "no new taxes" commitment as a condition of Japan's participation in talks on the trade imbalance (the so-called Structural Impediments Initiative) dramatically demonstrated the degree to which the country's fate rested in the hands of others. By the 1988 presidential election, a declinist school had formed in the United States among liberal intellectuals and the leadership of the Democratic Party who derided Reagan's emphasis on the nation's foreign political commitments at the expense of domestic social and economic progress. How could the United States be "standing tall," as Reagan reassured, when it ranked last among the world's advanced industrialized states in infant mortality, male life expectancy, and equality of income distribution?[8]

America Triumphant

The rising chorus of support for Kennedy's bleak assessment of the future aroused the ire of conservative writers and politicians. Georgetown University professor and former U.S. Ambassador to the United Nations Jeane Kirkpatrick maintained that there was no correlation between past empires and the United States, whose spending on defense as a percentage of the total national product had decreased since the 1950s. If anything, the decline in the economic gap between the United States and Europe was a sign of America's strength. Had the United States not nurtured Europe's postwar recovery? Columnist Charles Krauthammer scornfully dismissed the popularity of the American malaise, which ignored the more than threefold increase in GNP since 1950, the collapse of the Soviet empire in Eastern Europe, and the efflorescence of liberal-democratic values around the world. In political and military terms, "America is still number one," *The Economist* asserted. The American economy was suffering from a cold, not cancer. An editorial in the *Wall Street Journal* likewise encouraged a proud nation to shake off its hypochondria. Considering America's record of achievement, it stated reprovingly, the public should be cheering the end of the Cold War and the integration of the world economy, not lamenting it.[9]

This was precisely the view of a conservative paladin who rode into the policy thicket in the summer of 1989. In a daring article published in *The National Interest,* Francis Fukuyama, deputy director of the State Department's Policy Planning Staff and former Rand Corporation analyst, challenged the notion that the United States was a declining power. All the hand-wringing about the decline of America had failed to recognize the global triumph of ideas over matter. The eclipse of Marxism-Leninism in Soviet Russia and Eastern Europe, he jubilantly asserted, heralded the universalization of the liberal-democratic ideal embodied in the United States and thus the end of history's ideological evolution.[10]

Fukuyama's provocative thesis created an international sensation. "The End of History" was headline news in *Time* and *Newsweek,* the featured subject of clatter on the ubiquitous talk shows, and an intellectual curiosity in the Washington think tanks that treat public policy agendas as the storehouse of all relevant thought. The popularity of Fukuyama's thesis derived from two coterminous developments: the rhetoric of American decline and the end of the Cold War. Fukuyama provided intellectual and psychological relief from the depression that had settled over the United States in the previous decade. America's trade imbalance with Japan and its diminishing dominance in international affairs in no way constrained the spread of its liberal-democratic ideals, which were inexorably uniting the world in a homogeneous state. The outbreak of democratic revolutions reinforced this optimistic outlook. Even the Soviet Union now genuflected at the altar of liberal-democracy. Moreover, the democratization movement in China that was brutally suppressed in Tiananmen Square and parallel movements in South Korea, Burma, and Chile amply testified to the power of the democratic light that shone from the American city on the hill.[11]

Even so, skeptics questioned whether the crumbling of the Berlin

Wall, and the Cold War victory it symbolized, was the epiphany that Fukuyama imagined it to be. Some speculated that reemerging nationalism or Islamic fundamentalism might well extinguish liberalism's shining moment.[12] European intellectuals noted that there was still considerable debate between socialists and conservatives on the ideal society, the end of the Cold War notwithstanding, not to mention the raging dispute, as the Maastricht Treaty of Union later revealed, on the parameters of Continental unity. "History may have ended for the Rand Corporation," British journalist Ian Davidson pointed out, "but on this side of the Atlantic it is boiling most actively."

But Fukuyama insisted that his idealistic edifice could only be toppled if one could show that nationalism or religious fundamentalism or some other ideological force were likely to be buttressed by an explanatory framework that superseded liberalism. Hegel said that we created our own nature in the course of our evolution, Fukuyama pointed out, and the long historical process toward the liberal-democratic consciousness that was revealing itself in the world could not be dismissed as an accident of history.[13]

ANTITHESES

The dawn of the Pacific Century, the theory of great-power decline, and the prophesied end-of-history are unidimensional, mythologies of change that promise more than they deliver. None provides much insight into the broad expanse of historic change. As theoretical constructs, the new ideologies offer facile, monistic explanations of the dizzying flow of events that the international community has experienced during the past decade, leave aside past centuries. In addition, they betray a presentist preoccupation that reduces the future to a simple extrapolation of current developments.

Pax Nipponica

The current fascination with the Pacific Century is not new. America has been captivated by Asia ever since it began trading there in the late eighteenth century. The easily forgettable President Millard Fillmore waxed enthusiastic about the Pacific over 150 years ago. William H. Seward, President Abraham Lincoln's secretary of state, also predicted that the future lay in the Pacific. And by the end of the nineteenth century, dispirited by the prolonged economic contraction that followed the depression of 1893 and the disappearance of open space in the once limitless frontier, Americans perceived China and Japan, rather like they do today, as glimmering El Dorados. "The Mediterranean era died with the discovery of America," Theodore Roosevelt proclaimed at the turn of the twentieth century. "The Atlantic era is now at the height of its development and must soon exhaust the resources at its command. The Pacific Era, destined to be the greatest of all . . . is just at the dawn.[14]

Roosevelt's prophecy proved to be wrong, at least half wrong. It was the United States, not Japan or China, that became the dominant power in the twentieth century, in the Pacific as well as in the Atlantic region. History is not predictive, however; the dawn of the Pacific century to which Roosevelt referred may only now be breaking, as the current generation of Asia-watchers maintain. Nevertheless, there are plenty of contemporary factors that suggest otherwise, starting with the continued vitality of the United States.

The mind-numbing statistics about America's trade and payments deficits aside, it is premature to conclude that the United States is about to be economically overrun by Japan and the newly emerging Asian states. True, the savings and investment rates are appallingly low in comparison with those in Japan or South Korea or Taiwan, and capital costs have tended to be higher. As a result of lower interest rates, however, the cost of acquiring new capital has dropped dramatically in the United States, while it has correspondingly risen in Japan. In addition, the United States did succeed in reducing its trade deficit with Japan in the period 1987 to 1991. Helped by the slumping dollar, U.S. exports to Japan rose by 113 percent between 1985 and 1991, more than half of which were manufactured goods. To be sure, Japan's surplus, which is currently approaching $70 billion, has risen steadily since 1992. But the surplus has resulted largely from the recession-induced reduction in imports—a condition that the government has attempted to correct through the partial opening of its markets, interest-rate and income-tax cuts, and other stimulatory programs such as public-spending packages and the dramatic depreciation of the dollar against the yen.[15]

The discussion about the penetration of the U.S. market by Japanese companies fails to take into account the success that Motorola, Boeing, McDonalds, and other American corporations have had in Japan. IBM Japan contributes more to corporate profits than any other subsidiary of the American corporate giant, and Coca-Cola earns more money in Japan than it does in the United States. Tower Records has opened outlets throughout Japan, and Levi Strauss, the jeans maker, has built its own distribution center. While cultural trade barriers still exist, laws excluding foreign companies from doing business in Japan have been relaxed, and trade disputes from supercomputers to play toys to auto parts have been settled or are on their way to being settled as part of the Structural Impediments Initiative. U.S. companies have gained market share in the semiconductor industry, investment firms such as Salomon Brothers have become active traders in the Japanese bond market, and credit card companies such as American Express have begun to exploit the burgeoning consumer market.[16]

Even if the American economy failed to sustain its present vigor, it is fanciful to believe that Japan Inc. will maintain an uninterrupted cycle of economic growth. As a result of sagging industrial productivity, economic growth in fiscal 1994 rose by only 0.6 percent, barely greater than in the previous year, when it shrank by 0.2 percent. Although industrial production has recovered somewhat from the 87-percent drop it registered in the year ended March 31, 1993—the biggest annual decline since 1974–75—Japanese manufacturing plants are still operating at only around 70 percent of capacity. In the future, the former president of Matsushita, Akio Tanaii, observed, Japanese companies can at best look forward to "stable" growth of 5 percent or less. For some, even this is overly optimistic. In the absence of efforts to deregulate the economy, some economists aver that Japan faces a protracted deflationary cycle that could stifle growth through the end of the century.[17]

In the spring of 1992, as the soaring real estate prices that had propelled stock investments plummeted, Japan's stock market plunged to its lowest levels since 1987. Periodic rallies since then aside, stock values have yet to recover. Worse still, given the depressing effect of a muscular yen on corporate profits, the market may continue to decline. The bursting of the market's bubble portends rising capital costs for Japan. In the past, corporations were able to rely on retained earnings, surplus income, and subsidized loans to finance expansion. In the future, they will be forced to obtain funds from equity and bond markets. Not only will the end of cheap money circumscribe corporate investment in new technology, it will also retard Japan's acquisition of foreign assets. Indeed, Japanese financial institutions have already begun to shed some of the American properties they acquired in the late 1980s. The cost of credit will further increase pressure on the Japanese financial system to make more efficient use of capital.[18]

Confronted with a rising tide of nonperforming loans collateralized by property whose inflated value had precipitously declined, the banking system began to creak by the end of 1992. Since then, the number of bad loans accumulated by Japanese banks has risen to dangerously high levels. The problems of financial institutions have been compounded by the mounting number of bankruptcies from the Kobe earthquake in January 1995, a steady pattern of declining loan growth, and a sagging stock market, all of which are intensifying pressure on the system's capital reserves. Although no bank failures have occurred thus far, a run on Japan's vast network of credit cooperatives and housing loan companies could deplete the resources of the nation's deposit insurance fund. Meanwhile, major lenders such as Mitsubishi Bank and Bank of Tokyo, whose recent merger has created the world's largest bank, will probably continue to be called on by the government to bail out troubled institutions. If the banking crisis worsens, however, the government may have to launch a major rescue operation of its own to stave off financial collapse.[19]

The end of easy money and fast growth have induced industries from plywood makers to software companies to petition the government for subsidies to retain workers. Worse yet, as a consequence of the contraction in domestic sales and increasing price competition in foreign markets, including the United States, the vaunted Japanese auto industry has begun to gear down. Ignoring the predictability of future trade conflicts with the United States, the pricey yen is bound to take its toll on weaker companies. Nissan and Mazda Motor Corporation, along with a host of vehicle-parts makers that will be affected by Japan's June 1995 agreement to purchase more American components, may be forced to merge with stronger competitors in what is likely to be a major restructuring of the auto industry. This is not to say that Japanese automobiles will become less visible in world markets. Auto imports alone still account for nearly two-thirds of America's $60-plus billion deficit with Japan. But the shrinkage of global market share, domestic deflation, and the inability of Japan's roads to absorb more cars suggest that the auto industry has in all likelihood entered a phase of consolidation, if not retrenchment.[20]

Slow growth, the collapse of the real estate market, and nagging corporate restructurings have, in turn, adversely affected Japan's philosophy of lifetime employment. Faced with declining profits, manufacturing and investment companies have also been forced to reduce the wages or hours of employees. Workers have been relocated, transferred to menial jobs, and, in some cases, released or retired. The dimming prospect of lifetime employment will undermine much of the social cohesion that has been responsible for Japan's economic success. And, as the public expectation of guaranteed employment wanes, consumer spending is also likely to decline. The conspicuous consumption of French wines, German cars, and Italian fashions has just as conspicuously declined, as have travel and opulent dining.[21]

An aging population will also impose greater burdens on the Japanese government to absorb welfare costs once largely assumed by Japanese corporations. By the year 2000 the percentage of people 65 and older in Japan will be greater than in the United States and roughly the same as in Germany. Thanks to the world's longest life span, Japanese senior citizens are projected to account for 25 percent of the population by 2020—a higher percentage than in any other country—as compared with between 5 and 8 percent during the expansionist 1960s and 1970s. The comparable portion of medical spending to care for the aged is expected to increase to 37 percent, compared with 18 percent in 1980. An aging population will, among other things, reduce the national savings rate from the current 15 to 16 percent of disposable income to as little as 3 to 5 percent, according to some estimates, or roughly the level of savings in the United States. Even assuming a greater share of wages to finance pensions, the government will be forced to borrow to defray the social cost of the elderly at the expense of its acclaimed fiscal prudence.[22]

Until the 1990s, rising productivity enabled governments and corporations to provide for people in their old age. But the celebrated Japanese work ethic is also changing. Japanese executives have been increasingly less inclined to pay homage to their corporate masters. Some have willingly left companies in pursuit of more attractive jobs. Others have decided to work for foreign companies, where opportunities for creative independence, advancement, and leisure time are greater. The younger generation of Japanese—the *shinjinrui*, or, "new humans"—altogether reject the work ethic of their abstemious parents. Theirs is a generation of voracious consumers and sybarites. The reality that they will never be able to own a home further diminishes the incentive to work.[23]

Foreign competition will also constrain Japanese growth. Although the momentum toward European integration has slowed noticeably in the wake of the tepid public reaction to the 1991 Maastricht Treaty on economic and monetary union, a borderless Europe will eventually become a reality. With a combined population of 370 million people and a gross domestic product of $7.3 trillion—slightly more than that of the United States and more than twice the national output of Japan—the European Union will exert a powerful political and economic influence in the world. The expansion of the Union will further enhance its economic power. Although the recently completed GATT agreement can be expected to ease European quotas on Japanese automobiles and other products, the geographic concentration of production and its effect on transaction costs will create more or less natural obstacles to market penetration by Japanese industry.[24]

The newly industrializing economies of Asia also pose problems for Japan. As a result of the rise in the yen and surging investment in Southeast Asia, Japan began to import television, videotape recorders, and other consumer appliances from the "Four Tigers"—Taiwan, Hong Kong, South Korea, and Singapore—in the mid-1980s. Although Japan still has a comparative advantage in capital goods, the Tigers now enjoy a competitive edge in consumer durables. In addition, they are becoming serious competitors in shipbuilding, steelmaking, and electronics. Moreover, China is looming on the horizon. With a savings rate of 35 percent, a steady stream of new private businesses, and growing foreign investment, China is Asia's fastest-growing economy. China's economy has averaged annual growth rates of 10 percent since Party leader Deng Xiaoping instituted reforms in 1978, and nearly 13 percent from 1992 to 1994.[25]

Asia's burgeoning economies are on the verge of producing high-tech companies that will gradually weaken Japan's economic domination of the region. Largely because of the strong yen, Asia's exports to Japan have risen by roughly 150 percent since 1985. So long as Japanese firms remain opposed to foreign competition and the yen continues to climb the heights, this trend is likely to persist. On the other hand, economic deregulation is not likely to arrest the flow of high-quality/low-price Asian goods, the importation of which could force weaker Japanese firms out of business and thus incite trade frictions. Not surprisingly, Japanese businessmen are becoming more concerned about intra-Asian competitive pressures, especially about the challenge posed by China. Assuming that management inefficiency, corruption, and inflation can be kept under control, China's emergence as an economic power in Asia will dramatically alter regional relationships. For some Japanese, China promises to cast an even longer shadow. In a survey conducted at the end of 1994 by the Tokyo Broadcasting System, CBS News, and the *New York Times*, one-fourth of the Japanese public identified China as the emerging dominant power in the world.[26]

One must be careful, however, not to exaggerate the implications of the apparent slowdown in Japan's economic growth. Current recessionary conditions in Japan have had a large impact on the securities and real estate markets, but the unemployment rate has remained low (though rising to 3.2 percent in 1995), automobile sales have headed higher, and consumers are beginning to benefit from the importation of cheaper goods. Moreover, the savings rate remains enviably high, and the country's huge trade and budget surpluses allow the government to reflate the economy through fiscal stimuli and public works programs such as those instituted between 1992 and 1994 by Prime Ministers Kiichi Miyazawa and Morihiro Hosokawa. In addition, Japan is taking steps to ensure its continuing influence in East Asia. Japanese companies are increasing their direct investment in the region, either through the establishment of affiliates or joint ventures, and are beginning to transfer technology to local businesses. Japanese foreign aid also continues to pour into Asia. Furthermore, as Ezra Vogel and others have pointed out, superior technology, education, and management techniques buffer Japan against prolonged economic downturns.[27]

Unquestionably, Japan will continue to be an economic power and, for the foreseeable future, the engine of expansion in the Pacific Basin. At the same time, its meteoric postwar growth is coming to an end. Ironically, its reentry into the earthly economic orbit will be propelled by the dialectics of its own expansionism. The soaring yen that has resulted from mercantilist policies and the $130 billion global surplus they have produced has begun to depress exports, thereby reducing corporate profits and worker security. The Asian recipients of Japanese investment and business tutelage that are on the verge of joining the front ranks of the world's developed economies now pose the same economic threat to Japan that Japan posed to the United States and Europe after World War II. Moreover, as illustrated by the recent auto trade pact between Washington and Tokyo, Japan's major trading partners appear to be increasingly less inclined to tolerate its protectionism. No sooner had the United States signed the agreement giving American companies greater access to Japan's auto-parts market and its domestic dealerships than the Clinton administration formally issued a complaint against Japanese restrictions on the import of photographic film. In future disputes, the United States might be joined by the European Union, whose member states are no less exasperated by Japan's persisting market regulation.[28]

Such political pressure may yet have a salutary effect on Japanese attitudes. Corporate leaders such as the late Sony chairman Akio Morita and Tadahiro Sekimoto, president of NEC Corp., have urged business executives to temper their market expansionism and to employ the more profit-oriented focus of American companies. Some Japanese writers have encouraged greater economic liberalization, the removal of structural impediments to trade, and a more active leadership role in the

Asian–Pacific Economic Cooperation organization set up in 1991 to facilitate a trans-Pacific dialogue on trade, investment, and macroeconomic policy. External pressure is also likely to influence the thinking of Japanese who want to stand for something other than making money.[29]

As a founding member of the Group of Seven (G-7) leading industrialized nations, a major contributor of developmental aid to the world's have-not countries, the economic and even cultural cynosure of Asia, and increasingly the paymaster of American military forces in the region, Japan has developed a degree of prestige and political gravitas that it probably would not want to jeopardize by the resort to "inward-looking exceptionalism" or the "GNP-ism" of the postwar governments that preceded the leadership of Prime Minister Yasuhiro Nakasone in the 1980s. Japan's postwar economic success has reinforced national pride and a sense of cultural distinctiveness, which have, in turn, fostered a new nationalism of the sort expounded by Shintaro Ishihara. Internationalism, however, has not been abandoned, particularly on the part of those Japanese who want their country to play a more active role on the world stage. Indeed, it is in Japan's national interest to pursue an internationalist course, including the continued development of mutually rewarding relations with the United States and Europe.[30]

The Rise and Fall of Empires

Japan's economic ascendancy in the 1970s and 1980s reflected the loss of U.S. competitive vitality. Can one then expect Japan's decline from the heights to be accompanied by a resurgent America? Before Bill Clinton's election as president of the United States, the new pessimists would not have bet on it. As Paul Kennedy argued, the combination of global military commitments, the secular decline in productivity, and the massive national debt was leading the United States to the same abyss of hegemonic decline into which all previous great powers had eventually plunged. The pessimism and organicism of Kennedy's thesis are reminiscent of Oswald Spengler's brooding ruminations about the decline of the West after World War I. In contrast to Spengler, however, who likened the rise and fall of different cultures to the predictable growth and death cycle of organic beings, Kennedy's theory of great-power decline is driven by economic reductionism.[31]

However salient, economic prosperity and stagnation are only part of the explanation for the rise and fall of the great powers since the sixteenth century. Non-economic factors must also be taken into account. In the case of Hapsburg Spain, for example, there is no doubt that military expansionism and the protracted warfare against the Ottoman

Turks and the rebellious Dutch provinces concealed considerable economic erosion during the end of Philip II's reign. But the decline of Spanish hegemony was not solely the result of "imperial overstretch." As Kennedy himself suggests, the failure to achieve political cohesion in the culturally and geographically disparate dominions of the Hapsburg empire severely hampered the collection of taxes. The profligacy and bureaucratic ineptitude of the government in Castile further contributed to Spain's decline.[32]

In the case of Holland, geography and population, not "imperial overstretch," proved to be more salient factors in its loss of great-power status. It was their physical distance from Spain's escapades in the Mediterranean that allowed the autonomous provinces of the Hapsburg Netherlands to imbibe the socially transforming economic and religious ideas of post-Reformation Europe. By the same token, it was the combination of Holland's unfortunate location between England and France and its size—both its land mass and its population base—that led to its loss of empire. Even in the case of Britain, the idea of imperial overextension is overstated. In fact, Britain's economic success derived in large measure from its military prowess, which forced defeated rivals such as Spain and Holland to accept unfavorable trade treaties.[33]

It is true that after the mid-nineteenth century the increasing costs of empire and the emergence of the United States and Germany as trade rivals began to erode Britain's hegemony in the international system. But given the diffusion of technology and the growth of industrialization in Europe, the United States, and Japan, how could one expect Britain, empire or no, to maintain the supremacy it enjoyed in 1860, when Kennedy says it reached its economic zenith? Besides, the cost of empire notwithstanding, defects in the educational system, the changing social ethos, the growing disaffection with liberalism in nineteenth-century Britain among the working class, and the autonomy issue in Ireland also adversely affected productivity and competitiveness.[34]

The case for the decline of the United States is still harder to make. Depending on the statistical grab bag from which data are selected, it could be argued that the United States is a declining power. The country is living beyond its means, as the albatross of a $4.6 trillion national debt demonstrates. The United States could not even finance the Persian Gulf war without the infusion of some $54 billion from its allies. A rickety primary and secondary education system, urban blight, and a widening income gap between the rich and the poor: this is the oft-repeated sad commentary on late-twentieth-century America.[35]

Bleak as the future appears, however, it may be premature to consign the United States to the dust bin of history. Over the past quarter century, the American share of world output has remained remarkably stable at about 25 percent of the total product. Indeed, as Joseph S. Nye Jr. points out, the gradient of American economic decline was steepest from 1950 to 1973, a period of acknowledged American political and military hegemony. Per capita gross national product rose by 17 percent during the decade of the 1980s, and manufacturing productivity also increased. Moreover, investors are experiencing the longest bull market in American history, and the budget deficit has been reduced from $290 billion to $203 billion during the first two years of the Clinton administration. And as for the nation's bloated military establishment, the share of American defense outlays as a percentage of GDP has actually declined during the past three decades, including the Vietnam War period, from 10 percent to slightly more than 5 percent today.[36]

Granted, the United States does not today cast the economic, political, or military shadow it did in 1950, when it reached its apogee of power. If power takes into account nonmaterial factors, however, including the internationalization of beliefs and values, the United States may not yet be headed down the slippery slope of decline. Hegemony, Marxist philosopher Antonio Gramsci argued, manifests itself in subtle cultural and ideological ways. A group, or class, or state may continue to exercise "dominant" political influence, even though it may no longer be what Gramsci called the "determinant" of the material conditions that define its power. Witness the influence of Italian culture long after the city-states of Venice, Genoa, Florence, and Naples were shunted to the side of the European stage after 1500.[37]

Culturally and intellectually the United States still defines the politico-economic-security structure of international relations, as attested by the global trends toward decentralization, privatization, and democratization and by the power it wields through multinational institutions such as the International Monetary Fund, the World Bank, and the United Nations. In addition, American popular culture continues to pervade the world. British political scientist Susan Strange calls this cooptative capability the "nonterritorial" power to influence political developments.[38]

The Spirit of Progress

If America is caught in the vise of history, and, like all other previous great powers, is experiencing the death-grip of inexorable decline, such affirmations of its continuing global influence would be meaningless attempts to resist destiny. Curiously, however, the declinists do not seem convinced that America's demise is inevitable. Quite the contrary, they advocate the reallocation of national resources from the defense-oriented policies of the past to domestic programs in an effort to revitalize the United States. America might have lost its way, Kennedy stated in a response to his critics, but there still was time to avert the grim future he predicted.[39] As it turned out, the future had already arrived, or, at least, so its messenger proclaimed. In contrast to Kennedy's gloomy historicism and the persistent pessimism of the twentieth century, Fukuyama rejoiced in the triumph of liberal democracy, the self-contained ideal that gave history its content, direction, and ultimate purpose.

For Fukuyama, who, like Hegel, presupposes the rationality, unity, and self-transparency of history, the history of the world is the progressive unfolding of Freedom through a dialectical process in which it repeatedly asserts itself against the material world in a recurring cycle of creation and destruction until it manifests itself as liberal-democracy. While the process of history would continue, he explained, History, the animating idea that gives ordered meaning to events, had finally come to an end. With the collapse of communism, human beings everywhere now would be able to transform the benefactions of science and technology into capitalist enterprise, and form the kind of liberal society that fulfilled their deep-seated desire to be recognized as worthwhile individuals. Liberal-democracy, then, is the meaning of History.[40]

The end-of-history thesis is the mania to declinism's depression, and Fukuyama is the Dr. Pangloss to Ronald Reagan's Candide. Just as Kennedy's liberal defeatism appealed to political liberals, Fukuyama resounded the hopes and beliefs of conservatives who extolled the universalization of American ideals. The "long historic search for ways to organize human society" was over, Hudson Institute fellow and author George Gilder gushed.[41]

It may come to pass that the end of the Cold War is the historical cataclysm that transforms the world. The repudiation of communism may herald the final ideological challenge to the liberal-democratic ideal. On the other hand, it may be only an interlude in the human drama, when, as Hegel would say, "the antithesis is in abeyance." If history is any guide to History, it would seem at least intellectually risky to predict the future on the basis of the collapse of communism and the apparent outbreak of democracy in Eastern Europe.

Certainly Fukuyama's is not the first end-of-history revelation, and it will probably not be the last. Hegel believed that Napoleon's victory in 1806 over Prussian and Austrian forces at Jena signalled the beginning of the final stage in history that would lead to human freedom. Karl Marx later perceived the mobilization of the working classes as history's overture to the timeless socialist state. As it turned out, the French Revolution did not usher in the stage of universal human freedom that Hegel envisioned. The flowering of democracy in the nineteenth century was supplanted by authoritarianism in the twentieth. Nor did socialism fulfill its promise of human redemption, even though Marxist-Leninist eschatology continued to mesmerize intellectuals in Europe and in the developing world long after the romanticized workers had become cynical about the Utopia that awaited them.

Besides, liberalism, at least liberal-democracy U.S.-style, may not be suitable for everyone. Some states may prefer the European social-democratic hybrid. Others might prefer statist models. For cultural, geographical, and racial reasons, Singapore, Thailand, and Malaysia have emulated Japanese state-capitalism, or what Fukuyama calls "market-oriented authoritarianism," not liberal-democracy. Humanistic-distributive variations of the liberal idea could also plausibly arise from ideological differences among democracies. "The history of ideology," as Samuel Huntington has pointed out, "is the history of schism." Competing ideologies based on racial or religious factors may also eventually reemerge. Fukuyama is probably correct in stating that Islam has little global appeal, but the intensifying struggle between Sunni and Shi'a branches of the faith would nonetheless present major obstacles to the spread of liberal-democracy in the Middle East, North Africa, and parts of Southeast Asia. And, however remote it may seem at the moment, might Islam not spread?[42]

Liberal-democracy may prove to be especially unassimilable in semi-developed and underdeveloped countries, which lack the infrastructure, educational and technical resources, capital base, and value system that are necessary for its development. Economic privation and social inequality are hardly likely to be conducive to the spread of liberalism, and there is no assurance that the advance of technology will normalize the differences between haves and have-nots. We may be headed for a fragmented international order in which nations, especially in the developing world, may reject the imposition of Western liberalism and the homogeneous state in favor of welfare-nationalist forms of government that seek to preserve immemorial cultural traditions and local autonomy. Welfare-nationalist forms of government may also find fertile ground in the former Soviet republics and in Eastern Europe, depending on the speed and breadth of economic progress.[43]

The unbridled optimism of the end-of-history thesis further pays short shrift to the demonic and irrational forces in human nature that threaten order and liberal-democratic progress. Fukuyama acknowledges that wars, dictatorships of the right or left, and social upheavals are bound to occur as states grapple with political and economic change, but he cannot imagine that such perturbations will divert History from its transcendent course. He is more worried about humanity's increasing decadence (as though that were a novel development), which will undermine its willingness to struggle and sacrifice and weaken its spiritedness, self-esteem, and self-actualization, freedom, creativity, and recognition, or its *megalothymos*.[44]

But the glories of technology and the disparagement of communist ideology will not purge humanity of the alienation, insecurity, and parochialism that breed hostility. Malevolent leaders with more than their share of *thymos* may reappear and redirect the flow of history away from Fukuyama's Promised Land. Another Hitler may not revisit the world, but one cannot assume that the world will be spared other, and possibly worse, tyrants. Eastern Europe has resumed the process of de-Ottomanization and de-Magyarization that was interrupted by a half-century of German and Russian domination. Thus far, the corrosive admixture of nationalism and economic deprivation has not eroded the "liberal idea." But that could change swiftly. The ethnic hatred that made a corpse of Yugoslavia could recur elsewhere in Eastern Europe, the Caucasus, and Central Asia. Thousands have already fallen victim to ethnic violence in the former Soviet republics of Moldova, Georgia, Azerbaijan, Tajikistan, and Chechnya. The future may not be boring, it may be unimaginably destructive.

Even the most advanced post-historical societies may succumb to violence. Citing Michael Doyle's statistics on the history of warfare among democracies, Fukuyama has concluded that liberal societies are "fundamentally un-warlike." Their aggressive instincts have been sublimated in the pursuit of economic prosperity and social equality. But Doyle also points out that warfare between democratic states could occur if the deterioration of their liberal foundations were to destroy the stability of the international system. Fukuyama is not blind to the prospect. "If men of the future become bored with peace and prosperity, and seek new thymotic struggles and challenges," he allowed, "the consequences threaten to be even more horrendous. For now we have nuclear and other weapons of mass destruction, which will allow millions to be killed instantly and anonymously."[45]

Not to worry. Fukuyama is confident that any relapse into bestiality will be short-lived and, in any event, confined to societies that are still stuck in history rather than those that liberal-democracy has transported beyond its horizons. Like the philosophies of Hegel and Marx, Fukuyama's liberal-democratic eschatology is surreal. It is beyond the coordinates of time and space. Such a priori reasoning, as Daniel Bell once said of socialism, may be in but it is certainly not of this world.[46] In the end, Fukuyama has no more appreciation for historical complexity than Kennedy does. Where Kennedy exalts historicism and objectivism at the expense of ideas, social processes, and the diffusion of culture, Fukuyama disembodies history. He idealizes reality at the expense of the material world. One lives in a Hobbesian jungle, the other in Plato's cave.

The real danger in believing that the liberal ideal is the apotheosis of mankind's evolution—"free of contradictions" and thus of dialectical transformation—is that it is likely to foster political complacency. In Fukuyama's post-historical world, just as in Marx's classless society, who are the custodians of freedom and justice and equality? Upon reflection, however, such matters are not likely to command urgency in the foreseeable future. History is not a closed process, a tautology of preordained truth. It is relative, contingent, unpredictable, and frequently irrational. No one can say how the liberal democracies, let alone the less fortunate states of the underdeveloped world, will respond to the changing realities of the post–Cold War era. Even Fukuyama ironically concedes as much. In the enigmatic conclusion to his book, in which a wagon train converges on a town that is the metaphorical liberal-democratic Promised Land, some travelers, after looking around, choose to move on.[47]

Endism and the American Self-Image

Despite their questionable value as road maps for the future, the Pacific Century, America-in-decline, and end-of-history constructs have nonetheless stirred powerful emotions in the United States. There is an evangelical, even apocalyptic, tenor to the debate about the new ideology, whether in the rarefied air of universities and think tanks or in the communities of small-town America, which suggests that its significance lies more in its implicit than its explicit content—in what it symbolizes rather than in what it says.

Superficially, Asia-rising, America-declining, and America-triumphant are different constructs. The first foresees the emergence of an Asia-centered international system in which the United States and Europe will play important but less influential roles than they have in the past. The second predicts an increasingly diminished role for the United States in the future, whether that future is centered on Asia or some other part of the globe. And the third awaits Godot-like the efflorescence of liberalism and the universal escape from the vortex of history.

At a deeper psychological level, however, what appear to be different formulations are really three variants of the same phenomenon: endism. Each of these constructs sends the same message to Americans, namely, that their culture and history—indeed, their great revolutionary experiment—are, as idealized rather than in reality, coming to an end. Whether America is being supplanted, effaced, or consumed in the universal realization of its liberal godhead, it is being cut off from its past and its future, and thus from itself. It is the fearful prospect of its impending demise as exemplar, great power, and archetype that grips America. America-chimerica, America-invalidated, America-consummated. That is the unsettling underlying message of the new ideology. That is its power.

Endism is integral to the American historical experience. The early migrants from England who established settlements along the Atlantic seaboard believed that they were charged with the celestial task of redeeming a wayward world. They and their descendants accordingly set out to build a just and orderly society that other peoples would behold and imitate. At the same time, they feared that their social experiment might not withstand the ravages of a corrupt, rapacious world. Conspiratorial fantasies about fiendish plots to defile the nation were constant companions of Americans throughout the nineteenth century. Evil lurked everywhere: in the form of Jesuit subversives under the satanic command of the Pope and his Hapsburg legions, in Freemasons, Mormons, utopian movements, or in the culturally unrecognizable newcomers to the land.

Anxieties about endism reached a crescendo in the final decade of that century. The disappearing frontier, industrialization, urbanization, immigration, and economic depression engulfed the nation in a tidal wave of change, transforming society and the distribution of power and prestige in its wake. As it turned out, the fin-de-siècle depression that gripped the United States at the end of the last century was short-lived. Progressivism and Wilsonianism transported America to new heights. The former reaffirmed the integrity of the democratic experiment; the latter internationalized it. Inspired by the Allied victory over the Axis powers and by the restoration of economic health at home, the United States exported its liberal-democratic values to the world with renewed fervor after 1945. By the beginning of the 1960s, largely because of America's defense of the free world against the scourge of international communism, endist fantasies began to assume the apocalyptic character that would find consummate expression in Fukuyama's end-of-history musings.

Long before the Berlin Wall came crashing down, sociologist Daniel Bell exposed the illusion of Marxism in his eulogy to the pragmatic, liberal values that were America's birthright. However, Bell's pronouncement that ideology had ended turned out to be premature. The subsequent breakdown of social order and public authority during the turbulent decade of the 1960s mocked the triumph of pragmatic, pluralist, laissez-faire liberalism. Liberalism, wrote political scientist Theodore J. Lowi, had become anachronistic, both in its nineteenth-century and New Deal variants. Lowi's advocacy of government planning and a rule-based juridical democracy was an effort to reform a political system that, in his view, had become socially dysfunctional. But in his appeal for a new public philosophy, Lowi sounded the death knell of liberalism, thereby reviving the pessimistic strain of endism in American society that has resonated so powerfully in declinism and, less transparently, in the message of the Pacific Century.[1]

AMERICAN GENESIS

America is sui generis. Unlike other nations, whose identities derive from geographical propinquity, ancestral traditions, and immemorial ways of life, the United States of America is the culmination of an idea, the society "born free," as Louis Hartz described it. America is its own beginning and end. It emerged outside of history on a divine errand and entered the world to redeem it. It self-consciously set out to show others—by its example and by its militant defense of liberty—the way to salvation and, in so doing, to fulfill its promise. As Tocqueville observed, "the whole destiny of America [is] contained in the first Puritan who landed on these shores, as that of the whole human race in the first man."[2]

The Puritans who made their way from England to the New World in the Great Migration of 1630 perceived themselves as a chosen people who, like the ancient Hebrews, had been summoned by God to establish the long-awaited millennium prophesied by the Old Testament. Their flight from bondage in Europe also had worldly significance. Europe was the new Babylon, which denied the lower social orders access to the material comforts and social prerogatives of the nobility. In contrast to the other-worldly, redemptive character of Catholic eschatology, the English Puritans believed that salvation was also a secular undertaking.[3]

As God's elect, the emigrants who boarded the good ship Arabella en route to the New World believed they had embarked on a providential journey that would come to an end in the unity of the universal and the particular, the timeless and the historical. Inspired by its divine vocation, the Puritan migrants to America referred to their settlement as a "city on a hill." That city was to be a reflection of both the religious and political aspects of their calling. It was intended to harmonize individual needs and societal obligations in a visible union between church and state, which they called a "theocracy," that would forever enshrine virtue within a finite political form.[4]

The Puritan mission provided considerable solace from the dangers that lurked in the Gethsemane of the New World. But the human impediments to the construction of a saintly community proved to be formidable. Three decades after the Great Migration, materialism, corruption, and pestilence had begun to take their toll on the Puritan theocracy. At the same time, the failure of the Puritan Revolution in England prompted fears of reprisal from the restored Stuart Monarchy. As a consequence of these developments, the Puritans adopted the Half-Way Covenant, which relaxed the terms of membership in the congregation by conferring on the baptized children of the original settlers the same chosen status as the elect, the visible saints who had experienced a spiritual conversion. Following God's pact with Abraham's posterity in the Book of Genesis, the children now shared in the covenant of grace as lineal descendants of the Puritan divines.

More important, the new covenant secularized the Puritan settlement: it transformed the colony from an aristocratic theocracy to a middle-class meritocratic order. In time, the franchise of the "social church" expanded to include a variegated army of Protestant sects, all of which shared the faith in America's future. By the end of the seventeenth century, the growth of towns and financial speculation markedly weakened the attachment of the Puritan community to the social and religious piety that had characterized its founding, as the Massachusetts witch trials bore testimony.[5]

The failure of the Puritans to transcend their historical bounds produced two conflicting but, paradoxically, mutually reinforcing effects. Barely concealed apprehensions that the Christian journey might be diverted from its heavenly course now found expression in public lamentations about the failure of the grand design. "O, New England," William Stoughton exclaimed in 1668, "thy God did expect better things from thee and thy children." Descendants of the original emigrants wondered whether the New World "were doomed to stand not 'as a Cite upon an hill,' [but] desolate and forsaken."[6] At the same time, the children's fall from grace reinforced their redemptive mission. To assuage the feeling that they had dishonored the fathers, the children immortalized the Great Migration into legend and socialized their offspring in the mythology of America's Promise to redeem a profane world.

The jeremiad, which would recur time and again in America, was a Janus-faced elegy and eulogy. It was an act of expiation for the inconstant fulfillment of the Puritan covenant with God. It was also a form of praise for the noble mission on which the fathers had embarked. True, the Puritan Dream had failed. But as the renown minister and social philosopher Cotton Mather said in the early eighteenth century, the original settlers and, for that matter, their children "have given great examples of the methods and measures wherein an evangelical Reformation is to be prosecuted."[7]

At once self-deprecatory and self-congratulatory, the jeremiad fostered an ideological consensus that socialized Americans in the ideology of exceptionalism. It legitimated the emerging nation's material progress as a sign of God's benevolence by reviving the primal memory of its failure to live up to its calling. Sacvan Bercovitch points out that the jeremiad was not intended to be destructive, but rather constructive; suffering was a sign of society's continued commitment to its errand.[8] Besides memorializing the primal experience, the jeremiad of promise and disappointment served another purpose: it provided subsequent generations of Americans with a self-image that distinguished them from the rest of the world. The ideology of perfectibility, or exceptionalism, was an abstraction of the beliefs and values of the original settlement. The recounting of the Great Migration and the effort to build a model society—ritually reenacted annually in the nation's birthday and in the national day of thanksgiving—invested the primal Puritan experience with a mythical quality that became the organizing theme of American culture.

Repetition of the myth by the Yankee descendants of the original settlers redeemed the Dream of the fathers and symbolically consecrated the American political experiment in liberal democracy from the War of Independence as a "holy commonwealth," in J. G. A. Pocock's words, the success of which thereafter became the test of the nation's fidelity to God's commission. John Adams traced the American revolution to the Great Migration. The first Fourth of July celebration in 1778 hailed the revolution as an act that symbolized "the universal redemption of the human race." Two hundred years later, Ronald Reagan exhorted the electorate to "begin the world over again" and build "for all mankind a shining city on a hill."[9]

American writers and scholars reinforced the ideology of perfectibility. "Let us realize that this country, the last found," declared Ralph Waldo Emerson, "is the great charity of God to the human race." Herman Melville and Henry David Thoreau denounced America's periodic transgressions precisely because they diverted the nation from its sacred errand. "For America," Walt Whitman wrote after the Civil War, "if eligible at all to downfall and ruin, is eligible within herself, not without; for I see clearly that the combined foreign world could not beat her down."[10]

Historians too helped to instill the nation's mission to mankind in society. Guardians of the nation's traditions and interpreters of its fluctuating moods, scholars from George Bancroft to Bernard Bailyn to Daniel Boorstin socialized successive generations in the mythology of American exceptionalism, both in its born-free formulation and in the historiography of the republican synthesis. Henry Nash Smith, whose Virgin Land inculcated a generation of Americans after World War II in the lore of the frontier, later revealed in a self-critical essay that he had been far more influenced by the ideology of America than he realized at the time.[11]

Fortified by the myth of a virtuous people born free in a society that emerged uniquely outside of history and time, the American army of "citizen-saints," as David Noble has referred to them, went about the business of taming the wilderness and proselytizing the heathens they encountered in the spirit of manifest destiny. That the Founding Fathers placed political power in the hands of the propertied classes and condoned slavery in no way detracted from their consensual belief in the universality of freedom and equality. Indeed, the boundless frontier and the promise of an inheritable freehold in land reconciled any temporary disparities between individual freedom and social equality, at least for those who were not forced to endure the ascriptive inequality imposed by race or national origin. As Bercovitch has observed, "the land belonged to them before they belonged to the land, and they took possession, accordingly, first by imposing their own image upon it, and then by seeing themselves reflected back in the image they had imposed."[12]

Happily detached from the vicissitudes of change in the world beyond its shores, Americans pushed their settlement westward. The combined rise of textile manufacturing, the introduction of the railroad, and the development of agriculture, including the plantation system of the South, spawned a new entrepreneurial class of nouveaux riches. As Tocqueville discovered during his travels in America, in a society that set out to do away with class distinctions and to ensure equal opportunity for all citizens, "the desire of acquiring the comforts of the world haunts the imagination of the poor, and the dread of losing them that of the rich."[13]

Between the Civil War and 1890, the United States experienced a stunning social and economic transformation that reinforced the public's belief in its divine mission. Largely because of the efficient railroad and communications network that linked national markets, the gross national product doubled. Gleaming factories in bustling urban centers unleashed a torrent of goods that exceeded the output of the major European powers. Despite periodic economic downturns, Americans grew richer; and those who had not yet participated in the gospel of success preached by Horatio Alger and Russell Conwell were fortified by the almost limitless opportunity to advance beyond their social station. Anyone could join the elect in the "fee-simple empire," to borrow Henry Nash Smith's phrase, as long as one believed in America's redemptive mission. Commerce was virtue, and virtue was commerce. In such an era of plenty, it was not hard to fantasize that the nation was in control of history.

For all the optimism it engendered, prosperity also bred discontent. Wordly wealth became more and more the object of humanly pursuit rather than a sign of one's salvation. As the rich got richer, the old social elite—the repository of American culture and virtue—lamented the nation's wayward course. For this was also the Gilded Age of "robber barons," political corruption, and social indifference toward poor, rural Americans uprooted from their farms and the strange hodgepodge of immigrants who streamed into cities that were ill equipped to provide basic public services. The coterminous depression of 1893 and the disappearance of the frontier exacerbated the end-of-century social crisis and demoralized the nation's belief in itself. Time, a despairing Henry Adams concluded, had run out on America.

The social turmoil of the 1890s and the closing of the frontier had another significant effect: they dragged the United States into the wilderness beyond its shores. Until this time, Americans had heeded George Washington's admonition to steer clear of foreign entanglements, especially in the Old World. Aristocratic, decadent Europe, after all, was the antithesis of the United States—the iniquity that reinforced America's chosenness. Owing to the spread of Social Darwinism and the revival of manifest destiny, however, the pre–Civil War flirtations with expansionism beyond the national borders became more frequent in the last quarter of the nineteenth century.

In 1889 the nation narrowly averted a war with Germany over vaguely defined rights in Samoa; in 1895 it nearly squared off with Britain over a boundary dispute in Venezuela. Finally, in 1898, besieged by social and economic upheaval, emotionally aroused by the journalistic sensationalism of William Randolph Hearst and Joseph Pulitzer and a jingoist elite eager to restore the nation's former glory, the American public gave vent to its passions. In the aftermath of its war against a proud but declining Spain, the United States had not only lost its innocence, it had, much to the chagrin of anti-imperialists, also acquired an empire in the Pacific and the Caribbean.[14]

The nation reacted ambivalently to the acquisition of foreign territories. True, expansionism conferred the blessings of liberal-democracy on more of the human race. Americans, after all, came "as ministering angels, not as despots." But it also glorified power and the state at the price of law, morality, the individual, and, not least, America's virtue. The nation's imperialistic fling and the socioeconomic transformation of the domestic landscape combined to produce a new jeremiad of atonement. As they had done in the past, and as they would do again in the future, Americans rehistoricized—indeed, rationalized—their experience in order to propitiate the fathers for their moral lapse or, in the case of their imperialistic foray, what later historians would apologetically dismiss as "the great aberration."[15]

The social reform ethos of turn-of-the-century Progressivism and Wilsonian foreign policy was self-consciously intended to restore the national virtue that the materialistic degeneracy of late nineteenth-century America had tainted. Rather than deny the social effects of industrialization and urbanization, or worse, recoil from them, Progressive reformers paid homage to industry, much as their forebears glorified the land, as the fecund new frontier of American social and economic progress. Rather than retreat from the Babylon beyond the nation's borders, President Woodrow Wilson chose to reform it.[16]

In the first two decades of the twentieth century, the United States underwent a massive social reformation that would serve as the model of reform for the New Deal legislation of the 1930s and the Great Society program of the 1960s. City governments were reformed, public services were instituted, and a host of laws were passed to regulate the industrial workplace, the treatment of children, the production of food and drugs, and the concentration of capital in cartels and monopolies. Progressivism reenacted the nation's revolutionary experience, in order to restore its belief in its own redemptive mission, its perfectibility.

Wilsonianism, the eponymous foreign policy that has broadly defined America's relations with the world in the twentieth century, internationalized the nation's religiopolitical mission. Whether in the Americas, the Caribbean, or Europe, force was permissible only insofar as it served liberal-democratic values. That moralistic Wilsonianism also advanced the nation's material interests was in no way contradictory. Quite the contrary, self-interest and morality were perceived as mutually reinforcing. America's redemptive mission abroad, like its reform agenda at home, was simultaneously self-serving and selfless, reflective and projective. International as well as domestic reform reassured the nation that its revolutionary experiment remained intact. Both confirmed the nation's prophetic destiny.

So armed, the citizen-saint became the citizen-warrior crusading against the anti-Christ of amoral Europe, heathen Asia, and, in due course, atheistic communism. The moral standards of Woodrow Wilson's new diplomacy, like those set by the domestic reformers, were never in dispute. Once the United States sailed into the world beyond its shores, its identity became as inextricably connected with its proselytizing mission abroad as with its civic virtue at home.

Alas, the myth of perfectibility that the Puritan divines bequeathed to their children is an impossible burden to bear. The fear that the redemptive mission will end has been the obsessive companion of every successive generation of Americans. Since perfectibility is limitless and, therefore, beyond human attainment, there can be no acquittal of the American mission. The most one can expect is temporary relief from its oppressive demands and from the anxiety of endism it generates.

THE PACIFIC CENTURY: AMERICA, CHIMERICA

Almost from the moment it entered American consciousness, Asia was viewed simultaneously as an opportunity and a threat, a hope and a challenge. By the end of the nineteenth century, Asia was perceived as the new frontier of westward expansion, the new wilderness, the new test of the nation's journey with destiny. Asia had changed little during the previous two millennia. More despotic than Europe, but, after the sixteenth century, technologically and institutionally less advanced, Asia was a fertile ground for commercial and religious proselytization. So the United States, as God's anointed agent of progress, undertook the task of liberating Asia from its backwardness and thus of completing the process of civilization that had begun there more than two thousand years earlier.

Captain Alfred Thayer Mahan, the great military strategist, called the new states of Asia "sheep without a shepherd" whose growth must be stimulated by "external impulses." One of the impulses was the spread of commerce, which helped the United States as it helped Asia. The other was the inculcation of "ideals which in ourselves are the result of centuries of Christian increment."[17] Such was the transcendent purpose that underlay Secretary of State John Hay's diplomatic efforts to prevent the dismemberment of China in 1899–1900.

Indeed, the dissolution of China by imperialist Europe provided a providential opportunity to advance America's gospel of salvation. Since God had "placed us like Ismael of old in the center of nations," a lecturer at the Union Theological Seminary solemnly intoned, it was America's duty "to make the Pacific Ocean the chief highway of the world's commerce" and to "[fulfill] the manifest destiny of the Christian Republic."[18]

Japan seemed even more receptive to American liberation theology. After the Meiji Restoration of 1868, a generally peaceful transformation from the authoritarian shogunate of the Tokugawa era to an emperor-centered, samurai-dominated system, Japan welcomed Western technology, education, and organizational technique. Moreover, unlike other Asian countries, it was politically independent, sort of European. Japan was "the flower and concentrated essence" of Asia, Paul R. Reinsch wrote in the early twentieth century. "Like her great English counterpart, Japan has assimilated talent of the highest order" and [moulded] the influences to which she has been subjected into a harmonious whole."[19]

Despite its racial and cultural distinctiveness, Japan was perceived by Mahan and others as a "willing convert," as a kind of American apostle and would-be tutor of other Asian societies, "the prepared soil, whence the grain of mustard seed, having taken root, may spring up and grow to the great tree, the view of which may move the continental communities of Asia to seek the same regenerating force for their own renewal."[20] At the same time, Japan was perceived as a threat to America, much as the untamed and vaguely menacing wilderness had been viewed as a danger to early Puritan and Yankee settlers. Perhaps because of its assimilation of Western ways, but certainly after its successful war against China in 1894–95 and, more dramatically, its defeat of Russia a decade later, Japan was seen as a potential adversary of the United States. Less than four decades after the Meiji Restoration—roughly the same span of time that it took to assert its economic might after World War II—Japan had become an imperial power. Its acquisition of Taiwan and Korea and its control of Manchuria not only contributed to the dismemberment of China, they also imposed barriers to American commercial expansionism in the Pacific.

The Japanese challenge affected the United States in several ways. In the first instance, it redoubled the American commitment to the Open Door policy in China. In addition, it fostered a more confrontational attitude toward Tokyo. Diplomats and businessmen viewed Japan's restrictive trading practices in the areas it controlled as a threat to American interests. Roosevelt's much publicized decision to send the American naval fleet on a Pacific cruise, which took place in 1909, was as much a muscle-flexing exercise as it was a demonstration of national vanity. Two years later, the navy created War Plan Orange, which envisaged the possibility of a military conflict with Japan.[21]

More troublesome still, Japan's emergence as a Pacific power inflamed racism in the United States. The San Francisco school board's segregation of Japanese students in 1905, although overruled by the Roosevelt administration, was a precursor to the immigration restrictions that followed World War I. Egged on by the Hearst press, which exploited Japanese massacres of Chinese at Port Arthur and the murder of the Queen of Korea, public antipathy toward this Asian upstart, tumescent with pride after its defeat of Russia, mounted. "They get upon your nerves!" remarked one politician. Japanese protestations about the white race's misuse of power were all too often dismissed as arrogance by British as well as American critics. They contended that Japan owed the West a debt of gratitude for the independence it enjoyed ever since the arrival of Commodore Perry's "black ships" in 1853, for teaching it how to live, for overlooking its "peevish fits of infantile irritability and anger."[22]

Japanese social practices and cultural forms—concubinage, the disrespectful treatment of women, the refusal to assimilate other peoples in society—exacerbated the stereotype. Besides, they were corrupt. Cleansed of the stain of the Gilded Age by Progressivism, Americans condemned the bribery and electoral fraud in Japanese politics, the scandals in the military services, political parties, and the ministries. "Rotten to the core!" one writer fumed. "An ulcer on society!" said Senator Hiram Johnson of California.[23]

Japan and, to a much lesser extent, China posed a deeper, more insidious threat, however, one that struck at the core of the American identity. Americans believed that the reformation of Asia would reaffirm their moral mission, their chosenness. Conversely, the failure to reform Asia would be a sign of America's spiritual degeneracy. Failure, Pocock has brilliantly written, would imprison the chosen people in earthly versus heavenly time and consequently corrupt their providential mission.[24]

As it turned out, China was not destined to become either a Christian society or a thriving commercial marketplace. Following the overthrow of the Manchu dynasty in 1911 and the inability of the Kuomingtang, Chiang Kai-shek's Nationalist Party, to provide political stability, China fragmented into warlordism and widening social divisions between the commercial-urban elite and the peasantry, which the Communist Party exploited. Notwithstanding China's admirable resistance against Japan and the herculean American efforts to halt the resurgence of civil war between the Nationalists and the Communists, China remained incorrigibly unreformable, a prisoner of political disorder and corruption.[25]

The Communist victory was more than a setback to American prestige. It was perceived as a blow to American virtue. Unable to accept the fantasized implications of the Chinese Communist victory, the United States idealized the "real" China of Chiang Kai-shek as a struggling democracy victimized by the pernicious power of communism and its fellow travelers in the United States. As for the fellow travelers, they became the sacrificial victims of Senator Joseph McCarthy's modern-day witch trials, who were sacrificed, in the same spirit of condign retribution that must have gripped Salem, to restore America's faith in itself.

Until recently, America's image of Japan produced little of the hand-wringing that China induced. In a society that enshrined the divinity of the emperor, Christianity had never found much favor. Japan's brief interlude with Christianity in the sixteenth century came to a bloody end when the Tokugawa Shogun Toyotomi Hideyoshi crucified a group of Jesuit missionaries he suspected of being the advance guard of Spanish expansionism. And the subsequent spread of science in the nineteenth century fostered agnosticism among educated Japanese.[26]

Nonetheless, the prospect of converting Japan into a disciple of American liberal values and beliefs had always been more encouraging. According to one writer, the virtues of loyalty, generosity, and bravery had forged an impressive national unity in the "New Japan," even though it was "apparent that a code made for knights in a militant age [bushido] does not meet all the moral difficulties of a modern industrial society."[27] Besides, early Asia-watchers paradoxically believed that Japan's militancy might be salutary, if properly channeled. Indeed, Japan emerged in the minds of some observers as a surrogate American tutor and political codefender of Chinese territorial integrity against the ravages of the European powers, especially Russia.

After its military defeat of Russia, however, Japan seemed bent on becoming the "comb of the Oriental cock" and a threat to the nation's redemptive mission in Asia. This image of Japan hardened after World War I, partly because of Tokyo's insistence on equal status with the other world powers and partly because of its intention to establish a new order in East Asia. The Japanese invasion of Manchuria in 1931, and the subsequent creation of the puppet state of Manchukuo, shattered the fiction of preserving China's territorial integrity and set political-military planners in Tokyo and Washington on what turned out to be an unalterable course toward war.[28]

The post–World War II social transformation of Japan assumed especial importance to the United States in light of the "loss" of China. The "reeducation" of Japan reaffirmed American innocence and perfectibility. Freed of the devil of militarism, if not reborn in the values of political and economic liberalism, Japan, like Germany, became a living legatee of the American revolutionary experience. Until the 1970s, Japan was perceived as a diligent student of American tutelage, a reassuring symbol of the nation's eternal mission. Under terms imposed by America's postwar military occupation, Japanese society was finally reformed. The new constitution renounced the right to wage war and safeguarded democratic institutions. School textbooks were rewritten to expunge emperor worship. Commercial expansionism, facilitated by the access to American markets, became the new basis of national power. As a consequence of the devaluation of Japanese politics and the ascendancy of the bureaucrats, mercantilism replaced militarism. For Japan, too, salvation lay in partnership with the United States, which became both its protector and moral exemplar.

After 1973, however, the symbiosis between the United States and Japan steadily weakened. The explosion in the Japanese economy had begun to take a toll on American exports, triggering U.S. protectionism. In retaliation, the Nixon administration persuaded Japan to accept "voluntary" quotas on its imports to the United States. Further, in the wake of détente and the normalization of relations with China, Japanese economic expansionism, particularly in Southeast Asia, lost its value to the United States as a stabilizing element of American Cold War strategy. As bipolarism slowly gave way to multilateralism, Japan was viewed increasingly as a threat to American global dominance.[29]

Japan's rise as an economic power coincided with the brutalizing effects on the American psyche of the Watergate scandal and the Vietnam War. During the prolonged depression that lasted until the Reagan years, the nation relapsed into an unconsolable jeremiad, tormented by the sins of Watergate and Vietnam and, worse, the anxiety that its redemptive errand, hence, its identity, was a chimera. Not only had Japan assiduously assimilated American know-how, it had achieved in a brief quarter-century a level of productive efficiency, technological innovation, and market penetration that had become the envy of the capitalist world. As Vogel and other exponents of the Pacific Century pointed out, Japan, not the United States, was the messenger of hope and salvation in the postindustrial era.

For many Americans, however, acceptance of the Japanese industrial model is tantamount to admitting that the United States is no longer relevant to the world. For a nation that sees itself in deliverance of a celestial errand, such a state of mind cannot be tolerated for long. The United States can only be diverted from its mission by sinister forces, as the modern-day Japan bashers, heirs to conspiratorial tradition in American history, remind us.

The Japanese challenge strikes at the heart of the American identity. To meet that challenge by adopting Japanese social forms and methods, as advocated by American trade experts who lobby for an industrial policy, is to sever the nation from its cultural moorings. Industrial policy, bureaucratic centralism, and communal allegiances have as much resonance in the United States as laissez-faire, corporate autonomy, and individualism have in Japan.

Culturally unsuited to the structure and regimentation of Japanese society, but painfully aware of their worsening balance of trade, Americans have therefore developed a powerful resentment toward the Pacific challenge because they fear its implications for change. For those who are unwilling to face the future—and the past—the Pacific Century is a mirror of America's spiritual and physical exhaustion.

DECLINISM: AMERICA-INVALIDATED

The perceived economic displacement of the United States by Japan is symptomatic of the deeper concern that the country as a whole is languishing. Declinism is the antithesis of the exceptionalist ideology from which Americans derive their national identity as the beginning and end of humanity's evolution. At the same time, declinism reflects America's historical pessimism, the penitential, self-negating side of its cultural character and the source of its frequent descents into despair.

There has been plenty to feel bad about. The economic rise of Japan and, to a lesser extent, Europe, signaled the end of American supremacy in international commerce. Even the domestic market has come under siege. Trade quotas and other economic barriers offer little protection against the penetration of high-quality, competitively priced Japanese products. Japan's economic invasion aside, the incubus of Watergate and Vietnam has continued to assail American society long after Richard Nixon and Indochina have lost their notoriety. In appearance, if not in reality, Watergate and Vietnam returned in the guise of the Iran–Contra scandal of the 1980s and the surrogate war against the Sandinistas in Nicaragua and their Marxist-Leninist co-conspirators in El Salvador.

Ironically, both actions were undertaken in defense of the exceptionalist values and beliefs they were corrupting.

The United States also seems to have lost its way at home. Cities have succumbed to the ravages of crime and drug gangs, while the social, educational, and industrial base of the country has steadily deteriorated. Meanwhile, mirroring the policies of the Reagan–Bush administration, the public has continued to live beyond its means. And despite the business recovery under Clinton and the reduction of the federal budget deficit, the nation remains unwilling or unable to make the sacrifices required in the longer term to arrest its socioeconomic decline. Middle-class America has become an increasingly stratified society; in contrast to Japan and Germany, the gap between rich and poor has widened rather than narrowed.[30] Perversely, the unemployed, underemployed, the menially employed, and the homeless form a potentially subversive counterculture that silently mocks, the nation's exceptionalist belief in the compatibility of economic progress and participatory democracy.

Shackled by the redemptive ideology of the fathers, Americans responded to Kennedy's prophecy of decline with cries of contrition. It was not their sense of perfectibility that was amiss; rather it was their failure to live up to the standards of the fathers that had been consecrated in the revolutionary experience and ritually reenacted in the process of progressive reform. And nothing could more vividly demonstrate the profligacy of the United States than the diminution of its preeminence in the world, which, in keeping with its sacred errand, it was duty-bound to liberate. The perceived failure to redeem the world, in turn, implied that the national experiment itself might also be doomed.[31]

For the American public, Kennedy's decline thesis conveyed both sacred and profane overtones. Declension signified not only a this-worldly contraction of influence and power but also the evanescence of the nation's redemptive mission, hence, its reason for being. Indeed, given the nation's vision of the future as but the continuation of the present, the notion of decline invalidated the American self-image, reduced it to an illusion. To be sure, history would not end, but its direction would thenceforth be determined by the vicissitudes of the profane world—by the actions of great powers such as Japan, or perhaps a European entity, or by some as yet unknown force—rather than the sacred mission of the United States.

In his conclusion, however, Kennedy suggested that it might not be too late for the United States to stop its slide into the recesses of history. But this poses a dilemma for Americans. If the country undergoes a major transformation in the way it thinks and acts—acknowledges, say, that it is at best primus inter pares in an increasingly multilateral world order and, therefore, reduces its international involvement—it will be forced to abandon its exceptionalist self-image. If, on the other hand, it persists in believing that its current difficulties are, like other episodes in its history, temporary deviations from the nation's providential course, it runs the risk of creating ever-widening fissures between the world and its idealized view of its place in it. In the first instance, it will be forever suspended in historical time and thus at the mercy of the forces of corruption. In the second, it will become a lonely prisoner of its own timelessness, increasingly cut off from the world.

END-OF-HISTORY: AMERICA-CONSUMMATED

Fukuyama's provocative excursion into the essence of history endeavors to resolve the dilemma posed by Kennedy's jeremiad of decline: it rouses a dispirited America to celebrate the fulfillment of its errand. Fukuyama's apotheosis of America is part of a large body of literary and historical writing that seeks to reconcile the nation's ideals with the material world, the metahistorical with the historical. Kennedy conjures up the image of Captain Ahab's titanic battle with the great whale, Moby Dick, Melville's metaphor of America's struggle to fulfill its destiny in a turbulent and evil world. Fukuyama evokes Billy Budd's accomplishment of that quest, the reconciliation of the temporal and the universal. What makes Fukuyama's treatise so captivating is its subliminal message that the United States was honoring its Promise and fulfilling its heaven-sent mission in the worldly wilderness. The end-of-history, in short, is the consummation of America.

The global competition between liberal-democracy and communism was a long and wrenching struggle that tested the mettle of the American people and the durability of the nation's revolutionary experiment. Following the loss of China and the infestation of Marxist-Leninist dogma in the newly emancipated states of the Third World, the forces of darkness appeared to be advancing. In the end, however, communism proved to be a false god. In their liberation from Marxism-Leninism, Eastern Europe and the developing world also liberated the United States. Their apparent conversion to liberal-democracy revalidated the American national experience and the universalizing values and beliefs that underlay it.

The collapse of the Soviet empire was more than the end to the Cold

War. It meant that the United States had once again withstood the challenge of a benighted world, thereby reinforcing its special calling and preserving its innocence. The end of the Cold War was the final stage of history's progressive synthesis, and the culmination of America's religio-political errand.

Whatever Fukuyama's intentions, the end-of-history thesis deflected the American public from its obsession with the country's decline and restored its exceptionalist identity. The retreat of Soviet power in Eastern Europe and the end of the Cold War seemed to trivialize the litany of the nation's shortcomings invoked by Kennedy and the declinists. If the United States was intellectually and socially in decline, why was the rest of the world so eager to emulate it? After all, the nation was watching the ideological and institutional replication of the American revolutionary experience in Eastern Europe, Latin America, and Asia, a mitosis of virtue, liberty, and culture. The good ship Arabella was sailing unfettered through placid seas to the shores of countries that had seen the light of America's revolutionary flame and entered the community of the chosen. As the British philosopher John Locke had predicted, just as in the beginning all the world was America, so in the end the world would be America again.[32]

America-consummated is, however, both a reassuring and an unsettling concept. Just as the euphoria that attended the end of the Cold War has given way to concerns about renewed international instability, the immediate appeal of Fukuyama's pronouncement has generated ambivalent feelings about the end of history. Nominally, the United States is experiencing the inexorable transformation of the world from Europe to Asia to Africa into its own likeness. Its regeneration is not merely self-actualizing, however, it is self-consuming.

Americans view progress in apocalyptic, not dialectical, terms. If the democratic revolutions of 1989–90 signified the end of history, if America is the world and the world is America, then the United States is no longer unique, outside of historical time. But if Americans continue to believe that the United States remains distinguishable from the world, then either the world has not been liberated or the ideology of exceptionalism is a fantasy. In the final analysis, Fukuyama's end-of-history message is irreconcilable with reality. Given the real and perceived decline of the nation's social and economic structures, most Americans do not believe the future has arrived. In fact, the American Dream is under assault. But even if that were not the case, in American mythology the future never arrives. The errand of the fathers is unfulfillable. The American quest for perfection is futile. If it were attainable, as Fukuyama suggests, if heaven and earth were to converge in the United States, the nation would cease to exist.[33]

Historic Change and National Identity

Before the twentieth century, there were few challenges to America's exceptionalist self-image. Geographically isolated from the world beyond its shores, the United States scrupulously avoided all but the most superficial encounters with corrupt and corrupting influences, particularly in Europe. Its untamed territorial expanse provided an outlet for social advancement that reinforced its liberal-egalitarian values and thus regenerated the primal experience of the fathers from which the national identity derived. America was the embodiment of the schismatic spirit of individualism and human liberation that originated in Europe. It was a youthful rebellion against the fathers of the Old World the original settlers left behind.

Sustaining the national identity has been more difficult in the twentieth century. Both the frontier and the isolation from the world it provided have vanished. Industrialization, urbanization, and bureaucratization have all but effaced the virtue of agrarian simplicity and the mythologized innocence of the yeoman farmer. The incorrigible amorality of the international political system has been unreceptive to the mission of a country that believed it was uniquely endowed for global preeminence.[34]

Now the world's frontiers have disappeared. As it has become more enmeshed in the world, the United States has found it more difficult to preserve its exceptionalist self-image, Ronald Reagan's politics of nostalgia notwithstanding. The end of the Cold War is part of a global transformation that has been imperceptibly taking place since the end of World War I. It is reconnecting the revolutionary children of the United States with the Old World fathers that the Puritan settlers left nearly four centuries ago. The world in which America and its Promised Land vision took root and blossomed is receding into history.

To be sure, the United States continues to inform the world with its ideals. But the world is also informing the United States, at the very least imposing limits on its universalizing mission. This is not to repudiate American ideals. It is to say that a new era is emerging, the evolution of which cannot be predicted by America's exceptionalist ideology. Indeed, the reverse is more nearly true: the changing world order is more likely to redefine America's identity.

Throughout much of its history the United States has defined itself by what it was not; for the most part, it maintained a careful detachment from the world around it. Now it must redefine itself in the consciousness of its inescapable immersion in the surge of global events. "The text is historical," historian Michael Warner has stated, but "history is textual."[35] In short, the meaning we ascribe to the world and the identity we derive from it are produced by context. And the context is changing.

The Meaning of
Historical Change

Talk of change is everywhere. Corporations, think tanks, agencies of the federal government, they all agree that the world is undergoing dramatic change. Radical, revolutionary, transfiguring change. Pundits, talk-show hosts, and writers of books such as this one solemnly toll the passing of time, of eras, of history. But how do we know that we are standing on the precipice of change? that today is qualitatively different from yesterday? How do we know that the transformation of international society that academics and policy analysts noisily debate is not simply a cliché, a ruse, an illusion? Certainly we cannot rely on the exhortations of the ideologists of endism to explain the process of historic change. They are caught up in mythology. And when we seek to go beyond mythology we tend to become entrapped in the straitened circularity of historicism or positivism.

"The trouble with change," stated sociologist Ralf Dahrendorf, "is that it is so hard to pin down. It happens all the time. But while it happens it eludes our grasp, and once we feel able to come to grips with it, it has become past history."[1] Indeed, change is usually imperceptible. Even when it is socially disruptive or traumatic—as in the case of wars or natural disasters—it eventually subsides, and societies resume their ingrained patterns of behavior. The globalization of United States foreign policy after 1945 was a major departure from America's congenital avoidance of international entanglements. But it did not alter the national self-image. Whether internationalist or isolationist, the United States remained faithful to its liberal-exceptionalist calling.

If the past is prologue, the storm of international change that is currently buffeting the post–Cold War world should eventually pass. Yet the international community seems to be awaiting the future with considerable apprehension, as if it anticipated that it was about to be cut adrift, separated from customary social and cultural beliefs and practices. Judging by the endless stream of academic and journalistic futurology, Americans are especially concerned about the shifting international landscape. Endism, in any of its variations, offers solace because it provides an ideological tether to the world. Regardless of their validity, the notions that the United States is in eclipse, in mortal collapse, or in a post-historical process of linking up with other nations in veneration of some "world-Idea" serve as intellectual and emotional anchors for publics that are struggling to cope with the implications of global change.

That the new ideology reduces global change to simplistic explanations hardly detracts from its appeal. Just the opposite. At a time when the expected is the unexpected, formulaic explanations impart a pseudoauthoritative quality, indeed, a fictional reality, to complex, unintelligible events. In periods of cataclysmic change, however, the fiction cannot be sustained; the chasm between the world as it is and as one fantasizes it to be becomes impossible to bridge or rationalize. Eventually, the harsh reality of the world invades the senses.

During such periods of change, the values, beliefs, and norms that once gave meaning to the world cease being relevant. Without a map to find our way in a strange and terrifying environment, we become disoriented. This is the condition that currently afflicts the states of Eastern Europe in their painful transition from state socialism to economic and political pluralism. Moorless, societies either drift in the sea of change that surrounds them or deny reality and take refuge in old ideologies, old convictions, in a past that offers little shelter from the present or the impending future.

They may cling to religion, like the ancient Greeks who sought shelter in world-weary Stoicism and neo-Platonic mysticism, or the Indians who fled from the Moslem invasion into Hindu spiritualism, or twentieth-century Americans who anesthetize themselves from the world in pietistic evangelism. Or they may construct new ideologies, however false or potentially destructive, to tranquilize or negate or avenge the force of change, relapsing into atavistic barbarity, as is unhappily the case in former Yugoslavia, until the falsity of the convictions and the futility of the barbarism impels them to devise new frameworks of belief that make the world meaningful again.

ART AND CHANGE

The artist lives on the edge of society in a chronic state of contrariety with convention and conformity. Unlike the vast preponderance of people who define their identities on the basis of social and cultural commonalities, the artist is acutely sensitive to developments or attitudes that depart from the commonplace, the accepted, the expected. Art and, to a lesser degree, popular culture provide prisms through which one can anticipate historical change.

Mannerism, for example, which spans the period from 1520 to 1590, was more than a reaction to the symmetry and balance of Renaissance art. It was also the exploitation of cultural forms that, in themselves, were symbolic of the emerging trends of individualism and the secularization of society. Mannerist art scorned proportion and order in favor of spatial and figural distortion. Its painting and architecture reflected an uneasy tension that sharply contrasted with the serenity of Renaissance innocence. It evolved at a time of massive social upheaval—plague, economic decline, religious schism, and the shift in the fulcrum of power from the Mediterranean to northern Europe.

As captured in the restless, distorted, and sometimes grotesque canvasses of El Greco, Rosso, Pontormo, and Hieronymous Bosch and the asymmetrical, ornamentally excessive architecture of Sanmicheli and Giulio Romano, tormenting doubt, dread, and an eerie expectation of terror had replaced mankind's faith in the verities of medieval order. Caught between the passing era of faith and reason and the impending age of science and individualism, mannerism, like the society it mirrored, had lost its faith in the convictions of the old order and in mankind. It was, in the words of art historian Nikolaus Pevsner, "the first Western style of the troubled conscience."[2]

Four centuries later, Cubism introduced a radical fusion of space and mass that anticipated the beginning of another transformation of the human spirit. In contrast to the multiperspectival approach of Renaissance art, Cubism flattened space into two dimensions. Rather than precisely locate objects in an illusory depth, as the art of the Renaissance, including the Mannerist distortions of the High Renaissance and the Baroque had done, Cubism presented objects as illusory elements in indeterminate space. Cubism precluded certainty and the absolute. Tables, books, and human limbs appeared and disappeared in dismembered planes. Seemingly opaque, recognizable forms metamorphosed into one another or into the void of space. Foreground and background were interchangeable.

Cubism had little respect for art as a representation of nature. Nature was ambiguous, protean, and paradoxical. Renaissance art symbolized human extroversion, a turning outward to explore the world. Cubism is the art of human introversion, a turning inward to discover one's subjective interpretation of an otherwise unintelligible world. With Cubism, the vertical dimension that pointed humanity to God or science no longer exists. The human spirit is left to confront the world alone.[3]

Art and popular culture similarly serve as barometers of contemporary change. It may be going too far to say that the trivialization of politics is any reliable gauge of change, although the toleration of a bare-breasted pornography star in the Italian parliament and the presence of raffish, bizarrely attired members of the Green Party in the German Bundestag is at least a curious departure from convention. A more important sign may be the powerful disaffection of electorates with elected officials as a whole, regardless of party affiliation. The wholesale change of faces in the U.S. Congress in 1992 and 1994, the growing appeal of narrowly focused regional parties like the Northern League in scandal-plagued Italy, political reform in Japan and the splintering of the Liberal Democratic Party, and the antiestablishment, antielite movements that are gaining momentum in Third World countries in Africa and the Middle East are all reflections of this attitude.

Cultural decadence is another index of social change. It is curious, in an era when the AIDS epidemic threatens to revive Malthusian economics, that the glorification of polymorphous sexuality pervades popular culture in virtually every corner of the world. The universal emblem of decadence, and of its underlying materialism and social decay, is the pseudonymous Madonna, the sexual shaman whose omnivorous carnality is not merely a direct assault on convention but also a commentary on the irrelevance of the values and beliefs that once bound modern societies into cohesive structures.[4]

Modern society. It is already a relic of the past for the artist who contends that the world has entered the postmodern era, an opaque future-world that remains indistinct except in its repudiation of modernity. True, there have been other times when societies have rejected or lost faith in the traditions of the past—the post–World War I period, for example—only to rediscover them. Unlike previous "lost generations," however, the postmodernist generation is, altogether incongruously, self-consciously experiencing the end of one era and the start of another.

In comparison, there seems to be no evidence to suggest that Mannerist painters consciously knew that the Renaissance was coming to an end or that Romantic poets such as Wordsworth and Coleridge were aware that the publication of *Lyrical Ballads* signaled the end of the neoclassical period in literature. Nevertheless, it may be hasty to dismiss the narcissism of postmodernism, its moral relativism, and its rejection of contemporary culture as a lack of spirituality, as Aleksandr Solzhenitsyn has done. For in the "paleomodern" world of the late twentieth century the cultural traditions that formed the basis of national identities in the past have lost their meaning in the emergence of an interdependent world culture, the outlines of which are barely visible.[5]

What postmodern painting and architecture reveal is an absence of universals—of form or line or geometrically informed space—in favor of a sometimes primitive, sometimes surrealistic collage of disintegrated themes and images that meet the eye. Postmodern art is a self-conscious liberation from the authoritative standards and values of the past and a search for a new social order. It is easy to dismiss or reject the kind of art that dallies with the past, desacralizes values and social institutions as stiflingly conformist, or ideologically eschews aesthetic evaluation as an elitist-defined tool of social control. There are no moral or aesthetic standards in postmodernism; there is no "first-class" art because there is no "first-class" culture. Nothing is sacred, as architect Michael Graves' design of Walt Disney's corporate offices in Glendale, California exemplifies: a parody of classicism, with columns formed in the shape of the fabled seven dwarfs. And as the "Arcades du Lac" housing project near Versailles, France, suggests—an oxymoronic public chateau—nothing is meaningful or, at least, unambiguously meaningful.

Jarring as postmodern art may be, however, syncretism is a metaphor for the metamorphosis that is taking place in the international society. Postmodernism's visual desecration of the past, its inherent ambiguity, and its eclecticism are intended to challenge the anxious conformity of the late modern era. It goads society to be innovative, to see itself and the world in which it lives in different ways, even though those ways are not yet apparent. The perceived negation of the past is really the artist's attempt to free society to plunge into the future and, in so doing, to see the past in a new way.[6]

Like the world of the late Renaissance, contemporary international society is straddling the threshold of a widening cleft in history. And if art is a metaphor for impending, socially transforming change, it will not be able to maintain its balance indefinitely. Local and regional economic parochialism, the ineradicable blight of poverty and hunger in an overcrowded world, the challenge to political authority, and the persistent dangers of nuclear and ecological disaster are eroding the belief in limitless progress.

Signs of disquietude abound. In Europe, historic hatreds darken the lofty expectations of economic integration and political unity. On Europe's periphery, newly independent states and would-be independent states struggle to maintain their autonomy, if not survival. Economic mismanagement and the burden of indebtedness threaten to destabilize further the Third World. And states, new and old, developed and underdeveloped, squander scarce resources to build sophisticated arsenals of destruction in the name of God, national honor, and political self-determination.

THE PROCESS OF CHANGE: EVOLUTIONARY CHANGE

Change is constant. Nations exercise greater or lesser power and influence in world affairs. Wars, civil insurrections, or natural disasters temporarily interrupt social processes. Economies expand and contract. Politicians and the parties they represent are voted into and out of office. Institutions appear and disappear; they flourish and atrophy; they mutate.

Change of this nature is evolutionary. It is for the most part incremental, predictable, quantifiable, a variable function within understood social parameters. Changes in employment statistics or domestic product or mortality rates are further examples of evolutionary change. Societies may not be able to forecast the precise magnitude of economic recessions or the outcome of political elections, but the collective judgment of experts provides a framework that makes it possible to anticipate and bound change. Even breakdowns in domestic order and military conflicts are evolutionary, depending on the predictability, amplitude, and extensiveness of the interruption in social routines.

Evolutionary change is diachronic or longitudinal; it is homologous with familiar variations in social patterns and processes. Plainly, it interrupts, and possibly disrupts, social routines. But such interruptions do not necessarily undermine the beliefs, values, or norms that govern the way societies see themselves or the world around them, any more than the daily changes in one's physiology necessarily terminate life.

Of course, social change may have enduring consequences for large segments of society, or whole institutions, as did the Great Depression of the 1930s for those people who found themselves jobless and, in many cases, penniless. But the world view of society as a whole may nonetheless remain just as valid as it was before the calamity occurred. Its departure from *laissez faire* aside, the New Deal program of Franklin D. Roosevelt in no way eroded either America's progressivist beliefs or its exceptionalist identity.

In the case of Europe, the social devastation of World War I had a more profound effect on society. The Bolshevik Revolution aside, it accelerated the political polarization of left and right everywhere, intensified labor–management strife, fostered disillusionment among intellectuals, and, in the proliferation of the weak, unstable, new states it begot, sowed the seeds of the next war. Nevertheless, Europe was not bereft of all hope that it would recover from its illiberalism, although it would never restore its faith in endless progress. Indeed, warfare had often been the crucible in which social change was forged. The reforms that led to the union of Austria and Hungary in 1867, the birth of the Third Republic in France in 1871, and Russia's Octobrist Reforms of 1905 all followed military defeats.[7]

Moreover, World War I—a world war only in the European imagination—was confined to a geographically delimited area. It had little effect on other regions of the world. Nor for that matter did later upheaval in one part of the world necessarily throw into turmoil the whole of international society. Fidel Castro's revolution of 1959 violently turned Cuban society inside out, but it was not replicated elsewhere, including in most of Latin America. The Vietnam War wreaked havoc on millions of innocent people in Southeast Asia. Although the repercussions of the war in Indochina were felt in the United States for years after, they did not transmute American values and beliefs. Decolonization dramatically altered the sociopolitical culture of millions of Africans, Asians, and Arabs in the 1940s and 1950s, but the profile of the world maintained by Europeans, though indisputably truncated by their diminished international status, remained essentially faithful to the tenets of rational progress.

In the post–Cold War environment, the efforts to institutionalize liberalism in Russia and the Commonwealth of Independent States (CIS) and the dismantling of apartheid in South Africa have undeniably subverted inveterate beliefs and traditions in those societies. Isolated from the effects of other convulsive developments, however, they are not likely to wrench the entire international community from its cultural and ideological moorings. As far as the larger world order is concerned, socially isolated crises are culturally containable. Moreover, insofar as crises are generated by the spread of values embraced by the preponderance of the world community—rising economic standards and political pluralism, to cite two familiar illustrations—they are also culturally assimilable. Thus, structural change, whether intranational or international, is incidental to the perceived continuity of global affairs when it is containable and assimilable within preexisting social, cultural, and ideological parameters; or, stated differently, when its effects are peripheral to the core values, beliefs, and processes that connect the individual and society to the world.

EPOCHAL CHANGE

When events overflow the cultural and intellectual banks of the world we know, however, when the force of ideas and social processes is pervasive and disruptive of core values and beliefs, change is epochal. Epochal or historic change occurs when the dynamics of the institutions that provide social cohesion are simultaneously in flux or when historical time disappears.[8] At such moments in history, we are culturally and intellectually severed from the past, psychologically disoriented, estranged from the world we inhabit. Yesterday no longer has meaning for tomorrow, which seems almost insidiously its antithesis. Orphaned by the tide of change in which we are swept up, we are forced to recreate the past in the reality of the present in order to embrace the future. In connecting the past and the future, societies not only overcome their alienation from the process of change they confront, they give it authenticity and meaning.

Of course, there can never be a complete break with the past. The existential disjuncture of history does not stop the passage of time or the physical flow of events and experiences that give time spatial content. Men make history, as Treitschke said, but history makes men.[9] Epochal change, like evolutionary change, is not random. It too springs from a timeless river of individual and societal experience. The future always contains vestiges of the past. The past, however, imprints the future in ways that are not always immediately discernible. The Black Death that swept Europe in the fourteenth century and claimed the lives of one-fourth of its population only temporarily arrested the development of capitalism that had rudimentarily emerged a century earlier. The Napoleonic wars ushered in a new concert of power that kept the European states more or less in peaceful alignment, but it did not supplant the rivalry and conflict inherent in the balance-of-power system of international relations. The introduction of democracy, initially by the "restoration" of the emperor in 1867 and after World War II by military fiat, did not eliminate the vestiges of feudalism and oligarchic rule in Japan.

At the same time, epochal change is not the continuation of the past.

History is not a single story; it is many stories. It relates events that have meaning primarily for the people who have lived them. What differentiates intervals of history is the meaning they are assigned by human beings who strive to make sense of the changing world that defines their identity. History is the living interaction of the past and the future in the present. Shifts in historical patterns are not directed by the irrepressible logic of the past weaving its way through time in the guise of assorted human and institutional agents. Rather, they are courageous, creative leaps into the unknown by individuals, groups of individuals, and eventually society as a whole, who take the stream of the past places it has not gone, and who, by reinvesting it with the future, tell a new tale.

HISTORICISM AND HISTORY

Historicism is the view that "the history of anything is a significant explanation of it" or that "the nature of anything is entirely comprehended in its development."[10] Essentially, it maintains that all social and cultural phenomena are historically determined. Truth resides in the history of living reality rather than in nature or in the abstract formulations of philosophy or science. History, however, provides no lessons for the future. It simply presents the human account of the past in its irreducible uniqueness or for its own sake (*Einmaligkeit*), as revealed by the documentary and monumental records unearthed in the process of conscientious scholarship. As explained by Leopold von Ranke, the historian's task was neither to judge the past nor instruct the future but rather to reveal the record of human experience as it actually was. *Weltgeschichte ist das Weltgericht*: the history of the world is the world's court.

Historicism emerged in the first half of the nineteenth century, inspired by the Enlightenment's faith in the progressive evolution of humanity. As exemplified by the late eighteenth-century writings of Johann Gottfried von Herder, it was a reaction against rationalism, an intellectual awakening of the diverse emotions and subjective stirrings of folklore that gave concrete perspective to the past. Although historicism originated as a critique of natural law doctrine and its belief in the unchangeableness of time, it was not unscientific. Quite the contrary, it embraced the Enlightenment's commitment to methodological rigor and adopted the belief that history can be objectively studied in conformity with scientific rules and methods of inductive inquiry.[11]

Imbued with the Enlightenment's faith in science and human progress, historicism assumed that material reality was the phenomenal manifestation of reason, either in the Hegelian sense or, in the view of Ranke or Johann Gustav Droysen, as a representation of divine will. By immersing oneself in the documentation of the actors who crossed history's stage—the enlightened, the celebrated, the commonplace—one could reinhabit the past, relive it, as it happened (*wie es eigentlich gewesen*). Whether the revealed past proved to be inspirational or disheartening, it constituted the objective record of human experience. It was both the necessary and sufficient account of the only present that was possible.[12]

Following the collapse of the liberal challenge to authoritarianism in the revolutions of 1848, however, and the incipient cultural pessimism that appeared in the writings of Aleksandr Herzen and John Stuart Mill, historicism began to depart from the humanistic values that gave meaning to the universe and purpose to the course of history. Late nineteenth-century historicists rejected Hegel's notion of Spirit as "otherness" as being no less subjective than the scholasticism of the medieval Christian church. Good Cartesians, they instead called for empirical investigation of the scientific "facts" of the past, without really divesting themselves of Hegel's religious belief in the unity of history. As George Iggers explained, they shed their faith in the past as the repository of value and reason and increasingly adopted the view that all values were historical.[13]

Disillusionment with the belief in history's purpose led to the atomization of historical inquiry, on the one hand, and to scientism, on the other. To be sure, the basic concepts of historicism formulated in the writings of Herder or Goethe and developed by Ranke—the ideas of individuality and individual development through time—contained spiritual and romantic elements. The secret of existence, in Herder's view, could only be penetrated by immersing oneself in the self-development of national culture. By the latter part of the nineteenth century, however, scholars such as Jacob Burckhardt concluded that the individuality of a people or culture was the only reality of history, a view that sharply diverged from the principle of generality or historical universality that continued to inform Ranke's historiography.[14]

The emphasis on national or cultural individuality became still more pronounced in the twentieth century. Influenced by the devastation of World War I and the crisis of consciousness in postwar Germany, Friedrich Meinecke and Ernst Troeltsch maintained that the discovery of the past lay in the individual spirit or national soul of peoples spontaneously expressing their freedom in unity with God and nature. In contrast to Ranke's focus on the general and the universal, these writers emphasized the individual and the specific. According to their interpretation of historicism, science could not reveal the spirit of a people, its inner life, its national character. The unity of history was the assemblage of unique races and cultures coexisting in inimitable variations on the theme of humanity. Philosophical generalizations about human nature or scientific explanations such as those advanced by Marx or Herbert Spencer that claimed universal applicability, hence, validity, were considered meaningless because they derived from nonhistorical knowledge.[15]

Other scholars, however, turned their attention to the search for the underlying laws of history. Those who wished to demonstrate the scientific rigor of their research compiled mountains of data drawn from archival sources on narrower aspects of historical reality. The quest for objectivity, in turn, led to increasing scholarly specialization. Scholarship became "a labour of bricks and mortar, manipulated by armies of diligent labourers among records," as Geoffrey Barraclough remarked, insensible of history's wholeness, its meaning. But the massive accumulation of historical facts produced by the quest for scientific objectivity rendered history purposeless and devoid of all objective meaning.[16]

The conceptual response to the lack of coherence of history was scientism, which emerged in the writings of Oswald Spengler and Arnold Toynbee. And what gave the laws of history impetus was the calamity of World War I and its destruction of the belief in progress. In contrast to the evolutional views of Marx or Spencer, which were predicated on the faith in progress, scientistic historiography attempted to recreate order in a world that had dissolved into a disorienting flux through the formulation of organic theories of cyclicality and recurrence. In subjecting distinct cultures to uncontrollable organic processes of life and death that recur with mechanistic regularity, scientism had denied the continuity and unpredictability of history. History had ceased to exist.[17]

Whether the past is viewed scientifically or romantically, however, historicism is time bound. Although the past may not be governed by universal laws, its evolution is nonetheless inevitable; it could not have been otherwise. History pursues its own course, unfettered by human involvement. What appears to be spontaneous and free is prefigured in the intersection of events that precede it, or it surges from the primordial strivings of the national soul or character.

Historicism assumes that history is linear, the perpetuation of an uninterrupted process, the expression of which can be objectively determined because objective knowledge is within history itself, that is, it resides in the discoverable facts of the past. But historical facts do not simply fall into some coherent order; we arrange them. Moreover, the past is more than its own facticity. Such reasoning further fails to differentiate between enduring, containable change and transformative change. To posit that today is the indissoluble sum of all the yesterdays is to normalize change. If the present were predictable, indeed, preordained, history would have no existential meaning. Change would be illusory. The present and the past would be indistinguishable; the future a vacuum, an irrelevancy. Contemplating the future would be idle, a subjectivist fantasy. If the future were controlled by the seamless past, there would be no reason to think about it, study it, attempt to shape it.

Because historicism is fundamentally retrospective—preoccupied with becoming as such and with the culturally predetermined beliefs and behavioral patterns of diverse peoples—it is remarkably oblivious to the spatial or synchronic dimension in the evolution of the human experience, the why as opposed to the what. Those who subscribe to the view that history is an ungeneralizable chronological narration of the past blithely ignore the developments and trends—including the irrational and the self-destructive—that interrupt its flow and that, in challenging traditional views and practices, necessitate a new synthesis of the past. What is meaningful to societies in one period of time may be meaningless to those in another. To assert that the past is either the linear progression of fixed, immutable events or the self-contained spirit of peoples who can only be understood in their unique cultural contexts does not clarify our understanding of historical change, it obscures it.

Positivism and Science

Like historicism, positivism has also been differently interpreted since Auguste Comte coined the term early in the nineteenth century. Positivism, according to Comte's historiosophical theory of human development, was the formulation of laws of social progress. To be sure, Comte's explanation of humanity's evolution reflects the philosophical romanticism of an age that produced Hegel and Marx. It was also influenced by the same concern with scientific rigor that inspired historicism. What separates positivism from romantic idealism and historicism is its faith in the unity of the social and physical sciences, its pure phenomenalism, its reduction of all knowledge to a single formula, and its interpretation of knowledge as having practical value.[18]

In the aftermath of the failed revolutions of 1848 and the eclipse of the utopian socialism of Henri de Saint-Simon, whose reformism influenced Comte's thinking, the search for a scientifically based social order was replaced by a more empirical approach to social phenomena. Drawing on the strict empiricism of David Hume, philosophers such as John Stuart Mill defined their task as the formulation of the rules of reasoning. One could not make assertions about the world that were not informed by immediate observations. Moreover, the meaning of knowledge, as Hume had earlier explained in his attempt to discredit the legitimacy of inductive reasoning, was purely pragmatic; it was judged in terms of its ability to increase society's body of information about itself and thus facilitate the experience of living. What was socially useful was socially valued.[19]

By the late nineteenth century, biology began to exercise a growing influence on positivism. Darwin's theory of evolution contributed to the view that biological regularities could be applied to all aspects of human existence. The belief that all behavior could be reduced to biologically driven utilitarian rules thus expanded the application of positivist thinking to organic nature and to creation itself. In Herbert Spencer's theory of evolution, all human conduct, regardless of apparent social, cultural, and historical differences of development, was attributable to the mechanical operation of biological forces undergoing the same process of evolution in accord with a unifying set of laws or cosmic force to which all knowledge could be reduced.[20]

Even before World War I destroyed the search for a general theory of progress that embraced all humanity, positivist thought began to retreat from attempts to rationalize the world and to return to the study of pure experience. Analogous to the turn-of-the-century trend in historicism, empiriocriticism both relativized and dehumanized experience. There was no objectively determined knowledge, hence, no generalizations or universally valid science, no "truth." In reducing subjective experience to its component parts, it destroyed the subject or self.[21]

Empiriocriticism, in turn, was supplanted by logical positivism, which sought to unite rationalism and empiricism through the logical analysis of the syntax and semantics of language. Positivism thence confined itself to the testing of hypotheses and the evaluation of inferential reasoning in scientific thinking. Logical positivism, the emergence of which coincided with and was influenced by the post–World War I emphasis on technological efficiency, is the precursor to the scientism that is rampant in the technocratic culture of the late twentieth century. Scientism asserts that questions that cannot be answered by the natural and deductive sciences are improper and that putative answers to them are inherently meaningless.[22]

Just as historicism is more of an orientation to the nature of reality than a theory, positivism is more a method of analyzing what is observed about the world than a doctrine. Both are preoccupied with process. But where historicism describes what is, positivism focuses on analyzing the validity of the propositions that underlie perceived reality. Unlike historicism, positivism is concerned with presuppositions rather than outcomes; with the disaggregation of concepts into their analytical components rather than their synthesis into holistic constructs. In its zeal to achieve logical clarity of observation, however, positivism pays short shrift to the content of thought.

Positivism asserts that meaning inheres in the scientific affirmation of the observable natural world; in the correspondence between the structure of the propositions we advance about experience and the facts they assert. The aim of such an approach is to posit laws from which the meaning of contemporary events can be deduced. Conversely, if a proposition cannot be verified, it is invalid. If it is invalid, it is meaningless. And if it is meaningless, it is necessarily devoid of any predictive value. This is the basis of Karl Popper's criticism of historicism. For Popper, who narrowly defines historicism as the nomothetic development of social processes that operate independent of human involvement, historiosophical systems such as those propounded by Hegel, Marx, and Toynbee were devoid of value because they did not lend themselves to the study of their component parts or to an analysis of their practical utility.[23]

In contrast to historicism, which believes that historical knowledge is the only requirement for understanding the human condition and contemporary problems, positivism is only interested in what can be empirically deduced, experimentally reiterated, and operationally refined. Positivists like Popper dismiss historically derived knowledge as being truistic. Where historicism reduces contemporary spatial reality to the extension of the temporal, positivism excludes the temporal from any consideration of the present. Indeed, it is antihistorical in Kahler's sense that it is antievolutional. It purports to transcend history and its arbitrary logic by imputing cognitive value only to those efforts that are measurable in terms of their practical effectiveness.[24]

Consequently, emphasis is placed on technical efficiency, or what Lyotard calls "performativity," in the assessment and management of social processes. Nontechnical expertise—the narrative tradition of explaining social change in its historical and cultural context—cannot be legitimate because it does not lend itself to scientific experimentation and validation. By restricting knowledge to the denotative, or that which is susceptible to proof, positivism further severs society from its traditions—the beliefs and myths that provide continuity with the past and meaning for the future.[25]

The fascination with technique and technology has led to the development of a mechanistic approach to social inquiry, or social "science." This, in turn, has encouraged professional specialization and the compartmentalization of research into narrower categories in the name of science and epistemology—or what Christopher Chase-Dunn appropriately refers to as "methodological sectarianism"—but generally at the expense of any intellectual or cultural synthesis. Sociologist Talcott Parsons' self-regulating system, a functionalist model of society in which processes contribute to or detract from the operation of the whole organism, and modern-day cybernetics, which reduces thought to the workings of a machine, are exceptions to the rule of compartmentalization. But they similarly restrict their understanding of social processes and social change to the operation of phenomena under controlled observation.[26]

By imputing meaning to the efficiency of operation, positivism not only severs humanity from its past, it also removes it from the world around it. It abstracts knowledge from society, confines it to a preserve of detached experts or social engineers. Rather than clarify the changing rhythms of modernity, positivism makes it harder to apprehend social change. It does not address questions of ontological meaning, or tradition, or justice, all of which are dismissed as unscientific conventions.

But the technocratic elite cannot share knowledge without being immersed in the process of change, and thus in the flow of history. As Lyotard has pointed out, knowledge cannot assert its own truth without resort to narrative explanation. To do otherwise would be to presuppose its own validity, which would be unscientific. Worse, positivism's cultural disconnectedness and its emphasis on certitude imposes constraints on knowing. Because it cannot say what the world is really like, positivism undermines the foundations of science. Descartes could not be sure that cognition mirrored reality, so he relied on his belief in God to link reason with the world.[27]

In its emphasis on social engineering, positivism breeds conformity. It narrows the universe of influences that shape the way society interacts with the world. It rejects social instabilities as dysfunctional deviations from the management of social process rather than as precursors to invention. In its emphasis on performance and social unity, positivism is also dehumanizing. The complexity of human intentions, aspirations, anxieties, and the other dimensions of personality are discarded as opaque mentalistic concepts. Positivism believes that human behavior, in emulation of physical nature, can also be ascertained and predicted on the basis of scientifically determined responses to social variability.[28]

At the same time, positivism embraces a not-so-scientific faith in the socially therapeutic power of science. Contemporary social engineers, no less than their utilitarian predecessors, believe that the spread of ideologically neutral science through education will enhance human rationality and ultimately eliminate intolerance and warfare. Such an attitude, however, naively ignores the demonic aspects of human nature, which cannot be attributed solely to defective thinking.[29]

Knowledge and understanding are not reducible to mechanistic models. Events, physicist Fritjof Capra has written, do not always have a well-defined, predictable cause.[30] Nor does human behavior. The acquisition of knowledge is speculative. Its value does not lie in its apodictic nature. Science may provide consensual agreement in the observations we make about nature, but it cannot produce truth. Truth is accessible only to God. For mortals, knowledge is at best truth-approximation, that is, the representation of limited minds. Knowledge implies a memory of the past and an openness toward the future.

The real value of knowledge is emancipatory; it bestows freedom on human beings to understand their lives in the context of their beliefs and traditions and the contemporary social processes they confront. Stated differently, knowledge is humanity's perpetual dialogue with itself about its existence at any point in time. It is what Benedetto Croce meant when he said that all history is contemporary. It enables society to continue telling its story, recreating the narrative, and thus itself, in the process. It is humanity's search for meaning in the world and the reciprocal imposition of the world on humanity's self-identity.[31]

In so doing, however, the historical dialogue does not aim either to reproduce the past or to rewrite it willy-nilly but rather to recreate it in the questions we pose. Knowledge of the past is a composite of past and present, or what Louis Mink called "history-as-past-actuality and history-as-present-knowledge." Knowledge is not only the understanding of one's being-in-the-world, as Heidegger put it, it is also the projection of that understanding toward the future and its indeterminate possibilities. Knowledge thus requires an understanding of the past and the present and their implications for the future, the whole of which is greater than the sum of all the parts.[32]

The Lived Experience of Change

History provides a compass to guide society into the future. Although there is a direction in history, a general trend in which events are moving, it cannot be determined a priori, and certainly not with finality. It is a composite of the objective course of events and the subjective interpretation of those events by individuals whose personal beliefs are influenced by the collective culture—the *Zeitgeist*—in which they participate. History is at once continuous and discontinuous. It is not merely the inexorable flow of time. Existence is more than a process, or a chain of processes, that systematize life in a state of "universal simultaneity" or "spatialization," as Kahler put it. Events, ideas, and interruptions of social processes may disrupt the world's trajectory and propel it outside its accustomed path, giving rise, like shifting geological plates, to new ages or epochs. At such cleavages in the progressive temporality of experience, societies may either repress the change swirling about them or, unshackled from the burden of history and positivism, plunge headlong into it.[33]

Such divestment, or "unlearning," or "creative negativity," as Palmer calls it, liberates society from the determinism of the past and the conformity of scientism in order to experience the present and the indeterminate future. By "forgetting" the past and escaping the presentist preoccupation with process, societies discover the future. This, in turn, makes it possible to reintegrate the past with the future from the vantage point of the changing present. The dialogue between the present and the past, or between paradigms, reconnects society with its traditions, with its story. "The shift from one paradigm to another," Richard Brown points out, "is not merely a psychological shift of gestalts or an unreasoned leap in the dark. Instead, it is a leap into the logic of narrative, a construction (or reconstruction) of a cognitive tradition in order to make sense anew."[34]

Historical change is both objective and subjective. To be sure, the validity of one's interpretation of epochal change must be subject to some method of evaluation, if not empirical investigation, if one is to distinguish between reality and whimsy. At the very least, the parts should show share a relationship with the whole, lest one fall into the postmodernist fallacy that there are no standards of evaluation, or, at least, no meaningfully applicable standards, and that aesthetic, moral, or intellectual judgments are elitist contrivances. It should also elucidate a theme or leitmotif and address issues in the proper historical context.[35]

Methodological standards facilitate the rational description of change between paradigms or ideologies. They provide an existential reference point between one set of realities and another. Empirical investigation defines knowing in explicit terms. Knowledge is whatever one can reduce to mathematical formulae or, at least, to statistical probabilities of certitude. What cannot be fitted within the formal construct of logic is unscientific, illusory, or what systems analysts call "background noise." Imagination is merely the reordering of sensory information in one's consciousness. Knowledge is representational, a mirror of the world.

Such standards of evaluation cannot be applied while change is taking place, however. When it is occurring, historical change is mainly perceptual. We know it even when we cannot describe it. Knowledge, then, is also implicit and indeterminate. The background noise inevitably contains patterns that help to focus one's awareness of the world. To be sure, the patterns in the background may not be readily apparent. They are likely to be revealed in clues that may at first be ignored, screened from cognition, or rejected because they do not fit within the existing ideology or paradigm that encompasses reality.

Historical events may not be reproducible, but this does not make them incomparable. If this were the case, history would be useless in comprehending the present. In fact, discrete, unreplicatable experiences are simultaneously observable cases in a broader pattern of developments that permit synoptic judgments—indeed, generalizations—about otherwise unique and, therefore, irrelevant occurrences. Historians implicitly acknowledge this duality when, in addition to maintaining the uniqueness of history, they also stress its criticality in contemporary decision making.[36]

Few, if any, American analysts, for example, altered their views of the Soviet Union on the basis of Communist Party leader Leonid Brezhnev's 1978 speech in Tula, in which he voiced Moscow's concern about the state of economic decline, or the coincident devaluation of the Third World in the calculus of Soviet interests. Yet these developments were harbingers of the "new thinking" that preceded Soviet military retrenchment and political restructuring a decade later. Nevertheless, the persistence of clues during Yuri Andropov's brief tenure as party leader and especially following Mikhail Gorbachev's emergence in 1985 increasingly attracted analytical attention to the still indeterminate reality of a transformation in Soviet foreign policy. What beckoned a closer view was the intuition that the clues concealed a pattern of change that was about to emerge.[37]

Although conceptually vague, the awareness of change in the Soviet Union preceded the understanding of its particular elements. Sovietologists apprehended the connotation of Gorbachev's repeated references to mutual security or peaceful coexistence in 1985 and 1986 without knowing their denotative meaning, that is, without integrating the particulars into a new framework of understanding. What made the particulars meaningful was the coherence of the whole of which they were a part. What made the whole intelligible was intuitive judgment—Kant's "mother wit"—the inscrutable procedure that etches the conceptual profile within which the rules of formal logic can be applied.

There are places science cannot take us, the "boundary situations" Karl Jaspers refers to, where neither theory nor empiricism can provide answers to the human experience. There is no law of science or explicit procedure that defines phenomena in universal terms. Science explains relationships; it does not provide a formal procedure for induction. We derive meaning from the whole by apprehending a background of clues on which we have not focused our attention. It is the recognition of the whole that permits identification of the parts. Indeed, it is the recognition of the whole that gives meaning to the parts.[38]

When we see the whole, we see the parts differently. Concentration on the identified parts, in turn, clarifies their relationship to the whole and thus deepens one's understanding of it. We can identify the scene in impressionist art—Monet's haystacks, for example, or Manet's water lilies—if we stand away from the painting. As the focus of our attention becomes less tangible, the meaning of what we apprehend becomes more conceptual. In other words, although we are fully aware of the particulars of the scene, we focus from them to what they mean. By drawing closer to the canvas, however, focusing on the relationship between light and color, and concentrating on specific objects, we integrate the elements of the painting and intensify our understanding of the whole scene.[39]

In effect, then, we "tacitly" know change, to use Michael Polanyi's term, in all of its indeterminacy, before we know it empirically in its particulars. We know the unexpected by the unattended or unfocused or subliminal awareness of particulars in a comprehensive entity. To illustrate the point, the laws of science and gravity enabled Newton to explain the importance of the heliocentric system, but the concept that the sun was the center of the planetary system was anticipated 140 years earlier by Copernicus. But Newtonian mechanics and the belief that the universe moved according to immutable laws failed to explain electrodynamics and wave theory. Indeed, the subsequent discovery of subatomic units of matter and the emergence of quantum theory have shown that the apprehension of the whole precedes an understanding of the interrelatedness of the parts. Further, quantum theory has advanced the view that events, even scientific events, may often be probabilistic rather than causative. "Even the physical world is not completely determined,"

Kenneth Boulding has observed. "The coming together of a group of atoms into a complex molecule, for instance, may be highly improbable, but if it is not impossible, it will eventually happen," as it has in human history. "The more complex a system, the more the actual happening of improbable events dominates its history."[40]

Understanding change, whether in science or in society, is phenomenological; it is one's access to the prereflective givenness of phenomena derived from sense perceptions and undistorted by anticipatory ideas. There is no pure perception, as Gadamer points out, because one's consciousness and the object of that consciousness are not separated. Understanding change is not an act of pure objectivity or subjectivity, it is a mode of being. It is the fusion of being and existence.[41]

The integration of one's life into the whole of life that is unfolding is the ontological expression of knowledge. It is, to use Kierkegaard's phrase, the "illumination" that comes from one's existential commitment, one's immersion in the process of life in all its diversity. By immersing ourselves in the process of change, we also become aware of the prejudices and preconceptions that have obscured the understanding of change. Rather than stand outside of experience and history, in good Cartesian fashion, we are ontologically integrated by the objective reality we confront. The subject and object of inquiry are fused.

The same is true of historical change. Awareness of the whole similarly facilitates the integration of past and present in the emerging future. "The problem of history is not to be found in the relationship between painter and painting," Fernand Braudel has written, or "in the relationship between painting and the landscape. The problem is right in the landscape, in the heart of life itself."[42] Historical change is not something we discover, manage, or control. It is its own happening in which we are imbedded. Historical change is fraught with terrifying anxiety. Manifestly the continuation of the past, it is existentially the dislocation of society from its convictions. It throws humankind, individually and collectively, into a time warp that makes it seem as if one were living in different places at the same time. The pain of separation can only be overcome by leaping into the unknown and, in being what Nietzsche refers to as "unhistorical," risking the future by choosing tomorrow at the expense of yesterday. Implicit in this process is a negation, not of the events of the past, but of meanings assigned to them that are no longer relevant to the reality of the present.[43]

We know or understand from the perspective of the past, that is, by engaging in a comparative dialogue with the beliefs that mediated experience in the past and the new reality that looms before us. It is the integrated accumulation of recognitions that make sense out of what is being experienced and nonsense out of what has been experienced. Once we implicitly recognize the coherence of the events we are experiencing, we cannot unlearn them; they dwell within us. Change is *lived experience; it is being-in-the-world.*[44]

Change is dialectical. As we see the profile of the present, an indeterminate range of future possibilities open up that also illumines the past. Just as the traditions of the past transport us into the present, the present recreates the past in ways that make it meaningful for the nascent future. Ontologically, history has no other meaning. There is no irreducible element or elements, the unearthing of which will reveal the "objective" truth of an age. Nor is truth the objectification of an idea that is history itself. The past is no more definitive than the future. It does not exist for itself, it exists for humanity. Both are subject to the meaning imputed to them. Like the future, the past is also an inexhaustible source of possibilities on its trajectory toward tomorrow.[45]

Lived experience makes it possible to understand change and thus to construct new ideologies that reconnect the human community with the world. Shorn of its normative debris, ideology is simply the conceptualization of reality. It is a "matrix of meaning" that, for better or worse, gives cognitive and affective content to reality by symbolically reaffirming society's lived experience in a defined social order. Ideology legitimates historic change. Its "truth" or "falsity" is a function of the human experience from which it derives and to which it seeks to ensure society's allegiance.[46]

PATTERNS OF HISTORICAL CHANGE

Evolutionary history compartmentalizes time. Its focus is on the discrete and the particular. It is slice-of-life history, history as vignette, *l'histoire événementielle,* as Braudel called it, a narration of events within a constricted time span. It endeavors symbolically to capture the society's ethos and belief system in the events it relates, the authenticity of which lies in a documented record. Its aesthetic is comparable to the "beautiful" in art.[47]

Epochal history, in contrast, is panoramic. Its focus is on the cultural structures, both material and intellectual, that underlie specific events in the broad expanse of time. It is *la longue durée,* a composite of the synchronic and the diachronic. Unlike evolutionary history, it is not learned through immersion in the events of the past. Rather, epochal history requires distance from the events of the past and an openness to the complexity of forces that give meaning to culture and society as a whole. Its authenticity lies in its interpretation of the patterns or rhythms of the past. Its aesthetic is the sublime.

By definition, epochal change is infrequent. Including the shifting tectonic plates on which the world is presently teetering, I can identify only two other such transformations in history. The first is the long sweep of time extending from the period of antiquity preceding Christ to the mid-fourteenth century, in which geographically remote and culturally insulated societies struggled to establish physical security and a peaceful social order in the world they experienced. For these societies, order was fragile; disorder, destruction, and the dissolution of peoples and cultures commonplace. Theirs was a world of observation, classification, and consolidation.

The era of order gave way at the midpoint of the fourteenth century to the age of progress that has lasted to the present time. From its inception it was an era of rebellion against the other-directed order and dogmatism of the past. Science was enthroned as the new God whose boundless power would lead to the perfectibility of humanity. Exploration, experimentation, and expansionism have been the hallmarks of the epoch of progress.

But science, alas, has not perfected humanity. Even as it has removed the social and physical barriers that once segregated peoples from each other and greatly enhanced their productive capacity, it has culturally alienated societies that have lagged behind in the race for status and prestige from themselves and the world around them. Partly because of the growing estrangement between peoples, partly because of the dawning realization that traditional structures of social and political organization no longer inspire confidence in our ability to ensure human progress, the world, as we shall see, is undergoing another transformation. We are entering an epoch of mutualism in which autonomy, interdependence, and the harmonization of interests is likely to provide a new, holistic framework of understanding and behavior.[48]

These epochal changes, of course, cannot be precisely fixed in time. There is no clearly demarcated moment when one era ends and another begins, no cultural big bang, so to speak. In addition, the timing of epochal change does not follow a chronological sequence. The twentieth century, for instance, appears to have begun in 1917, not 1900, just as the modern era—for the West but not for Asia or the Middle East—

probably started in the mid-fourteenth century rather than with the bloom of the Renaissance or the institutionalization of science two centuries later. Furthermore, the signs of epochal change are visible in different societies at different times. China, for example, was immune to modernizing developments in Europe until the Ching period in the seventeenth century.

Nor are successive epochs indistinguishably different in form and content from those that preceded them. The search for stability, for example, has not been absent from the epoch of progress, any more than the epoch of order was devoid of discovery. Likewise, the epoch of mutualism is not likely to extinguish the quest for human progress. Nevertheless, order or progress or mutualism will be more characteristic of the ethos, defining nature, or behavior of one age than of another. The quality, degree, and extensiveness of different values and beliefs, as well as the forms they take, inevitably change as societies ascribe new meanings to the changing reality they experience.

Finally, there is no linearity to historic change. The transition from the epoch of order in the West to the secularization of the epoch of progress was a tortuous development. Witness the European church–state crisis of the twelfth century. At the mid-point of that century, Holy Roman Emperor Frederick Barbarossa temporarily restored the absolutist order and unity of Charlemagne's empire, which was itself a continuation of the legacy of ancient Rome. In the twentieth century, the welfare state became the institutional repository of the belief in progress that World War I and the Great Depression had all but shattered.

The dynamic that produces change is still more elusive. How people will respond to disruptions in the way they see the world cannot be predicted. There was no immanent force or law of nature or historical totem rising Excalibur-like from the recesses of time that compelled Europeans to redefine their view of the world in the fourteenth century. Nor is there, in the final analysis, any assurance that the emerging epoch will be characterized by a mutuality of interest rather than by some other, possibly pernicious, ideology. The literature is filled with theories that confine change within predetermined paths. Oswald Spengler's dreary biological metaphor for life, Toynbee's challenge-and-response dichotomy, the nomothetic ahistoricism of Marx and neo-Marxist theorists like Immanuel Wallerstein readily come to mind.[49]

Historic change, however, like individual change, is not the residue of the past. Toynbee may be right in calling life the recurring attempt to reconcile liberty and necessity. But the social profile that such reconciliation produces is always contingent on the inherently unpredictable behavior of individuals whose creative leap into the unknown is the impetus for the future. They create the possibles—the "what will have been," in Lyotard's term—the reality of which can be experienced only after it has occurred.[50]

What will have been is the societal distillate of the human response to change. It is the reinvestment of life with meaning that permits humanity to reconcile itself with a world from which it is no longer estranged. Understanding historic change lies in the recognition that life is a moving human portrait. As Dorothy discovered in the Land of Oz, we are the wizard. For better or worse, we define our future.

The Search for Order

From the dawn of civilization to the stabilization and predictability of economic life that gradually set in after the fifteenth century, humanity waged a constant struggle for survival in a world of mystery, wonderment, and arbitrary destructiveness. The relentless regularity of death and devastation were part of life's natural rhythm. Only the fittest survived. The fragility of existence, not surprisingly, compelled early peoples to establish some semblance of order amid the disorder that enveloped them. For those peoples from antiquity to modernity who built great civilizations, as well as those whose imprint on history is barely decipherable, the creation of order entailed the development of religious myth and ritual to make sense of a vast and incomprehensible cosmos, the formation of agricultural communities that increased the odds of outlasting the ravages of plague, pestilence, and famine, and the fortification of society against the onslaught of barbarians on the periphery of civilization.

The paramountcy of order, both in cognitive and material terms, defined humanity's social and intellectual orientation to the world until the eleventh or twelfth century. Thereafter, as reason gradually replaced religion and technology and new forms of human organization rescued societies from the vicissitudes of mere subsistence, the ideology of order began to lose its explanatory power. By the fourteenth century, the conception of order was no longer a meaningful referent for societies that were undergoing the onset of convulsive social change. Bereft of beliefs to fathom a suddenly strange and terrifying world, humanity was forced to reinterpret the conditions of its existence in response to the new realities it confronted.

The absence of a written record and scarce physical remains shroud the prehistoric past in darkness.[1] Absent evidence to the contrary, one can only assume that the human transition from savage predator to hunter-gatherer that predated the beginning of civilization was a brutal evolution. The origins of civilization, in its most rudimentary form, date from around 4000 B.C. in Mesopotamia. As far as one can tell, farmers in search of arable land migrated from hillsides to the confluence of the Tigris and Euphrates rivers, where they established a relatively specialized social structure. Both to ensure social cohesion and to defend against bands of roving barbarians, proto–city-states gradually emerged in the lower Mesopotamian valley plain of Sumer and, later, farther north in Akkad, a land of semitic tribes that coalesced under the warrior Sargon into the world's first empire.

In time, internal conflicts, repeated plunder by outsiders, and, according to recent evidence, a 300-year drought in the Akkadian empire beginning in about 2200 B.C. eventually laid waste to these societies until Mesopotamia was united by the Amorite leader Hammurabi around 1700 B.C. in the rising city of Babylon. The Babylonian empire eventually fell prey to Hittite and Kassite raiders. They, in turn, were succeeded by the Assyrians, who also absorbed the Egyptian empire on the Nile, the Chaldeans, who created the second or neo-Babylonian empire under Nebuchadnezzar, and the Achaemenids of Persia, whose empire extended from the Nile to central Asia.[2]

The same cycle of generation and extinction is visible in other early civilizations. Roughly coeval with the emergence of Sumerian society, an Egyptian community was taking root along the banks of the Nile River. On the basis of the fragmentary record, Egyptian civilization under the pharaohs, to which the great pyramids bear monumental testimony, appears to have been remarkably cohesive and sophisticated. Here, too, however, faults in the social structure began to weaken its foundation in the second millennium, and by 1800 B.C. Egypt was overcome by the Hyksos.

Meanwhile, in about 2500 B.C. a metropolitan civilization similar to that in Mesopotamia had also emerged in the Indus Valley. Partly because of the export of cotton from the cities of Mohenjo-Daro and Harappa to Sumer society, it flourished until 1500 B.C., when Aryan invaders from the steppes of southern Russia infiltrated the region and obliterated it. As the great cities of the Indus Valley were disappearing, a

Mycenean empire was forming in Asia Minor. At the same time, Chinese civilization was emerging in the Yellow River valley, isolated by geography and by roving bands of barbarian warriors that separated the Middle East from Asia. The earliest dynasty, the Shang, lasted until about 1000 B.C., when conquering tribes established the Chou empire, whose loss of power to local princes predated by nearly two millennia the later emergence of feudal potentates in Europe and Japan.[3]

All early civilizations from Sumer onward were ruled by a king or overlord. In the perilous, unstable environment that these early societies faced, both within and without their settlements, autocratic control was in all likelihood a condition of survival. It was surely necessary to erect defenses against barbarian invaders. Arguably, autocracy also preserved social order by establishing a connection between the rigors of daily existence and the spirit world. Indeed, the rulers of these societies were king-priests, intermediaries between the gods and the natural world. According to scholars of early civilization, the agricultural output that resulted from social control and organization propitiated the gods, whose disfavor, manifested in floods or droughts, frequently meant the difference between life and death. The same pattern of productivity and propitiation probably influenced the development of other temple societies in early human history, whether the priest-rulers functioned as human agents of deities or, as in the case of the pharaohs, as their incarnations. The more insecure one's environment, the more powerful the ruler's control.[4]

Because of their inherent weakness and the dangers that lurked on their peripheries at every turn, the civilizations that emerged from barbarism were physically and culturally isolated. But as societies expanded and grew into city-empires, the probability of contact with strange peoples perforce increased. The trade that seems to have taken place between Sumer society and the city-states in the Indus valley is illustrative. By the end of the second millennium, warfare, diplomacy, and commerce accelerated the frequency of contact between Mesopotamia and Egypt and the societies in the Aegean region. There is even archeological evidence of contacts between China and the peoples of western Asia and the Middle East. Such interaction, however, was sporadic and irregular. For all the examples of cultural syncretism that students of antiquity may adduce, it seems safe to say that the early civilizations were culturally autochthonous, largely independent, and, in some cases, impervious to the influences of other societies they encountered.[5]

Greek civilization, for example, which emerged after a hiatus of three centuries from the ashes of Mycenae, was influenced by contacts with Phoenicia and Persia. Vestiges of Phoenician and Persian culture have been found in Greek art, religious rituals, even in the alphabet. Nevertheless, the development of Greek civilization—from the Peloponnesian settlements of either Dorian tribes or Mycenean descendants to the Aegean cities established by the Ionians—was largely self-contained. Despite the periodic intersection of societies, the "refusal" to embrace beliefs or social characteristics that could not be assimilated within indigenous cultural patterns was common. Indeed, King Darius I, who ruled the Persian empire from the end of the sixth century to the beginning of the fifth century B.C., paid little heed to the Greek societies that had developed in the Peloponnesus and across the Aegean Sea on the Asia Minor coast.[6]

Like other ancient civilizations, the Greeks were preoccupied with the need to establish order in an unstable and mysterious world. For the Greeks, order meant the preservation of self and society against the ravages of nature and other peoples, civilized or barbarian: the creation of structures and processes to provide for the sustenance of communities and the erection of defenses to guard against invasion. Order also entailed the formulation of convictions and beliefs that imparted meaning to the unpredictability of the present and the uncertainty of the future.

In addition to providing a this-worldly communion with the heavens, religious rites and ceremonies also united peoples from different cities in a common culture. As reflected in the Orphic cults and the transcendental teachings of Pythagoras, mysticism and religious ritual permeated Greek society. Despite the absence of an organized priesthood, rituals of homage to the deities were frequent occurrences in ancient Greece's democratic as well as imperial phases. From the rise of the polis in Periclean Athens to the empire of Alexander the Great, however, there was an undeniable intellective aspect to the maintenance of order. What distinguished the Greeks from earlier civilizations was their ability to make the world apprehensible to reason.[7]

Among the educated, the priesthood and the presence of anthropomorphic deities of the temple societies were replaced by philosophers and a reason-based cosmology that harnessed the unpredictable power of the gods to the laws of nature. Their task was to understand, organize, and explain the immutable laws that regulated the rational operation of the world, including the individual and society, as the plays of Aeschylus and Sophocles demonstrate. For the Greeks, and for later peoples in the Mediterranean and beyond who shared in their intellectual inheritance, order was not defined solely in phenomenal terms of physical and social survival. Order was also noumenal, a creation of the mind; the intuitive understanding of the world as it essentially is rather than as it appears.[8]

From Thales to Aristotle, Greek philosophy proceeded on the assumption that behind the apparent disorder of life lay a timeless order, regularity, and permanence, the material aspects of which were subject to observation, explanation, and classification. Life was cyclical. Human history mirrored the repetitive pattern of nature, and there was little expectation of any future that differed from the past.[9]

The harmony of polis life was consonant with Greek cosmology. The polis was a microcosm of the world. The citizen-based, open form of democracy in the polis reinforced social solidarity and equality. Attic citizens could speak and vote in the assembly, and some might be chosen to sit on the council of five hundred magistrates annually chosen by lot from the wards *(demes)* of Athens and Attica. Upwardly mobile peasant farmers—the hoplites—commonly received plots of land in exchange for military service. To be sure, Athenian democracy did not extend to women, noncitizens, or helots. Nor could it withstand Athens's arrogation of power to itself.[10]

After the defeat of the Persians, Athens began to encroach on the freedom of the neighboring cities that had joined with it in 454 B.C. to form a defensive alliance known as the Delian League. The outcome of Athenian imperialism, the Pelponnesian War against Sparta, was the prelude to protracted warfare among the Greek city-states and the demise of the polis. In the fourth century, Philip of Macedon and his son Alexander absorbed the once-proud city-states, spreading Hellenic culture in the far-flung Greek empire that stretched from the Mediterranean to the Indus River and from the Caucasus Mountains to the Nile. But the Greek empire proved to be short lived. By the middle of the third century, Greek dominance in Italy collapsed before the mounting power of Rome, a city-state like Athens and Sparta. Thereafter, the Greek states, eager to arrest the growing social disorder of their faction-ridden cities, became subjects of the Roman Empire.[11]

One does not have to agree with Arnold Toynbee's view that Rome was simply the universalization of the Hellenic state to acknowledge that its pattern of development from city-state to republic to imperium strikingly parallels that of Greece. Undoubtedly, Rome was influenced by

Hellenic culture. Roman mythology and religion, with such notable exceptions as the fable of Remus and Romulus, is almost a transposition of Greek practices and beliefs. Roman thought and literature, enriched by the writings of Plautus, Seneca, Cicero, and Tacitus, reproduced the orderliness of Greek cosmology. The Roman conception of society in the early Antonine period of the Republic emulated that of the polis. Whether patrician or *pleb*, the citizen was subordinated to the state, to public service, and to the common good.[12]

At the same time, distinctive elements in Roman society both broadened and extended the parameters of classical culture and its search for order and stability in the world. The practice of government was rationalized. Bureaucracies were formed to administer financial affairs, collect taxes and take the census, and preside over the courts in a governmental system that became increasingly differentiated and specialized. In addition, Roman law, the origins of which date from 450 B.C., codified the rights of citizens, or *civitates*. Until the late second century, when Roman rulers ceased to honor the law, this assured the plebs of some influence in the Assembly. Judicially sanctioned norms of behavior also facilitated the process of assimilating newcomers into Roman society.[13]

Of course, Roman law did not have universal applicability. As was the case in Greece, no rights were accorded to slaves. Nor did it conduce to the formation of a real representative system of government. For the Romans as well as the Greeks, as P. A. Brunt has observed, liberty denoted privilege and immunity from arbitrary coercion more than political influence. And by the time the Republic turned despotic, in around 120–100 B.C., liberty was little more that a facade that legitimized oligarchic control.[14]

The Romans also spread urbanization. They imposed political and administrative order on the teutonic tribes they conquered. Cities—architectural and social microcosms of Roman civilization—sprouted in the hinterlands of the civilized world in the wake of military expansion. Although one may comfortably assume that barbarians did not welcome their colonial status, they eventually assimilated the culture and refinement of Rome. Moreover, in contrast to Athens and the later Greek empire, Rome granted citizenship to all subjects, barbarians included. Indeed, conquering legions permitted the peoples they overran to retain local customs and self-government within a Romanized municipal structure, thereby reinforcing the empire's cosmopolitan unity and lessening the risk of instability on its ever-expanding borders.[15]

Paradoxically, however, the civilizing influence of military expansionism undermined the domestic order of Rome. Increased wealth corrupted government officials and the military and debased the concept of *civitas*. The importation of grain and other products from Africa and Egypt economically dislocated the citizen-farmer, who was the backbone of the republic and the army. Riots and military reprisals alternated with destructive regularity until 31 B.C., when a tired, bloated pseudo-Republic gratefully acquiesced in the autocratic control of Augustus.[16]

The recentralization, indeed, militarization, of political and administrative authority under Augustus and his successors, notably Trajan and Hadrian, restored the integrity of Rome. But the Augustan system masked a military despotism. Senators were now agents of the emperor rather than independent magistrates. The more power vested in the person of the emperor rather than in the institutions he controlled, the less the empire was able to withstand the divisive forces in the army and the bureaucracy that undermined imperial unity.[17]

By the third century, Rome had become a divided empire, both socially and geographically, a victim of what Gibbon called its "immoderate greatness." The shortages of manpower and material resources to manage its sprawling domains and the increasing income gap between the urban aristocracy and the oppressively taxed farmer deprived Rome of its social cohesion as well as its revenue base. In the aristocratic West, an apathetic and senatorial oligarchy became increasingly estranged from the more trade-oriented, egalitarian society of the East—the Danubian provinces, the Rhineland, Egypt, northern Africa—where one's sense of personal and social identity as a *romanus* remained surrealistically intact.[18]

The Greco-Roman struggle to impose order on the world mirrored the historical development of Asian civilizations. Centuries of warfare in China similarly created a need for some centralizing authority. Like the temple societies in Mesopotamia, early Chinese civilization established a link between the natural and supernatural worlds in the form of an emperor who exercised political authority in accord with the wishes of Heaven. The imposition of imperial order was legitimized by sanctioned violence on the part of the ruler—military conquest, hunting, and religious sacrifice—and by the teachings of philosophers that reinforced state authority.[19]

Among the philosophers of the "hundred schools" of thought that sprang up between the sixth and fourth centuries B.C. was Confucius. Like the classical Greek philosophers, particularly Aristotle, Confucius paid scant attention to religious speculation. The virtuous society, in his view, was one that demonstrated wisdom and courage and the fidelity to the rituals and responsibilities that accompanied the different stations in the social hierarchy in accord with the cosmic order of which it was a part. This was just the opposite of the Taoist view, which attributed rules of social propriety to the inherent moral disorder of the world. Taoism idealized the harmomy of interests between ruler and ruled and thus rejected the state's emphasis on proper conduct in favor of *laissez faire.* Confucian philosophy also differed from the Legalist school's authoritarian emphasis on rewards and punishments to preserve order and obedience to the state.[20]

Following Confucius's death in the fifth century B.C., Chinese society introduced a money-based relationship between the gentry and the peasantry that replaced the obligations of the feudal period. Nevertheless, the struggle for power among the nobility thrust China into renewed instability until order was restored in 221 B.C. by Shih Huang-ti, whose autocratic rule was the antithesis of Confucianism. Following his death in 210 B.C., the empire disintegrated until the Han rulers appeared on the scene four years later. The Han united China's fractious principalities and dispersed Chinese culture and influence from Western Asia to Mongolia, Annam, Korea, and the fringes of the civilized world. To be sure, Legalist methods of bureaucratic control persisted even after the Han emperors restored Chinese unity. Indeed, as the violence in Tiananmen Square in the spring of 1989 demonstrated, they remain to this day powerful instruments in the state's control over society. But bureaucratic power was now combined with Confucianism's emperor-based moral cosmology, thereby instituting what John King Fairbank referred to as "imperial Confucianism."[21]

Unlike China, which was indirectly connected to the civilizations west of Asia through trade along the Silk Road, Indian civilization had come into direct contact with the Mediterranean world as a consequence of Alexander the Great's expansion into the lower Indus Valley. Further Greek advances after Alexander's death were repulsed, however, by Chandragupta Maurya, who united India from the Indus to the Ganges rivers within a single empire. The Mauryan empire reached its apogee in the third century under the rule of the reformer Ashoka, who sought to bring internal order to a society that was torn between the elaborate ritual of Brahminism, the unadorned enlightenment of Buddhism, and the more ascetic Jainism that appealed to the imagination of urban dwellers. In contrast to the temple societies that preceded Mauryan rule, Ashoka became a devout adherent of Buddhism, which he propagated throughout India and parts of central Asia.[22]

As was true elsewhere in the world, the Mauryan order proved to be ephemeral. Ashoka's death ushered in a prolonged period of internal turmoil and invasion by steppe nomads, which was temporarily interrupted at the end of the first century A.D. by Kushan tribesmen from the central Asian steppe who briefly consolidated power in northwest India. The collapse of the Kushan empire preceded the emergence of the Gupta states in the fourth century and the restoration of order based on the imperial rule of the Mauryan empire.[23]

LATE ANTIQUITY

By the third century A.D., the classical civilizations that had forged an imperial order out of the chaos that surrounded them were in process of disintegration. In their place, new civilizations formed. Whether led by patricians, tribal chiefs, lower-class usurpers of power, or feudal families, these societies were absorbed in the same struggle to establish and preserve orderly ways of life in an uncertain, arbitrary, menacing world. Like civilizations before and after them, they too had to brave the natural and human hazards of existence: disease, the scarcity of food, and unexpected disaster. Both to explain and seek relief from the human misfortune they chronically encountered, they also found solace in religion. In its magical, ascetic, or redemptive aspects, religion invoked a supernatural order that transcended the earthly environment and therefore endowed the faithful with some control over it. Societies appeared and disappeared. Whatever the exact causes of their demise, they all eventually succumbed to the parasitism of natural or human predation, either to the gradual decomposition of frail social structures or to the sudden extermination of entire civilizations.[24]

In the West, the combination of political fragmentation, declining economic growth, and social disaffection progressively depleted the moral and material resources of post-Augustan Rome. Besieged by Sassanid invaders from Persia and by an array of German tribes, a sagging empire desperate to stave off its demise entered into nominal alliances with the barbarians inside its gates, who cast covetous eyes at its domains. The efforts to defend porous borders were of no avail against the Huns, however, who steadily advanced from the Black Sea and the Danube to the Rhine valley, Gaul, and, in 410, to Rome itself, which they pillaged in retaliation for a feckless aristocracy's refusal to pay tribute to the barbarian hordes. Under the increasing control of German military chieftains, the colossus of Rome ceased to exist by the end of the fifth century, its proud traditions and culture having become the preserve of the eastern empire—and the Christian Church—in Constantinople.[25]

In East Asia, intrigue and factional strife among the ruling Chinese elite weakened the influence of the Han emperors over their provincial patrimony. The breakdown of centralized authority further exacerbated divisions between landowners and peasants, which erupted into popular revolts that were exploited by local warlords and roving barbarians on the periphery of Chinese civilization. Protracted internal instability and penetration by nomadic tribes ensued until 589, when the Sui dynasty, in alliance with Turkish tribes from the eastern steppe, managed to bring the independent provinces under imperial authority. Reunification did not resolve social tensions between the ruling elite and the masses, however. Three decades later, the Sui gave way to the T'ang dynasty, whose efforts to expand China's territorial ambit to Tibet, Korea, and Japan disrupted the empire's fragile social cohesion and thus resumed the cycle of disorder that followed the collapse of the Han dynasty.[26]

While Rome and Han China imploded, Sassanian rulers were busy reviving Persian civilization from the Oxus River valley to Arabia to the eastern borders of the East Roman, or Byzantine, empire. The Sassanid dynasty that formed in the third century established a centralized administration that became a repository of Hellenistic culture and an intellectual mecca for scholars from Europe and Asia. Farther east, in India, another powerful empire was rising phoenix-like from the ashes of the Mauryan state whose ideal of unity had been preserved in the intervening three centuries. By 320 the consolidation of Gupta power from the Himalayas in the north to the Deccan Valley in the south and from the Bay of Bengal to the Arabian Sea had assured a secure physical environment in which Indian culture flourished.[27]

Political and military order, in turn, facilitated sociocultural development, including the creative fusion of the caste system and religion. The institution of caste, which had been introduced in pre-Mauryan times by light-skinned Aryan invaders and given religious sanction by the Brahmin priesthood, established roles and relationships that, as in Confucianism, defined socially acceptable behavior. Hinduism joined the conflicting religious strains that had emerged in response to the protracted upheaval in peoples' lives prior to the Guptan period with Brahmanic behavioral codes and rituals. The tolerant, accommodative character of the Hindu omni-faith and the contrastingly structured inflexible caste system that it also spawned were the domestic complements to the order that Gupta rulers imposed on the world just beyond India's gates.

The Gupta empire was the apogee of Indian civilization. Missionaries and merchants carried Indian culture from the familiar locales of southeast Asia with which early traders had established contact to the foreign lands of China and Africa.[28]

Human survival remained precarious, however, even for the most sophisticated and powerful societies. Indeed, civilization, however developed and refined it may appear against the backdrop of history, continued to coexist in a tenuous relationship with barbarity. Warfare, plunder, and pillage were part of life. As the discovery of weapons in peasant graves shows, the warrior was accorded the greatest status in society. Culturally rich and peaceful India under the Guptas fell victim to the scourge of the Ephthalite Huns in the sixth century. The Sassanian dynasty lasted until the mid-seventh century, when it was destroyed by Islamicized Arab conquerors. Moreover, warfare was usually brutish. The Mongol warrior Genghis Khan and his descendants repeatedly and wantonly slaughtered the Christian and Muslim societies they happened upon with a ferocity that breaches credulity, stacking the heads of their victims in pyramids and, in one account, pouring molten gold down the throat of a Muslim governor. Under fortuitous circumstances, the civilizer subdued, or tamed, the barbarian. Or he coopted him, as the late Roman emperors, the post-Han warlords, and the Byzantine rulers coopted the Germanic, Turkish, and Arabic tribes with whom they were forced to live in a primal symbiosis.[29]

While the artifacts of war—the use of wheels turning around a fixed axle, armor, the crossbow, the stirrup—improved the odds of overcoming less-sophisticated adversaries, little could be done to prevent the depredations of nature. Pestilence, disease, and natural calamities decimated societies with ghastly regularity. Even after early civilizations managed to protect food supplies against raiding bands of barbarians, climatic changes and the inadequate tools and agricultural know-how at human disposal before the introduction of the moldboard plow in the fifth and sixth centuries imposed formidable constraints on society's ability to feed itself.

Societies subsisted at the margin. For a variety of reasons, land was rarely under continuous cultivation. Droughts and floods imposed enormous obstacles on the productive capabilities of the societies in the Yellow River region, the Ganges Valley, and along the Mediterranean coast. The combination of ineffective storage facilities and the exposure of supplies to rodents worked further hardships on malnourished communities. Famine lurked in the best of times. In sixth-century Gaul, civilized society desperately strove to make bread out of anything that could be milled, including fern roots. The graves of tenth- and eleventh-century Hungarians, among others, reveal a high rate of infant mortality attributable to food deficiencies. To compound the insecurity of life from antiquity to feudalism, warfare and disease routinely devastated societies, despoiling the land and reducing the supply of animal and human agricultural labor.[30]

Disease frequently accompanied the human disorder of warfare and famine. The mutual exposure of peoples from different regions transmitted infectious diseases that parasitically exploited the dietary and immunological deficiencies of host societies. Although there is some evidence that infectious diseases were not uncommon before 500 B.C., epidemics appear to have been a later development, the spread of which resulted from the growing density of populations in urbanized areas and the more frequent encounters with strange peoples through trade and warfare. Hippocrates apparently recorded the outbreak of epidemics in ancient Greece. Livy has similarly documented the outbreak of pestilence in Rome, which occurred with greater regularity and intensity after the second century A.D. Indeed, the bubonic plague that ravaged Rome between 541 and 543—the worst such outbreak until the Black Death of 1348—probably contributed to the failure to restore imperial unity to the lands of the Mediterranean. Infestation disrupted Chinese society as well, as the writings of the Sung dynasty disclose.[31]

The fragility of physical existence placed great importance on social organization. The more cohesive the society, the more likely it was to mobilize its resources and endure the disruptive effects of invasion and the capriciousness of nature. Ancient society—from Sumer civilization to the ordered life of feudalism—was hierarchical. Whether patrimonial or nomadic or city-state in form, early societies invoked the allegiance of the masses to a potentate or tribal council or, as in Periclean Athens and Republican Rome, a political elite to overcome the internal turmoil and strife that reduced their chances of survival. Adumbrating the later contract theories of Locke, Hobbes, and Rousseau, the leaders of ancient societies promised peace and stability in exchange for a monopoly on decision making.[32]

To be sure, leadership also required political legitimacy in the eyes of the ruled, the more so as economic development and social differentiation increased individual autonomy. Autonomy, of course, is not to be confused with equality. The practice of slavery persisted throughout the civilized world. The societies of ancient Greece, Rome, and China were dominated by a wealthy, landowning, hence governing, class. The peasantry and the artisanal classes fared less well. The former, who paid rent to till the landowners' soil, existed at the behest of the aristocracy. With some exceptions—China, for example, where state monopolies prevailed and the merchant was relegated to a lowly status in society—the rents peasants paid sustained the artisans who crafted luxury goods for the wealthy.[33]

For the most part, however, the life of the peasant or the townsman was wretched. Even in the Byzantine empire, where villages individually owned land in a preformation of the kolkhozes of later Russia, the free peasant was ignorant, uneducated, and often alienated from his society; he was constantly buffeted by the awesome power of nature, barbarian invaders, and the arbitrary encroachment of his social superiors and the state on his limited domain. The effects of natural and social disorder were especially burdensome for the peasantry. As warfare and disease dwindled populations and rulers exacted greater taxes to maintain their imperial control, agricultural overlords accelerated their demands for greater productivity from the peasantry, who were fungible with and, in respect of their utilitarian purpose, indistinguishable from the chattel animals that were also annexed to the land.

In Europe, some landowners encouraged the marriage of peasants and slaves to reduce the cost of staff maintenance and to extract greater productivity from the enthusiasm the extrication from one's servile status was expected to generate. But there, as elsewhere, the lowest classes of ancient society became increasingly alienated from the social community to which they were denied membership. Periodic peasant uprisings that erupted as early as the second century in Rome and China were cries for deliverance from social oppression. So was the peasantry's retreat into religion, through which it sought to impose an order of a higher kind on the turbulence of its daily life.[34]

To be sure, appeals to the spiritual world were hardly new. As noted earlier, mysticism permeated pre-Mauryan India and challenged the rationalism of the Ionian Greeks. In China, too, the animistic, naturalistic beliefs of Taoism presented an alternative to Confucianism. Even in the best of times, such as they were, religion gave refuge to people who sought respite from the arbitrariness of life. During periods of protracted upheaval, however, societies on the verge of dissolution appear to have embraced spiritualism, doctrines of individual holiness, and the belief in personal salvation with greater fervor.[35]

In the waning days of the Greek empire, the mysticism of neo-

Platonism, along with world-weary stoicism and Epicureanism, replaced the rationalism and conceptual order of Plato and Aristotle. Following the collapse of Gupta society and the subsequent Muslim invasion of the Indian world, Hinduism underwent a revival; Indians searched for order in an inner world of atavistic traditions and magic rituals that increasingly isolated them from the outer world over which they had little control. In China, during the tumult of post-Han warlordism and the barbarian invasions that followed, Buddhism virtually eclipsed Confucianism. In this time of turmoil and toward the end of the T'ang dynasty, the dispossessed sought release from suffering in the quasi-mystical passivity *(wuwei)* of Taoism, the salvatory succor of Mahayana Buddhism, and in the emergence of new sects such as Chan (Zen, in Japanese) that professed enlightenment through meditation.[36]

In the same measure, the disintegration of communal order and foreign invasion fostered the spread of Christianity in the Roman Empire. By the second century, the enslaved, the putatively free, and the socially aspiring artisans and merchants had retreated into communion with a personal God inherited from Judaism and Persian Zoroastrianism. The pagan belief that a pantheon of gods imposed an impersonal order on the universe could no longer be reconciled with the pervasive disintegration of society and the oppressive rule of an aristocratic elite. Christianity and the organized church that emerged in the third century provided a new sense of community for the socially alienated and a spiritual escape into the divine embrace of a deity who promised a better world to come.

With the Emperor Constantine's acceptance of Christianity in 312, and more importantly, the subsequent conversion of the senatorial aristocracy, the Christian Church became the conservator of Roman culture and traditions and, after the last emperor was deposed in 476, the living symbol of its civilization. A Christian elite replaced the pagan aristocracy. Papal Rome became eternal Rome.[37]

For Constantine, Theodosius I—the first true Christian emperor—and the early Church Fathers, Christianity saved the classical age and the Roman Empire from extinction. In form and substance a new order, it was emotionally and culturally a continuation of the world bequeathed by the Greek and Roman empires: the guarantor of civilization and the promise of a new social community in which all people, the powerful and the weak, the educated and the ignorant, the aristocracy and the peasantry, could equally share. In the revised cosmology of order that anticipated Hegel by nearly two millennia, Greece and Rome were, in the minds of theologians, divinely ordained stages in human development the culmination of which was the culture, or *paideia,* of Christianity.

Notwithstanding the efforts of Saints Jerome and Augustine and the Emperor Justinian to build a new community, however, Rome became increasingly divided geographically and culturally after the fifth century. Following the loss of the western provinces to German tribes, contact between Rome *aeterna* and the "new" Rome in Constantinople, the former Byzantium, diminished. The latinized West became culturally distinct from the Greek-speaking and "orientalized" Byzantine empire in the east. Worse, religious disputes revolving principally around the human versus divine natures of Christ exacerbated the cultural and geographical cleavage in the Roman world. The bishops in the West, the successors to the aristocratic traditions of the senatorial elite, imposed their dictatorial views on the more egalitarian, prosperous, hence, resentful, East, whose bishops, in turn, claimed jurisdiction over the eastern Church through the patriarch of Constantinople. With the encroachments of the Slavic tribes and Muslim conquerors on the Byzantine empire in the seventh century, the link between East and West was all but broken.[38]

Islam provided the same catalyst to social order in the Arab world. What began in the mid-seventh century as the religion-based tribal order the prophet Muhammad brought to Bedouin society on the fringes of the Sassanian empire in Arabia soon became a powerful movement that united the combative Arab world in a socioreligious crusade of national conquest. Weakened by incessant fighting, both the Sassanid and Byzantine empires proved easy prey for the advancing Arab armies, which spread in the seventh and eighth centuries under the Umayyad- and Persian-dominated Abbasid caliphates from Spain and North Africa to the former Roman territories in the Middle East, northwest India, and the borders of China.[39]

Islamic expansionism left an indelible imprint on the societies the Arab-Persian forces encountered. Peoples from the Byzantine empire to southeast Asia, especially in Malaya and Indonesia, had become acculturated in a religious order that superimposed the social sanctions of a fearsome God on the traditional communal ties and tribal conflicts of an earlier time. By 655 the Persian empire no longer existed. By the same token, Islam prompted societies they had not conquered either to retreat further within the spiritual order of their own beliefs, as was the case in India, or to reaffirm their religious allegiance with comparable militancy, as later happened in Christianized Europe.[40]

In different ways, religion provided a renewed sense of order for societies that were mired in interminable instability. India took solace in the expansive temple of Hinduism. China increasingly blended Buddhism and other religions of salvation with indigenous religious beliefs in a neo-Confucian, hence less other-worldly, synthesis that emerged toward the end of the first millennium in the late T'ang dynasty. In the case of Europe and the Islamicized Arab-Persian world, religions inspired zealotry and expansionism.

The peace of mind and the perception of order that religious conviction provided, however, also raised impenetrable barriers between civilizations, each of which took comfort in the belief that the outlying world had little redeeming value. Muslim expansionism physically reinforced the intellectual and cultural isolationism of civilizations. As it turned out, however, Muslim dominance of the Indian Ocean was a blessing in disguise, for, in impeding communications and trade among different civilizations, it encouraged economic growth within them. This was particularly true in China after 960, which, having overcome the internal rivalries of the provincial potentates, embarked on a period of great commercial progress, technological innovation, and cultural development during the reign of the Sung emperors. In Europe, too, the effects of Muslim expansionism had unexpectedly propitious consequences. Admittedly, the monopolizing effects of Muslim sea power on Mediterranean trade deprived Europe of commercial contacts with the East. But they also accelerated the trend toward agrarianism that spurred European economic growth in the eleventh century.[41]

FEUDAL ORDER

Partly because of the Muslim penetrations of the world, partly because of the breakdown of social structures, human societies everywhere turned inward after the seventh century. A combination of immemorial traditions and supernaturalism imbued life with a social and intellectual integrity that rendered the particular indistinguishable from the universal. Resurgent Hinduism in India, replete with Tantric superstitions and primitive rituals, the neo-Confucian synthesis in China, and Byzantium's self-image as a Christian island in a heathen world were institutionalized psychological defenses against the mutable, the unfamiliar, and the unknown. In the Islamic world, too, the Persian element in Umayyad society revived Sassanian cultural traditions and embraced the Shi'a rather than Sunni form of Islam.

In all of these societies, the belief in a transcendent power—whether expressed in magic, sorcery, or religious faith—and immemorial tradition, more than reason, determined reality within the straitened ambit of one's experience. In these detached, self-sufficient recesses of humanity, earthly time had little meaning. The sameness of life precluded any expectation that tomorrow would be different from yesterday. People took comfort from the dreary repetitiveness and cyclicality of life in the ancient traditions that created a sociohistoric unity of past, present, and future, and in world-escaping religious ritual.[42]

In the post-Roman Western world, however, religion reconnected humanity with the past. Unlike Byzantium, where the clergy was subordinated to imperial authority and the classical legacy was gradually diluted by the influence of Islam, the Church of St. Peter and the bishops who succeeded him formed the chrysalis of ancient Rome's rebirth. As the Germanic tribes in the West converted from paganism to Catholicism, Peter's apostolic successors claimed authority over the spiritual life of all Christians, including those in Byzantium. At the same time, the Church set out to renew ancient Roman culture. Descendants of old noble families such as Pope Gregory the Great self-consciously spread learning and social reform in an effort to preserve Rome's cultural patrimony. Roman culture and Christian unity coalesced in the order of the Carolingian empire, which expanded in the eighth and ninth centuries to Spain, the Baltic Sea, and south of Rome. The empire served simultaneously as the protector of the Roman Church and as the agent of its influence in the lands it conquered. Although the legitimate Roman emperor continued to reside in Constantinople, an informal alliance between the Roman Church and the Frankish kingdom was gradually forged, symbolized by Charlemagne's coronation as Emperor in 800. The coronation was important in two respects. It effectively ended the Byzantine empire's putative authority over the pope. In addition, it created a politicoreligious order within and without the Carolingian empire that linked the emerging European civilization with the classical era.[43]

This is not meant to convey that the mass of European humanity faithfully adhered to Christianity. Magic, witchcraft, and thaumaturgy were widespread practices among the poor. Animism and heretical beliefs such as Catharism and Albigensianism also competed with Catholicism well into the fourteenth century. For practicing Christians, however, the Church was a powerful force for social change. Indeed, religious order was more than devotion to duty, just as political order was more than the power exercised by Charles as the sovereign and successor to Roman emperors. The order of the Roman Empire, in whose image all barbarians chose to rule, commingled with the tribal order of lordship derived from the conquest and settlement of new lands. As it turned out, the feudal form of political order was destined to outlive the Carolingian kingdom, which collapsed under the fragility of centralized government control, the inability of Charles' sons to maintain the integrity of a partitioned kingdom, and the ninth-century invasions by the Danes and other Scandinavian tribes, the Saracens, and the Magyars.[44]

Feudalism was the institutional response to the perpetual disorder and political fragmentation that afflicted Europe after Charlemagne's death and the concomitant shift of economic life to the countryside. It revived the ethos of church-state order expounded by the Carolingian rulers. Power rested in the hands of the Church, the vehicle of human salvation, and the princely class of knights who assumed the duty of defending the Church and the masses against the infidels who threatened Christianity's borders. Productive tasks were left to the peasants, whose free status belied their obligation to the lords, and an inchoate class of merchants and artisans that subsisted on the largesse of the nobility. Despite the social inequality, the enormous productive burden placed on the peasantry as a result of the vagaries of nature and the decline of pillaging in the tenth century, and the persistence of seigneurial exploitation, there was an inherent order in the feudal system, which functioned, through its hierarchical orders, in the service of God.[45]

It would be erroneous to leave the impression, however, that all of Europe coexisted in the self-contained community of the Carolingian manor. As Georges Duby has demonstrated, there was considerable variation in the institutionalization of feudalism in post-Carolingian society. Indeed, the old monarchical-ecclesiastical order persisted until well into the nineteenth century. It was only after the Carolingian empire expanded, the threat of invasion receded, and pillaging gave way to the cultivation of new lands and improvements in agricultural technique that the roles of nobility, clergy, and lay society became more sharply defined. Even then, feudal structures varied. The obligations of the servile class appear to have been greater north of the Alps and comparatively lesser in Italy and in southern France. Moreover, the exchange of leaseholds for labor services and some portion of agricultural harvests can be traced as far back as the eighth century.[46]

The standard of small estates that coalesced into larger comital and viscomital units or duchies was set in the former West Frankish kingdom, or feudal France. In the East Frankish kingdom, the independence of the German states and the relative success of the king's representatives in protecting the exposed frontiers to the Slavic and Magyar lands circumscribed the emergence of smaller principalities and sustained the monarchy, which, in contrast to France, also controlled the Church. In Italy, where cities emerged as the citadels of defense against invaders and power gradually consolidated into a small number of powerful families and bishoprics, feudalism lacked the fertile environment for growth that existed in France. In the English version, the monarchy was especially resilient.[47]

The feudal system that emerged between the tenth and thirteenth centuries in Europe satisfied the need for order in other societies as well. In the increasingly truncated Byzantine kingdom, lands too were given as reward for services to the beleaguered empire, although without the right of primogeniture permitted in the West. In Kievan Russia, feudal forms followed the spread of Christianity and the Byzantine Church's efforts to restore order amid the political divisions of the late eleventh century. In contrast to the West, however, lord–vassal relations, codes of chivalry, and rights of primogeniture were absent even before the concentration of power by Tsar Ivan III.[48]

Feudalism also planted roots in Asia, some of which scholars have traced as far back as Mauryan India and Shang China. Its appearance became more conspicuous in China only after the tenth century, however, as the social tide shifted in favor of landed versus urban-commercial interests. Still, Chinese feudalism lacked the institutionalized structures and obligations of Europe or, for that matter, of Japan. In the exchange of land for the pledge of military allegiance, Japanese feudalism, which emerged during the Kamakura shogunate, bore a striking resemblance to the European variety. What distinguished Japanese feudalism from its European counterpart was the existence of an emperor and a civil administration and the family nature of social relations. As the role of the emperor gradually diminished to that of a symbolic sovereign, the concentration of power and authority devolved to the shogun and his princes (or *daimyo*). And after the advent of the Tokugawa period in the seventeenth century, Japanese feudalism became increasingly centralized.[49]

In the East as well as the West, feudalism was also a response to the general instability of imperial or other institutionalized authority. The factionalization of social and political life was a pervasive phenomenon throughout the world after the tenth century. The struggle for power among competing aristocracies continuously disrupted social order in post-Carolingian Europe, as vividly demonstrated in the twelfth and thirteenth centuries by the contest between the Hohenstaufen and Guelf families for German kingship and control of Italy. Similar social upheaval eroded the legitimation of authority in Asia as well. In Japan, for instance, the rivalry among aristocratic families persisted throughout the Heian period (784–1156). The eventual emergence of a warrior elite in the Kamakura and Tokugawa shogunates eventually restored order at the expense of the emperor, who ruled in name alone.[50]

The nobility was not the only source of disorder. Peasant uprisings and mob demonstrations were widespread, as the lower classes rebelled against their feudal incarceration. In Europe and in Byzantium secret societies began to form, precursors to the class-consciousness that would later animate the working masses. Furthermore, the practice of simony and other ecclesiastical excesses of the Roman Church aroused the ire of servile publics, sowing the seeds of religious regeneration that would ultimately be harvested in the Protestant Reformation. Fearful that the righteous order of society was in jeopardy, bishops and monarchs repressed the unruly toilers and their loyal clergy, in some cases expropriated the wealth they had accumulated, and imposed obedience to royal power.[51]

The disruptive challenge to social order that societies from Europe to Asia experienced after the tenth century was exacerbated by the expansion of nomadic hordes from the surrounding steppe areas into the civilized world. Indeed, it was the spread of Turkish warriors from the Middle East into Byzantium that incited the Crusades. Having grafted the Islamic faith and the idea of *jihad,* or holy war, onto their warrior traditions, the Seljuk Turks posed a formidable threat to the integrity of the Christian world, particularly after they hived off most of Anatolia from the Byzantine kingdom in 1071. Alarmed by the encroachment of Turkish power on Greek lands, the Byzantine emperor summoned the pope, Urban II, with whom the Greek Orthodox Church had irreparably severed political and ecclesiastical ties in 1054, to the rescue. The pope, in turn, roused a public motivated as much by the opportunity for plunder as by religious ardor to save the Holy Land, not to mention Spain, from the Muslim infidel. For the next two centuries, Christians and Muslims hemorrhaged their religious devotion to their respective jihads on battlefields from Byzantium to the Middle East.[52]

Islamicized Turks also expanded their power eastward to Iraq and Iran, Central Asia, and beyond the Oxus River to the upper Ganges Valley. But they were no match for the Mongol nomads who swept down from the steppe north of the Gobi Desert in the early thirteenth century. Under the leadership of Genghis Khan and his successors, the confederated Mongol tribes ferociously assaulted the Turks in Central Asia, the Middle East, Eastern Europe, Russia, and China. In their wake lay the

Abbasid caliphate and the glory of Baghdad, Christianized Eastern Europe and southern Russia, and, by 1279, all of China.[53]

In time, the civilizing effects of indigenous cultures and the internal disintegration of the steppe warrior empires into less formidable adversaries combined to tame the ferocity of the barbarian interlopers. The fragmentation and domestication of Genghis Khan's empire led to the eventual expulsion of the Mongol intruders in Russia. In India, spiritualism and the social routines it reinforced buffered society against the alien presence of Islamicized Mongols even after the Mongol potentates suppressed Hinduism in the sixteenth century. Indeed, the efforts of the Sikh sect to blend Islam with ancestral religious forms aside, Hinduism experienced a revitalization during the Mongol empire. For China, which had been repeatedly invaded throughout its history, the Mongol horde was just the latest uninvited guest in the Celestial Kingdom. Besides, long before their ejection in 1368, the Mongol Khans had become culturally sinicized. In each of these civilizations, however, the protracted stay of the barbarian invaders left lasting effects. In the case of India, it reinforced the political passivity and social immiscibility of religion and caste that have characterized Indian society from the post-Gupta period to the present. For Russia and China, protracted tribute status contributed to the bureaucratic centralization and xenophobia that influenced subsequent historical development.[54]

THE CHALLENGE TO ORDER

Meanwhile, in Europe, the effects of barbarian expansionism, Christian militancy, and feudalism left a different imprint on society, one that would later dramatically affect the lives of peoples in every part of the world. Having been spared the devastation of barbarian conquest, post-Carolingian society developed, if not *in vacuo,* at least with the relative freedom that allowed the uninterrupted evolution of social processes. Incipient trends began to emerge by the thirteenth century that did not conform either to the convictions that European society embraced or to the institutions that reinforced those convictions. What may have appeared to be another shift in the cosmological cycle of order and disorder that had defined human existence since time immemorial was really the beginning of a process that was antithetical to the beliefs and social conditions that historically had ascribed meaning to life.

By the beginning of the thirteenth century, four mutually reinforcing trends began to emerge in social contradiction of the familiar ways and customs of life. One major departure from the past was the rise of a precapitalist economy from the confluence of the barbarian invasions and agricultural expansionism of the previous three centuries. The Slavs, Hungarians, and Danes who pillaged the former Carolingian empire ultimately settled the land, converted to Christianity, and expanded the productive base of the European economy through increased trade, urbanization, and the widespread use of money as the medium of commercial exchange. As the frontier expanded, beckoning slaves and peasants to leave the manor in search of arable land, the great feudal estates correspondingly shrank. Serfs who settled the frontier at the behest of their masters provided a portion of their production to the estate in exchange for their freedom. The growing output of the new agricultural settlements and of the monasteries that were also intensifying their cultivation of the land created a surplus product, the proceeds of which were used to expand into such enterprises as wine making and the mining of iron ore.[55]

The loosening of the social nexus between lord and peasant was not the only repercussion of economic expansionism. The superiority of the aristocratic class also began to wane. Increasingly in debt to the obligations of feudal largess, the profligate aristocracy was forced to sell off parts of its estates, not to mention its noble lineage, to uncultivated, newly rich upstarts. In addition, as moveable wealth increased the prospect of riches, materialism and greed supplanted the rustic preoccupation with God and the supernatural. No where was this attitude more evident than in Italy, where urbanization had limited the development of feudalism.

Unlike other Europeans, Italian merchants reinvested their capital and, along with the Jews, pioneered accountancy and joint associations. By the mid-thirteenth century, Florence already boasted 80 banking houses and a population in excess of 100,000. Large-scale wool manufacturing was also emerging in Italy as well as in Flanders and northern France. In contrast to the prevailing ethos, profit, not the munificence of God, was now equated with good citizenship. Moreover, as pillage gave way to trade, the economic impetus of the Crusades diminished. Italians and others were increasingly inclined to trade peacefully with the infidel, thereby linking the Mediterranean with cities in northern and eastern Europe that were providing new vitality to human intercourse.[56]

Clearly, agricultural growth and the economic boom it stimulated would not have occurred without improvements in technology. Population growth in the post-Carolingian period imposed added burdens on productivity. As a consequence of the discovery of iron ore in the Tyrol,

Carinthia, Bohemia, and Sweden, materials heretofore used solely in the production of weaponry were now assigned dual usage. Starting in the eleventh and twelfth centuries, iron that was forged into swords was grafted on to the wooden moldboard plough, thereby increasing the tillage of intractable clay soil. The increased frequency of ploughing, triennial crop rotation, and the substitution of horses for oxen enhanced output. As peasants settled the wilderness, they introduced the new techniques to the nobility in the eastern and northern reaches of Europe, who, eager to participate in the new prosperity, replicated the process of social and economic decentralization that had taken place in the western lands.[57]

Comparatively, of course, European technological prowess lagged far behind Chinese inventiveness. Chinese production of silk, porcelain, paper, and gunpowder were all well-developed activities by the twelfth century. Europeans, however, were good students, as the multifarious military use of gunpowder that so decidedly shifted the global power balance in their favor after the mid-thirteenth century would demonstrate. Through the Crusades and the resulting contact with Arabs who had established trade ties with the Orient, Europeans divined the mystery of Chinese technique and technology. Marco Polo's path-breaking travels to China in the last quarter of the thirteenth century were no less important in removing the veil of ignorance that shrouded Eastern civilization from Europe.[58]

The socioeconomic and technological changes that were taking place further attenuated the centrality of the Church in European society. A spirit of inquiry and learning that drew its inspiration from classical Greece was also beginning to gain adherents in the monastic orders and in the universities that sprang up in the twelfth century. This is not to say that the Church no longer commanded social allegiance or that religious piety was suddenly languishing. Just the opposite. Amid the social transformation and rampant materialism of the twelfth and thirteenth centuries, villagers and urban dwellers alike clung to their belief in divine intervention—whether it was the Church or the local sorcerer that sacramentally dispensed supernatural power—to ease the insecurity of their lives. Myths such as the appearance of a great religious ruler—the legendary Prester John—who would overthrow Islam were also preserved. And the Church continued the reforms instituted by Pope Gregory VII in the eleventh century to remove itself from the feudal control of Holy Roman emperors and from the political and moral degeneracy such control fostered.[59]

Nevertheless, the Church could not stop the rash of heresies that erupted at the end of the twelfth century in reaction to the perturbations of social change and to the lingering perception that the institutionalized clergy had lost spiritual touch with the world. Not since the fifth century, when, in the collapse of the Roman Empire, Arianism questioned the mystery of the Trinity, had the Church experienced such a challenge to its authority. Unlike previous departures from religious doctrine, the chiliastic fervor of the twelfth century reflected an uncontainable need for spiritual deliverance from a world that had become a battleground between what Friedrich Heer calls *civitas dei* and *civitas diaboli*.[60] Such spiritualism was the first wave of a social assault against intellectual orthodoxy and the class structure that perpetuated the wretched conditions of the masses. It was agitated by the heretical views of Franciscan monks, who rejected the abstract scholasticism of St. Thomas Aquinas and, for those who embraced the radical views of theologians like William of Ockham, reposed ecclesiastical sovereignty in the community of the faithful rather than in the pope.

The rumblings of discontent among the laity and the creation of new religious orders such as the Franciscans and the Dominicans coincided with the formation of universities in the twelfth century. As cities sprang up and competition between craft and merchant guilds intensified, urban centers of learning, the earliest of which emerged in Bologna in the late eleventh century, began to replace the rural monasteries as places of study and specialization. Here students came into contact with the remarkable scientific discoveries of Arab scholars and, through the teachings of Avicenna and other Muslim scholars, with the rationalism of Aristotle and the classical Greek philosophers.

In universities in Italy and France, in newly formed centers of learning in thirteenth-century England and in Germany, Bohemia, and Poland in the next century, interest in technical and scientific knowledge—itself a function of urbanization and the formation of merchant and craft guilds—was gradually superseding feudal Europe's Church-centered emphasis on letters and the humanities. Just as European society was witnessing the incipient emergence of capitalism, it was also beginning to experience the emancipation of knowledge from religious dogma.[61]

Although Frederick I (Barbarossa) and his Hohenstaufen successors tried mightily to restore its unity, the secular authority of the Holy Roman Empire was also being assaulted by the effects of social and political change. The absorption of the countryside by the cities and the formation of new states in Eastern Europe and in Scandinavia—tacitly encouraged by the papacy as a counterweight to German imperial power—

fostered the development of national identities that resisted centralized control. After 1254, the Holy Roman Empire was a hollow shell that had virtually no influence in Italy and little more in the collage of German states that geographically redefined the former East Frankish kingdom.

In England, Spain, and, within the limits that feudalism would allow, in France as well, the increasing consolidation of royal authority adumbrated the formation of the nation-state and the foundations of constitutional government. By the thirteenth century Bohemia and Poland had become independent, semifeudal states, as had the Scandinavian kingdoms of Denmark, Norway, and Sweden. A Russian state was forming around Moscow in spite of the continuing Mongol occupation, and the Byzantine empire was fast receding. Hungary and a reconstructed Bulgarian empire had emerged from the ecumene of Byzantium, the remains of which had broken into shards of autonomous aristocracies that paid little regard to the emperor. What the Turks, Mongols, Bulgars, Serbs, and Christian crusaders did not militarily consume, Venetian merchants commercially controlled.[62]

Elsewhere in the world, equally dramatic changes were occurring. In 1279, at about the same time the Ottoman Turks were beginning to ingest the remains of Byzantium and France and England were emerging as embryonic national powers in the West, the Sung empire in China fell to the Mongols. For nearly the next century, China was ruled by the *soi-disant* Emperor Kublai Khan and his sinicized successors, who expanded their control into Southeast Asia and Korea. Eventually, in 1368, a Buddhist monk, Chu Yuan-Chang, led a rebellion that expelled the Mongols and reunited China under the Ming dynasty in the conservative, anti-merchant Confucian traditions of the landed gentry.[63]

Although the Ming rulers expanded their control over Annam, Korea, and Japan, the nascent trend toward national autonomy that was forming in Europe was also visible in Asia. Foreshadowing the turbulence that would later afflict Chinese–Vietnamese relations, the leaders of Annam bridled at their client status and tried to preserve their cultural independence. Japan, which had earlier demonstrated its mettle by resisting Mongol suzerainty, was still more recalcitrant. By the thirteenth century, Japan had overlaid the importation of Chinese civilization with the feudal-warrior-merchant forms that set it apart from China both politically and culturally.[64]

On the surface, the world did not look unrecognizably different in the late thirteenth century from the preceding millennium-and-a-half. To be sure, greater agricultural productivity vastly improved the level of subsistence. Increased output also accelerated economic intercourse, which, in turn, advanced the process of urbanization. Trade, the minting of coins, and the prospect of prosperity further contributed to closer and more peaceful contact among disparate cultures. On balance, however, life was still perilous, as demonstrated by the savagery of the Turkish and especially Mongol steppe invaders of the civilized world and the ceaseless disruption of social cohesion and continuity. For the most part, societies struggled, as they always had, to maintain order and social stability in a treacherous and unpredictable world. In the worst of times, when physical and social order collapsed, people everywhere immured themselves in the security of religious rigidity and in the timeless traditions and beliefs that distinguished them from the outsider, the foreign, the alien, the heretical. As late as the thirteenth century, in spite of the commingling of cultures that was the residue of invasion, the civilized parts of the world engaged in no sustained interaction.

Below the surface, however, trends were already discernible that would irreversibly alter the social patterns to which human society had become accustomed, not least of which was the spirit of inquiry and discovery that wafted from West to East. As time passed, it would become harder either to tame the alien invader or spiritually to insulate oneself from his proselytizing presence. Long-held beliefs and immemorial traditions, reinforced by religion and feudal social structures, would no longer provide refuge from the storm of change for societies that could not escape the ideology of progress that European merchants, missionaries, and military men carried as their standard. It was not yet apparent to the thirteenth-century world, but the mythologized glory of a golden age—whether that of Rome, the Baghdad caliphate, Gupta India, or Han China—was fast disappearing into an irretrievable past.

Modernity and the Messiah of Progress

Precisely when in the fourteenth century the modern epoch began is hard to determine. On the surface, the major features of the preceding century remained visibly intact everywhere. The immemorial struggle for order—indeed, survival—had not changed. Nor had seemingly indelible social structures and rituals. There was an inescapable order to the disorder of life, a timeless rhythm the majesty of which poets, philosophers, and priests reverently enshrined. At a deeper level, however, the skeptical unbundling of old verities and the reconsolidation of human communities along functional, as opposed to personal, lines were slowly shifting the center of historical gravity from the local to the metropolitan; immemorial traditions and ascriptive relationships were giving way to expertise, institutional dynamism, and the extension of relationships across time and space. The modern epoch was forming.

Social and intellectual change combined to create the modern epoch. The movement of capital, the scope and diversification of human organization, and the rise of geographically delimited and mutually exclusive territorial units made the landmarks of civilization—initially in the West but eventually everywhere—increasingly indecipherable. The seed of capitalism that germinated in the twelfth and thirteenth centuries nurtured economic opportunism and, in turn, trade expansion, urbanization, and a business class, all of which disrupted the cooperative nature of manorial life and the system of craft and merchant guilds. Individuation and social differentiation eroded the timeless customs and practices of the epoch of order. Reciprocal sovereignty and the balancing of interests among competing states replaced the insular cosmopolitanism of antiquity and feudalism's tessellated system of overlapping rights and manifold allegiances.

At the same time, rationalism and the scientific method freed societies to question the absolutes they had accepted on faith and to explore faraway lands. The expansion of humanity's intellectual and geographic horizons was mutually reinforcing: the discovery and conquest of new lands stimulated new ways of conceptualizing the world; the rationalization of structure and process encouraged geographic expansion. Detached or liberated from the hoary past, Europeans, from the fourteenth century onward, began to experiment with new methods of inquiry and new techniques in the quest of human mastery of nature and society; to explore the world beyond their shores; to expand, by dint of reason or military might, the domains of their civilization to the farthest reaches of the ecumene.

To be sure, the best possible of all worlds that European intellectuals, entrepreneurs, and adventurers built was not inviting to everyone. For the peasantry and for the factory operatives who were both psychologically and materially denied the privilege of social inclusion, life was still a grueling ordeal. Until the mid-nineteenth century, however, the plight of the poor had little effect on the attitudes of the elite, who set out to inculcate in the benighted masses of the world beyond Europe the blessings of modernity. For the most part, they experienced little resistance. The Ottoman empire remained a military force until the seventeenth century, and for a time China and the outliers of Asia managed to isolate themselves from the expansionism of the West. By the eighteenth century, however, they were no longer formidable obstacles to Western military and cultural supremacy. Transported in the confidence of their own superiority, Europeans gradually superimposed their values and beliefs on the civilizations of the Middle East, Asia, and the Americas in insouciant disregard for the peoples and traditions they encountered and, by the beginning of the twentieth century, in amoral disregard for each other. Although it was not yet apparent, by this point the epoch of progress had begun its denouement.

Until then, of course, the West had little reason to alter the course on which it had providentially set sail. Its political, military, and commercial accomplishments bespoke the success of its liberalizing, humanizing mission; its colonization of the world offered the promise of the same felicitous future to peoples who emulated its ways. Where order— both in this world and, for the redemptive faiths, in the next—provided meaning and an ethical standard for ancient civilizations, material and spiritual progress defined the ethos of modernity. Ancient civilizations trusted in the natural ordering of things. Modern societies placed their faith in reason. In antiquity, the past was never ending. In the modern era, the future was ever becoming. For countless generations from the dawn of time, humanity stood at arm's length from the world, in whose wonders it ontologically acquiesced. In the modern era, humanity penetrated the world; it investigated it, experimented with it, manipulated it to serve its immediate needs and its future happiness.

THE EUROPEAN WORLD: THE MERCHANT AND THE STATE

October 1347 is as good a place as any to begin. In that month several Genoese ships carrying diseased sailors sailed into Messina harbor in Sicily. The ships had sailed from the Crimea, where its crew had been infected with bubonic plague through the bites of rats either that lived on the ships or fleas that lived on the rats. By 1348, the plague had spread from the Mediterranean northward, across the Alps and the English Channel, and eastward, into the Danubian plain, similarly transported by ships that plied the great trade routes in the Levant and Asia along the coasts and inland waterways of Europe. Instantaneously, or so it must have seemed with a disease that claimed its victims with such ferocious efficiency, Europe became a charnel house. Paris lost half its population, Florence somewhere between 60 and 80 percent, and numerous smaller cities such as Venice, Hamburg, and Bremen as much as two-thirds.

Helpless to contain the unsparing extermination of humankind, European society concluded that it was experiencing God's wrath for its debauchery, greed, and self-indulgence. Both remorseful for and resentful about the perceived end of the world, they vented their wrath on the Church and on the Jews. Public discontent with the Roman Church manifested itself in dissent, flagellation, and the appearance of mystical sects that provided the popular base for the great schism that would in due course destroy the unity of European Christendom. For the Jews, whose isolated status in society had progressively deteriorated since the Crusades and the growth of commerce in the twelfth and thirteenth centuries, it took the form of pogroms. No matter that the scourge indiscriminately swept up all humanity in its pestilential rage, frenzied mobs intent on gaining retribution for God's refusal to forgive them slaughtered Jews by the thousands. Entire communities were exterminated in Antwerp, Brussels, and Erfurt. Those who survived fled eastward and only began to return a decade later.[1]

The Great Mortality, or Black Death, which reappeared less savagely on five more occasions from 1361 to the end of the century, exacerbated the slowdown in the European economy that began at about the midpoint of the fourteenth century. The plague's decimation of the European population compounded the adverse effects of colder, longer winters on agricultural productivity. The straitened economic circumstances in which the land-owning as well as the landless peasantry found itself inspired an incipient class consciousness, and provoked widespread revolts against the nobility, such as the Jacquerie that occurred in France after the Black Death, and uprisings in England, Flanders, and elsewhere that erupted periodically over the course of the next three centuries. At the same time, the prolonged economic contraction gave impetus to the rationalization of economic activity that had begun in Italy after the eleventh century. As the fury of the plague subsided, and population growth and economic productivity resumed, the reinvestment of commercial and agricultural profits into productive enterprise stimulated the growth of capitalism.[2]

Capitalism benefited in the first instance from the removal of socio-religious restrictions on private enterprise. Partly because of its dependence on bankers during the Crusades, the Church's historic prohibition on the charging of interest, or usury, long the business of Jews and other non-Christians, faded in the fourteenth century. In addition, the traditional controls of craft and merchant guilds on business activity loosened, as larger commercial and manufacturing entities penetrated markets outside the local community and hired labor that was free of guild restrictions.

Technical advances also fostered capitalism. Although the great innovations in technology were still two centuries away, profit calculations spurred modifications in agriculture such as crop rotation. Increasingly, land became a marketable commodity. New techniques in mining and in the weaving and finishing of cloth were similarly driven by the profit motive, as were improvements in naval vessels. The Italian inventions of double-entry bookkeeping, maritime insurance, and commercial banking were soon copied by others, thereby enhancing the commercialization of human enterprise. In 1370, German capitalists from cities such as Hamburg, Bremen, and Leipzig formed the Hanseatic League, which set up trading posts throughout the Baltic region and as far east as Russia.[3]

As the development of banks and trading houses and improvements in commercial and manufacturing techniques expanded European trading markets, they also effectively destroyed the institutions of feudal society. To be sure, the structure of feudalism varied greatly; in some places—urbanizing Italy, for example—it was almost nonexistent.

Structural differences aside, by the fifteenth century the extant principles of reciprocity and redistribution that had governed relations between landlord and serf began to lose their hold on communities increasingly motivated by personal gain. Traditional relations between peasant and lord were supplanted by the emerging business ties between urban merchants and manufacturers and the legalized usurers in the banking community who greatly expanded the commercial intercourse of the medieval trade fairs among traders into what was rapidly becoming an integrated European market. New structures of society were emerging. A growing and increasingly prosperous middle class, or *bourgeoisie*, had formed, on which kings and princes relied for funds that were previously supplied by the feudal nobility.

As a consequence of the steady stream of financial support from a growing merchant class, the diffuse nature of political control under feudalism also gave way to centralized government. Following the so-called Hundred Years' War, which raged from 1337 to 1453 over control of lands in the French fief of Aquitaine acquired through marriage by the English King Henry II, national monarchies emerged in England and France. The Spanish monarchy centralized control after 1469, although not before it was forced to suppress rebellions by local lords opposed to King Ferdinand and Queen Isabella's union of the principalities of Aragon and Castile. In each of these countries, a national consciousness arising from the perception of territorial space as "homonomous," to use John Gerard Ruggie's term, that is, as "territorially disjoint, mutually exclusive, functionally similar [and] sovereign," replaced the medieval view of territory as the nonexclusive, personalized, segmented formations in which rule was legitimized by the shared commitment to the laws and customs derived from natural rights.[4]

The consolidation of monarchical powers in national states accelerated the process of political, economic, and social change in fourteenth- and fifteenth-century Europe in several ways. In order to finance the administration of their kingdoms and constant warfare, monarchs became increasingly dependent on the new commercial class. The alliance between kings and men of commerce enhanced the political influence of the bourgeoisie at the expense of the nobility—as the Magna Carta and the French Estates General had earlier reduced the power of the monarchy vis-à-vis the nobility. Eager to extend royal control over the sources of finance, English, French, and, to a lesser degree, Spanish rulers granted favors to native capitalists in furtherance of economic self-sufficiency. Although the Industrial Revolution would later reverse the relationship between government and financier, at this embryonic stage in the modernization of society capitalists were the captives of powerful monarchs and their state-centered policies of mercantilism, the zero-sum system of trade in which nations hoarded wealth by exporting as much as possible and importing as little as necessary.

Mercantilism indisputably enhanced the ties between the well-to-do and the monarchy. The more the business community prospered, the more it identified its interests with those of the state. The fusion of business and politics, in turn, facilitated monarchical control over commerce and industry. By the late fourteenth century, England began to regulate trade and industrial production through the creation of government-supervised trading companies and monopolies. France, Spain, and Portugal followed suit. Mercantilism served still another purpose: it facilitated the exploration of the lands that lay beyond the uncharted seas and the rich treasures they held in store.

By the fifteenth century, the power of both the Italian city-states and the German Hanse had begun to wane. Internal conflicts, the French invasion of 1494, and the advance of the Ottoman Turks had seriously weakened Italian city-state domination of the Mediterranean. Faced with the secession of some members and increasing competition from England, the Netherlands, Poland, and other rising nation-states, the once mighty Hanse was similarly hobbled. Attention had turned elsewhere. The widespread acceptance of maritime codes of conduct, the construction of larger and more seaworthy ships with improved instrumentation (such as the compass and astrolabe) imported from China and the Arab world, and the map-making brilliance of Portugal's Prince Henry the Navigator prepared Europeans who were reaching the limit of their internal commercial expansion for journeys that would not have been possible in an earlier time. No less important, Europe benefited from the imagination and derring-do of intrepid sailors like Christopher Columbus, Vasco da Gama, who made the first voyage around the Cape of Good Hope to the Indian Ocean, and John Cabot, an Italian in the service of England. Miraculously, so it must have seemed in sixteenth century Spain, Portugal, and England, El Dorados of riches lay within grasp only oceans away in India, the Spice Islands of Southeast Asia, Africa, and in the "new world" across the Atlantic.[5]

THE WORLD BEYOND EUROPE: GOD AND SPICES

At first, non-Western peoples were little affected by the penetration of European explores, traders, and missionaries into their changeless world of ritual and routine, magic and mystery. But time would eventually dislodge them from the familiar. Try as they might, they could not retreat from the ruthless expansion of European economic, technological, and military power. Unable to insulate themselves from the material and cultural force of modernity spread by Europe's religious faith in human progress, non-Western civilizations were forced to acquiesce in their own transformation.

The westernization of the world was not predictable before 1500. Judging from the empires built by the Turks in Asia Minor and the Eastern Mediterranean, the Safavids in Persia, and the Ming in China, the easternization of the world would have seemed more probable. While the European world was in the throes of political and economic change, the Ottoman Turks had methodically expanded their influence from Asia Minor into eastern Byzantium. By the end of the fourteenth century, they had overrun Bulgaria, Thrace, Macedonia, and the Serbian kingdom. In due course, the once majestic Byzantine empire, impoverished by centuries of financial mismanagement and commercial exploitation by Venetian, Genoese, and other merchants, was reduced to a fragile outpost on the European side of the Bosphorus before it too was absorbed, in 1453, along with Constantinople, thence Istanbul, into the Ottoman empire.[6]

Like the Europeans, the Turks were also self-conscious agents of God who believed that civilization and religious rebirth followed their path into Europe. Led by Suleiman the Great, the Turks marched through Hungary in 1526 and, three years later, laid siege to Vienna, whereupon they met the formidable Charles V, Holy Roman Emperor, King of Spain, and defender of the faith. The undulating tide of battle that ensued reached a crescendo in 1571, when Spain, now ruled by Charles' son, Philip II, inflicted a crushing defeat on the Turkish fleet of Selim II in the Gulf of Lepanto. Thereafter, Turkey turned its attention to Asia and the prolonged but inconclusive conflict with the Shiite Muslims in Safavid Persia. For its part, Spain focused on the Atlantic. In 1593, the old gladiators returned to the Mediterranean for one last joust—indeed, the last crusade—which culminated in a peace treaty in 1606.[7]

The treaty of Sitvatorok was the beginning of the end for the Ottoman empire. To be sure, it was not until the second failed siege of Vienna in 1683 that the Turks were forced to cede territories to Europe. These capitulations, however, were foreshadowed in the progressive social and economic deterioration of Turkey that set in after 1500 consequent to the loss of trade to the northern European states and their settlements and the infusion of gold and especially silver from America that inflated prices and debased the Ottoman currency. Equally significant was the refusal to alter immemorial practices and traditional values. Although the Turks assimilated Western improvements in firearms, Ottoman receptivity to technology, commerce, and industrial organization was inhibited by feudal inheritances that limited "knowledge" to war, government, religion, and agriculture. As in China, trade and industry were not honorable occupations for a superior civilization, the more so as they were identified with Christian and Jewish pariahs. "Primitive techniques of production, primitive means of transportation, chronic insecurity and social penalization, combined to preclude any long-term or large-scale undertakings," Bernard Lewis has written, "and to keep the Ottoman economy at the lowest level of competence, initiative, and morality."[8]

Farther away from Europe, in India, another Muslim empire flourished. Muslim invaders had begun to establish a presence in northern India as early as the tenth century. As time passed, large parts of central and southern India fell under the sway of diverse Muslim rulers, who formed distinct principalities. In the north, however, territories conquered by Muslim warriors from the central Asian steppe were integrated in an imperial organization that gradually expanded its yoke southward.[9]

The emergence of the Mogul dynasty coincided with the Renaissance and Reformation in Europe, the Ming restoration in China, the zenith of Safavid rule under Shah Abbas, and, of course, the Ottoman empire of Suleiman the Magnificent, which it soon rivaled in power and cultural refinement. The Moguls were hardly cowed by the presence of Portuguese traders and missionaries who followed da Gama's path to the Indian Ocean. They tolerated Portuguese control of Goa, Malacca, and other ports in the region but, aided by their coreligionists in Turkey, Egypt, and Persia, managed to keep Portuguese power at bay, a task that was eased by Portugal's forced union with Spain in 1580. The Dutch and the English proved to be more formidable. Little interested in the religious proselytism of Portugal and Spain, they concluded treaties with the Moguls and other Muslim rulers that enabled them to gain a commercial toehold in the Indian Ocean from which they could supply Europeans with indigo, cotton, tea, and silk.[10]

Although it was not apparent at the time, the growing European control of native production gradually created markets for export goods from Europe. Inconspicuously a division of labor was emerging between what Wallerstein calls the core and peripheral states of the emerging world economy. Long before the Mogul empire crumbled in the eighteenth century and the British Raj was established in India, commercial and technological innovation had also begun to alter political relations between Europe and the surrounding world. The Mogul emperor and the other Muslim rulers of India and Southeast Asia could not withstand the onslaught of European commercial power because their rigid systems of religion and ethics did not permit either the social differentiation that had taken place in Europe after the fourteenth century or the comparable spirit of inquiry and discovery that stimulated economic and political expansion.[11]

Similar social and cultural impediments also constrained Chinese commercial and military power. Until the fifteenth century, Chinese traders had established commercial beachheads in southeast Asia, the Indian Ocean, parts of the Persian Gulf, and even east Africa. China's expansionism benefited from the construction of larger and (after the introduction of cotton sails) faster ships, the invention of the compass, and the high social status accorded to merchants by the later Mongol rulers in the thirteenth and fourteenth centuries.[12]

But Chinese attitudes toward commerce changed in the early Ming period, just as Europe was beginning to focus its attention on East Asia. Following the overthrow of the Mongols, the Ming dynasty reinstitutionalized the primacy of Confucian principles, which elevated the status of the learned and the landed classes and consigned the urban bourgeoisie to the lower rungs of social respectability. Nothing more dramatically illustrated the reassertion of deep-seated cultural traditions than the Ming emperor's sudden proscription of the great maritime expeditions of Cheng-ho, which had commercially ensconced China in the Indian Ocean and beyond long before its markets were discovered by the Europeans. Indeed, the Ming government went so far as to ban the construction of new ships, the effect of which was to weaken the Celestial Empire against the depredations of stronger, if, as the Chinese believed, culturally inferior, foreigners, including those from Europe.[13]

Europe's growing interest in Asia was influenced by Marco Polo's accounts, which date from the end of the thirteenth century, its romanticized treasures, and the fantasy, encouraged by the success of Jesuit missionaries in the Philippines and Japan, that a heathen world eagerly awaited the glories of Christianity. As they soon discovered, however, the early success of the Jesuit missionaries in the Philippines and Japan proved to be illusory. Confucianism and Taoism were deeply ingrained belief systems in China, as was Buddhism in Siam, Ceylon, and elsewhere in Southeast Asia. The Jesuits' early religious victories in Japan also turned out to be fleeting. Partly because of a military setback in his war against Korea, and partly because of mounting apprehension that the Christian missionaries were the stalking horses of the Spanish conquistadores, the warlord Toyotomi Hideyoshi savagely tortured and executed the Jesuits at the turn of the seventeenth century, a practice that was repeated by the Tokugawa shoguns until Christianity was all but extirpated in the late 1630s.[14]

Cultural obstacles and local conflicts in which the Europeans were sometimes unintentionally involved also encumbered accessibility to Asia's treasures, at least in this first encounter. To be sure, the Portuguese, Spanish, and Dutch all developed trade networks in Asia from their settlements in Macao, the Philippines, and the East Indies. Unlike the Americas, however, the apparition of glittering oases never materialized. In China's case, sinified, culturally parochial Manchus swooped into Beijing from southern Manchuria in 1644 and set up the Ch'ing dynasty that, if anything, was even less receptive than had been the Ming rulers to the barbarians from the West. As for Japan, its socially valued commercial interests, openness to foreigners, and European-like feudal society aside, the Tokugawa shoguns who ruled in nominal fealty to the emperor severed contact altogether. Intent on consolidating their power against domestic rivals, the Tokugawa shoguns abandoned their belligerent policies and piratical ventures against China and Korea. Like the Ming emperors, they too prohibited shipbuilding in order to seal Japan off from the outside world.[15]

In a way, the cultural and political introspection of Asia mirrored the sociocultural involution of Europe. Whatever Europe meant to peoples who were experiencing the disintegration of old routines and inheritances that infused the world with meaning, it was no longer a civilization with a clearly defined center. Trade expansion, social differentiation, and the spirit of discovery were in process of creating many Europes, or, more accurately, many parts of a yet-to-be-defined Europe, the protean shape of which was nearly as culturally unfamiliar to Portuguese, Spanish, Dutch, and English as they were to the civilizations of India, Asia, and the Americas.

In the century-and-a-half between the Lutheran Reformation and the Treaty of Westphalia, which ended the Thirty Years' War, the face of Europe changed dramatically. Politically and economically, the fulcrum of power shifted from the Mediterranean northward to England, Holland, and France. Following the French invasion of 1494, the Italian city-states were relegated to the periphery of European politics, for all intents and purposes a battleground on which the Spanish Hapsburgs and the French Valois vied inconclusively for dominance. For its part, Spain lost an empire, when it immoderately resumed its quest for religious unity and political hegemony against Turkey, England, and its rebellious Dutch and German possessions. Neither the religiously divided Hapsburg empire nor the collage of contentious Italian city-states could compete with the technical organization, administrative efficiency, and financial rationality of states like England.[16]

The Treaty of Westphalia not only ended more than a century of religious warfare in Europe; in its enshrinement of national sovereignty—dramatically illustrated by the more than 300 German states that signed the accord—it also laid to rest once and for all the creation of a universal empire, Hapsburg or otherwise. The basis of Westphalia was the principle of *cuius regio, eius religio* that had been vainly articulated a century earlier in the inaptly named Peace of Augsburg between Charles V and his German possessions. European acceptance of this formula had profound implications. The divisibility of sovereignty along national lines banished any hope of restoring the political unity of Europe under the leadership of Rome. Moreover, the absence of universally shared religious beliefs invited a nonconsensual latitudinarianism in thought and practice that fostered individualism, on the one hand, and broad social participation, on the other.

Calvinist asceticism, which defined worldly success as a sign of salvation, gave moral succor to entrepreneurship and the acquisition of wealth, effacing the social and cultural palimpsest that, until then, had ensured a sense of social situatedness. By complicating the task of affirming the "truth" of any single religion, Protestant sectarianism also hastened the secularization of reform; it facilitated the mobilization of human and technical resources on a scale unmatched by other civilizations in the search for socially uplifting—indeed, "progressive"—expressions of humankind's rationality and generosity. Entrepreneurs, corporations, and stockholders appropriated the social status once accorded to the guild masters and their apprentices. As capitalism was integrating distant markets in a division of labor that was a natural function of specialization and product differentiation, multinational enterprises such as the Dutch East India Company rendered obsolete the international fairs of the feudal era. New commodities from Asia such as tea, tobacco, and china became symbols of social mobility in an increasingly differentiated society.

Underlying the accumulation of wealth and the specialization of the marketplace was the liberation of the individual from the ordered medieval world. Individualism destroyed the network of relations and obligations that had heretofore bound the Church, nobility, and peasantry in a common community. The "I-form of speech and the use of subjective perspective in Renaissance art symbolized the separation of the individual from the world and from each other. The rich increasingly set themselves apart from the poor. Privacy became socially valued and differentiated from public activity. Space became symbolic rather than concrete, an abstraction from the territorialessness of feudalism and the social order of antiquity.[17]

To be sure, the material benefits of social change were not symmetrically distributed. In contrast to the traditions that bound the princely class and the peasantry to each other, there were no longer any mutual obligations between the acquisitive parvenus and the legions of destitute and socially disconnected for whom beggary was often the difference between life and death. Employers, sanctioned by law, restricted the rise of wages for those who were gainfully employed and punished those who demanded more. Where order was socially liberating, not least for those who performed fewer labor services, individual freedom was societally incarcerating, especially for those who could neither participate in the rewards of capitalism nor seek solace in the rules and rituals of a simpler time. Where once there was a belief in supernatural intervention to ease one's earthly pain, there was now an implacable world.

The Sedition of Reason

God, at least the personal God whom the ancients believed united heaven and earth, began to lose His hold over the lives of Europeans long before Nietzsche pronounced His death several centuries later. Sorcerers, soothsayers, and other purveyors of chthonic magic competed with the Christian God for the hearts and minds of the poor throughout post-Carolingian (and post-Renaissance) Europe. For many, the supernatural power of magic and witchcraft counteracted the misery of life and the uncertainty of survival. Others, of course, especially the educated, placed their faith in the tenets of Christianity and the sacramental role of the Church as *mater et magister*. For the godly, who faithfully participated in the conjurations of the Church and believed that prayers, penance, and pilgrimage would relieve their worldly suffering, the social upheaval that began in the fourteenth century was cataclysmic. Having been forsaken by their God for their perceived sinfulness, they repeatedly revolted after the Black Death against the irremediable insecurity of their lives, and, above all, the Church and its priesthood, whose sale of benefices and other forms of simony all too often fleeced those least capable of paying for their salvation.[18]

The teachings of theologians contributed to the public's antagonism toward the anti-Christ of Rome. Beginning in the last quarter of the fourteenth century, the English priest and scholar John Wyclif championed the restoration of the unadorned, unmediated church of early Christendom. The Bible, Wyclif argued, was the source of divine authority, not the papacy and the legions of priests who manipulated public credulity to aggrandize the Roman Church. Such heresy was embraced by the poor, many of whom joined Wyclif's disciples in the Lollard movement, the new merchant class, some of the aristocracy, and priests like the Bohemian Jan Hus and the Dominican friar Girolamo Savanarola, both of whom were burned at the stake, and the incendiary catalyst of politicoreligious liberation from Rome, the Augustinian monk Martin Luther.[19]

Luther's theology of salvation through faith alone rather than through the combination of faith and good works stressed by the Church redeemed humanity's faith in God's compassion and justice. No cathedrals, no good works, no ritual acts, no impersonal absolution, no rational verification of the divine order by Thomistic Schoolmen could equal the existential identification with God's human sacrifice. Salvation by faith was not only a religious phenomenon, it was also a political statement. As Friedrich Heer stated, Luther was to the masses of Germany what Joan of Arc had been to the French. For them, and for the Slavic peoples of Eastern Europe, including the Russian heirs of Byzantium, Luther symbolized the repudiation of the culture and traditions of the "Heavenly Jerusalem" of Rome. His protest permitted culturally, ideologically, and politically subject peoples to throw off the yoke of the West and its pretensions of politicoreligious unity.[20]

What Luther began in Germany as a personal theological rebellion the French theologian John Calvin transformed into a political revolution. Calvin's manichaean division of humankind into the elect and the damned was only a step removed from the creation of holy communities, including the formation of nation-states that fortified themselves against the Roman anti-Christ by their godliness. Although it surely contributed to the growth of capitalism in Europe, Calvinism saw wealth as a means to promote the kingdom of God. In contrast to the ancient world's perceived unity of the spirit world and the cosmos, Calvinism redefined life as a battleground in which humanity, in the interest of salvation and in the name of progress, was locked in combat with the profane forces of nature. Calvinism justified the secularization of society.[21]

The deracination of humanity from its convictions of the world was prefigured in the Christian existentialism of Renaissance Europe, where modernity began. "The Renaissance," Erich Kahler observed, "marked the beginning of man's settling down on earth for good." To be sure, the Renaissance also represents a return to the past; to a reverence for antiquity and a belief in the cyclicality rather than linearity of human affairs. But during the second half of the fourteenth century, and especially in the fifteenth century, a change occurred. The demonstration of dissident tendencies on the part of Italian humanists began to emancipate the individual from social conventions. It was their desire for unmediated knowledge that inspired the scientific inquiry of Thomas More, Francis Bacon, and René Descartes and the secularization of life.[22]

Before he died from the ravages of plague in 1349, the English Franciscan William of Ockham had already parted company with Thomistic Scholasticism. Like fellow Franciscan Duns Scotus before him and Marsiglio of Padua, William rejected the notion that society and the individual were earthly manifestations of divinely inspired reason. Reality, Ockham argued, was not a representation of universal concepts; universals were terms that only nominally represented a plurality of similar events or objects in the world. Reality, he insisted, derived from experience, which meant that God's existence could not be demonstrated, but, as Scotus had maintained, had to be accepted on faith. Like Marsiglio, Ockham drew a distinction between spiritual power, which issued from divine law, and secular power, which emanated from natural law and the consent of the governed. By separating the worldly from the divine, Ockham provided grist for Luther's justification of God by faith and for the scientific revolution that followed.[23]

Renaissance artists and intellectuals also contributed to the secularization of society. Renaissance humanism liberated the individual, who, in seeking to overcome his estrangement from society, became his own emperor. Writers such as Dante, Petrarch, and Boccaccio were also skeptics. As Descartes would do more than two centuries later, they questioned everything except themselves. Because they wrote in the vernacular rather than in ancient Latin, their views became the first shapers of popular culture. After the introduction of Gutenberg's printing press, which appeared with cosmic irony in the same year that the Christian citadel of Constantinople fell to the Turks, writers in France, England, Spain, and eventually in Eastern Europe similarly spread their views of society and its possibilities in the national tongues of audiences eager to be educated and, in time, radicalized. Just as the compass had reduced the physical distances that separated peoples, the printing press reduced the social and intellectual distance.

Political liberalism emerged—or, more accurately, reemerged from its pre-Christian cocoon—in the civic humanism of the Renaissance. Like Renaissance art, the political thought of Machiavelli and Guicciardini aimed to restore the ancient unity between heaven and earth. They sought to revive the sense of *civitas* that had atrophied in the course of time. Society, they argued, could only possess moral integrity if individuals assumed the responsibility of controlling their own destiny. The alternative was to become the victim of Fate, or *Fortuna,* and those who would sully the community's virtue.[24]

Such views, which contradicted the inherent dependency of feudal society, were decidedly revolutionary. The skepticism of Renaissance thought departed from the regularity and finitude of the past. As the French essayist Michel de Montaigne later postulated, the inability to establish the certainty of something precluded certainty about anything. In the epoch of order, the individual's social identity was never in question; one's place in society was assigned on the basis of custom and tradition. In the gestating ideology of progress of the Renaissance and Reformation, however, one's social identity was now open to discovery. Although it was not yet discernible, this intellectual milieu was giving rise to the creation of what Pocock refers to as "romantic man," for whom "political action is revolutionary, a transformation of the self, a reconstruction of the conditions under which selves are to be created, and an engagement in the presumed self-creation of others."[25]

That process of self-creation still lay in the future, of course. The spiritual force of the macerated Holy Roman Empire and the splintered Church continued to provide psychological sustenance for those who were suspended between past and future in the form of the Baroque. The Baroque was a final, furious effort to recapture the mystical unity of an earlier epoch and the brilliance of Mediterranean culture, the celebration of naturalism and the ecstasy of religious redemption that inspirited the Counter Reformation and reaffirmed the certitude of God's divine purpose in an otherwise chaotic world.[26]

Paradoxically, the Baroque was also the artistic adumbration of the scientific and philosophical developments that lay ahead. The sense of infinity expressed in the treatment of space, light, and time had clear religious overtones, but it also symbolized the contemplation of limitless nature. In the rational order of Nicolas Poussin's scenery, the illusion of undefined space in the interiors of cathedrals and Dutch homes, and the chiaroscuro depth of Caravaggio's and Rembrandt's settings, Baroque artists extended the mathematization of space introduced in the Renaissance in ways that anticipated the breakthroughs of the natural sciences in the last third of the century.[27]

To be sure, rebellion against the classical verities that germinated in the Renaissance and blossomed in the scientific discovery of the late seventeenth century unsettled the Baroque's defenders of order. In 1633 the Catholic Church condemned Galileo Galilei's mathematical proof of the heliocentric theory advanced by the Polish astronomer Copernicus nearly a century earlier. Disturbed more by the challenge to their authority as priest-kings than by the methodological repudiation of Aristotelian formalism, the Church sentenced Galileo, who disingenuously renounced his views, to prison and thence to house arrest for the remainder of his life. Although the Inquisition into Galileo's heresy stifled scientific research in Italy, the power of discovery unleashed by his revolutionary research in the dynamics of motion stimulated considerable intellectual activity in Protestant Europe and paved the way for Isaac Newton's *Principia,* a synthesis of the laws of mechanics that would shape intellectual inquiry of all kinds for the next three centuries.[28]

Vestiges of the Baroque, however, and of the ancients' belief in the universal harmony of God and the cosmos, also persisted into the eighteenth century, perhaps because of the prolonged paroxysm of the Thirty Years' War, notably in Leibniz's *Theodicy,* the geometrized validation of God's justice in the world. Their God was a remote God, however—not the personal, always righteous, sometimes punitive God of Augustine or Calvin—the product of the same formal rigor that rationalism demanded in the natural sciences. Their God was the God of deism, who set the world in motion and left it to operate according to the mechanical laws, timeless structures, and general principles that underlay the material and social mutability of life. It was humanity's duty to ferret out the clarity and permanence in God's universe. In so doing, Galileo, Descartes, Bacon, and Newton departed from the skeptical inquiry of Renaissance humanism. Armed with the certainty of reason, they embarked on a future of unlimited possibilities and progress.[29]

SCIENCE AND PROGRESS: THE BEST OF ALL POSSIBLE WORLDS

In 1662, a group of English scientists who had been meeting informally to discuss their research received a charter to form the Royal Society of

London for Improving Natural Knowledge. The founding of the Royal Society, prodded by Bacon's insistence on the organization of the new learning into different areas of inquiry and investigation, was an event of major importance for the development of science and for the continuing transformation of social attitudes of which it was a reflection. The Royal Society, which preceded by four years its French counterpart, l'Académie Royale des Sciences de Paris, fostered the specialization of scientific inquiry into discrete areas of research, the practical or cumulative effect of which was intended to improve the condition of humanity.[30]

Aided by the introduction of the telescope, microscope, barometer, and other instrumentation, scientists in England exchanged views with colleagues elsewhere in seventeenth- and eighteenth-century Europe, where the spirit of enlightened learning similarly glowed. In addition to the theory of gravitation, broadly acclaimed as the greatest single achievement in the history of science, Newton also developed the theory of optics and, along with Leibniz, differential calculus. Robert Boyle's research on the variation in the volume of gases helped to establish modern chemistry. Thanks to the new microscope, the Italian anatomist Marcello Malpighi described the movement of the blood through capillaries. The Swedish botanist Carolus Linnaeus and the French biologist Georges Louis Leclerc de Buffon set up systems of classification for plants and animals. Science had become an institutionalized subculture of Western society and a secular model for social change. Science was the fashion. It was a sign of cultivation, as Benjamin Franklin, Thomas Jefferson, and others in the New World were all too aware, and a subject of drawingroom conversation.

At a deeper level, scientific discovery cultivated the view that humanity had finally fathomed God's design of the universe. The universe may have been created by God, but it could be understood only according to the laws of nature, or what Leibniz called "the preestablished harmony." For Newton and Leibniz, revelation supplemented what humanity had learned about a world that God continued to govern. For their students, it was a mythological surrogate for the scientific explanation of natural phenomena. As explained by British philosopher David Hume, who sought to reduce all of life to quantifiable properties, man created God in his image. For intellectuals as a whole, science had dethroned religion, and reason had replaced faith.[31]

Just as rationally endowed individuals could discover the laws of nature, so too could they ascertain the societal structures and processes that ensured human progress in the best of all possible worlds. So, at least, concluded the so-called contract theorists: John Locke, the Baron de Montesquieu, and Jean-Jacques Rousseau. In his appeal for a society that vested authority in the consent of the governed, Locke deviated from the dismal portrait of Thomas Hobbes, who, influenced by the English civil war of 1640, defended authoritarianism as the only way to control the incorrigible belligerence of human nature. For Locke and, in time, Britain's American colonies, revolution was lawful if the state failed to discharge its obligations to protect the rights, including property rights, of the governed. Rousseau went even further, arguing that humanity was naturally good and thus capable of preserving its freedom by establishing a government that was consonant with the popular will.[32]

REVOLUTION AND PROGRESS: THE RIGHTS OF MAN

The first fruits of social progress, or, given its ambiguity, social dynamism, appeared in the Glorious Revolution of 1689. That conflict, which turned out to be bloodless, was the product of both the ascendancy of science and individualism and the culmination of the religious strife that had plagued Europe throughout the seventeenth century. It was also the beginning of the relocation of political authority from the monarch to the parliament. To be sure, England was hardly democratic. The religious tolerance that was granted to dissenting Protestant sects was not extended to Catholics, and parliamentary power, limited as it was, lay in the hands of the aristocracy and the wealthy bourgeoisie, not the general public. Nevertheless, a powerful transformation in governance had taken place that would influence both the French and Russian revolutions. Humanity, not God or His royal agent, was now responsible for its own destiny.[33]

At the dawn of the seventeenth century, this intoxicating idea had not pervaded the European continent, which remained captive to the fearsome and uncompromising power of Louis XIV of France. No prisoner of moderation, Louis ruled in the capacious self-confidence of an absolute monarch who, in the tradition of the Baroque, saw himself as a celestial king accountable only to God. Alarmed by France's hegemonic ambitions and the revocation of the Edict of Nantes that had given Protestants their religious rights in 1598, England formed a coalition of forces in Protestantized Europe that extinguished Louis's dominance of the continent and the *ancien régime*'s dominance of France. The domestic costs of Louis' insatiable ambition—excessive taxes, trade disruption, insolvency, and the enfeeblement of the aristocracy—sowed the seeds of revolution in the hearts and minds of a succeeding generation of *philo-sophes*—intellectuals, writers, philosophers, and scientists—who aspired to the rational regeneration of French society and humanity as a whole on the basis of limited government, religious toleration, and social equality.[34]

Although it is difficult to draw generalizations about a movement of intellectuals and ideas that transcended national distinctions, it seems reasonable to say, as other scholars have, that the French *philosophes* radicalized the antiauthoritarianism of the English and, to a lesser degree, American revolutions, which served as their models. English intellectuals questioned the existence of God. The French believed that religion had to be extirpated in order to achieve a free society. English intellectuals like Edmund Burke were political conservatives who subscribed to a government of cultivated elites separated from the lower classes. For their French counterparts, the common good was the residue of individual sovereignty. In any case, what began as a patrician reaction to the king's abrogation of the aristocracy's tax-exempt status became a middle-class rebellion of the men of law and commerce against the vestiges of feudal privilege and, before it was over, an explosive release of centuries of indentured rage by the shopkeepers, artisans, and the working class, the *sans-culottes* in whose rejection of all authority lay the seeds of nihilism.

The French Revolution was far more than the liquidation of the old order of aristocrats who commanded the promontories of European social life. It was at once the final breach of order and the herald of a homocentric epoch of progress that began in the Renaissance. Shopkeepers, workers, and artisans were no longer in thrall to kings, nobles, or even God. Henceforth all people could make and remake their lives in accord with the revolutionary principles of liberty and democracy. Progress was the measure of change. Empowered by the belief in the universal equality of humanity, men and women of all stations charged political leaders with the responsibility of distributing the benefits of economic prosperity and social mobility to the whole public. The inseparability of the governed from the government further strengthened the bonds of nationhood and patriotism; it imbued citizen-revolutionaries with the belief that the fate of a nation lay in their hands. In due course, patriotism gave rise to a cultural exclusivism that was inimical to eighteenth-century society's cosmopolitanism and its self-conscious imitation of the elegance, stability, and restraint of classical forms. In the radicalism of the French Revolution and the *levée en masse* there also lurked the demonic specter of aggressive nationalism that was the social and political antithesis of the ideology of progress.

When the orgy of terror finally subsided in 1795 and, with the help of an obscure general by the name of Napoleon Bonaparte, order was restored, neither France nor any other society that came into contact with the values and beliefs that inspired the revolution would ever again derive inspiration from the transcendental verities of the past. In its Declaration of the Rights of Man, the French Revolution expanded and enshrined the political transformation that had occurred in England 100 years earlier. Even more important, it redefined the cultural trajectory of the human community. Unshackled from theocentric cosmology and the unvarying cyclicality of life, people looked to the future and to the infinite possibilities of social and economic development it held in store.[35]

The State and Progress: The Struggle for Dominance

The quest for progress also dominated Europe's relations with the external world. Like the politically charged bodies-in-motion in domestic society, the state system of Europe that emerged from the cauldron of religious warfare in 1648 was forged in the same intense climate of rationalism and secularism that was transforming quotidian social life. The laws of nature applied to the interaction of states just as they did to the interaction of individuals within states. The sovereignty of the nation-state was consonant with the sovereignty of the individual. Individual rights were microcosms of *raisons d'état.*

Because of the potentially anarchic nature of world politics, national survival could only be assured, as Machiavelli had written two centuries earlier, through a balancing of interests among the competing states. Whether in the international or domestic context, the balancing of power implied a trade-off between the unconstrained aggrandizement of one's interests at all costs and the loss of one's possessions, not to say national existence. Shifting coalitions of forces or alliances were a constant feature of the European scene after the seventeenth century, as states, in emulation of the planets in the solar system, sought to establish some constellary equilibrium in their struggle for power.[36]

At a time when the states of Europe plunged headlong into the future in search of power, glory, and riches, however, international equilibrium was inevitably a transitory condition. Warfare was a perpetual part of life in the vertiginous environment of shifting alignments and alliances. Still, despite their acquisitive impulses, states restrained their bellicosity in respect of the dictates of history and natural law until Frederick the Great of Prussia appeared on the scene. For Frederick, whose cynical disregard for the historical rights and traditions of other states foreshadowed the aggressive nationalism of the nineteenth and twentieth centuries, there were no moral bounds on the state; space was there for the taking. Frederick's expansionism, in contrast to that of, say, Louis XIV, was the unslakeable thirst for power of which the seizure of Austrian Silesia was the ominous harbinger of the first partition of Poland in 1772 and thus of the demise of the European state system. Frederick's was the diabolical face of homocentric progress.[37]

Rapacity, however, was not confined to Europe's turf. The constant search for raw materials and markets to enhance the economic sinews of power created a zero-sum game of international relations that was increasingly played after the sixteenth century in faraway lands and usually at the expense of native peoples. In addition to its possessions in the West Indies, Holland extended its colonial control over the Spice Islands (modern Indonesia) and, after the Portuguese were driven out, established a small trading post in Japan. Portugal continued to exploit Mozambique and other parts of East Africa, just as Russia, under Peter the Great and Catherine II, expanded its commercial dominions in North America, Central Asia, and the Black Sea region.

The Anglo–French rivalry that dominated the European stage from 1689 to 1815 centered on North America, where both countries had developed extensive colonial possessions, the economic control of which was perceived as the key to political dominance in Europe. By the mid-eighteenth century, Britain had begun its industrial revolution, and it was fast on its way to becoming an economic leviathan, an entrepôt for the reexport of goods from its colonial possessions to Europe. Britain's economic efficiency facilitated the construction of a powerful navy, which, in turn, redounded to its commercial interests in the recurrent transfer of property that followed European warfare. France, for its part, had dramatically expanded its commercial presence in the Americas and in India and West Africa as a consequence of Louis XIV's appointment of Colbert de Croissy to manage its financial and economic affairs. Matters came to a head in the French and Indian War of 1756–63, the New World theater of what Europeans refer to as the Seven Years' War. That rivalry not only confirmed Britain's ascendancy over France, which lost its North American possessions, it also marked the beginning of the British imperium.[38]

That empire-in-the-making already extended as far East as the Indian subcontinent, where the British East India Company, helped by the collapse of the Moguls, assumed economic and political sovereignty over territories such as Bombay and Calcutta, which English traders had penetrated in the sixteenth century. In some cases, the British ransacked the land in search of products that could be traded in other markets. In Brazil the attraction was gold; in the West Indies and Africa, it was slave labor. In others—North America and the Caribbean—settler colonies provided a constant supply of raw materials such as tobacco, cotton, sugar, and indigo and a market for British manufactured goods. Gradually, a culture of trade integrated Britain and the world in a network of relationships that anticipated the informal empire of the nineteenth century.[39]

Initially, the societies that were the sacrificial hosts for the commercial parasitism of enlightened, progressive Europe reacted impassively to such intrusions. In the eighteenth century, the culturally invasive forces of westernization had not yet disrupted traditional patterns of life. The cultural onslaught was still to come. In some places, of course, the Western invasion accelerated social disintegration. Certainly this was the case in India, where the once unchallenged Mogul dominance had deteriorated into a *pasticcio* of independent principalities. Indeed, the fragmentation of authority facilitated European exploitation; the British and French exchanged their military support of local warlords for territorial concessions. After their defeat by Russia in 1774, the Ottoman overlords increasingly struggled to maintain control over an empire that was plainly no match for the European interlopers, either militarily or economically. By the eighteenth century, European manufactures had substantially replaced Muslim goods in the bazaars of the Ottoman Empire, just as European ships had taken control of the surrounding seas.[40]

In those parts of the world where the Europeans had not yet established a presence, life kept harmony with familiar rhythms. The Manchu rulers of China instituted a period of sustained political and economic stability in the eighteenth century and self-aggrandizing tributary relations with the peoples on its borders. European merchants who came to China coveting its silks, tea, and other riches were obliged to conduct their business with the government monopoly at Canton expressly set up to quarantine them from Chinese society. In Japan, by contrast, Westerners interacted directly, though sporadically, with merchants and intellectuals, who were quite independently beginning to question the virtue of a social system in which the Tokugawa shoguns retained a monopoly of power. In both societies, as it turned out, the socioeconomic gap between the landowners and bureaucrats, on the one hand, and the peasantry, on the other, was inconspicuously generating potentially explosive social tensions. At the end of the eighteenth century, however, Europeans were not aware of the latent energies that remained concealed behind the facade of Oriental isolation. Nor were they aware of the suppressed rage in their own societies among the lower classes of people who could no longer tolerate their involuntary exclusion from social status, power, and privilege.[41]

SOCIETY AND PROGRESS: DEMOCRATIZATION AND ORDER

The forces of reactionary conservatism that defeated Napoleon in 1815 hardly extinguished the ardor of revolutionary reform in Europe. The liberal ideals of the revolution to which the exiled former emperor paid homage in his memoirs burned brightly wherever Napoleon's armies carried the gospel of liberal-national regeneration. In 1830, armed insurrection erupted in the restored monarchy of France and forced the abdication of the last Bourbon, Charles X. The restarted French Revolution incited national uprisings in the Belgian Netherlands, Germany, Italy, and Poland. Worse still was the revolutionary wave that swept Europe in 1848. This time liberal-nationalist firebrands such as Louis Kossuth in Hungary and Giuseppe Mazzini in Italy and socialists such as Louis Blanc in France succeeded in forcing the old guard on the defensive. The Second French Republic was formed, and liberal governments were proclaimed in Hungary, Bohemia, and the German Confederation at Frankfurt. Aided by Russia, the forces of reaction in Austria and elsewhere eventually regained control of their rebellious subjects, but they could not suppress a restive public's desire to participate in the same progressive flow of events that was transforming the lives of the social and intellectual elite.[42]

The radicalization of European publics was incited only partly by the reformist democratic ideals of the French Revolution. It was also a by-product of sociological change. Ever since the British parliament authorized the enclosure of common lands in the eighteenth century, the peasantry that had historically farmed the open pasturage of the village community was forced to eke out an existence as farm hands or to migrate from the land to the city or, as many did, to the New World. For a time, the monarchy attempted to relieve the plight of the dislocated. But such assistance diminished in the state-less formalism of laissez-faire, which argued in favor of the diminution of state involvement in the natural, therefore, rational and inherently good, workings of the marketplace.[43]

In Britain, the combination of capitalist values and new technologies—coke smelting, the spinning jenny, the steam engine, the power loom, the introduction of railways in the 1830s and 1840s—sped the industrial revolution that had begun in the previous century and, in so doing, transformed human labor into an economic commodity, a factor of production like land and capital. Crammed into unhealthful cities and unsafe factories, shackled by economist David Ricardo's so-called "iron law of wages" that, even with the Poor Laws, barely met subsistence standards, the peasant or rural artisan sacrificed the communal ties and social serenity of the village for the depersonalized existence of a factory hand, an operator, as Carlo Cipolla put it, of " 'mechanical slaves' fed with inanimate energy."[44]

Social conditions on the continent mirrored those in Britain. Belgium, France, and Germany imported the techniques of British industrialization and the utilitarianism of philosophers Jeremy Bentham and John Stuart Mill, which equated the good of the community with the self-interest of the individual. Clearly, the state played a far more intrusive role in the continental economies, which generally favored protectionism over free trade. Assisted by huge tariff barriers, industrialization nonetheless proceeded apace. In the first half of the nineteenth century, as machinery increasingly replaced handwork in the production of textiles and railways began to link remote villages to the centers of production, the peasantry left the countryside and streamed into the cities of Europe. There they confronted the dreary conditions of factory life, urban squalor, and the congeries of health, sanitation, and welfare deficiencies that the well-to-do preferred to ignore.[45]

Socially excluded like the peasantry throughout history, with whom they shared spiritual communion, the human jetsam of industrializing Europe began to band together in a search for community, justice, and social progress. Workers associations—surrogates for the informal support structures of the village—appeared in Britain in 1825. Stimulated by the Chartist movement in the late 1840s, which sought the social and political equality of all classes, workers established trade organizations, lobbied for political suffrage (which was granted in the Reform Act of 1867, as it had been extended 35 years earlier to the middle class), and, in the 1890s, joined the Labour Party of Fabian socialist intellectuals and middle-class reformers. On the continent, trade unionism assumed a more doctrinaire cast. There workers turned to socialism, first the utopian variety that flourished between 1830 and 1848, and later the so-called scientific version foreshadowed by the painter and anarchist Pierre Joseph Proudhon but systematically formulated by Karl Marx in the Manifesto of the Communist Party.[46]

In the end, the incontestable improvement in living standards obviated a proletarian revolution. Despite the dislocations produced by the depressions of 1873 and 1893 and the insouciant response of the scions of nobility to the hapless conditions of the urbanized masses, the accretion of wealth expanded the church of social progress. The pell-mell rationalization of business that compartmented enterprise into specialized industries steadily improved the economic futures of workers who sullenly churned out its production after the mid-nineteenth century.

As a result of improvements in agricultural technology, famine no longer haunted humanity's horizons. The peasantry, still the largest segment of society in late nineteenth-century Europe, was better fed, dressed, and housed. No less impressive were the innovations in communications: railways and steamships, newspapers, the telegraph and telephone, and, by the end of the century, the radio, which linked hitherto disparate societies in an increasingly unified world. The security of peoples' lives had also dramatically improved. In Britain, Germany, and elsewhere on the continent, the enactment of a staggering array of legislation improved sanitation and social services, regulated the safety of factories, and provided health and welfare insurance to the destitute. Free compulsory education, immunization against disease and other advances in medical science, and nearly universal male suffrage all bore the mark of the irresistible march of science and social progress.[47]

The engine of progress was the state—socially and economically—not the idealized self-regulating market. The poorer classes relied on its largesse to alleviate the strains and stresses of economic perturbations and to stave off the specter of pauperism. The university-educated better classes shared a sense of social duty to promote its interests and thus to help stifle the clamor for revolutionary change that periodically emerged from the slums and shanties of Europe's great cities. After 1870 the welfare state gradually became a fixture on the European social landscape. Bureaucratic appurtenances of generally gentrified character expanded everywhere to minister to its needs, not least of which was its ability to increase its productive capacity, thereby ensuring the social stability that was a prerequisite to progress.[48]

IMPERIALISM AND PROGRESS: LA MISSION CIVILISATRICE

The importance attached to expanding the economic base of society incontrovertibly gave impetus to the feverish imperialist expansionism that seized the imagination of all Europe in the last two decades of the nineteenth century and beyond. Colonies offered a secure source of cheap food and raw materials and a captive market for the export of goods. No less significant, by creating space for Europe's burgeoning population, particularly the unemployed and potentially rebellious classes, imperial conquest reinforced the social network that undergirded the ideology of progress. As the British adventurer and colonizer Cecil Rhodes put it: "If you wish to avoid civil war, then you must become an imperialist."[49]

Certainly, territorial expansionism was not new. Britain's imperial claim on India, Canada, and Ireland, like Spanish, Portuguese, and French expansionism in the Americas and Asia, predated the era of liberal reform. What distinguished late nineteenth-century imperialism from its earlier incarnation was its underlying ideology of Social Darwinism. For elites and publics alike, imperial conquest was part of the natural struggle for survival; it was seen as a vindication of national superiority and a badge of honor. Motivated by national pride as much as by the introduction of universal military service (save in Great Britain), young men thronged to the armed forces.[50]

Imperialism also contained a moral dimension that was almost wholly absent from Europe's earlier penetration of the outside world. In the past, economic motives had propelled expansionism, as Britain's wars against China from the late 1830s to the late 1850s, its dominion in India after 1857, and France's conquest of Algeria in 1840 attested. During the last quarter of the century, however, Europeans believed that they had a duty to civilize a primitive world. No matter that the colonizer imposed autocratic control over his subjects or that the extirpation of local traditions and customs would retard, if not preclude, the development of effective self-government.[51]

The imperialist forays of the late nineteenth century began on the fringes of the European ecumene in what was left of the Ottoman Empire. Although weak and increasingly impecunious rulers had been ceding territory to Russia and Austria since the seventeenth century, it was the Congress of Berlin, in 1878, that formally sanctioned the divestiture of Ottoman territories, notably in the Balkans, where Britain, France, and even the newly created state of Bulgaria ravaged a spavined empire. The engorgement of the Ottoman lands was the appetizer for the feeding frenzy that followed in Africa. Following the treaties between Belgium's King Leopold II and the native chiefs of the Congo, the European powers, in 1884, again congregated in Berlin to settle their competing claims. A decade later, virtually all of Africa had been apportioned. In the feverish climate of acquisition that had settled over Europe, however, the gen-

tlemanly demeanor that attended the partitioning of Africa did not resolve all territorial disputes, as demonstrated by the near war between
France and Britain over the Sudan and the actual hostilities from 1898
to 1902 between Britain and the hardy Boers who claimed squatters'
rights to land in southern Africa they had colonized in the seventeenth
and eighteenth centuries.[52]

The rush for colonies was no less frantic in Asia, which was the last
remaining area of exploitation after the partition of Africa. The small
Pacific island chains—Fiji, New Guinea, the Solomons, the Gilberts, and
Tahiti—were devoured first. Pickings on the Asian mainland were politically more complicated, particularly in China, which was saved for last.
Here, imperialistic competition was fierce, hence, more dangerous. The
British and the Russians nearly came to blows over Afghanistan; the British and the French exchanged heated words over the Kingdom of Siam.
In the end, warfare did erupt over China, the choicest and most appetiz-
ing fruit in Asia's orchard, between westernized combatants who were
late entrants in the quest for empire, but with unexpected results.

In 1868, fifteen years after Japan was opened to commercial and
cultural contact with the outside world by American gunships, a group
of merchants and intellectuals revolted against the feudal rule of the established Tokugawa shogunate and established a constitution that guaranteed individual liberty. With extraordinary speed, Japan emulated
Western educational and health practices and, as in Germany, fused
capitalism and feudalism in a state-directed oligarchic structure. In Japan's case, however, the merchant-manufacturer, under the patronage of
the state, was the driving force of progressive reform, not the burgher, as
was the case in most of Western Europe.[53]

Japan also assimilated European military conventions, especially
Prussian strategy and tactics, and the vogue of imperialism. In 1893, not
for the last time, Japan invaded Manchuria and the Liaotung peninsula
and forced a devastated China to surrender Formosa, among other islands, and to accede in what was implicit Japanese control of Korea.
Japan's invasion both initiated the dissection of China and, in the evolution of that process, brought the expansionist craze to an end. In short
order, all of the European powers laid claim to Chinese territory. But
Russia's dominant role in Manchuria cast an ominous shadow over Korea that sowed the seeds of tension with Japan and led, in the war of
1904–5, to the end of tsarist expansionism in the Far East. More important, as a consequence of the Russo–Japanese war, the bloom was off the
rose of imperialism. Coming on the heels of the American victory over

Spain in 1898 and Britain's protracted struggle against the Boers, the defeat of a European power by an occidentalized Asian country was a felicitously ironic, if not yet fully appreciated, check to Western hubris. In any case, imperialism had lost its allure.

Europe's real suffering lay ahead, however; for the acquisitive frenzy set the stage for subsequent developments that gradually debased the ideology of progress and the belief in human perfectibility. Imperialism and its brutal aftermath were to the ethos of progress what greed and individualism had been to the belief in order. In the first instance, imperialism was the deathbed of the Concert of Europe, the decline of which began with the Crimean War of 1856 and the open season on the doddering Ottoman Empire it ushered in, the short-lived Anglo–Prussian efforts to preserve its territorial integrity notwithstanding. The incontinent impulse to conquer and control induced a pell-mell scramble for security on the part of the Great Powers, which resulted in the formation of mutually exclusive alliances that posed Europe against itself in an unforgivingly militarized environment. The calamity that erupted following a Serbian nationalist's assassination of the heir to the Hapsburg throne was not inevitable. But Austria was intent on going to war; and the rest of the European states impassively honored the rigid, pseudo-fraternal obligations that gave murderous force to the confluence of barely understood emotions—ideals, if you like—in which they were swept up in the most perfect of worlds.

International polarization mirrored the widening domestic cleavage in Europe. For all the rhetoric of progress, the material benefits of modernization had not significantly narrowed the gap between the wealthy and the lower orders of society that stoked Europe's furnaces and fed its teeming population. Although living conditions had generally improved wherever capital and industry had spread, the spirit and form of life remained the same to the bulk of humanity. The laboring class still lived in existential bondage to the aristocratic upper class and the lords of the industrial manor, the *arriviste* men of commerce whom, Gramsci argued, the gentry had socially coopted and exploited. Worse, the authority of the expanded ruling class had become depersonalized in industrialized, urbanized Europe. In the medieval era (and before), the nobility and the peasantry constantly interacted in a symbiosis of order that transcended reason and barbarism, Christianity and paganism. In the industrial age, however, even as the world economy was integrating the nation-state and its colonial possessions into an intricate process of production and distribution, the working class was losing touch with its society, with its past, with itself.

Having lost the anchor of personal relationships that once provided social connectedness, it is no wonder that the working classes gravitated toward the communal embrace of socialism at the close of the nineteenth century. At the manifest level, the class struggle preached by Marxism, both in its revisionist form and in the radicalism of Vladimir Ilich Ulyanov, better known as Lenin, promised to correct the social inequities that kept the working class in a perpetual state of fealty to the nobility. Psychologically, socialism provided a new community, a new "we-ness," or what Giddens calls a new situatedness of place, to replace the ontological alienation of industrial progress. The revolutionary was the religious heretic of old in modern guise, a secular priest who employed the talisman of reason to free society from its ideological shackles, that is, the false consciousness of religion or capitalism.[54]

Paradoxically, however, the more the working class embraced the ideology of revolutionary change, the more estranged it became from the society in which it sought inclusion. Caught up in the romanticism of revolution, socially marginalized workers vowed to destroy the institutionalized appurtenances of a decadent society. In doing so, the individual's sense of self, the professional elite excepted, was slowly effaced, his I-ness expropriated by a shared revolutionary identity that descended into the darkness of nihilism.[55]

The sense of alienation that accompanied progress for those who did not share in its social and economic benefits was no less palpable in the colonized extremities of the European world. In transforming the ecumene into its own likeness, the metropolis of the West gradually separated subject peoples from their cultural traditions. Just as the social gospel of Marxism inflicted ideological orthodoxy on its converts, European and American imperialists imposed their beliefs and values on non-Western peoples as a universal standard that they had little choice but to accept. Severed from their traditions, the technologically backward peoples of Africa, Asia, and the Middle East were inevitably forced into dependency on their colonial masters that gave rise to feelings of helplessness and inferiority. Dependency simply reinforced the West's self-serving belief in its own superiority and in its perceived duty to instill in uncivilized peoples the virtues of material and moral progress.

The westernization of the world exported agricultural and commercial knowledge to less developed societies. It exposed non-Western peoples to advances in medical science, sanitation, and the construction of roads and railways that undoubtedly improved the quality of their lives. The seeds of education and government planted by colonial administrators and missionaries produced increased literacy, political stability, and self-managing, if not self-directing, societies. Despite its benefits, however, colonialism left a legacy of injustice that was the antithesis of the ennobling aspects of its mission. For the colonized, like the industrial workers in urbanized Europe, modernity was the deprivation of autonomy, independence, and cultural identity. Unable to escape their feelings of inferiority, colonial peoples began to harbor anti-Western attitudes, even as they attempted to modernize their societies in imitation of the West. The day was not far off when subject peoples would direct their suppressed fury at their colonial masters in the name of the ideals of democracy and national self-determination the West had inculcated in them. Ironically, the impetus for the independence movements that lay ahead also derived from Western models; in this case, the totalitarianism of illiberal westernization—communism and fascism.[56]

The End of Progress

The ideology of progress died in Europe, long before its demise in the United States, in the great climacteric of 1914, alongside hundreds of thousands of unsuspecting crusaders who carried its colors into battle. Miraculously, it has twice reappeared, albeit in less utopian guise, from the rubble of war and social upheaval, first in the 1920s and again in the 1940s. As the twentieth century draws to a close, however, the belief in endless material progress, though no longer in human perfectibility, cannot be reconciled with the specter of disease, poverty, and human brutality that continue to stalk the world. Science, democracy, and industrialization have not produced the global peace, happiness, and human equality that Immanuel Kant and other Enlightenment philosophers had predicted. Just as reason, science, and individualism had shattered the epoch of order of the ancients, the unperfectibility of human nature and thus of the political, economic, and social institutions humanity has created have undermined the belief in the inevitability of progress that has been the bedrock of modernity. That we need encomiums to the end of history to validate the ideology of progress bears witness to its fading luster in a world that has lost faith in its message of secularized salvation.

PROGRESS ENTHRONED

"If ever in history there was a time when human objectives supported by an infinite amount of good-will heaped catastrophe upon catastrophe upon mankind," said Protestant theologian Paul Tillich, "it was the twentieth century." Ironically, the twentieth century had begun amid great fanfare of indefinite human progress. After all, the cumulative effects of science and technology seemed to have validated the optimism of seventeenth- and eighteenth-century rationalism, which viewed history as a unilinear process of human development. For some, the progressive course of history was the revelation of God's divine plan. Most people, however, defined progress in worldly terms of material abundance, social equality, and the liberation of the individual. The church's hold over humanity had been broken; the "true and only heaven," to borrow Christopher Lasch's phrase, was on earth. The state had been harnessed by the growth of industrialization to serve society.[1]

The origins of the belief in progress are debatable. According to J. B. Bury, who attributed the expectation of continual becoming to the theory of evolution and to the socially and economically transforming effects of industrialization, the concept of progress as limitless and universal does not predate the nineteenth century. Critics of Bury, however, rejected the idea that the notion of progress was an invention of rationalism; they traced its origins to the beginnings of Christianity and earlier to classical Greece. To be sure, Bury paid short shrift to developments before the nineteenth century. But those who claimed to have located the intellectual foundations of progress in antiquity or early Christianity exaggerated the historical record in their zeal to equate the blessings of modernity with religion. If the concept of progress is simply an extension of Judaeo-Christian or classical ideas, it cannot be examined as an independent construct. But, if one conceives of progress in its most rudimentary form as the development of a historical consciousness of a forward-looking, earth-bound, secular undertaking that improves our knowledge of ourselves and, therefore, of the human condition, its origins can be more accurately traced to the Renaissance.[2]

Prior to the Renaissance, people looked either backward to the divine for commemorization or forward to heavenly eternalization. During the fourteenth and fifteenth centuries, however, intellectuals and artists from Petrarch to Leonardo began to challenge the efficacy of religious belief as an explanation for the natural world and, in the course of time, to liberate the individual from tradition and convention. This is not to suggest that Renaissance societies began to look forward to inevitable or unlimited progress. Clearly, Renaissance intellectuals adhered to the classical belief that history was a recurring cycle of recovery and degeneracy. At the same time, however, they separated humanity from the divine order that defined the ancient cosmos.[3]

Starting with the Renaissance, humanity's interests became more this-worldly than other-worldly. Life became a more human-centered process than a finite, divinely ordained plan, the badness or goodness of which owed more to reason than to miraculous intervention. It was the emancipation of the individual in the Renaissance that led to the Enlightenment's exaltation of human dignity and to the utilitarianism of Jeremy Bentham, John Stuart Mill, and Herbert Spencer. It was the transformation of the relationship between subject and object that made it possible to explore and exploit the world in perpetuation of a process that romanticized historical development as the progressive approximation of an unattainable ideal. As a consequence of intellectual and social developments that began in the Renaissance, science became the religion of modernity, and faith in the future increasingly meant faith in the possibility of human endeavor.[4]

Stimulated by scientific discovery and the hopes of human perfectibility it aroused, Western intellectuals broadly believed that progress was historically preordained. They nonetheless interpreted its blessings differently. There was considerable disagreement about the form progress might take and, in some quarters, about its illimitability. Idealists defined progress in humanistic terms. The Abbé de Saint Pierre, Marquis de Condorcet, and Kant, as examples, believed that society was infinitely improvable. In their view, humanity was destined to achieve a condition of universal peace and well-being. For the eighteenth-century philosophers, Carl Becker pointed out, faith in the creation of an earthly utopia was a secular modification of the Christian doctrine of redemption. Conservative admirers of the English Revolution like Voltaire and Leibniz, however, believed that progress was inevitably bounded by the finitude of science. One could not go beyond the natural workings of the universe the Clockmaker set in motion.[5]

For most intellectuals, progress was synonymous with the material development of society. Just as the trial and error of scientific investigation contributed to the store of human knowledge, economic competition would foster ever-increasing material prosperity and, in so doing, improve the social and moral fabric of society. The affinity between progress and economic growth was particularly evident in the writings of Adam Smith and the French physiocrats, including Anne Robert Turgot, Louis XIV's finance minister. Condorcet, Kant, Locke, and the scientist Joseph Priestly were also proponents of laissez-faire. The socially meliorative role of commerce and manufacturing even influenced the thinking of Voltaire, who believed that liberty and wealth were inseparable.[6]

During the nineteenth century, growing numbers of intellectuals began to question the perceived social benefactions of economic prosperity.

Even John Stuart Mill deplored the social ills that resulted from relentless economic advancement. In time, the seamier side of industrialization condemned by novelists and artists was accompanied by the appearance of trade unionism and by a social radicalism that redefined the utopian character of progress. Echoing the radical idealism of Rousseau and Henri de Saint-Simon, Marx, Engels, and Spencer too stressed the importance of social engineering to promote educational and moral reform and thus social harmony. For the most part, these philosophers sought to liberate Progress from Providence (although Saint-Simon later recanted his atheism, and Hegel was a devout Christian). Moreover, none of these theorists opposed industrialization or technological change. They simply wanted to channel its course in such a way that it benefited society as a whole.[7]

Such differences in the conception of progress, however, in no way undermined the widespread belief among intellectuals and a growing educated elite that the steady advance of science and the accumulation of knowledge would lead to an increasingly rational and ethical human order accompanied by industrial expansion, social harmony, and individual dignity. Conservative or idealist, laissez-faire capitalist or social engineer, all paths converged in the certitude that tomorrow would be better than today for all of humanity. Progress, as Spencer put it, was "not an accident but a necessity."[8]

Everyone would progress. Neither the German states, suffused with transcendent idealism nor the even more authoritarian Russian monarchy could escape the force of predetermined social progress. For the new rich, the real ideologues of progress who materially benefited from the blessings of science and technology, this meant taking equal place in society with those born to privilege. For the lower classes, it meant perseverance and forbearance and the rising expectation that the gains of material and spiritual progress would in time trickle down to them, once science and reason removed the remaining caprices and restrictions of ascribed status that precluded their elevation into the elect of the new secular church.

So confident was the Western world about the course of human progress that the European states extended its trajectory to alien societies and cultures. Bearing the sanctimonious mantle of the white man's burden, Europeans and Americans alike sallied forth to inculcate the laws of political and economic liberalism on cultures they reckoned to be but a step removed from barbarism. Given the perceived backwardness of the peoples the West confronted, few questioned that the tutorial would require a prolonged and quite likely indefinite presence. Fewer understood that the feelings of confusion, impotence, and inferiority that their unwanted cultural proselytization produced would provoke such anti-Western sentiment on the part of peoples suspended between traditionalism and modernity.

PROGRESS DETHRONED

Not everyone, however, rejoiced in the confidence that progress would lead to freedom, social equality, and the advance of civilization. Doubts about the inevitability of human progress are discernible as far back as the Enlightenment. Voltaire and Diderot were by no means certain that the future did not portend a renewal of barbarism and the decline of civilization. And Montesquieu was reluctant to concede the future to the regenerative properties of science and the acquisition of knowledge; like Vico, he envisioned humanity's development as the outgrowth of individual organic cultures rather than some preordained process. Sounding the same note of skepticism a century later, Tocqueville worried that affluence and political independence would undermine the human community and Western culture along with it. Even as he ennobled democracy and modernity, he feared that they might lead to the emergence of social homogeneity and political despotism. The Swiss historian Jacob Burckhardt, who shared historicism's antirationalist temper, prophetically observed that the faith in progress would lead to colossal human evil. The same skeptical views of progress were expressed by Schopenhauer and Kierkegaard.[9]

By the end of the nineteenth century, doubt, disillusionment, and even despair became more widespread in intellectual and artistic circles in Europe and in the United States. Nietzsche's revulsion against the "decorative culture" of an age that appeared content to let its clock wind down or to await the universalizing world-historical process was a call to action in the service of cultural values. Similar appeals were sounded by American writers Brooks Adams and Henry George and by the English philosopher and political economist John Stuart Mill, all of whom feared that the aggressive pursuit of progress and prosperity masked a social and moral degradation that would one day explode with violent intensity.[10]

The emergence of realism in the novels of Gustave Flaubert, Emile Zola, Fyodor Dostoevsky, and Henry James and in the plays of Henrik Ibsen and George Bernard Shaw rejected the bourgeois vulgarity, idealism, and conformity that suppressed irrational, passionate, violent urges. Similar attitudes were given representation in the expressionism of Paul Cézanne, Vincent Van Gogh, and Paul Gauguin, the Cubism of Pablo Picasso and Georges Braque, and the Italian Futurists, French Fauvists, and German Expressionists whose unstably arrayed artistic compositions bore no relationship to the apparent stability of the external world.[11]

Neither visionary nor conformist, however, could have anticipated the devastating consequences of World War I and the volcanic fury of social dissatisfaction that it disgorged. Indeed, Bury's paean to the ideology of progress, which was written before the outbreak of warfare, appeared in 1920. The idiosyncratic episode that triggered the fighting notwithstanding, World War I was not a bolt from the heavens. It was the final destructive discharge of competitive tensions that had been mounting for several decades. The nation-state, romanticized upholder of traditions and guarantor of political and economic liberty in harmonious constellation with humanity and nature, had destroyed the European balance of power in the consummation of its own egoism. Nor was the social turbulence that roiled European and, to a lesser extent, American society a wholly unexpected departure from the quotidian nature of life. For those who were willing to recognize the signs, the polarization of states in competing alliances, the spiraling arms race, and the intensity of national pride ominously challenged the image of cosmic peace and progress to which the West faithfully clung.

The literature of postwar pessimism made this depressingly clear. Books such as Austin Freeman's *Social Decay and Degeneration* and Spengler's theory of cultural decay echoed the despair of Henry and Brooks Adams, who had written about the decline of Western civilization earlier in the century. Not all intellectuals had forsaken the idea of progress, of course, as the work of Albert Schweitzer and the mid-twentieth-century books by Teilhard de Chardin, C. P. Snow, and Margaret Mead testified. Nevertheless, there could be no denying that the message of these latter-day prophets of optimism had to compete for public receptivity with the dystopian writings of T. S. Eliot, James Joyce, Samuel Beckett, and George Orwell.[12]

In any event, when the dust finally settled, more than four years of combat in conditions of virtual military stalemate had produced staggering losses. Millions upon millions of young men who cheerily marched to war for the honor of being Germans, Frenchmen, Englishmen, Austrians, Italians, and Russians never returned. Physically and psychologically bled by the massive human and economic costs of total warfare, the

European world faced itself shorn of its convictions about the past and its faith in the future. The bickering and mistrust that accompanied the Paris Peace Conference, the illiberal demands of the victors against Germany and its allies, and the implacable hostility that such behavior aroused left the European states, the postwar treaties aside, in a persisting state of conflict, or in the condition of what Kenneth Boulding has called "unstable war."[13]

Domestic tranquility was also shattered. Class tensions, revolutionary rhetoric, and urban violence mocked the ideal of social harmony propagated by the ideology of progress. Patriotism aside, the pervasive social and economic effects of prolonged war and the growing centralization of government decision making took their toll on European publics, especially the working classes. Although European publics had faithfully supported the war, the combination of the ideological fervor fed by the Bolshevik revolution, postwar uprisings in Germany and Hungary, and widespread economic recession unleashed long-suppressed resentments about the widening gap between rich and poor that destroyed the myth of social harmony through the natural, self-equilibrating dynamics of the marketplace. Just as nationalism had sent the international political equilibrium careening off course, the social inequities of unregulated economic liberalism provoked massive strikes and domestic violence. In an effort to curb the violence, publics tolerated increasing governmental intervention in society. In the end, the cure was worse than the illness: the emergence of fascism in Italy and Germany led to the cooptation of the capitalist class and ultimately to the destruction of the market economy that the aristocratic and bourgeois champions of progress sought to preserve.

THE PERVERSION OF PROGRESS

For all their ostensible differences as ideologies and systems of governance, communism and fascism were strikingly alike. Both sprang from the debris of World War I and, more fundamentally, from the disaffection and disconsolation of exclusion from the culture of progress. The brutalizing consequences of protracted warfare hardened attitudes toward liberal society. In the case of Russia, where liberalism was in its infancy, the real war was with an imperial system—represented by the tsar, the landed estates, and the orthodox church—that had stripped working men and women of their social status and deprived them of the basic necessities of life. In the West, men who had gone to war in the patriotic bliss that they were cleansing the world of its impurities were disillusioned with the materialistic societies to which they returned and contemptuous of those who were indifferent to their sacrifice. Communism and fascism became the new cathedrals of progress for the dispossessed. They provided a new eschatology, a new certitude for those without a place in society, as science and the belief in unlimited progress had earlier given meaning to peoples that had ceased entrusting their faith in the future to chiliastic hopes of deliverance.

Paradoxically, even as communism and fascism heaped scorn on liberalism, they were no less committed to the underlying ideology of progress. Communism and fascism contributed to the flow of history they were in revolt against through what von Laue calls "substitutionism," or the application of totalitarian means to achieve progressive ends.[14] Sociologically, the lower classes of Western society from which Lenin, Stalin, Mussolini, and Hitler arose were expressing atavistic resentments against the upper classes and, in the process, vindicating their own perceived inferiority and impotence. They were the descendants of the archetypical anti-Western westernizers: Peter the Great, who singlehandedly dragged a feral Russian state into the main currents of European life, and Frederick the Great, who no less ruthlessly avenged the cultural and political humiliations imposed on the Prussian people by its Romanized masters.

Feelings of inferiority and resentment likewise commingled in the reactions of the non-Western world to the ideology of progress. Just like the lower orders in Europe, the non-Western beneficiaries of progress—whether formally colonized or informally exploited—were simultaneously attracted to and repelled by the values and beliefs of their putative civilizers. Japan was an exception, at least a partial one. In the five decades between the Meiji Restoration and the end of World War I, Japan had sedulously assimilated Western technology and techniques. Its industry and powerful military establishment bore the stamp of westernization; its business and political leaders the imprint of Western culture and practices, including the diplomacy of imperialism. When World War I ended, a rich and powerful Japan took its place in the pantheon of world powers.

But the Meiji modernizers were not confident of their equality with the West, much less of the West's acceptance of Japan as an equal. This perception, and the related anxiety triggered by renewed Western domination, induced Japan, during the period of Taisho democracy in the 1920s, to cooperate with the European powers in the Washington Conference system. It also provided a convenient foil, especially after the onset of the Great Depression, to the nationalistic attitudes of the post-Meiji generation of political, business, and military leaders who, like their fascist and communist counterparts in Europe, opposed the West while embracing the values of westernization. It was this group of militant nationalists who gained influence after World War I and who set out to demonstrate Japan's cultural superiority by replacing Western power in Asia. After 1929, the militants ascended to power, like the ancient shoguns, in the name of the emperor.[15]

In the less-developed parts of the non-Western world, attitudes toward westernization were not as complex. Sun Yat-sen's Three Principles—nationalism, democracy, and the people's livelihood—also reflected the ambivalence of Chinese leaders toward the West. Intent on abrogating the unequal treaty system imposed by Europe and on recovering its sovereignty, Chinese revolutionary nationalism was unquestionably fueled by animosity toward the haughty barbarians of the Western world. At the same time, the state-directed modernizing efforts undertaken by the Kuomintang and the Communists equally betrayed the desire to westernize Chinese society. In India as well, where Mohandas Gandhi infused modernization with Hindu asceticism and pacifism, and in Turkey, where Kemal Ataturk's reforms extended a process of secularization that began in the late eighteenth century under the Sultan Selim III, once proud civilizations sought to recoup their self-esteem by cleaving to the very ideology of progress that had deprived them of it.[16]

The system of command modernization employed by less-developed societies was intended to quicken their reacculturation in the ideology of progress and thus to catapult them into the front ranks of the developed world. In most cases, it was the antidemocratic aberration of westernization. But while the liberal world and the new states carved from the former Hapsburg and Ottoman empires heaved helplessly in the gale of the Great Depression and the resulting political turmoil, the command societies of Europe and Asia stood out as islands of stability, seemingly untouched by its devastating effects. Below the glistening surface of rational planning and human engineering, however, was the refuse of human rot and misery that the anti-Western prophets of progress concealed from view of outsiders, especially in the West. There the devastating social and psychological effects of war and economic depression left little doubt that the era of faith in science and technical progress, much less in civilizing perfectibility, had ended. Inexplicably, the tape of the preceding five centuries of seemingly uninterrupted progress was being rewound to an earlier time. The force of some malevolent cosmic gravity was forcing civilization to retreat into a new dark age, one without compassion or hope. All the signs pointed in this direction—the overt warfare and material deprivation as well as the tacit, nebulous indicators of change, whose shadowy presence was only now beginning to emerge from the background of human consciousness.

Nietzsche, Dostoevsky, and the pioneering work in psychoanalytic psychology by Sigmund Freud exposed the naivete of the West's deification of rationalism. Until this time, the prevailing view of enlightened intellectuals was grounded in the self-conscious reflection and apprehension of an objectively knowable world. This was the intellectual legacy of Galileo and Descartes by way of Plato and the later empiricism of Locke and Hume that reduced knowledge to the acquisition of and reflection upon sensory data. Existentialism and psychoanalytic theory focused on the prereflective givenness of reality that existed without the mediation of anticipatory ideas or the objective apprehension of sensory stimuli. They took humanity into a nether world it had never known, in which hidden sources of thought revealed reason's limits.

Psychoanalysis exposed the dark side of human nature, the depraved, destructive, demonic urges of an immortal unconscious that defied reason and society. Existentialism mirrored the European condition after World War I. It was a reaction to the specialization of rationalism and scientism that divorced humanity from the ordinary understanding of the daily events of life as a whole and thus from active participation in them. It too invited humanity to scale the citadel of reason and to discover in the valley that lay beyond the inescapable reality of death, anxiety, and the alienation of the individual struggling for self-realization in a faceless, Godless world.[17]

The post–World War I encounter with human alienation and despair provoked different social reactions. One was the flight from rationalism that was reflected in the emotional flatness and unintelligibility of abstract art, in existential philosophy's preoccupation with the absurdity of life, and in the writings of such diverse thinkers as Karl Mannheim, Oswald Spengler, and Vilfredo Pareto. Another was the self-immolating embrace of nothingness. In a way, nihilism was the logical opposite of eternal progress. Its desperate pursuit of power for the sake of inexhaustible power was the fateful coda of an age that believed in limitless progress for the sake of progress. For the individual and for society as a whole, it was the drunken grab for power on the part of the backward and the underdeveloped, who, not unlike the *sans-culottes* of the French

Revolution, sought to wrest control of their fate from the hands of the privileged and refined, no matter the cost.

Nihilism resulted from a loss of faith in the absolutes of reason, including God, and in the value of the past in which progress resided. The repudiation of reason undermined humanity's convictions about the intellectual coherence of the world it inhabited and thus about itself. The reduction of the past to one's roots relativized history and disconnected humanity from its attachment to a larger evolutionary process that seemed inconsequential. The resulting alienation and purposelessness encouraged the exaltation of power, the self-reaffirming need for which fostered nationalistic experiments that were designed to create universal truths to fill the void of historical tradition. The will to master nature that emerged in the scientific revolution of the seventeenth century was now the arbiter of civilization's advance. Nihilism was extreme individualism turned against freedom in the name of liberty. It justified materialistic excess, removed the human content from the functional capacity of society, and, therefore, rendered life inert.[18]

The disaffection from truth, justice, or morality "freed" the individual from the perceived discredited values of a degenerate society. The devaluation of progressive values and thus of the society that was shaped in moral and ethical reflection of them led to the loss of self. Severed from society, the homeless sought communion with others who had also extricated themselves from their social fetters. They found communion in the messages of racial superiority, social revolution, and nationalism that merged in the nihilism of totalitarianism, in whose name they rediscovered their social identities, hence, their lives. The revolutionary state became the new master of the "homeless" individual and its leader the avatar of progress.[19]

As the demonic lurking in the human unconscious flaunted reason, and nihilism perverted freedom, so developments in science also undermined society's ability to shape its own future. According to Newtonian mechanics, the universe consisted of a collection of building blocks, the gravitationally induced movement of which was the basis of all matter. All one had to do was to ascertain the laws that set the great machine God had designed into motion to understand the immutable workings of nature.

By the end of the nineteenth century, however, scientists began to question the material foundation of Newtonian theory. Experiments conducted in 1881 by two American scientists, Albert Michelson and G. W. Morley, revealed that light was composed of a series of waves without substance, which traveled at a fixed speed. The subsequent discovery of the quantum by the German physicist Max Planck, which demonstrated that radiated energy was emitted in discontinuous quantities, paved the way for Albert Einstein's theory that particles were simultaneously matter and waves of energy, or photons. In 1915, while Europe was eviscerating itself, Einstein, in the general theory of relativity, was razing the foundations of scientific certainty by reconceptualizing the universe in space-time coordinates that associated mass with energy rather than matter.

Quantum mechanics revolutionized science. In doing so, however, it also assailed the intellectual underpinnings of progress on which Western society had rested since the Enlightenment. The uncertainty of scientific absolutes reinforced the loss of faith in human perfectibility that was the legacy of the world war and the subsequent political and economic meltdown it precipitated. As if to ensure that no relapse into the determinism of progress would occur, the German mathematician Werner Heisenberg introduced the uncertainty principle in 1927. Derived from calculations that demonstrated the impossibility of knowing both the momentum and location of an electron at the same time, the Heisenberg principle not only put the final nail in the coffin of Newtonian physics, it also renounced the belief in causality. The movement of electrons from one atomic orbit to another could not always be explained in unequivocal terms. Hereafter, even the natural sciences were forced to base the outcome of discrete events in the universe on statistical probabilities.[20]

Worse, as scientists delved deeper into the mysteries of the subatomic units of matter that composed the elemental forces of energy, it became less clear whether they would be able to control the awesome power their research had unleashed. Danish physicist Niels Bohr discovered that atoms were constantly in motion and that their collision with one another caused their electrons to move unstably from one orbit to another. The greater the collision, the greater the electronic excitation; the greater the excitation, the greater the atomic instability. Bohr's formulation of the theory of atomic structure inspired the research of scientists elsewhere in Europe and the United States, which culminated, as World War II erupted, in the discovery of fission, or the splitting of the atom.

In 1942, American and European scientists working in Chicago as part of the Manhattan project successfully initiated the first self-sustained nuclear chain reaction of fissile material. The atom bomb was born. Originally intended as a security hedge against the possibility that Germany would develop and deploy such a weapon, it soon became a doomsday machine, a Frankenstein monster, the lethal perfection of which threatened the existence of all humanity. Science's quest for certainty had produced the ultimate uncertainty. Any advantage that the United States gained from its possession of nuclear weapons, a somber Niels Bohr told President Franklin Roosevelt in 1944, would be "outweighed by a perpetual menace to human security."[21] Rather than manipulate nature, as the Enlightenment sages had prophesied, modern society was being manipulated by it, like its ancient forebears.

THE ILLUSION OF PROGRESS

Still, ideology dies hard. Long-held beliefs about the world in which we live, reinforced by experience, social convention, and mythology, do not change either instantly or easily. There is no single moment, no neat separation of physical reality, that signals the end of one epoch and the beginning of another, much less one that affected everyone everywhere at the same time and in the same way. The belief in endless progress that originated in the West and gradually spread to traditional societies has been no less resistant to its passing than was the ancient world's acceptance of the natural and unvarying order of life. The knowledge that the aspirations and expectations in which meaning has been vested no longer provide a road map for the future is a slow, tortuous, uneven process. Even when we are aware of its presence, historic change is never welcomed. Its message is ignored, distorted, rationalized, and rejected.

Fascism and communism were the perverse responses to the loss of hope in the future. They promised a new and surer path to the Utopia that lay ahead. They mesmerized the socially dispossessed, the lower classes that sacrificed their independence for the community attachments they so desperately desired. They aroused politicians and intellectuals from the languor of lapsed liberalism. Some Europeans and Americans even flirted with the idea of abandoning liberalism for state-directed models of social engineering. But these systems took far more than they gave. Eventually, the absence of freedom exposed the hypocrisy of the false prophets of progress. As time would show, the heretical ideology of progress formulated by Fascism and Communism, unlike its orthodox variant, died from a paucity of optimism, not from a surfeit of it.

A second and more enduring attempt to revitalize the ideology of progress was undertaken by the United States. The youthful innocence and insouciant optimism of the United States contrasted dramatically with the somber, disconsolate mood of post–World War I Europe. It was as if Americans had not fully understood, let alone appreciated, the magnitude of the disaster that had befallen the civilized world. Of course, even America had its Cassandras. Long before World War I, as we have already seen, more than a few intellectuals feared that the twentieth century portended a cataclysm of biblical proportions. Gloomy musings about the end of progress were no match, however, for the faith in human perfectibility that Progressivism restored. To speak of the declining vigor of Western civilization was to languish in despair and defeatism, the very antithesis of the United States.

This is not to say that World War I or, more accurately, the peace talks that followed it, had not affected American perceptions of progress. Shocked by the revelations of the secret treaties that had been negotiated before and during the war and by the persisting mistrust and antagonism that marred the postwar peace, Americans too had lost faith in the corrigibility of humankind, in the utopian ideal of progress. The seemingly irremediable European decadence that was disclosed in the postwar peace discussions ultimately decided the Senate to reject American participation in the League of Nations, Woodrow Wilson's parting tribute to the moral universalism of the Enlightenment and to the myth of human perfectibility.

Even so, the disillusionment that the United States experienced after World War I was brief, certainly nothing comparable to the sense of devastation and death that haunted Europe during the interwar years. Part of the explanation for this lay in America's youth. By the early twentieth century, Europe dominated the world militarily, politically, and economically; its culture pervaded the world. The United States, in contrast, having only recently tamed its own frontier, was just beginning to experience the world beyond the Americas. While Europe, which stood on the promontory of human progress on the eve of World War I, basked in its global self-reflection, the United States was still in a state of self-discovery.

Moreover, the disillusionment that the United States experienced during the peace negotiations (and on countless occasions since) was rationalized in such a way as to protect the American self-image. Indeed, the perception of an immoral, unregenerate Europe illuminated American virtue. In fact, the decision to spurn membership in Wilson's peace league reenacted the primal American experience of fleeing the debauched world of the fathers. The despair of post–World War I Europeans appeared to reflect the decline of a dissolute civilization withering in the final stages of decomposition. But Americans were no more willing to accept the incongruity between an incorrigible world and their universalizing mission than they were able to assimilate the symbolic disappearance of the once limitless frontier into the national self-image. Instead, they intensified their faith in limitless material progress, which became the symbolic surrogate for the progressive vision of human perfectibility.

The politics of abundance was the policy correlate of the redefinition of progress. The gospel of material progress was reinforced by industrialism, the new engine of democracy, and by the applications of science and positivism to daily life. Efficiency and productivity were the hallmarks of modernity, and everything that contributed to their development contributed to global progress. Technological innovation, scientific management, and specialization fueled the politics of abundance. The corporation, the state, and the international system were modeled on the workings of a huge machine that (in anticipation of cybernetics) could be continuously engineered to achieve social mobility and international harmony. As the world's most productive and prosperous nation, the United States continued to see itself as the exemplar of progress.

Caught up in the delirium of postwar prosperity, the United States carefully avoided political involvement with the wobbly Eurocentric world order. Nevertheless, it supported the League's disarmament agenda, including its prominent participation in the war-renouncing Kellogg-Briand pact of 1928, and visibly championed the outlawry of force in the resolution of international disputes. Even after the depression ridiculed Herbert Hoover's promised "chicken in every pot," Americans succumbed neither to despair nor to the illiberal alternatives of the left or the right. Sheltered from the world by its born-free mythology and the infectious optimism of Franklin D. Roosevelt, Americans placed their hopes in the prosthetic capitalism of New Deal welfare economics. On the basis of their experience, Americans still believed, as Europeans no longer could, that tomorrow would be better than yesterday—not just for Americans but for everyone who followed the liberal-democratic path to material progress. And, more or less, it was.

The Second World War and its aftermath justified the American society's faith in progress and its mission to clone the world in its likeness. Physically unscathed by a war that was fought thousands of miles away from their shores, infatuated with the boundless prospects of prosperity that lay ahead, Americans enthusiastically spread the gospel of progress to the diverse peoples and cultures of the world. Not only had the fascist perversion of progress been defeated, the societies from which it sprang had been rejuvenated, reincorporated in the mainstream of liberalism through the generosity of American postwar reconstruction aid and political tutelage.

Former subject peoples were now free to chart their own future. Undoubtedly, their liberation was hastened by the implosion of the European imperial oligarchies; but it was also influenced by the Roosevelt administration's unwavering advocacy of decolonization and political self-determination. To safeguard against the renewed disruption of global peace and thus ensure a peaceful environment in which the nations of the world could develop and prosper, the United States rebuilt the League of Nations into a collective security organization. Unlike the League, which had no enforcement mechanism save the rule of law, the United Nations armed reason with the military might of democracy's defenders, notably the United States. The League was the handmaiden of the utopian belief in progress, and Woodrow Wilson the embodiment of that ideal. The United Nations was an association to promote material progress, and Franklin Roosevelt was its chief publicist.

The Soviet Union's unwavering allegiance to its own conception of progress elevated the American mission to a crusade. The evangelistic fervor of American internationalism was not politically insignificant. Without it, postwar administrations would have faced considerable difficulty in mobilizing broad support for policies from a society that preferred to lead by example rather than by entangling obligations to the world. For most Americans, Soviet Russia was not perceived as a rival for power in the bipolar international system that was the residue of Europe's collapse; it was the allegorical face of the devil, the sinister and destructive wilderness impeding the progress of a virtuous community in the American morality play. Providence and the recurring compulsive need to justify the nation's chosenness required the United States to play St. Michael to the communist dragon.

Four-and-a-half decades later, the dragon was subdued by a combination of military resolve on the part of the United States and its allies and the gradual deterioration of a system whose hypocrisy undermined its putative legitimacy. In this conflict, the United States did not leave unscathed. One casualty of the Cold War has been the loss of American exceptionalism. The righteous nature of the Manichaean conflict with the Soviet Union justified the resort to measures that contradicted the nation's virtuous self-image. Americans could excuse their government's clandestine removal of ideologically tainted foreign leaders such as Mohammad Mossadeq or Salvador Allende, the periodic violations of international law, the support for authoritarian strongmen who governed in defiance of the public will, and the counterinsurgencies and undisguised wars such as Vietnam as aspects of the struggle for liberal-democratic progress that in no way vitiated the nation's ideals. If anything, a society periodically in need of reassurance was reminded, the defense of the free world indelibly demonstrated the nation's commitment to its ideals.

As the United States became enmeshed in Vietnam and later in the politics of liberation in Central America and Africa, however, foreign observers, including its friends and allies, could not help but note the similarity between the means the United States and the Soviet Union used to achieve their objectives. Whether such transgressions of the principles of self-determination or the rule of law were unavoidable concomitants of the Cold War, the myth of American innocence could no longer be rehistoricized.

The irreconcilable nature of the conflict with the Soviet pretender to the throne of progress further obscured America's view of the sociocultural complexity of the world. Rather than see other societies as they saw themselves, the United States all too often superimposed on other peoples, particularly in the developing world, the template of its Cold War contest with the Soviet Union. United States policy rewarded its friends and punished its enemies.

Such a zero-sum approach to international relations inevitably alienated the neutral and nonaligned states. Having recently emerged from colonization, these states were intent on maintaining their distance from the two superpowers. But the ideological filter of the Cold War obscured the visibility of the social turmoil in the developing world that pitted the forces of modernity against the forces of tradition. Suspicious of the socialist political programs and agendas that were at once a compromise with traditional values and a desperate effort to accelerate the pace of modernization in emulation of the West, the United States tended to see leftist regimes—even those that professed not to be communist—as Soviet pawns on an ideological chess board rather than as indigenous expressions of self-determination on the part of newly emerging societies.

Now that communism has been discredited virtually everywhere, the United States finds itself in the uncomfortable position of having to familiarize itself—in some cases, for the first time—with a host of societies to which it had been heretofore exposed only abstractly in the chiaroscuro light of the Cold War. Eager but ill equipped to improve their material conditions without assistance from the industrialized West, these societies, including those in the former Soviet empire, aspire to participate in the culture of progress. For the United States, a new set of challenges unlike those it has previously experienced awaits.

The Cold War struggle to decide the course of progress ultimately took its toll on American society as well. For the generation born after World War II and reared in relative material comfort, the culturally invasive conflict for the hearts and minds of the world diverted Washington's attention from the inequities and injustices in the United States. The militarization of foreign policy devoured public funds that might have been used to eradicate the blights of poverty, segregation, and crime. The war in Vietnam was a lightening rod for blacks and other outsiders in the United States, who, in repetition of the historic pattern of social inclusion, demanded membership in their society.

Politicized by Vietnam and the constitutional breaches of an imperial presidency, the dispossessed joined forces in a social revolt that continues today against the culture of material progress and the breakdown of society it was abetting. The fascination with Mao, Che Guevara, and the other symbols of the socially disinherited is gone, but the cultural subversiveness that shocked American society in the youthful rage of the 1960s persists in the spread of drugs, violent crime, and disease and in the more insidious and lethal forms of ignorance, greed, and moral indifference. Ronald Reagan's attempt to relive the folklore of an uncomplicated past was a palliative that ended with the Cold War. We now have to face the future and ourselves in a society that is in some ways as foreign to the political leadership of the nation as the peoples beyond our shores.

REVOLT AGAINST PROGRESS

The ideology of progress has been kept alive by the belief in a limitless frontier of human opportunity and the expectation of ever-rising material standards for the peoples of the world. As the twentieth century comes to an end, however, one cannot help but acknowledge the end of the world's frontier as well. Granted, we have neither plumbed the oceans nor probed the heavens. Futurists like Kenneth Boulding and Herman Kahn looked forward to the development of nutrients from reprocessed waste in space or from the sea or the production of energy from shale and tar sands. Scientists have recently discovered rocky oases on the ocean floors that, some believe, promise an eventual bonanza of mineral and biological riches, including deep-sea gold, not unlike that offered by China and the New World centuries ago. Doubtless new discoveries lie in store for future generations. For all we know, we will be living in pods below the sea or in space stations. But the once horizonless world we inhabit and its immeasurable store of riches no longer exist.[22]

For much of the world, tomorrow will not necessarily be better than today. The post–World War II faith in progress inspired in the 1950s by the Bandung Conference of nonaligned states and revived in the 1970s no longer excites the imagination. Political instability, economic inefficiency, and resource scarcity have slowed the process of modernization. With some exceptions—notably China and Southeast Asia—ambitious programs to industrialize and westernize petered out in the oil crises of the 1970s and the government mismanagement of the 1980s. Today, many counties are under siege to maintain minimal standards of living. In large parts of the world, particularly in Africa, natural resources are rapidly being depleted and the environment devastated in a struggle for survival. And, given the insufficiency of global investment capital, help does not appear to be forthcoming. For a variety of reasons—the cost of German reunification, the recession in Japan, the low savings and investment rates in the United States—the developed world is presently incapable of generating the capital required to help develop Eastern Europe, the former Soviet Union, China, and the rest of the Third World simultaneously.[23]

The failed promise of material progress has precipitated a revolt against modernity. Large segments of societies in the Third World that have not benefited from the politics of abundance and that remain culturally antagonistic to the specialization, compartmentalization, and acquisitiveness of modernity have retreated to the familiarity and security of time-honored traditions. The uprising against the Shah of Iran in the late 1970s and similar public discontent in other poor societies in the Middle East and Africa are reflections of antimodern sentiment in the developing world. The resistance to modernity also underlies the revival of suppressed traditions and customs in the Central Asian republics that have emerged from the former Soviet empire.

In some cases, unfulfilled expectations have elicited violent reactions from peoples who have chosen either to inflict retribution on the advanced industrialized world for its perceived indifference to their conditions or to seize by force what they believe is rightfully theirs in contempt of international law and human decency. Terrorism and civil wars are the legacies of such unrequited hopes. Still others have taken refuge from modernity in religious radicalism and the occult.

The religious fundamentalism or revivalism of the late twentieth century is both anti-Western and antiwesternization. Wherever it thrives, it contributes to the cultural context of the reaction against modernity. In the urban villages of Christian Europe and Latin America, in Hindu and Buddhist Asia, and, of course, in the Muslim world, supernaturalism provides a comforting balm to those whose lives seem controlled by powerful forces of technology. In the United States, too, revivalist faith-healers have multiplied in response to the excess of materialism and the spiritual barrenness it produces. Jonestown, Waco, Texas, the doomsday Order of the Solar Temple in Switzerland, and Aum Supreme Truth in Japan are simply the pathological extremes of supernaturalism.[24]

Progress and Despair

Despite the widening economic gap between the developed and developing worlds, and the growing social polarization between haves and have-nots, much of humanity continues to repose its faith in the ideology of progress because, one may conjecture, it staves off despair. For many, Christopher Lasch has observed, progress is still the secularized version of Providence.[25] The belief that the trajectory of material progress will propel humanity toward freedom and equality is spiritually comforting to societies that would otherwise be unable to endure the chronic scarcity and political turbulence they confront. The ideology of boundless progress is the illusion of a secular divinity that protects those who internalize it from lapsing irretrievably into self-fulfilling prophecies of pessimism.

Paradoxically, however, the ideology of progress has contributed to the very psychology of despair that it has sought to avert. Like Fascism and Communism, it too is a false messiah. In the contemporary world of increasing competition for fewer resources, the mantra of endless progress has an especially hollow ring. The expectation of ever rising prosperity proves self-defeating; it breeds depression. It further attenuates the bonds of social cohesion, both domestically and internationally, without which shared sacrifice in pursuit of common goals is impossible. It is the silent accomplice of polarizing religious fundamentalism and gratuitous violence. It is the source of strength of charlatans and demagogues, such as American evangelist and Christian Coalition founder Pat Robertson, whose political power is fed by the anomie of the socially excluded.[26]

The inescapable reality is that the world is no longer a universe of physical frontiers, the discovery of which will ensure a future of boundless material progress. Rather, it is quickly becoming a community whose development is dependent on a realistic acceptance of human limitations as well as possibilities. To be sure, it is no more sensible to conclude that the international community has reached the limits of human ingenuity to respond creatively to the formidable material and societal obstacles it faces than it is to assert that history has come to its blissful end in the utopia of liberal-democracy. For better or worse, the creative imagination that the international community exercises in charting the future, however, must be guided by an understanding of the complex realities it confronts. What is required is a new conceptual framework—indeed, a new way of living that will provide meaning to the objective flow of events that people everywhere are simultaneously encountering in the context of shared experience.

This is no easy task. As has been the case in past periods of epochal change, the unpredictability of the future is impelling contemporary societies to turn inward and to cling to the stale beliefs of another time. In the developed as well as the developing world, people are recoiling from the globalization of everyday life that is the bestowal of the twentieth century. The retreat into sociocultural exclusivism, however, reinforces parochialism and myopic self-absorption. Only through the perspective of the larger tableau of life in which all humanity is depicted can we apprehend the outlines of the future.

Neither positivism nor historicism can be relied on to illuminate the contours of the dawning postmodern world. Positivism is inherently system preserving. It is concerned with process and technical efficiency and the optimization of function within fixed social parameters. Its emphasis on the acquisition of knowledge constricts human awareness. By reducing individuals to interchangeable integers of political or professional or national or ethnic collectivities, it dehumanizes society and thus deprives it of a moral dimension. Conversely, historicism, in its romantic, post-Rankean form is preoccupied with the one rather than the many. It views the social development of peoples and cultures as discrete, historically incomparable experiences. Historicism worships the "supremacy of uniqueness;" nation-states are the distillates of the inimitable genius of a people and its customs. Antiscientific historicism is incompatible with the integration of different cultures in a common sociopolitical system. In its emphasis on national character and cultural uniqueness, it interprets human behavior in narrow, reductionistic terms.[27]

The search for the meaning of change is not discoverable in either the compartmentalization and systematization of social science or the determinism of historicism. The ascription of meaning to social change is a reflective and reflexive activity that is fundamentally interpretive or hermeneutic in nature. It is the creative confrontation between human-kind and its heritage that forces us to redefine ourselves within the framework of new possibilities. History confronts us with facts, but facts assume meaning on the basis of the decisions we make about the future. As Kahler argued, the direction in which past and present events take us is inevitable only in the formal sense that "for it to otherwise happen the antecedent causes would have had to be different." But the ways in which such events define the future depends on the choices we make.[28]

Major deviations from the course of the past and from the logic of present events are unpredictable. The creative choices that redefine the meaning of existence at crucial moments in history are intuitive and ex-perimental, not inferential or deterministic. They result from an open-ness to the world in all its confusion and instability, not from a techno-cratic compulsion to compress it into the confines of some predetermined model or from a solipsistic indifference to it. The endowment of meaning to a seemingly disorderly world reflects the continuing discourse between humanity and its past, present, and future rather than the stifled dialogue of social conformity to an engineer's drawing or a belief in some mystical unity. The search for meaning is a search for values that emanate from rather than transcend human involvement with the world, values that instill hope in the future and overcome the loss of a disappearing past.[29]

The quest for meaning as lived-experience should not be confused with deconstructionism, which it superficially resembles in some way. Deconstructionism also purports to see reality in new ways through the culture, symbols, and language of discourse. It too subjects reality to temporal-spatial contingency. The culturally ex-post facto view of Machiavelli, for example, as an amoral archrealist preoccupied with international affairs is meaningless to contemporary scholars such as Po-cock or Skinner, who see him, in the context of his own time, as a hu-manist preserver of the classical value of civic virtue concerned primarily with the local political community. In addition, deconstructionism ac-cepts human finitude; it recognizes that the subject of Descartes' *cogito* cannot transcend the limitations of historical boundedness. Deconstruc-tionism further maintains that social reality is not some totalizing self-evident truth; it too asserts that human beings are unavoidably con-signed to live in a world of truth-approximation. And it acknowledges that social change necessitates a forgetting of the institutionalized prac-tices and meanings of another time.[30]

Deconstructionism, however, caricatures and trivializes the ontological nature of lived experience. It rejects all distinctions. Its self-congratulatory repudiation of rationalism, scientism, and method is all well and good, but it offers no intelligible alternative framework of knowing. It provocatively challenges conventional wisdom and intellectual elitism, but it provides no value-added alternative to understand social change of any kind, leave aside historic change. Moreover, in its attempt to go beyond the text and expose the arbitrariness of meaning, it destroys the human being's conscious relationship with the world. As reflected in deconstructionist art and architecture, there is no clear expression of personal meaning. What we are left with, then, is the absence of any social modifiers that ontologically (or semiotically) connect humanity with the world, thereby revealing some collective meaning in shared experience.

The imposition of meaning on the world without regard to morality, convention, or tradition is nihilism by any other name. Even deconstructionists themselves can only define themselves by what they are not. They do not purport to be a new school of thought or a new social identity or a "we" of any kind. They view themselves as the protagonists of critical thought "that becomes possible only when one cuts all ties and becomes a stranger to country, language, [and] sex" and begins to function "in the void" of nonspace, as Michel Foucault has put it.[31]

Lived-experience, however, is just the reverse. It is the reintegration of the individual in the society from which he has been detached. As we approach the end of the epoch of progress, we are at a loss as to how we should live. Humanity is desperately in search of new explanations to manage the immobilizing complexity of social, economic, political, and ethical problems that obscure its future. The new convictions that will provide meaning for the postmodern era will not miraculously appear in the self-perpetuating *Idea* of history. Nor will they emerge from the programmed instruction of the technologist's computer. Meaning derives from the unending human struggle with existence.

Sooner or later, we will need to find the courage to leave the past and face the future. Eventually, we will have to risk tomorrow, knowing that we cannot eliminate the consequences of our imperfections, and believe in ourselves. In time, we will find a "postmodern face," as playwright and current president of the Czech Republic Vaclav Havel has put it, that will explain the future that encroaches on the present.[32] But before we can explain, Havel has cautioned, we need to understand the emerging trends that will influence the shape the future takes.

The New Realities

The future has already arrived. The realities that have disrupted the belief in eternal progress have appeared in the early twentieth century as unsuspectingly as those that shattered ancient convictions of cosmological order and the predictable cyclicality of life. Through global acts of omission and commission, we have unwittingly accelerated the process of epochal change, the nature of which remains unassignable and inarticulable.

Signs of change intruded more palpably on human consciousness after World War II, long before the evanescence of communist ideology. Change was the incipient supranationalism championed by Jean Monnet and the other founding fathers of European economic integration. It was the release from Western cultural bondage, the liberation politics of Gamal Abdul Nasser, Frantz Fanon, Mao Tse-tung, and Che Guevara. It was Mohandas Gandhi's nonviolent demand for social inclusion in the international community and Yassir Arafat's rage of exclusion. Change was also the stupefying advances in technology, the noiseless transmission of productive energy in electronic enterprise, the automaticity of nuclear destruction. Change was the global village of the eponymous Marshall McLuhan, the dazzling speed of information flows that linked the world in an integrated communications network.

The future that we are shaping and simultaneously being shaped by, like previous periods of epochal change, is both a continuation of and a departure from the world in which we are currently living. Although the idea of progress as an ideology and an ethos that provides social cohesion can no longer be sustained in a world of resource scarcity and socioeconomic inequality, improvements in living standards or technical know-how will be just as much a part of the emerging epoch as social order was in the dynamic societies that emerged after the fourteenth century. At the same time, the impending future differs qualitatively from the past in several ways.

We are entering the era of the knowing society. Today, information propagates at an astonishing speed. Electronic transmissions of news events at the very moment of their occurrence place every person on the globe with access to television in immediate contact with one another. International developments are media shows. Transoceanic cables and satellites feed homes with up-to-date analysis on fashion, political elections, and sporting events. Video recorders permit programmed taping of reality for later browsing at one's convenience. Infomercials, informatics, and infowars are the cultural mutations of the electronic impulses that pump data into a postmodern world that is surfeited with information but wanting in understanding. In addition, the ease and accessibility of air travel increases the frequency of personal contact among friends, business associates, and political allies. The physical and intellectual movement through time and space further expands an awareness of a cosmopolitan world that is becoming interlinked but not necessarily socially integrated.

A polycentric and polyethnic world is also emerging, or reemerging. Culture, wealth, and power no longer radiate solely from Europe to the periphery of the world. Nor do the United States and the former Soviet Russia—the Europeanized surrogates of imperial France or Britain—preemptively define the rules and norms of international relations. Plainly, the United States still exercises greater influence in the world than any other single state. But it is hardly the model non-pareil that it once was. Pacific Century or no, Asianization is on the rise from the Pacific to the Indian subcontinent, as is Islamicization in the Middle East and North Africa, and Hispanicization in the Western Hemisphere.

Power is not only likely to become more broadly distributed in the future, it is also likely to reside in an array of institutional entities. In the epoch of progress, the state was sovereign. Polities conferred on the state the right to act authoritatively on their behalf in domestic and foreign affairs. In the future, authority relations will be far less hierarchical. As is already becoming evident, the nation-state will compete for authority with subnational and supranational actors intent on maintaining their autonomy. Private groups—"sovereign-free actors," as James Rosenau has described them—with interests in ecology or arms control or human rights or national self-determination will press their own agendas in the international marketplace, regardless of national policy directives, as will terrorist organizations and multinational agencies such as the International Monetary Fund (IMF) and the World Bank.[1]

In the future, national security policy making will be increasingly politicized, both domestically and internationally. Nation-states will accordingly be more constrained from taking independent actions, particularly those involving the use of force, that conflict with the interests of domestic groups or international organizations in an environment of constant tension between the forces of integration and disintegration, order and anarchy.

Declining national resources, the rising cost of technological inventiveness, and growing global demand for investment capital can also be expected to alter the heretofore unfettered nature of economic competition. Cross-border corporate mergers and alliances are harbingers of a future in which economic cooperation will become commonplace in an international environment of shared costs, shared risks, and shared benefits. At the same time, economic acquisitiveness will be tempered by cultural, ethnic, religious, racial, and other noneconomic considerations. Environmentalists, nonprofit social welfare organizations such as Oxfam or Habitat for Humanity, and the legions of students around the world who continue to crusade for political reform are not motivated by economic objectives. Nor, for that matter, are terrorist groups. This does not portend an end to economic growth as much as it does a redirection of economic needs.

As the international turmoil that has followed the end of the Cold War makes starkly clear, the international community is charting seas that are just as uncertain and unstable as were the swells of change that altered humanity's course in the fourteenth century. Then, as today, the forces of integration and disintegration were locked in a struggle to reimpose meaning on the world. The upheaval that we presently face is no less disquieting, the outcome no more predictable.

DYNAMICS OF CHANGE

Although the future remains murky, the direction it takes can be objectively bounded by the designation of certain enduring trends. At least five trends, or variables, all of which are clearly visible, can be identified amid the social debris of the post–Cold War era: technological diffusion, ecological erosion, migratory flux, political disaggregation, and economic consolidation. None of these trends alone would be sufficiently powerful to disrupt inveterate patterns of social behavior or long-held convictions about the world that derive from those familiar patterns. Their transformative power is the result of the volatility of their combined interaction, their critical social mass, so to speak. It is like the confluence of many streams into a raging river that alters the plain of time, recasts familiar landscapes into new shapes and forms, and impels new social orientations and beliefs.

The encompassing trends of historic change are also mutually reinforcing. Changes in any one parameter simultaneously affect all the others. Collectively, they may qualitatively and quantitatively contribute either to the integration or the disintegration of international society. Conceivably, historic change could be instantaneous, dramatic, and immediately evident, rather like the social analogue of the Big Bang. It is more likely to be a protracted occurrence, however, and one that the vast stretches of humanity who seek to preserve the present will endeavor to resist by rationalizing the events they are experiencing as temporary deviations from familiar patterns of life, ignoring or rejecting developments that are discrepant with their conception of the world, or by constricting their field of vision. Such efforts may help to make the present more intelligible and thus more manageable, but they obscure the view of the future, which can be understood only by immersing oneself in the flux of change that is transforming our lives.

Technological Diffusion

In the current age of push-button communication, technology is a pervasive purveyor of ideas, artifacts, and power. Although technology has been a stimulus to social evolution since the dawn of creation, its impact on society today is qualitatively different from anything that has preceded it. The computer has not only eliminated routine, repetitive, rote tasks from everyday life, it has freed the mind.

As witnessed by the anticommunist revolutions in Eastern Europe and the Chinese uprising in Tiananman Square, the instantaneous flow of electronic information is the handmaiden of political emancipation. To be sure, the liberating force of the Protestant Reformation (whose shadow hovered over the collapse of communist orthodoxy five centuries later) would not have been possible without Johann Gutenberg's invention of moveable type in 1456. Computerized access to information, however, has globalized Gutenberg's printing press. The microchip makes geography irrelevant. Developments in one part of the world are instantly communicated elsewhere. It is no longer possible to be removed from the world, as Tokugawa Japan or the Hermit Kingdom of Korea once were. The televised coverage of the crumbling Berlin Wall unquestionably reinforced revolutionary attitudes in other East European countries and beyond. That the cry for freedom in Eastern Europe could be heard in South Africa, Nicaragua, Nepal, and China was not surprising. Microelectronic circuity erases time and space with bewildering ease. Thanks to minitelevision cameras, microwave antennae, and satellite feeds, the drama of Tiananmen Square played to a world audience.

The technological diffusion of ideas further challenges the authority of the state. In a world compressed by the immediate accessibility to information, it is becoming increasingly difficult for states to maintain control over restive publics. The liberation of the human spirit that defied state domination in Eastern Europe has reappeared in other regions of the world. In Mexico and Brazil, public accessibility to the electronic imagery of events in Eastern Europe has diminished the power of state-centered political parties. The constant exposure of publics in one part of the globe to liberalizing change elsewhere has similarly affected political developments in the advanced world. The Japanese public's outcry against the Liberal Democratic Party and the election and subsequent collapse of a reform coalition of small parties mirrored the protracted political crisis in Italy and the massive transfer of power from the once dominant but now defunct Christian Democrats to an array of new parties like Forza Italia!, the Northern League, and the Network.

Not only has technology sped the transmission of ideas, it has also spread the artifacts of human ingenuity. Goods and processes once the preserve of the West now circulate throughout the world. The computer has completely reorganized commerce and industry. The instantaneous transfer of capital has integrated the world's financial markets. Where the sun once never set on the British empire, it now never sets on the world's trading system. The flow of new processes and techniques is similarly transforming manufacturing. Robotics, ceramics, metallurgy, laser-guided machine tools, and computer-guided design and manufacturing have enhanced the productive efficiency of industry. The centralized multinational corporation is giving way to the decentralized, transnational corporation. In the multinational enterprise, Peter Drucker has pointed out, the parent company developed the products that its subsidiaries manufactured and marketed. In the transnational organization, any subsidiary may initiate the design, research, and production of new products.[2]

Technological innovation has also greatly contributed to improvements in the quality of life for the peoples of the world. Wonder drugs have virtually eradicated diseases like smallpox and malaria that not long ago decimated populations. New vaccines have inoculated millions of infants in the developing world against life-threatening diseases. According to the United Nations Children's Fund, the immunization of children has increased fourfold since the early 1980s, thereby reducing the incidence of death from measles, diarrheal disease, whooping cough, and tetanus. Computer simulations of viruses enable scientists to design antiviral drugs, develop a greater understanding of immunological deficiencies, and improve the quality of clinical diagnoses and prognoses. Similarly, the commercial and scientific applications of remote-sensing satellites have advanced the human understanding of oceanography, meteorology, geology, agriculture, land management, city planning, and even real estate development.[3]

In some respects, however, the diffusion of technology threatens to undermine peace and constrict individual freedom. Clearly, technology has contributed to the globalization of military power. To be sure, the end of the Cold War has slowed arms production and procurement. Conventional arms transfer agreements between the major arms suppliers and Third World recipients fell to $20.4 billion (in current dollars) in 1993, or roughly half the value of the agreements negotiated in 1990. Arms deliveries of $15 billion were less than half of the total for 1990. This is the sixth consecutive year of decline in the value of all deliveries to the Third World. Still, there are worrisome signs that arms sales may be heading higher. Nationalist rivalries, economic pressures on weapons manufacturers, and the dissemination of technical knowledge to the developing world are likely to stimulate increasing activity in the arms trade.[4]

The East–West ideological competition may be a relic of the past, but the economics of arms exports continues to attract the interest of governments and defense contractors in the United States—far and away the leader in new arms agreements—cash-strapped Russia, and Europe, including former Soviet satellites such as the Czech Republic, Slovakia, and Poland. To complicate matters, criminal elements have begun to smuggle nuclear materials to foreign countries or terrorist organizations that possess the technical knowledge to build atomic weapons. Furthermore, the intelligence community in the United States suspects that Russia and Ukraine are transferring missile technology to China, whose continuing strategic modernization program not only dims the hope of progress on nuclear nonproliferation but also threatens to provoke a new high-technology arms race.[5]

Some encouraging developments, of course, have helped to impede the flow of arms, especially nuclear arms. In May 1995, the signatories of the Treaty on the Non-Proliferation of Nuclear Weapons agreed to the permanent extension of the 25-year-old pact, including the establishment of a comprehensive test ban by 1996. In addition, after much wrangling, Ukraine agreed to return all the strategic weapons on its territory to Russia, which permitted the START I accord signed in 1991 by the United States and the then Soviet Union to enter into force. Arguably, the end of the Iran–Iraq conflict, the recent peace agreement between Israel and the Palestine Liberation Organization, and growing competitive pressures from American and European arms makers will also make it harder for countries such as China, North Korea, and Brazil to maintain the level of sales they enjoyed before 1991.[6]

Neither treaty obligations nor the diminution of longstanding regional tensions have stopped the spread of arms technology, however. International protests and arms treaties aside, the world's acknowledged nuclear powers—the United States, Russia, France, Britain, and China—are clearly intent on retaining the right to conduct nuclear tests. Moreover, Russia has flatly rejected American appeals to terminate the sale of nuclear technology to Iran. So has China, which also appears to be providing medium-range M-11 missles to Pakistan, to boot. In a depressed arms market, these countries will have even less compunction than they have in the past about selling nuclear technology to potential rogue states, in disregard of international agreements such as the Nuclear Nonproliferation Treaty, the Missile Technology Control Regime, or the Chemical Weapons Convention.[7]

The spread of the implements of war, of course, is also a function of demand. Happily, South Africa, Argentina, and Brazil appear to have abandoned their nuclear programs, although the latter's purchase of technology from Russia will unavoidably arouse suspicions in Buenos Aires. South Asia remains a nuclear flash point, and the Middle East could become one, *pace* the Middle East peace accords, if Iran proceeds to build its offensive military capability. The Southeast Asian states, for their part, have embarked on a defense modernization program in part to replace aging equipment with state-of-the-art technology but also to protect themselves against prospective security threats from China, Japan, Russia, and each other. Internecine conflicts are further likely to accelerate the demand for arms. If the civil warfare in former Yugoslavia, Azerbaijan, Tajikistan, Georgia, Somalia, Angola, and Rwanda is any indication of what lies ahead, the future promises to be more violent than the Cold War period.[8]

In spite of its contribution to democracy, there is also no assurance that the technologically induced access to information will promote, or even safeguard, political liberties. Certainly authoritarian one-man or one-party rule has managed to resist the encroachment of electronically sped ideas of governance. With the exception of Zambia, Congo, and a handful of others, most African states are semidemocracies at best, military autocracies such as Nigeria or Ghana at worst. And, where technology has permeated the formerly hermetically sealed world of political authoritarianism, it is often subject to the manipulation of those who wield power. It is true that telecommunications, personal computers, and the new generation of electronic notebooks have complicated the task of centralized monitoring of public information. And in China, India, and the Middle East, the craze of satellite dishes is bringing people into closer contact with foreign ideas. But computers and electronic data banks are no less powerful tools in the hands of central authorities like those in Beijing, who have used surveillance cameras and other technology to restore social control, or international criminals. Centralized control is easier still in impoverished, semiliterate countries. Knowledge is becoming what Lyotard calls an "informational commodity."[9] Whoever acquires it will enjoy a competitive edge over potential adversaries, and possibly a disproportionate share of international power, not unlike the fictional megalomaniacal fiends that served as foils for supersleuth James Bond.

Where technological access cannot be stopped, it can be controlled in Orwellian fashion by distorting, falsifying, or screening out information that might otherwise limit a regime's hold on power. Lest we forget, the printing press that facilitated the rise of democratic liberalism subsequently became an instrument of dictatorship. Even in the advanced world, the torrential diffusion of information may overwhelm societies, making them prey to the subtle manipulation of political choices. Deluged by data that they have neither the time nor the interest in processing, publics may become victims of disinformation in the future. The profusion of information may be packaged in such a way as to polarize society, as the televised imagery of the Vietnam War did in the United States and as the carnage in Bosnia is currently doing throughout the world. The relentless diffusion of ideas and information could lead to intolerable social confusion and instability and prompt the consolidation of power by infomonarchies, or what RAND Corporation political analyst David Ronfeldt calls "cyberocracies."[10]

Just as bad, the diffusion of technology is likely to lead to cultural homogeneity. The ubiquitous access to the same points of view and social styles risks bleeding the cultural richness from the tapestry of life.

Technologically induced consensus threatens to produce a sclerotic uniformity whose rules preclude the invention of the conceivable and the idiosyncratic. Possessors of technology today instantaneously radiate their values, beliefs, and mores to remote corners of the world. It is no accident that Western attire and popular culture pervade modernizing societies and, no less surprising, that they catalyze struggles with the traditionalist opposition.[11]

Ecological Erosion

Even if the modernization of military arsenals ceased tomorrow, the world would still have to live with the ecological consequences of technological progress. The environmental detritus in the former Soviet empire is "living" testimony to its costs. The inland waterways and surrounding seas of Russia have all been contaminated from radioactive materials dumped by former Soviet governments who believed that natural resources were either inexhaustible or subject to the whims of the almighty state. Decommissioned naval reactors and scuttled submarines have reportedly been leaking nuclear pollutants into the seas from the Baltic to the Pacific. Local officials have indifferently polluted rivers and streams and farmlands. Untold millions of tons of toxic waste have poisoned the food chain and infected hapless residents with cancer and other chronic diseases. Millions of gallons of crude oil that seeped from deteriorating pipelines in 1994—reportedly eight times the size of the Exxon Valdez spill in Alaska—threaten to turn the waterways of Russia's Arctic into a purulating ecological disaster.[12]

Eastern Europe has not fared much better. From eastern Germany to the Black Sea, a ravaged land bears unfecund witness to the state-directed imperative of industrial progress. Whole cities like Cracow are dying. Rivers, forests, and farmlands throughout the region have been pronounced biologically dead, victims of acid rain; the air above the spires of Prague's cathedrals and quaint villages blackened from the polluting plumes of smoke and soot belched by coal mines and steel mills that for decades were harnessed in suffocating competition with the technologically superior West. Emphysema, tuberculosis, and hepatitis are commonplace throughout the region. Virtually everywhere rivers are open sewers of largely untreated waste, the water unfit for consumption.[13]

It would be easy to dismiss such environmental deterioration as one more illustration of a bankrupt ideology, but the harsh reality is that liberal democracies, in their unflagging desire for material comforts, have also mortgaged the ecological future for subsequent generations. Indeed, capitalism, consumerism, and the need to catch up with the advanced industrialized states have inhibited environmental protection in post–Cold War Eastern Europe, which, at the West's urging, has concentrated on economic development.

To be sure, environmental awareness has come a long way since the days DuPont promoted "better living through chemistry." Environmental advocacy groups and the departments of environmental affairs in national governments have instituted educational programs and lobbied for treaties on ocean dumping, whaling, and endangered species. The United States has banned pesticides such as DDT, purged gasoline of its lead content, and instituted recycling ordinances in municipalities. In 1994, the government was able to remove the bald eagle from the list of endangered species. In Europe, ecopolitics is on the rise, as the public furor over Royal Dutch/Shell's planned disposal of an oil platform in the Atlantic in 1995 attests. Green parties are proliferating, and parliaments, following Germany's lead, are passing recycling legislation to reduce disposable waste.[14]

Nevertheless, automobile emissions, pesticides and herbicides, acid rain, and chlorofluorocarbons (chemicals used in refrigeration, consumer products, and industrial processes) continue to take a toll on the natural habitats of prosperous and seemingly environmentally progressive countries as well. Species of wild life and fresh-water fish continue to disappear, and forests are still losing ground to developers and loggers. Ironically, the liberal-democratic West is effacing the frontiers that its progenitors so sedulously expanded in a mindless act of self-annihilatory materialism that differs only in form from the command politics of the former Soviet empire.

Earth Day 1990 and the second United Nations gathering on the environment two years later in Rio De Janeiro somberly concluded that the loss of forest areas, the depletion of the ozone layer, and the earth's rising temperature threatened the survivability of the planet. According to the Worldwatch Institute's report issued after the Rio conference, sulfur dioxide emissions had already destroyed 75 percent of Europe's forests. In the United States, radioactive waste from nuclear weapons facilities at Rocky Flats, Colorado, and Savannah River, South Carolina, have similarly contaminated streams and wooded areas. The deforestation produced by loggers and real estate developers has not only increased flooding and soil loss, it has also reduced nature's ability to cleanse itself and to generate the diversity of vegetation required to feed a growing population.[15]

Pollutants have also disrupted the compositional balance of the world's atmosphere. Depletion of the ozone layer, which was first discovered during scientific investigations of the polar regions in 1987, deprives the atmosphere of oxidizing agents that absorb quantities of ultraviolet light, the prolonged exposure to which can cause cancer and, some scientists believe, also destroy the plants and the ocean's plankton that are part of the natural food chain. Unlike the thinning of the ozone layer above Antarctica, which is surrounded by ocean, the newly discovered hole over the North Pole is surrounded by land and is thus likely to pose a greater risk to the ecosystem and to human life. Concerns about the ozone layer have prompted the international community to conclude several multinational agreements to ban CFCs, halons, and other substances by the end of the 1990s.[16]

More disturbing still is the threat of global warming. In a nutshell, gases such as carbon dioxide and methane are increasingly trapping heat that would otherwise be radiated back to the sun in the form of infrared waves in the atmosphere. In the bleakest scenario, some scientists have concluded that the continued emission of pollutants, including CFCs, could raise temperatures to levels that would melt the polar ice caps, raise the heights of the surrounding seas, and submerge lowland areas such as Bangladesh and the Netherlands. According to one account, in the next three decades, photochemical pollutants from automobiles and factories could substantially reduce crop yields in North America, Europe, and Northeast Asia, which supply 60 percent of the world's food.[17]

For all the concern the Rio summit aroused, however, little progress has been made toward reaching the target of reducing greenhouse gases to 1990 levels by the year 2000. At the Berlin conference on the environment in April 1995, the countries that signed the concluding declaration agreed in essence to disagree on the measures required to reduce emissions, in large part because of the economic cost such measures would entail. Poor countries were especially unwilling to make ecological commitments on grounds that the developed world bears responsibility for the pollution of the planet. No one appears to be taking the threat seriously. In the United States, for example, the Clinton administration's rhetoric of environmental awareness has produced little policy of substance. Besides, the current conservative Congress is hardly amicably disposed toward further government regulation of the marketplace.[18]

Scientific uncertainties further impede international action. Scientists differ in their views of the timing or severity of the so-called greenhouse effect, and some have challenged the reliability of computer models for failing to reproduce past warming trends accurately. Furthermore, some scientists contend that the emission of CFCs in the atmosphere is about to peak and slowly decline. On the other hand, after a two-year cooling period produced by the eruption of Mount Pinatubo in the Philippines, the temperature of the earth's surface resumed its warming trend in 1994. Those scientists who sound the alarms of global warming accordingly argue, like Pascal's famous wager, that the probability of recurrence in the next century is both necessary and sufficient grounds for the industrialized world to take some remedial action today.[19]

The world indeed. Developing countries bear as much, if not more, responsibility for global warming as the industrialized and newly industrialized countries. According to the International Energy Agency, the increase in greenhouse gases will be generated mainly by the developing world in the next century. This is not meant to apologize for the developed world. Clearly, the West's exploitation of Third World resources has accounted for some environmental spoliation. Just as clearly, however, it has not been responsible for the irrigation project that has led to the gradual disappearance of the Aral Sea, the depletion of fossil groundwater in Saudi Arabia as a result of efforts to grow wheat in the desert, the rape of Cambodia's forests by its warring factions, or the poaching of Bolivia's Amazon jungle by local loggers and coca growers. For the most part, explosive population growth, famine, and mismanagement have led to a massive degradation of the environment in the world's poor countries. From Africa to the Americas, multitudes of people barely subsist in conditions of squalor and deprivation that are reminiscent of the battle for survival humanity waged more than a millennium ago.[20]

Given the expected rise in world population and life-extending improvements in sanitation, little relief is in sight. Experts at the United Nations and elsewhere expect the world population to increase from its current 5.7 billion to 6.25 billion by 2000 and to some 10 to 11 billion or more by 2050. In the most optimistic scenario, the national delegates who met in September 1994 at the International Conference on Population and Development in Cairo reached agreement to stabilize world population at around 9 billion. It is questionable, however, whether the world's fisheries and farmlands will be able to sustain even a population of 9 billion people. As China industrializes and consequently reduces its arable croplands, it may be forced to import grain to feed its growing population, which is expected to increase from its current 1.2 billion to 1.6 billion in 2030.[21]

The environmental effects of a rising world population are potentially hazardous for both developed and underdeveloped states. In poor countries where rising populations impose greater burdens on exhaustible natural resources, there can be no capital growth. According to the World Bank, per capita economic growth fell in nearly 50 countries in the 1980s, comprising roughly one-sixth of the world's population, even though world economic growth rose nearly 3 percent. As population growth exceeds food production in the poorer countries of the world, peoples without technical skills or knowledge of resource maintenance will increasingly despoil the land, leading to ever-diminishing returns for successive generations, or what Lester Brown calls "the environmental equivalent of deficit financing." Unregulated deforestation will eventually exhaust the soil's ability to replenish itself, hasten the extinction of commercially productive croplands and grasslands and the diverse forms of animal, plant, and insect life that inhabit them, and contribute to global warming. In the opinion of the United Nations, carbon dioxide emissions in the Third World will quadruple by 2025.[22]

The demand for food also threatens the productivity of ocean and fresh-water fisheries, which will adversely affect the economies of rich and poor countries that farm the world's waterways. Some fisheries have already been exhausted. Thanks in large part to technology—lighter and larger nylon nets, on-board refrigeration, commercial satellite imagery, and spotter planes—the stocks of the world's fish are literally disappearing at the expense of the marine ecosystem and the growing population of people that subsist on them. In 1992 the oceans produced some 91 million tons of fish, about 5 percent less than their peak in 1989. Even at 1995 levels of 100 million tons, the seafood supply per person continues to decline. Harvests in the Caspian and Black Seas and even in America's Chesapeake Bay have dropped markedly. Furthermore, water tables are falling in the Middle East, Africa, Central Asia, India, and China. Many believe that some form of water sharing will be necessary to avert a potential clash between states such as Israel and Turkey that have exploited supplies through irrigation projects and the construction of dams and aquifers and resource-poor states such as Jordan and Syria that are tapping nonrenewable fossil water.[23]

To be sure, nature may come to its own rescue. Entropic forces such as famine, pestilence, and disease may drastically alter current growth projections. AIDS and the return of diseases such as malaria, cholera, and sleeping sickness, all of which would be accelerated by an increase in the world's temperature, could decimate Africa and other tropical regions. Further, new epidemics such as the Ebola virus in Zaire will add to the toll. Warfare, which may arise in part from the socioeconomic tensions caused by environmental blight, as apparently happened in Rwanda, could also help to relieve the ecological burden. Whether the scourge of disease, human predation, or the efforts of environmentalists from Chile to Malaysia can intervene before a burgeoning world population has exhausted nature's ability to regenerate itself is debatable, however. Time does not appear to be on humanity's side. The toleration of short-term pollution as the cost of long-term economic growth is a more perilous gamble today than it was twenty-five years ago when futurists like Herman Kahn waxed optimistically about unending technological progress. Some biologists have pointed to the sudden decline in the world's population of frogs—the canary in the coal mine syndrome—as a sign of looming ecological disintegration. Paleontologists such as Niles Eldredge believe we are on the verge of a seventh mass extinction in evolutionary time—but the first to be caused by humankind.[24]

Of course, one person's calamity may be another's hysteria. To those who place their faith in the ideology of progress and thus in humanity's ability to tame nature's aberrant ways, the rhetoric of extinction is at best alarmist. In his paean to the information age, George Gilder noted that we are witnessing the triumph of mind over matter, the most demonstrable sign of which "is a sharp decline in the value of natural resources" that characterized the Industrial Revolution. "What used to be called 'precious natural resources,'" he happily observes, are returning "to their previous natural condition as dirt, rocks, and gunk." Gilder may be right, but for the wrong reasons.[25]

THE DEMOGRAPHICS OF MIGRATION

The movement of peoples across international borders is the visible face of population pressure and environmental degradation. The 1993 United Nations report on population movement stated that some 100 million people, or 2 percent of the world's population, currently lived outside the countries of their birth. Two years later, only a small proportion of them have resettled in new countries. Some have left their homelands to improve the quality of their lives. But growing numbers—some 44 million since the end of the Cold War—are refugees who have fled the ravages of environmental destruction and political strife. Migration is also the expression of technology. It reflects the widespread access to transportation that has compressed the span of geography. It reflects the pervasiveness of television as well and the hope of new possibilities it has provided to countless millions of people throughout the world.[26]

People are moving in historically unprecedented numbers across borders and continents where throngs of other displaced peoples await the promise of new lives. Immigrants from Eastern Europe, including war-torn ex-Yugoslavia, and the former Soviet Union have poured into Austria, Germany, France, and Italy. Iranians, Lebanese, and Pakistanis are increasingly conspicuous in Scandinavia, as are North Africans in France, Italy, and Spain. Vietnamese and other Asians have streamed into Canada and Australia. Sub-Saharan Africans have migrated to Australia, the United States, and especially the United Kingdom. Immigrants from Mexico and Central America have thronged to the United States in increasing numbers since 1989.[27]

Some of this movement is temporary and geographically localized, the consequence of economic dislocation, political turmoil, or war. Some of it, however, constitutes the permanent resettlement in new lands, of which history furnishes numerous examples. But the size, speed, and scope of contemporary human transfers far exceed the circumscribed movements of peoples in earlier times. The globalization of migration is already altering the demography of Germany, Italy, Sweden, and Switzerland, where the flow of migrants exceeds natural population growth. Twenty-first century Europe will bear little resemblance to the Carolingian redoubt around which the European Economic Community was formed in 1957. Mosques already dot the skyline in Dusseldorf, Milan, and Moscow. Twice as many Britons now speak Urdu, Punjabi, or Gujarati as speak Welsh. In the United States as well, the admixture of Hispanic and Islamic cultures has diluted the Anglo-Saxon composition of Western and Southwestern society. The same is true in the Middle East, where Afghanis and assorted African refugees intermingle with host Arab peoples. A similar pattern is forming in the Asia–Pacific region, where Thais, Filipinos, and Vietnamese are relocating to Singapore, Japan, and Australia.[28]

Unlike the steppe nomads and other peoples without fixed societal patterns who came into contact with socially differentiated, institutionally developed civilizations such as China or the Arab caliphate, contemporary migrants bring with them a much more sharply defined social identity that may be incompatible with the values and beliefs of the host culture. Social tensions are already discernible in Germany and France, where publics view the surge of Turks, Arabs, and Africans in their midst as an ominous harbinger of their cultural disintegration.[29]

Xenophobia, racism, and nativism are the outward appearances of the loss of cultural identity. In Germany alone there were 2,584 confirmed acts of violence against foreigners in 1992, and some 1,609 in 1993. More recently, however, brutality has declined, as a result of public protests and prison sentences. Antiforeign rage has also flared in Britain, Italy, and Spain. In the summer of 1993, the Greek government expelled more than 2,500 Albanian immigrants on the pretext of the expulsion of a Greek Orthodox priest from Albania. Following the death of five of its citizens at the hands of Islamic extremists in Algeria, France has launched a campaign to detain suspected Muslim immigrants and, more recently, has banned the wearing of head scarves by Muslim girls in public schools.[30]

Racist violence has thus far been confined to the social fringe—unemployed youth, the ubiquitous "skinheads," and criminals. But the assault on foreigners is being abetted by right-wing demagogues who campaign against the culturally invasive threat of the *auslander*. The Austrian Freedom Party, the German Republikaners, the Vlaams Bok in Belgium, the Falangists in Spain, and the Northern League in Italy all have exploited the rise of xenophobia. In France, the success of Jean-Marie Le Pen's National Front in the industrial suburbs has pushed the country's respectable conservative parties further to the right. Le Pen broadened his popularity in the 1995 election, which, in addition to elevating the neo-Gaullist Jacques Chirac to the presidency of France, also proved to be a success for "family values" advocate Philippe de Villiers, among other candidates of the dispossessed. The Republikaners have had somewhat the same effect in Germany. In Austria, meanwhile, the Freedom Party won nearly one-fourth of the votes in the October 1994 elections; and in Italy, National Alliance party leader Gianfranco Fini is surging in popularity.[31]

Not surprisingly, many view immigration legislation as an antidote to social violence. In France, long a haven for those fleeing injustice or simply seeking a better life, the National Assembly passed legislation in June 1993 to establish a goal of "zero immigration." French-born children of foreigners no longer receive automatic citizenship, and, as a result of stricter residency requirements, it has become easier to deport immigrants and asylees. Germany passed a law at almost the same time that closed hostels housing some 600,000 asylum-seekers. The German government also tightened its refugee policies. Refugees seeking admittance from third countries have since been denied entry, as have those from states that Bonn has declared to be "safe," that is, free of political repression. As a result of the new legislation, the monthly average of asylum-seekers has plunged from 37,000 to about 10,000. Pressed by Conservative parliamentarians like the grandson of Winston Churchill, Britain has also moved toward a policy of "zero immigration" to "preserve the British way of life." The Asylum and Immigration Appeals Act, which was passed in 1993, has drastically reduced the number of refugees permitted to stay in Britain.[32]

Nativism is also on the rise in other regions where the mass movement of foreign peoples intrudes on local cultures. Hungarians, Poles, Czechs, and Romanians have vituperated against the threat to their cultural homogeneity posed by Jews, Gypsies, and other outsiders. The Baltic states have openly discriminated against Russians, who, in turn, have demonized Jews, Central Asians, and Caucasians. Ever since the ASEAN states began to push the Vietnamese and Cambodian "boat people" out to sea in the late 1980s, Asian countries have also gradually closed their doors to refugees. Nearby Australia similarly seeks to bar the influx of boat people. Ethnic Somalis have been required to prove their Kenyan citizenship or face arrest or deportation. India's Bharatiya Janata party, the reincarnation of the nationalist Rashtriya Swayamserak that was set up in 1925 to eliminate foreign cultural contaminants from Indian society, has abetted Hindu violence against the presence of poor Muslims from Bangladesh and Pakistan. The spectacle of Haitian and Chinese boat people huddled off America's shores has alarmed publics from New York to California that are already awash with immigrants, many of them illegal, from Asia and Latin America.[33]

Immigration further threatens to exacerbate social problems that feed racism and xenophobia. Where their presence threatens the social security and mobility of the indigenous poor, crime rates are likely to rise. Violence in London's East End, East Germany, or the urban ghettos of America have probably resulted as much from the perceived threat to jobs and welfare benefits as from racial, ethnic, and cultural differences. The prevalence of drugs—the analgesic of poverty—is also likely to accompany the migratory flow. Terrorism is another baleful byproduct. Extremist Muslim groups have expanded their influence in West and Central Africa, Europe, the United States, and Latin America. Although the local cell of the radical Lebanese group Hezbollah denied any involvement in the July 1994 bombing of a Jewish cultural center in Buenos Aires, its leaders have vowed to strike at Israel's interests anywhere in the world. Terrorist groups may set up operations under the cover of legal immigration or masquerade as international charitable or evangelical institutions, as Hezbollah does in Argentina, or as political asylees, as was the case with those who masterminded the bombing of New York's World Trade Center in February 1993.[34]

Increased immigration is also likely to hasten the propagation of potentially catastrophic communicable diseases. Somalis, Mozambicans, and other Africans who have fled warfare and poverty have brought with them malaria, cholera, and tuberculosis. A new strain of cholera in India and Bangladesh—the eighth such pandemic since 1817—has spread to Asia and Latin America, even as the strain that emerged in 1960 continues to rage. Although the estimates of mathematical modelers vary, AIDS is expected to surge with Malthusian malevolence in Central and East Africa. According to the World Health Organization, those infected will rise from the current number of roughly 15 million to between 30 and 40 million by 2000—possibly even to 100 million. Migration will not only transmit the disease to North America and Europe, but also to areas in the Middle East, Eastern Europe, Southeast Asia, and Australia, where, until recently, few cases had been reported. Drug use and prostitution—including the dramatic rise of child prostitution in the developing world—will ensure its spread.[35]

The socially destabilizing aspects of population movements and demographic change can be expected to raise social costs in host societies. Western Europe, which pays out an estimated 40 percent or more of GDP in social services (compared with about 30 percent in the United States and Japan), is already reeling under the burden of unemployment, social security, and medical insurance payments. Although welfare payments in the United States are significantly lower than in Western Europe, the prospect of a smaller economic pie has contributed to an anxiety of scarcity among younger people. Poll data suggest a growing fear that the influx of immigrants will deprive Americans of jobs, higher wages, and social services. Anxiety is especially acute among Americans born between 1968 and 1971. Similarly in Japan, which has not been historically hospitable to immigrants, the intractable realities of a maturing economy and an aging population are likely to exacerbate xenophobic attitudes.[36]

Poorer countries will face a massive and, in some cases, insurmountable obstacle, as governments such as those in Eastern Europe struggle to finance the cost of social programs bloated by the unemployed, the infirm, and the aged. Conditions in the developing world are still worse. In many nations, particularly in Africa, soaring debt-service ratios will surely preclude the availability of funds for social welfare programs without substantial humanitarian aid from developed donor countries. With a population growth rate of 3.2 percent per year, nearly 30 African states will double their populations in less than 25 years. A World Bank report noted that more than one of three people in sub-Saharan Africa cannot meet the basic needs of survival. The challenge is daunting. Population experts anticipate that developing countries will account for 86 percent of world population in 2030, compared with 78 percent in 1990. According to the Population Institute, 18 of the largest 20 cities will be in the Third World by the year 2000, and virtually all of these megalopoles will be aswirl with nonnative peoples who will add to the cacophony of conflicting political demands on what one can expect to be inefficient, economically overwhelmed, and possibly corrupt governments.[37]

Under the best of circumstances, competing demands for paltry resources is a recipe for domestic instability. The tide of European opposition to foreigners is rising. It is also mounting in the United States, the passage of NAFTA aside, as the California electorate showed in the 1994 congressional elections with its approval of Proposition 187, which denies publicly funded benefits to illegal immigrants. In Australia, a nation of immigrants like the United States, the Asianization of the population has raised cries of protest from a citizenry that is envious of the newcomers' rapid material success.[38]

Antiforeign sentiment may also portend growing international turmoil. Cries of discrimination by ethnic minorities will doubtless arouse the feelings of their kin in neighboring countries, as was the case in Hungary after Slovakian state television banned the use of Hungarian place names in its Hungarian-language programming. Such tensions could lead to cross-border clashes, as have occurred among tribes in sub-Saharan Africa. They could also inflame irredentism on the part of diaspora peoples (such as the Kurds) who wish to return to their native lands. Irredentism, after all, grows most immoderately where economic stagnation invites discrimination against strangers, who, in retaliation, seek the relocation—indeed, "renationalization"—of political legitimacy.[39]

Relocation of Political Legitimacy

The revolt against political authority that the world has been witnessing since Europe's democratic revolutions of 1989–90 is not a unique development in human history. Rebellions against arbitrary authority litter the record of the past. What distinguishes the current challenge to authority from past political upheavals is its pervasiveness. Never before have so many disparate groups in different parts of the world risen in polymorphous political protest against established governments. Three conditions form the structural backdrop of this trend. One is the variable geometry of political power to which regime theorists such as Stephen Krasner, Joseph Nye, and Robert Keohane have called attention. Since the end of World War II, the international political system has evolved increasingly into an interconnected network of governmental and nongovernmental entities. Multinational organizations with overlapping jurisdictions and subnational groups intent on asserting their rights or promoting single-issue causes from abortion to nuclear disarmament have circumscribed the exclusive authority over international relations heretofore accorded to nation-states. In order to establish a social consensus with powerful nongovernmental bodies, states have been forced to rely increasingly on negotiation rather than vested right, sovereignty, or fiat, thus diluting their command authority.[40]

The diffusion of information has "desacralized" national political authority. The emergence of knowledge-based societies has attenuated the governing elite's ability to wield power. In the postmodern/post-progressive age, it is the acquisition of information that secures power, regardless of who acquires it. Knowledge, particularly specialized knowledge, strengthens political autonomy, if not always civic responsibility, on the part of individuals and institutions that formerly acceded to or acquiesced in the standards and values set by political elites. Autonomy is the psychological correlate of knowledge. The politicization of heretofore apathetic or conformist publics is the political voice of autonomy that emboldens groups to challenge vested authority.

The growth of public activism in the process of governance, or what we might call the "politicization of politics," has further constrained the nation-state's use of coercion to counter challenges to its authority. To be sure, the state's ability to suppress dissent has not atrophied, as China's crackdown on the protesters in Tiananmen Square, Iraq's quashing of the popular uprising that followed its expulsion from Kuwait in 1991, Thailand's violent suppression of democracy advocates in May 1992, and Turkey's imprisonment of Kurdish parliamentarians for speaking their mind in 1994 unmistakably demonstrated. And it still controls the economic, technological, and military assets to assert its authority in foreign lands. But as the former Soviet Union and the United States discovered in their international adventurism of the 1980s, and as leaders like Nepal's King Birendra and South Korea's No Tae Woo were later to realize, the use of force also entails costs such as the loss of international prestige, the attenuation of alliance relationships, the imposition of economic sanctions, and the deterioration of the public's political allegiance to its authority. Of course, the politicization of politics works in reverse as well. Publics may take matters into their own hands when the state appears reluctant to act, as is unhappily the case in India, where militant Hindus, exhorted by the Bharatiya Janata Party, have inflicted violence on Muslim and Sikh minorities.

The challenge to political legitimacy may come from within or without. The challenge from within tends to be mounted by "insiders outside" the political establishment. Insiders outside are those who share the cultural traditions and social mores of the elite but who seek to reassert control over their lives by "downsizing" or "denationalizing" the political structure, that is, by localizing politics. The challenge from without is more likely to reflect the frustrations of those who see themselves as being "outsiders outside" the political process. Outsiders outside are those who do not share the cultural composition of the majority population and who accordingly seek to gain autonomy by "renationalizing" their identity, that is, by asserting their political autonomy or independence.

Insiders Outside. The fragmentation, even disarray, of political life in so many parts of the world reflects the localization of politics in societies that have lost faith in the ability of traditional parties to manage pervasive social change. Threatened by the persistence of structural unemployment, welfare cuts, and the influx of refugees, West European publics are that defected from mainstream political parties to grass-roots movements of protest against the loss of socioeconomic security and national identity. A profusion of new political parties are expanding the political landscape. Some of them—the Freedom Party in Austria, Republikaners in Germany, Le Pen's Front Nationale, Greece's Political Springtime—appeal to chauvinism and xenophobia. Outraged by the culture of corruption and patronage that was tolerated during the Cold War in the interests of political stability, local authorities in France, Spain, Belgium, and Germany have followed the Italian lead and have likewise begun to expose the abuse of power.[41]

Similar disaffection with vested political authority is evident in Asia. After four decades of Cold War–induced submission to the Liberal Democratic Party's (LDP) monopoly of power and its network of patronage and corruption that, like the Christian Democrats in Italy, wound itself in every nook and cranny of domestic life, the Japanese public resoundingly rejected the continuation of politics as usual by voting the

LDP out of office in 1993. The reform coalition (including the New and Renewal parties that defected from the LDP) that ruled the country has since given way to a Socialist–LDP government and, in the process, has reconstituted itself into a loose coalition called the New Frontier Party. Although the new government nominally represents the return of business as usual, electoral reforms enacted by former prime minister Morihiro Hosokawa, public disenchantment with the old guard, and the rumored dissolution of the Socialist Party promise to transform the traditional political culture.[42]

The same penchant for reform is visible in Taiwan, where the Kuomintang has lost its unrivaled authority, and in the anticorruption agenda of South Korea's Kim Young Sam, which has contributed to growing political liberalization. There are even signs of ferment in Southeast Asia. After two decades of dictatorship and political instability, the Philippines appears to be building a multiparty democracy. Undeterred by the slaughter of prodemocracy forces in May 1992, the Thai public vested power in a coalition of old and new parties, the so-called "angels." Three years later, that government was defeated in the nation's first election without the shadow of military intervention. And, in the summer of 1995, the military junta that controls Myanmar released Nobel Prize–winner Aung San Suu Kyi, the democratic reformer who had been jailed in 1989.[43]

Ideally, the new pluralism will strengthen democracy. The possibility cannot be excluded, however, that the disaggregation of political life could intensify the mood of introspection and national assertiveness that has also accompanied the end of the Cold War. In Eastern Europe, for example, a thicket of political parties have sprouted from the weeds of totalitarianism, suspended between the oppressive absolutism of Communism and the incoherence of democracy in search of clear rules of political engagement. Bewildered by the sudden transition from a command economy to a market system, European publics have also begun to retreat into the familiar and the local.

In Lithuania, Estonia, Poland, Hungary, and Bulgaria, former communists have returned to power in social democratic guise with quasi-paternalistic agendas that may lead to the reintroduction of managed economies. In Romania, the ruling social democrats have joined forces with the anti-Semitic Great Romania Party and the Socialist Labour Party, the old communist grouping. At the same time, most new-left coalitions have reiterated their commitment to economic reform. And in Hungary, where tens of thousands of people mourned the reinterment of former Nazi sympathizer Admiral Miklos Horthy in 1993, the public rejected the right-wing extremism of Istvan Csurka and the Justice Party. Nevertheless, continuing economic disparities, rising crime and corruption, and possible fissures in the major political parties could increase the appeal of statist or even authoritarian alternatives to democracy among the unemployed and socially displaced.[44]

Impatience with the parliamentary babel of democracy and intolerance of institutionalized political conflict have already resulted in two aborted coup attempts in Russia. Despite the continued support for Boris Yeltsin, public disillusionment with the messy process of democratic reform is growing. Spiraling inflation, declining production, the loss of public services, the growth of organized crime, and the open conflict between the executive and the Russian parliament have hardly instilled confidence in Moscow's leadership. Roughly one in four Russians supported the candidacy of dictator-aspirant Vladimir Zhirinovsky in the December 1993 elections. Current opinion polls (and history) suggest that most Russians place greater value on social security than on individual liberty and favor a strong leader as opposed to the disorder of democracy and the caprice of the marketplace. Indeed, some intellectuals confidently assert that the era of reform is over, a victim of Russia's totalitarian heritage and the monopoly of the state.[45]

By comparison with the changing political firmament in Europe and Asia, North America looks oddly stable. Even there, however, signs of political disquietude are not wholly absent. Witness the determination of Staten Islanders to reclaim their autonomy by declaring their independence from the dysfunctional pluralism of New York City and the secessionist fever in Northern California among citizens who resent the state government's disproportionate allocation of public funds to the more populous and welfare-dependent South. At the national level, disaffection has been registered in the public's support for H. Ross Perot's third-party challenge to Democrats and Republicans, its starry-eyed attraction to the suprapolitical mystique of former general Colin Powell, and, as demonstrated in the 1994 elections, its contempt for perceived congressional ineptitude. Next door, in Canada, an angry grass-roots movement in British Columbia and Alberta helped to defeat the ruling Tories in the 1993 national elections. In large measure, the nativist Reform Party is a reaction to the separatist Bloc Quebecois, which won two-thirds of the seats in Quebec, and is poised to achieve the kind of cultural autonomy that French Canadians have sought for the past three decades.[46]

In the Third World, where autocratic rule has been the political norm of decolonization, long-suffering peoples are also demanding greater influence over their lives. The most vivid illustration of political empowerment is in South Africa, where ethnic Africans, freed from the pseudocommunities, or "homelands," imposed by apartheid, are clamoring for self-determination. But less dramatic political transitions, some of which have been instigated by student-led protests, have occurred or are underway in Zambia, Benin, Congo, Togo, Ivory Coast, Cameroon, Niger, and even Nigeria, where military rule continues to thwart the spirit of democratization. Meanwhile, Arab governments from Algeria to Saudi Arabia have confronted more open public criticism of undemocratic processes. In South Asia, a prodemocracy movement ousted the monarchy in Nepal, and elections in Pakistan in the fall of 1993 redirected that country's political future away from the military's historic rule. In the Western Hemisphere as well, the relocation of political authority from military juntas to elected representatives that began in the mid-1980s has continued in Argentina and Brazil. Similarly in Mexico, where the public declared its preference for stability and continuity in the violence-marred elections of 1994, control of state governments no longer rests solely in the hands of the National Revolutionary Party (PRI).[47]

There is no certainty, of course, that the relocation of political authority from the control of entrenched interests or oligarchies to constituent publics will lead to greater social or political inclusivism in the developing world. The ostensibly reform-oriented opposition to political authoritarianism in Ivory Coast, Cameroon, and in North Africa may conceal no less antidemocratic ambitions on the part of those who have been denied power on the basis of their ethnicity or tribal affiliation or religion. Political rivalry, poverty, and intensifying violence in Karachi threaten to undermine Pakistan's inchoate liberalizing efforts. In India, the ethnic animosities that have accompanied the decentralization of political authority have factionalized party structures and fragmented national cohesion. Likewise in Latin America, as the Chiapas uprising in Mexico dramatically illustrated, the spread of democracy has masked the underlying tensions among groups who have differentially benefited from economic and political reform.[48]

Outsiders Outside. The relocation of political legitimacy will not be confined to existing national boundaries. Some outsiders will doubtless prefer to keep their distance from autonomy-compromising affiliations. Puerto Rican rejection of American statehood in 1993 is one illustration. For many minorities, autonomy will entail secession rather than power-sharing in a multicultural melting pot. Certainly this is the aim of Canada's Bloc Quebecois. Twenty-five years of sectarian violence and 3,000 deaths later, the Catholic minority in Northern Ireland continues to pursue its quest for union with the Irish Republic. Likewise, the Basques and Catalans still seek independence from Spain, as does Corsica from France. Nationalist firebrands in Scotland are also agitating for independence from England.[49]

The redrawing of national boundaries in former Yugoslavia and in the quondam Czech and Slovak Federal Republic is likely to recur in post–Cold War Eastern Europe. The Serbian majority in the Krajina region of Croatia is intent on union in a greater Serbia. Secessionist sentiment is rife among Albanians in Kosovo (who represent 90 percent of the population) and in western Macedonia, and it could arouse the Greek minority in Macedonia and southern Albania. Worried that its ethnic kin might be made scapegoats for failed government policies, Budapest has quietly promoted local autonomy for the three million Hungarians in Slovakia, Serbia, and Romania, even though the new government has called for an historic reconciliation with neighboring states. Smoldering irredentist passions in Moldova have focused on union with Romania, which, not surprisingly, is opposed by the minority Russian and Ukrainian populations living there, reinforced by Russia's elite 14th Army.[50]

Moldova is just one of the many cracks in the rickety foundation of post–Cold War Russia. In the republics along the Mongolian border (Tuva, Buratiya), in oil-rich Tatarstan and other lands in the Middle Volga, in the Siberian reaches of Yakutia (now Sakha), aglitter with gold and diamonds, the signs of separateness abound, as peoples seek to revive cultures that have disappeared from view over the course of the past four centuries. The assertion of political autonomy is also underway in the Caucasus and Central Asia, in bloodier fashion. Some republics, like Chechnya, are fighting for their independence; others, like Georgia, discovered that they could not contain separatism in the runaway regions of Abkhazia and Ossetia without Russian assistance and all that implies for their independence. To further complicate the vertiginous process of political *deroulement,* the Russian minority in Ukraine continues to demand greater autonomy and linguistic independence and, for those in the Crimea, reincorporation into Mother Russia. In Central Asia, an Islamic revival has renewed cultural connections and simultaneously kindled irredentist passions among peoples (Tajiks, Uzbekis, Turkmenis, Kyrghiz) arbitrarily displaced by Stalin's dismemberment of immemorial lands that could spread to Turkey and Iran like some reincarnation of the Sunni–Shi'a wars between Ottoman Turkey and Persia in the sixteenth century.[51]

Across the span of humanity in the developing world, separatist pressures also threaten national cohesion. Islamic radicalism promises to divide and dismember societies such as Egypt and Algeria that attempt to repress the effects of its militancy rather than address its socioeconomic cause. An endless war against an Islamic regime waged by Sudan's Christian and animist south could spread to neighboring Uganda. India faces multiple insurgencies in the northern state of Jammu and Kashmir, the Punjab, and in the Tamil-populated region of the south. Neighboring China confronts a Tibetan independence movement as well as separatist pressures in Inner Mongolia and in the Muslim region of Xinxiang among peoples who yearn to resurrect cultures suppressed by the Han Chinese. Meanwhile, in Southeast Asia, the Catholic majority in East Timor seeks independence from Indonesia, and a devout Muslim separatist movement flourishes in northern Sumatra. Although obscured by the first universal election in 1994, tribal fault lines in South Africa between the Xhosa-dominated African National Congress and the Zulu-based Inkatha Freedom Party could foment separatism, if not civil war. The hopeful prospect of unity that followed democratic elections in Angola has collapsed in renewed civil violence in spite of the United Nations peacekeeping force. Elsewhere in Africa, the separatist die has been cast: in Eritrea, which declared its independence from Ethiopia in 1993, and in the rest of Ethiopia, which has become a federal republic; in Zanzibar, which maintains a tenuous attachment to Tanzania; and in Liberia, riven by the competition between rival tribes.[52]

The Regionalization of Economics

Changes in the economic rules of the game are also diminishing the authority of the state. In the interests of competitiveness, efficiency, and capital accumulation, governments have privatized state-owned corporations since 1985 to the tune of more than $300 billion. In terms of sheer numbers, the privatization of national enterprises has been most conspicuous in Eastern Europe—particularly in the Czech Republic, Hungary, and Poland. But Italy, France, and other European countries, continuing the trend started in the 1980s by the British Conservatives under Margaret Thatcher, have also begun to sell state firms such as chemicals maker Rhone-Poulenc, Renault, Deutsche Telekom, Banco Credito Italiano, and Istituto Nazionale delle Assicurazioni. So have

Latin American governments, whose sale of state-held assets accounted for one-third of the value of global privatizations in 1992. In a sweeping divestment of state-owned companies, Argentina plans to sell off all government-run enterprises by the end of 1995. Countries in Asia— notably Japan, which privatized Nippon Telegraph and Telephone in 1986—and even in the Middle East have also begun to sell shares in state companies.[53]

This is not to say that the world is about to swear allegiance to the verities of nineteenth-century Manchesterian liberalism. Nor is the world moving toward the development of some supranational economy or world economic organization. This utopian view, which appeared on the eves of World Wars I and II, has resurfaced in the euphoria of the European revolutions of 1989–90. But persisting trade restraints, inadequate capital and infrastructure bases, Third World indebtedness, and the emphasis on solving problems at the local level (or what Europeans call "subsidiarity") preclude global economic federalism any time soon, if ever. Neither the liberal world economy of nation-states in harmonious competition nor the technoleadership of a World Economic Organization, much less the World Trade Organization, is a viable model for the future. The trend is instead toward the emergence of loosely federated regional entities in sometimes peaceful, sometimes hostile, competition with other economic alliances similarly organized to promote the mutual interests of their members.[54]

The archetypal regional economic unit is the European Union (EU). To be sure, the euphoria of unity that emanated from the passage of the Single European Act in 1986 has long since dissipated. National parliaments have not yet implemented all of the laws specified in the Act to create a unified market. National suppliers continue to monopolize public procurement contracts, and governments still subsidize local industry. And most member states do not meet the Maastricht criteria for monetary union. For the present, slow growth, high unemployment, fissures in the net of social services, and a flood of immigrants cloud the path toward unity. The incorporation of new entrants to the EU from the emerging democracies to the East adds to the haze. In thrall to their farmers, French politicians continue to block East European agricultural access to the EU. Besides, France and its Mediterranean partners are more interested in widening economic ties with North Africa. Moreover, the apportionment of voting power to smaller states will confront large members with the prospect of being impaled on the principle of majority rule. Aid-dependent states such as Greece, Portugal, and Ireland will run the risk of sacrificing some of their regional assistance to even poorer states such as Bulgaria, Hungary, and Slovakia or, worse, Romania.[55]

Some pundits believe the bogeyman of Eurosclerosis has returned. Eurobashers maintain that recession, an aging and increasingly welfare-dependent population, high labor costs and low worker mobility, and rising xenophobia have exhausted public tolerance for federalist visions of monetary union, a single currency, a common foreign and security policy, standardized social practices, or the free movement of peoples within the Union's confines. Fragmentation, *sauve qui peut* policies, and illiberality lie ahead, not union. For the moment, unity is fettered by a host of structural defects, but it is not likely to be hobbled permanently. In the first place, the same fear of nationalistic rivalry that provided the political incentive for the Treaty of Rome more than 35 years ago will prod Europe, no doubt kicking and screaming, toward regional integration in the future. With the merger of the EU and European Free Trade Association (EFTA) some widening has already occurred. Although Norway has rejected membership in the EU, at least for the time being, Austria, Sweden, and Finland voted to join the integrated market in 1994.[56]

Moreover, intraregional economic imperatives impel Europe toward a united-we-stand, divided-we-fall posture. For one, European states, within and without the EU, increasingly trade with one another, thereby blurring distinctions between national markets. Intra-EU trade has risen from 53 percent in 1958 to 70 percent in 1993. For another, the soaring costs of labor and new product research and development foster integration and economies of scale. Technology further connects financial and industrial centers and the people who service them, regardless of national boundaries. If that is not sufficient inducement, the establishment of the North American free-trade zone and the emerging economic convergence of Asia will create macroeconomic imperatives that Europe—both East and West—will not be able to resist unless it masses its financial, industrial-technological, and human resources. As an added measure of security, the EU has taken steps to establish a free-trade zone with Latin America and to improve economic relations with Asia.[57]

Ironically, it was the fear of Fortress Europe that gave urgency to the North American Free Trade Agreement (NAFTA), which the United States, Canada, and Mexico signed in 1992. Despite its endorsement by business groups, especially in the United States, who saw it as a mechanism to demand trade concessions from countries that deny access to their markets, more than a few hurdles had to be surmounted by the signatories, not least the diminution of sovereignty the agreement entailed. With the memory of past U.S. transgressions etched indelibly in their minds, Mexicans were understandably cautious about drawing too close to the colossus to the north. The loss of jobs to cheap labor also bothered the American public, as did the deterioration of the environment as a result of lax Mexican laws, the prospective surge of immigrants displaced by competition, and the decline of U.S. health and safety regulations. Canadians objected to the effects of further competition on unemployment and fears that American influence would erode their cultural distinctiveness and political independence.[58]

In the end, however, the same economic imperatives that drove the process of European unity since passage of the Single Act in 1986 propelled NAFTA past the shoals of public and legislative skepticism. For Mexico, a $6.5 trillion free-trade area represented the most sensible hedge against potential trading blocs in Europe and Asia and an accessible source of investment capital and technology to sustain its growth. For the United States, burdened by a massive deficit and equally worried about being caught in the economic pincers of Eurasia, Mexico and Canada offered markets for value-added capital goods that would spur technological innovation and the development of high-pay, high-skill jobs. Considering that the United States took three-fourths of its exports (and more than 80 percent by 1995), then recession-ridden Canada could not afford to isolate itself from North American economic integration.[59]

Clearly, the collapse of the Mexican peso and the economic debacle it precipitated in December 1994 prompted second thoughts about the viability of NAFTA, leave aside its expansion. For Mexicans, who suddenly faced a credit crisis, mounting inflation, and deteriorating living standards, NAFTA hardly seemed the harbinger of increased prosperity and a ticket of admission to the club of advanced industrial economies. NAFTA's promised creation of new jobs seemed to be no less a pipe dream for many Americans. Worse, the United States was forced to broker a rescue package that included $20 billion of loans and loan guarantees from Washington. American critics of NAFTA concluded that the United States was saddled with the responsibility for the Mexican economy. Some feared it would become a financial Vietnam.[60]

By the spring of 1995, however, as the combination of U.S. and IMF assistance and President Ernesto Zedillo Ponce de Leon's austerity measures restored confidence in financial markets, anti-NAFTA sentiment had markedly declined. Looking ahead, tight credit and high unemployment remain worrisome threats to social peace, but Mexican exports have begun to shift the trade balance to a surplus. According to some financial observers, the continued export recovery is likely to spur job creation on both sides of the Rio Grande after 1996, thereby rekindling confidence in the benefits of regional integration in both countries. Meanwhile, in Canada, which was a reluctant signatory to the free-trade arrangement, NAFTA has stimulated an economic boom. Employment has increased, and exports to both the United States and Mexico rose by more than 20 percent in 1994.[61]

Informally, the Asia–Pacific economies are also gravitating toward a regional orbit revolving around Japan. Deep-seated historical memories of Japanese aggression, concerns about the loss of national sovereignty, and persisting protectionist barriers presently preclude formal arrangements. Nevertheless, the 18-member Asia Pacific Economic Conference (APEC), which also includes the United States, Canada, Mexico, and Chile, and more localized arrangements such as ASEAN's Asian Free Trade Area (AFTA) provide frameworks to coordinate economic policies in response to European and North American integration. The perceived formation of global trading blocs, of course, has not been the sole impetus to Asian regional integration. Here, too, political and economic realities have spurred centripetalist tendencies. With the end of the Cold War, the West, and particularly the United States, is no longer as inclined as it once was to absorb Asian imports or to tolerate its closed markets.[62]

In response to these developments, countries such as Japan and South Korea are slowly starting to open hitherto closed markets in agriculture, construction, and auto parts. Largely as a result of Japanese direct investment, the Asia–Pacific region is being transformed into a peaceful and more successful economic version of the Greater East Asia Co-Prosperity Sphere. The spread of Japanese production facilities and technology and the growing importance of the manufacturing sector in the structurally transformed economies of Southeast Asia are already creating linkages in the pooling of regional interests. Owing to the adverse effect of a rising yen on the current-account balance, Japanese markets are likely to become increasingly open to lower-cost goods from Southeast Asia and China. As Asian economies develop, they also provide markets for Japanese exports. Although trade barriers remain high, exports within the Asian region are rising; intra-Asian trade increased to 43 percent in 1994, versus 32 percent a decade ago. Given continued economic growth in the area, the assimilation of the resource-rich Russian Far East into the Asia-Pacific ambit, and the eventual reunification of Korea, the halting process of regional integration should accelerate.[63]

At the same time, the Asian and Pacific states, Malaysia excepted, are also becoming aware of their growing economic interdependence with non Asian or Pacific economies. Most Asian countries export from one-fourth to one-third of their goods to the United States. Reciprocally, Asia provides an expanding market for American products. Moreover, the Asian states seek to participate in the common markets of Europe and North America. As reflected in the APEC meeting that was held in Indonesia in November 1994, the importance of these considerations was not lost on the summit participants. In a declaration that concluded the annual ministerial meeting, the APEC states issued a pledge to re- move all trade barriers and open their economies by 2020. Although the declaration is not binding, and problems from the exclusion of agricul- tural products to continued subsidization of favorite industries will com- plicate the attainment of a truly free-trade zone, the agreement sets a laudable standard that is bound to transform APEC from a talkfest where the "meeting is the message" into a more formal structure with a clearly defined agenda.[64]

Unsteady steps toward regional cooperation are also visible in the developing world. In South America, the five Andean nations have formed a trade grouping. Argentina and Brazil, along with Paraguay and Uruguay, have joined together in the Mercosur, a new common market that includes some 200 million people and roughly half of Latin Ameri- ca's GDP. Notwithstanding the Mexican crisis and its adverse effect on NAFTA enlargement, Mercosur could become the core of a hemispheric economic community that would incorporate the Andean states. Fur- thermore, the Central American economies, less Mexico, have estab- lished an Economic Community of the Central American Isthmus, and a new association of Caribbean states is linking island communities with major markets like Mexico. Intraregional trade has risen to some $26 billion, or nearly four times the amount recorded a decade earlier, and, almost everywhere, cross-border investment is on the rise.[65]

Elsewhere, at least the principle of economic cooperation has been embraced. The riparian states in the Black Sea region and the countries of North Africa have discussed the possibility of regional trade relation- ships. Some of the contumacious members of the Commonwealth of In- dependent States (CIS), their fears of Russian autocephalism notwith- standing, have come to realize that they cannot survive politically or economically without some form of financial and trade integration. Fol- lowing elections in July 1994 that brought pro-Russian presidents to power, Ukraine and Belarus broached the idea of creating a European

Union–like organization to replace the CIS. Even the Middle East has recently taken steps toward regional economic cooperation. At their summit in Casablanca in the fall of 1994, Israel and its Arab neighbors began to discuss ways to transfer the sinews of war into implements of commerce.[66]

Actions, however, have not kept pace with intentions. Little has been heard of the Black Sea pact since its formation in 1992, although working-level discussions continue between Greece, Turkey, and some of the other signatories, and neither Maghrebian nor Baltic economic cooperation has gone beyond the stage of rhetoric. Given the continued upheaval in Central Asia and the Caucasus and Russia's reluctance to subsidize the former Soviet republics, no one is talking seriously about economic integration in the CIS. Nevertheless, Russia and Belarus signed a customs union in May 1995, which Kazakhstan, Uzbekistan, Kyrgyzstan, and Tajikistan have voiced interest in joining. Under the leadership of Leonid Kuchma, Ukraine has steered clear of economic ties, preferring instead to pursue its own reform agenda. As for the Middle East, the obstacles to cooperation there are even more daunting. The Gulf States have resisted cooperation until Israeli troops leave all Arab-occupied lands. On the other hand, there have been some encouraging developments. Progress toward regional economic integration continues in the Western Hemisphere, and no one seems inclined to still the spirit of the Enterprise for the Americas initiative launched by the Bush administration.[67]

In the future, it is conceivable that developing countries with an abundance of resources or low-cost labor could become clustered on the periphery of one of the core economic areas in Europe, North America, or Asia. Since the end of the 1980s, investment funds have poured into the Third World, spurring privatization, trade liberalization, and growing foreign ownership of enterprise. According to a World Bank report, the flow of net private loans and investment to the developing world more than doubled in the period 1990 to 1992. Foreign direct investment jumped from $31 billion to $80 billion in the 1990–93 period. Improvement in the industrial and labor base of developing countries, in turn, will generate value-added technology, jobs, and exports in the core countries.[68]

Needless to say, the clustering of core and periphery countries into regional economic entities could result in protectionist trading blocs. But this is not inevitable. The accelerated movement of international capital is one inhibiting factor. The "Who Is Us?" query posed by Robert Reich with respect to the national identity of corporations may be overdrawn—home governments still intrude in the market to ensure domestic content in manufacturing and to protect the transfer of sensitive technology—but it is incontestable that multinational companies and financial consortia are increasingly traversing parochial attachments, whether at the national or at the regional level. Witness the surrender of the Gucci design house of Italy to a Bahrain-based group of international investors.[69]

Assuming the continued reduction of non-tariff as well as tariff barriers to the movement of goods and capital, rising economic growth rates in the developing world, and the absence of such calamities as another oil shock or financial crisis that would undermine investor confidence in emerging countries, trade-enhancing, two-way investment flows between core and periphery areas of the international economy will probably accelerate in the future, thereby reinforcing regional linkages. Moreover, depending on the changing source of investment and on transfers of ownership, developing countries might shift their ties from cluster to cluster, or they might participate in more than one regional cluster at the same time. Given the dependence of Europe and the Asia–Pacific region on Arab oil, for example, the Persian Gulf states could increase their ties with both the EU and the Pacific Rim. Chile has already become part of APEC, and it is likely to join NAFTA, once the health of the Mexican economy is restored.[70]

Strategic alliances between companies are also likely to impede regional insularity. Germany's Daimler-Benz and Japan's Mitsubishi Corp. agreed to share automotive, aerospace, and microelectronic technology in large part to ensure footholds in regional markets that could become more restrictive in the future. For the same reason, Japan has entered into similar arrangements with British computer makers, which will benefit from Japanese technology, and with companies in Chile. IBM and Siemens, Motorola, and Toshiba, and others have similarly joined forces. Italian eyeglass maker Luxottica purchased U.S. Shoe; Korean chaebols Samsung and LG Electronics have respectively acquired parts of computer maker AST Research Corporation and Zenith Electronics Corporation, the last American television manufacturer; and Polygram, the Anglo–Dutch entertainment group, has increased its stake in Music India, a Bombay-based record company. British pharmeceutical maker Glaxo Holdings PLC, Telefonica de España, ITT, and countless others are similarly seeking potential partners that are equally keen on ensuring their positions in foreign markets.[71]

To be sure, this is not the only form the internationalization of business is taking. Ford, IBM, and the Swiss–Swedish giant Asea Brown Boveri Ltd., among others, are centralizing product development in an effort to create manufacturing cost efficiencies that cannot be achieved by devolving operational responsibility to local managers. However, the risk in this approach—the failure to gauge the shifts in market demand—could be disastrous. Of course, strategic alliances are not foolproof either. They are the economic equivalent of political alliances, *mariages des convenances* that will not endure beyond their utility to the signatories. Where the benefits of cooperation are unclear or, in the case of the Swedish shareholders' revolt against the Volvo–Renault merger, in jeopardy, corporate collaborations are likely to be short lived. Nevertheless, strategic alliances ranging from ad hoc poolings of interest between firms to actual mergers are likely to become more common in the future, as companies seek more imaginative ways to share the costs and risks of product development and distribution in a global marketplace that is becoming more specialized and more competitive.[72]

The macroeconomic effects of international trade agreements—notably the General Agreement on Trade and Tariffs—are further likely to counteract protectionism. The surge in world trade in the roughly quarter-century between World War II and 1973 resulted in large part from the negotiated reduction of tariffs. The next 25 years were admittedly less productive. The two oil shocks of 1973 and 1978 hardly contributed to international cooperation either internationally or, prescinding OPEC, regionally. The subsequent imposition of non-tariff barriers, an array of import quotas and "voluntary" restraints masquerading as free trade, and bilateral extra-institutional mechanisms to adjust imbalances such as the U.S.–Japanese Structural Impediments Initiative further weakened multilateral resolve. With any luck, the recently completed Uruguay Round of GATT and the creation of the World Trade Organization, which was established to oversee the operation of the agreements put in place and to devise rules of market access in areas where differences remain, may start the pendulum swinging back toward international cooperation. Given the trend toward the relocation of political sovereignty that the end of the Cold War has accelerated, the liberalization of trade in agriculture and services that resulted from the Uruguay Round is probably not the precursor to a free and unfettered world trading market. But the economic effects of trade liberalization are likely to encourage intra- and interregional cooperation and thus inhibit the formation of exclusive trading blocs.[73]

Like it or not, the world is moving toward regional integration, economically as well as politically, and, in the most hopeful outcome, toward interregional cooperation. Economic regionalism is a logical correlate of the trend toward political autonomy. This is not to say that the ideal of a global economic order should be abandoned, only that its pursuit should not divert attention from the localization of politics that is taking place. As the debates over EC92 and NAFTA have illustrated, and as the predictable wrangling over free trade in APEC is bound to show, it will be difficult enough for diverse cultures to meld their interests and aspirations in regional entities, let alone global structures. Overt appeals for exclusivism such as the East Asian Economic Caucus urged by Malaysian Prime Minister Mohammad Mahathir remain temptingly near. In such a fragile environment, there is a danger that humanity will make the best the enemy of the good and that excessive expectations will divide the postmodern world against itself.[74]

The Epoch of Mutualism

Ends are always beginnings. The interval between the two may be insufferably long and turbulent, however, as is the case today, in a world that is undergoing the turmoil of social and political disaggregation. In developed countries, the splintering of society is visible in the "identity politics" of single-issue groups that narcissistically redefine human experience in terms of race, gender, sexual persuasion, or some other exclusivist orientation. In developing countries, it takes the form of cultural liberation or, with lamentable frequency, human destruction, as the carnage that Hutus and Tutsis inflicted on each other in Burundi and Rwanda and the clan warfare in Somalia and Georgia illustrate. Fragmentation is also discernible in the secessionist impulse of peoples. It is visible in Slovakia's divorce from its uncomfortable cohabitation with the Czechs, in the hodgepodge of Central Asia, Eritrea, and the gathering storm in Quebec. All too often it exposes the vengeful wrath of disgruntled peoples who seek to achieve by force what they could not accomplish politically.[1]

The disintegrative force of change is being propelled in large measure by ethnic passion. Peoples long submerged in centuries of great-power conflict and, more recently, in the permafrost of Cold War, have suddenly resurfaced like some fossils of another geological age long since forgotten by humanity. As they slowly warm to their own self-discovery, they are reminded by their collective awareness of past glories, unrequited dreams, and, in too many cases, implacable hatreds for neighboring peoples, tribes, and villages, whose different beliefs, practices, and customs pose unassimilable threats to fragile identities. Some will stay in the hallowed land of their fathers, defending it, like their premodern ancestors, against cultural interlopers, as the Armenians seem to be doing in Nagorno-Karabakh, and try to restore it against the insuperable odds of time and modernity. Others will migrate to new lands, driven by the cycle of death or impelled by the prospect of life, where they will add to the human flotsam of societies already burdened with the care of their own people and thus all the more inhospitable to strangers.

The widening gap between rich and poor in the global market place is also fraying the bonds of human cooperation. Peoples that have been denied their rightful place in society can be expected to displace their anger on cultural outsiders or on government leaders, as the Indians in Chiapas have done in Mexico, and to embrace the nativist, even demagogic, beliefs, which will polarize groups and states at the expense of consensual order. This is the politics of middle-class protest in the developed world. It is Silvio Berlusconi and H. Ross Perot. It is also Jean Le Pen, Jorg Haider, and Pat Buchanan. It is the fear of social exclusion and cultural deracination that inspires opposition to social processes of integration. It is the liberation from political oppression, if no longer bondage, in the developing world. It is the simmering conflict in Kashmir, the growing volatility between Sikhs and Hindus in the Punjab, the intermittent conflict in Yemen, the never-ending war in the Sudan. It is also the cry for cultural expression in East Timor, in China's Xinxiang province, in Moldova, and numerous other nominally independent states in what Russia calls its "near abroad." [2]

The uncertainty of human survival is bound to exacerbate the process of social disintegration. In much of the world, unremitting poverty, ignorance, and disease stalk the future. In drought-ridden Africa, but also in parts of Asia, Latin America, and the Middle East, some over-populated societies are left with little choice but to forage the land in order to subsist. Nature is one of the casualties of their deprivation. Civilization is another. For those societies that are being reduced to barbarism and the survival of the fittest, warfare will be the only basis of human organization. It is already stalking the land in Rwanda, Liberia, and other places in Africa where tribal animosities exacerbate marginal living conditions, in the killing fields of Central Asia, and in the Caucasus. In a world increasingly befouled by environmental decay and disease, humanity may wallow in its own destructiveness, not unlike the roving bands of marauders cinematically popularized a decade ago in the then incredible future-world of Mad Max. [3]

CONFLICT AND COOPERATION

The upheaval that currently afflicts the world has predictably prompted an outpouring of books and articles ranging from the alarmist to the hysterical that is quickly becoming the new intellectual fashion. [4] The more sensational make reference to a future of perpetual anarchy or even to the advent of a new Dark Age. That the world may be entering a period of prolonged turbulence does not presage perpetual chaos. To see the recrudescence of primitivism in the present turmoil is to ignore six centuries of civility and rationality. Moreover, it suggests that self-interest, indeed, self-survival, will impose no constraints on humanity's self-destructive impulses.

In the less febrile, but no less apocalyptic, view of Samuel Huntington, the world is headed for a titanic clash of culturally incompatible civilizations, or what one might call "ordered chaos."[5] Granted, cultural exclusivism of the sort that we have experienced in Eastern Europe or the Indian subcontinent or Southeast Asia is not conducive to international syncretism. Modernizing societies, as Huntington points out, are not necessarily westernizing societies. But cultural distinctiveness does not inevitably lead to ethnocentrism any more than ethnocentrism necessarily portends conflictual relations among civilizations.

In the first place, the social structures and processes of civilizations are not indelibly fixed. Historically, the reaction of the dispossessed to their social marginality—Toynbee's "external proletariat"—has been a source of the transformation of civilizations. The present-day Islamic world is rife with social and religious divisions. In Asia, too, adherence to Confucian principles does not ensure regional cooperation. Moreover, civilizations are not impermeable to outside influences. Civilizations "borrow" from each other, to use Braudel's terminology, just as they also "refuse" the cultural importation of certain unassimilable beliefs or practices. In the contemporary world, the diffusion of technology has created a culture-transcending technocratic community among the educated, who, in contrast to their poor and ignorant brethren that filter reality through the prism of immemorial traditions, can separate themselves from their cultural origins. Besides, the supposed impending conflict of civilizations is just another monistic variety of endism, which, in its West-versus-the-rest dichotomy, recreates in new form the morality play of the Cold War.[6]

At the other extreme are those who believe that a world of perpetual peace and harmony lies ahead. For Fukuyama, this is the last stop on History's self-fulfilling journey through time and space. For political modelers and theoreticians such as Richard Falk, Ervin Laszlo, and Rajni Kothari and their contemporaries in the peace studies field—Johan Galtung, Richard Smoke, Harry Hollins, among others—it is the formation of a norm-based transnationalism to which all humanity will assent.[7]

This is not to say that the futuristic visions of these writers are indistinguishable in every respect. Falk's advocacy of a supranational state replete with a parliament, judiciary, and police force is structurally the opposite of Galtung's international communitarianism, and both of these designs differ from Kothari's emphasis on Third World unity as a precondition of world federalism. Laszlo and Smoke, for their part, adopt a functionalist framework in which the resolution of common problems will foster a more or less self-regulating order of peace and international harmony. Conceptual and operational differences aside, however, these and other models of the future are nonetheless animated by a common set of assumptions and beliefs.[8]

In the first place, they all share an optimistic view of humanity, including the expectation of an increasingly denuclearized and eventually conflict-free world. They also all renounce the naked self-interest of balance-of-power politics, which, in view of the perceived decline of the nation-state, they believe is being supplanted by more constitutive global structures and a normative system of international relations that will delegitimize war. Indeed, values, not power, will become the determining force in international affairs. According to these futurologists, the inculcation of human rights and other democratic values in the world's polities will create shared interests among otherwise diverse peoples and cultures. Interests, Seyom Brown has noted, are informed by the moral worth of one's actions and not simply by their utility or practicality. Eventually, humanity will develop a new moral consciousness that will transform a once anarchic international system into a "feasible" or "relevant" utopia.[9]

Analytically, the values-based literature offers some useful insights into the trends that are shaping the world's future. At the level of social diagnosis, much of what these writers have to say echoes the more circumspect and less overtly sanguine views of Gilpin, Rosenau, Boulding, Kennedy, and others who have peered into the future. Furthermore, their assessments of technological, demographic, and socioeconomic trends and of the need to develop collective approaches to global problems in many ways parallel my own views. Seyom Brown's advocacy of "mutual accountability" shares certain similarities with my concept of mutualism. The importance of integrating the developing world into the larger international community described by Kothari and the growth of social movements that challenge the authority of the state discussed by Walker and Rosenau also coincide with ideas presented in these pages. The idealistic—and, in some cases, idyllic—vision of the future that underlies the reformist efforts to create a just and peaceful world, however, is a chimera. Indeed, at the level of social praxis, the values-based expectations of the future are naive.[10]

To begin with, the roseate image of society that colors value-based conceptions of global change distorts the human personality by choosing to ignore the dark side of our natures, the aggressive urges that exist within the human psyche. It is not simply corrupt political and economic institutions or ignorance that have produced international suffering and destruction, it is humanity itself. How is it that an essentially "good man could have produced corrupting and tyrannical political organizations [sic] or exploiting economic organizations, or fanatical and superstitious religious organizations," Reinhold Niebuhr asked rhetorically in his classic critique of liberal democracy's defense? It is admirable to hope that humanity will reject war as a legitimate means of achieving its objectives, but it would be folly to conduct one's affairs on the basis of such a belief.[11]

It is true, as Smoke and Harmon point out, that gunboat diplomacy is a long-discarded form of international intercourse and that democratic societies have been inclined to resort to war in self-defense, preferably far away from their national territories. No doubt, the emergence of nuclear weapons has helped to debase warfare. But this does not mean that the competitive interests and instincts of states and the desire to maximize power are waning. Nor does it mean that the structure of international relations that reinforces such instincts and thus induces states, even as they seek to increase their influence over others, to maintain power balances is about to metamorphose into a regime of norm-based federalism or a world state. Absent the satisfaction of all human needs, and probably not even then, and the rational distribution of power in the international system that Kothari wishfully envisions, states are not likely to subordinate their interests to the common good of the international community.[12]

Undeniably, the nation-state has lost some of its authority to multinational institutions, transnational corporations, and a host of national as well as international interest groups, as Rosenau, drawing on regime theory, has argued, but it is hardly on the verge of abandoning its cultural identity and thus its independence to the "general will" of a universal polity. Witness the continuing difficulty of European integration and the congenital American fear of sovereignty-threatening institutions like the United Nations or, the most recent illustration, the newly created World Trade Organization that was set up in the Uruguay Round of the GATT talks to officiate global trade relations.[13]

To believe that humanity can redefine its identity on the basis of its moral obligations to the world community is to misunderstand both the power of cultural particularism and political self-interest. In general, the values-driven approach to international cooperation assumes that Western forms of governance, economic pluralism, and human rights will gradually be embraced by the world's peoples, their different social and cultural experiences notwithstanding. This is an attempt to revive the ideology of progress and redemptive history. It also assumes that the indoctrination of such ideals as the prevention of war, social justice, and economic well-being will find receptive audiences everywhere and will overcome the frequent disorder of state-centered, amoral balance-of-power politics. But it is unclear how elites will translate such values to publics, especially those publics for which such concepts have no experiential referent. It is no less difficult to understand how states will be persuaded to act altruistically at the same time that they are being encouraged to exercise greater self-reliance and autonomy.[14]

Value-based formulations of world order require shared values. The world is a long way from the creation of a World Assembly advocated by Falk that would legislate behavior for an international, even transnational, public. Whose norms would apply? The liberal-democratic values of Jefferson's yeoman farmer? The precepts of Confucius? The social prescriptions of the uluma and the interpreters of the Koran? Who would have the authority to impose and enforce sanctions on groups or nations that violate the rules? Considering the inequality of capabilities, influence, and wealth among peoples and states, it is harder still to believe that some transnational consensus, let alone global unity, will result from the will of the governed. Even if the global unity of humanity were attainable, however, it is far from clear that it would lead to an idyllic world. It might reduce human beings to little more than the deindividualized receptors of centrally programmed instructions depicted in Aldous Huxley's *Brave New World* or B. F. Skinner's *Walden II,* which would be far worse than the boredom Fukuyama contemplates. Or it could result in the formation of an empire which, as Kant feared, would rule with tyrannical authority.[15]

As for the hopes of a feasible utopia, there is an implied, if not always stated, belief in the values-based literature that human beings can be taught to be peaceful, ethical citizens of the world. Ideas alone, of course, will not produce global harmony. Social engineering—notably structural changes in the distribution of power and resources—will also be required to achieve global governance and world community. Such visions of the future are both fanciful and potentially dehumanizing. No amount of moral exhortation is likely to prompt rich, developed societies to share their wealth with the needy if they are not otherwise impelled by necessity to do so. In any case, it is not clear who will mandate such altruism. "To a very great degree, the public must take precedence over the private," Robert Heilbroner wrote, "an aim to which it is easy to give lip service in the abstract but difficult for someone used to the pleasures of political, social, and intellectual freedom to accept in fact." [16]

Such notions of global peaceful convergence are, in spirit at least, postmodern transcriptions of Timoleon's gospel of *Homonoia* (concord), or Zeno's notion of cosmopolis, or, in the modern epoch, Kant's ideal of a "pacific union." And as was true in the past, they are psychological reactions to social transformation, warfare, and international disorder. Humanity, as the following pages suggest, may by approaching new forms of community, an "incipient cosmopolitanism," as Stanley Hoffman put it. Clearly, global problems will require global solutions. But such cooperation, if it comes about, will not result from the hope-based entreaties and reformist agendas of intellectuals who seek to reeducate publics and reengineer their societies to conform to some preconceived blueprint for global governance and planetary peace. Rather, it will result from the harsh reality of experience and the fear-based internationalism of peoples who, as they did at the Treaty of Westphalia in the mid-seventeenth century, will perforce agree to minimal constraints on behavior to contain their anarchic and self-destructive tendencies. [17]

Whatever the outcome of the current international upheaval, the contemporary augurers who would have us believe that the world is either about to implode or to unite in some state of harmonic convergence strain credulity primarily because they foreclose human alternatives. It is premature and even cynical to consign humanity to a future of perpetual conflict, and it is naive to believe that an ethically sanctioned global order awaits. To avert lapsing into either cynicism or fantasy, however, and the self-destructiveness both breed, will require a fundamental change in the way humanity defines its relationship with the world and with itself. It will require the West, in particular, to concede that it can no longer impose its values on a polycentric world order (as the Singaporean government has reminded the United States with its decision to cane a young American for the crime of vandalism). It will require the world's poor as well as rich to acknowledge that their survival is inseparable from the survival of other peoples with whom they coexist in a state of mutual dependency, if not always equality. It will require the diverse cultures of the world to purge themselves of their demons before we are all purged by them.

To be sure, such a transformative change in attitude and behavior will not occur, if it occurs at all, either quickly or quiescently. Given the natural resistance to change, especially life-transforming change, international conditions are likely to deteriorate further before humanity is prodded to redefine its convictions about the world in which it lives. As was the case during the protracted transition from the order of the ancients to modernity, we too will probably have to endure the disastrous consequences of warfare, or ecological crisis, or the pandemic spread of diseases such as AIDS or some other virulent virus, as Boulding and others suggest. It is hard to escape this fate. "Nor is it easy to foresee a willing acquiescence of humankind," Heilbroner soberly noted, "individually or through its existing social organizations, in the alterations of lifeways that foresight would dictate. If then, by the question 'Is there hope for man?' we ask whether it is possible to meet the challenges of the future without the payment of a fearful price, the answer must be: No, there is no such hope."[18]

On the spectrum between the extremes of anarchy and social unity, however, and between death-embracing and life-enhancing alternations of existence, there are signs that humanity is groping toward new forms of interaction based on the necessity of cooperative inclusion rather than competitive exclusion. Cultural and other differences aside, people seem to be gradually and pragmatically consolidating economic and even political interests in new institutional structures that, in some ways, supersede the authority of the state. Despite the setbacks of the diluted Maastricht Treaty, the collapse of the exchange rate mechanism, and the failure of most member states to get their monetary houses in order, Europe is moving toward integration. So are North America and Asia. Though fanatics and terrorists continue to intrude on the peace process, progress toward the resolution of differences between Israel and its neighbors has not been extinguished. In the seething tribal passions of Africa as well, one cannot ignore the prospect of integration in South Africa.[19]

In spite of the cultural parochialism and political self-absorption that have become all too apparent in the aftermath of the Cold War, there are also indications that humanity is beginning to see the world as an interrelated network of relations it cannot escape rather than as an object it can control. It is becoming apparent that states, supranational institutions, nongovernmental organizations, and local communities coexist in a mutually reinforcing relationship. Just as the parts shape the behavior of the whole, they are simultaneously being shaped by it in a dynamic system of interaction in which the parts tacitly comprehend the whole. Humanity may be on the verge of realizing, even as it reimmerses itself in a frenzy of egoistic ethnonationalism, that it can neither cultivate its garden at the expense of its neighbor nor seek salvation in some mythic past.[20]

The letting go or forgetting of the past that is implicit in the awareness of the future does not mean its repudiation. Quite the contrary, it is the acceptance of the past and its evolution in the context of the present that makes the future possible. The future, in turn, links the present and the past in a new framework of meaning. Nor will the increasing globalization of society lead to the disappearance of the nation-state. Just as the body is the visible manifestation of the human mind, the state will remain the visible expression of national culture. What is likely to impel the gestating epoch of mutualism is the overpowering existential awareness that the world will not last forever.[21]

In contrast to the belief in a static, balanced, deterministic universe that dominated scientific thought from Newton to Einstein, twentieth-century physicists have concluded that the universe is always expanding, but in an uncertain relationship with the gravitational field from other galaxies that threaten its extinction. Astrophysicist Stephen Hawking has pointed out that the universe may not recollapse for another billion years, but by that time the human race will have long since perished.[22] At some point, later rather than sooner, the human community will have to come to terms with the pragmatism of finitude. And if it chooses life over death, it will probably recognize, in its national and collective self-interest, that in an age of limited natural resources and international interdependence the benefits of cooperative inclusion far exceed those of competitive exclusion.

The Concept of Mutualism

Mutualism denotes a community of interests in which diverse peoples and states bounded by geographical, historical, and cultural affinities productively commingle in localized social, political, and economic associations reinforced by the acceptance of shared risks and rewards. In form, this sharply contrasts with the hierarchically arranged, order-defined, culturally segmented closed societies of antiquity, in which the repetitive cycle of life and death was controlled by nature and God. It also differs from the perpetual flux, egoism, and competitive conflict of modern societies, in which individuals and states, in unrestrained pursuit of endless progress and human perfection, seek to maximize power and control nature. In the lambent postmodern era of interdependent societies, there will be a greater propensity for individual and national interests to converge with the interests of the community as a whole.[23]

This is not to be mistaken with communitarian socialism, the self-contained cosmopolitan order of premodern times, or norm-based futurology's feasible utopia. The aggregation of states into localized associations will be inherently dynamic both intra- and interregionally, but the coordinates of change and order will differ from the past. In the ancient world, change was contained within order. Given the harsh demands of daily life, there was no temporal dimension to change. Change was spatialized. Beginning with the Renaissance, order increasingly became part of change. Space was a function of the trajectory of time. Change was thus temporalized. In the epoch of mutualism, change and order are likely to be convergent, if not synchronous. Ideally, change and order will be mutually reinforcing, virtually inseparable, interdependent elements of cooperative international interactions. In the epoch of progress, utilitarianism defined the common good as the residual of unfettered individualism. In the epoch of mutualism, self-interest will be consonant with the common good.

In the same measure, the regional concertation of interests does not preclude the prospect of progressive change in international relations. One may reasonably expect progress in arms control, the continuing eradication of disease, and environmental preservation. But in the future progress will be devoid of the cultural and ideological baggage that it has historically carried. Progress will not be seen as endless; it will be bounded by the limitations of nature, technology, and human generosity. Nor will it be universal. Persisting social and economic inequities within and among states will complicate the formation of consensual values and thus inhibit universal definitions of progress. Further, progress will not be inevitable. There is no scientific blueprint, no computerized program of artificial intelligence, that will overcome the unpredictability and perverseness of human nature. Depending on the choices we make, progress may also be reversible.[24]

ECONOMIC INTERDEPENDENCE

Mutualism departs from the premise that we can no longer entrust the future to the illimitability of progress. We may take flight from reality and persist in the belief that the next infusion of technology or capital or scientific discovery will save us, but we will do so at our own peril. If we are lucky, we will come to our senses before nature's unrenewable resources have been depleted and societies have plunged into anarchic competition. As NAFTA, APEC, and other such aggregations imply, however, national governments and multinational organizations are beginning to adjust to the new economic realities of mutualism. Influenced by the consolidation of enterprise within and across borders and the rising cost of social services, the harmonization of economic behavior is likely to increase in the future.

The rise of the transnational business enterprise and the global market date from the late 1960s. They have been spurred by both structural and functional factors. Structurally, the introduction of technological advances in the manufacturing and marketing process has not only increased the scope, method, and locus of the production and distribution of goods and services, it has also extended the geographical boundaries of corporations. In addition, the lowering of investment and trade barriers has accelerated the mobility of capital and goods in international markets. The combination of technology and capital flows, in turn, have fostered the concentration of industry and the emergence of huge multinational companies with the power to influence the behavior of markets.

Functionally, fewer companies can compete independently in such an environment because firms can no longer comfortably rely on the competitive forces of the market to set prices, as classical economic theory dictates. Increasingly, competition is becoming a function of the strategic choices companies make in an imperfect market that places value on the cooperative as well as competitive conduct of firms interacting in an integrated network of relationships. Economies of scale and the localization of production, efficiencies in the employment of capital, and the penetration of new markets have accordingly prompted growing numbers of companies to opt for either formal (mergers and acquisitions) or informal (licensing arrangements, joint ventures, research consortia) poolings-of-interest.[25]

To be sure, huge multinational enterprises will span regions; companies such as Philips, Alcatel, Toshiba, and Boeing will undoubtedly wish to continue their presence in the world's major markets in Europe, North America, and Asia. But most trade and investment is likely to be regionally concentrated. The reasons seem almost self-evident. Geographical proximity is more likely to enhance the cost efficiencies of manufacturing and market penetration. In addition, cultural familiarity is further likely to increase the effectiveness of international management and, with some global exceptions such as Coca-Cola, Mercedes-Benz, Armani, or Sony, facilitate product receptivity.[26]

No doubt, the process of economic integration will be tortuous. Political mistrust, social unrest, and the fear of cultural erosion will continue to litter the path toward mutualism, especially in the newly industrializing and developing states. A resurgent global economy may be a further disincentive. Given the sheer cost of doing business in an increasingly competitive world, however, most companies, and therefore most states, will find it hard to resist the logic of interdependence indefinitely. As economist John Dunning has pointed out, the progressivist, neoclassical assumption that companies coexist in a state of constant competition is no longer tenable in the emerging order of economic interdependence. The increasing tendency is for firms and states "to be part of a new form or entity, similar in concept to the group belief that for a specific purpose, or purposes, a merging of their identities will serve their overall individual interests."[27]

For all the bickering, economic and financial integration is already a fact of life in Western Europe. In Western Europe, not only have distinctions between domestic and foreign sales blurred, they have become less important to producers and consumers, who increasingly perceive the locus of economic activity in regional rather than national terms. It is probably only a matter of time before the alignment of trade and monetary policies lead to a European Bank and common currency. Moreover, the eventual extension of EU membership to the East European states will accelerate the process of economic regionalization in North America and Asia that it helped to set in motion and, where some measure of complementarity exists, stimulate similar developments in the developing world.

Regional integration will also ease the economic burden of social payments. In Western Europe, soaring welfare costs have priced many goods out of international markets. The modest reductions in cost-of-living adjustments and social subsidies are probable harbingers of more draconian cutbacks in the future, including mass layoffs. Recessionary conditions have challenged the principle of guaranteed employment in Japan and threatened the security of social benefits that corporations have historically provided. According to the Census Bureau, the number of poor people in the United States rose to 14.5 percent in 1992, despite social security payments and other noncash subsidies. A more recent study suggests that, not only are the poor continuing to increase, they are more likely to stay poor today than they were in the 1960s and

1970s. Indeed, the disparity of income between the top 10 percent and the lowest 10 percent of wage-earners has widened since the late 1980s, and chances of remaining in the middle class, particularly for younger people, have declined.[28]

The competition for dwindling social maintenance funds poses contradictory but equally unacceptable risks. Burgeoning welfare payments not only tend to produce higher budget deficits and inflation, they also lead to increased labor costs and eventually greater unemployment. Without corresponding rises in labor output or value-added infusions to the production process, persisting cyclical unemployment will eventually calcify into structural unemployment, as it has in Europe, which will send social welfare costs spiraling upward. Conversely, efforts to overcome structural economic defects and improve competitiveness through cuts in public spending programs run the risk of inflaming government opposition and potentially of fomenting massive social disorder.[29]

Faced with this Hobson's choice, national governments and corporations may find economic codependency a practicable social and economic alternative to their current predicament. Assuming that business consolidation and the convergence of macroeconomic policies enhance productivity and profitability, increasing national income will help to defray the cost of health and welfare programs. Economic integration may also facilitate the creation of regional social security funds that could be apportioned to poorer members on the basis of need, as the EU currently does. Such a reservoir of funds could supplant national welfare systems, including technical education and job training programs designed to increase the productivity of the work force, and thereby overcome structural encumbrances to economic growth.

Income redistribution, both at national and regional levels, is implicit in economic mutualism. This is not meant to suggest that the economically successful would be deprived of the fruits of their labor or that postmodern societies are likely to evolve toward some classless profile. Ineradicable human differences in abilities, skills, and effort preclude such a social order. Nor can one expect to see living standards in Bangladesh or Bulgaria approach those in Singapore or Sweden any time soon, if ever. But the economic distance between classes and between states may not be valued as a sign of intrinsic worth, as has been the case in the past. The willingness of the advantaged to share some portion of their income with the disadvantaged—in the form of debt relief, at the very least—will in all probability be motivated by a more realistic sense of self-interest in the future. Societal awareness of the limitations of progress is likely to impel a greater appreciation of social conservation on the part of people who see their interests and those of the entire community as being interrelated. As Prime Minister Poul Nyrup Rasmussen of Denmark put it, in an appeal to European governments to increase their assistance to the less fortunate, "If you don't help the Third World, if you don't help North African, if you don't help eastern and central Europe with a little part of your welfare, then you will have these poor people in our society." [30]

SOCIAL INCLUSIVITY

Mutualism implies a sensitivity on the part of political elites and the well-to-do to the socially alienated and disinherited, whose suppressed rage stirs the pot of social violence. In addition to reducing economic inequities, mutualism would also enhance the social mobility of lower-income groups, thereby creating more inclusivist societies. According to this logic, social insiders will need to give outsiders—immigrants as well as the native-born—a greater stake in social, political, and economic participation so that they too have some tangible attachment to the future. At the same time, racial and ethnic minorities will need to resolve their hostility toward their societies and overcome their defensive advocacy of caste virtues and social segregation. [31]

In the international context, advanced countries would likewise find it in their interests to bring states on the socioeconomic periphery of world affairs inside the institutional framework of mutualism. Analogous to the relationship between outsiders and insiders in the domestic context, advanced industrialized regions, along with international lending agencies, would accordingly need to provide assistance to developing countries to facilitate inclusion in regional associations. Such assistance might include the disbursement of developmental funds, the creation of technical education programs, debt–equity swaps, debt forgiveness, and access to the import markets of rich states.

In exchange, developing countries would be obliged to make concessions to the developed world. Now that the Nuclear Nonproliferation Treaty has become a permanent international fixture, Third World states should abandon costly military programs that threaten to proliferate nuclear and other weapons of mass destruction, as some have already done. Although progress in this area will depend on the willingness of the nuclear powers to agree to a comprehensive test ban, those states that do not possess nuclear weapons or weapons-making capabilities should be discouraged from acquiring them, as the nonproliferation treaty stipulates, either through political suasion or, if necessary, economic and even military coercion on the part of the larger international community. Those states that possess nuclear weapons should be encouraged to dispose of them, or, at least, to cap their arsenals through a combination of military, social, and economic incentives.

At the military level, such a framework of understanding would necessarily require the United States and Russia to reduce their arsenals to levels below the 3,500 weapons that START II allows them to retain, with the understanding that France, Britain, and, though far more problematically, China would make proportionate cuts. Were this to occur, it would improve the chances that Israel, India, and Pakistan, and, in time, possibly even North Korea, Libya, and Iraq, would cease to develop nuclear, chemical, and bacteriological weapons, as part of broad-based regional understandings tied to developmental aid and economic assistance from the industrially advanced states.

On the assumption that a nuclear-free world will evolve only if the concept of nuclear deterrence is deprived of its meaning, hence, social utility, arms reductions talks stand a better chance of success at the regional level, where interdependence is more likely to foster the kind of cooperative, inclusivist relationships that would redress competitive tensions. Optimally, regional economic cooperation would reinforce social and political collaboration among independent states, thereby lessening the suspicions that have heretofore invited the spiraling militarization of foreign affairs. The cessation of the nuclear programs in South Africa, Argentina, and Brazil are illustrative in this regard. At some point, similar trade-offs could be undertaken to control the transfer of sophisticated conventional weaponry, including intra–Third World sales.[32]

Similar regional agreements could be established to alleviate the spread of infectious diseases and other effects of poverty and to preserve the global environment. Social pressures to feed growing numbers of people will intensify the exhaustion of croplands and water tables, the depletion of which will force the starving masses to pillage the land and to migrate to neighboring countries barely able to minister to the needs of their own people, thereby exacerbating ethnic, religious, and tribal tensions. Even if population growth were to decline to replacement levels, the huge number of young people in developing countries under the age of 25 would preclude a global equilibrium for some time to come.[33]

Technological innovation and conservation measures are not likely to arrest the degradation of the environment. At some point, rich and poor alike will be forced to take action to ensure their own survival and to safeguard the prospects of future generations. Environmental mutualism might take the form of a collective body composed of representatives from the developed and developing worlds that would devise strategies to confront the challenge of population and pollution in a program of shared obligations and shared rewards. Developmental aid, financed through regional assistance banks and multinational organizations such as the IMF and the World Bank, could be provided to Third World states in exchange for programs to protect tropical forests, lessen the use of fertilizers, or restrict the conversion of arable land to nonfarm usage, or what some have called "debt-nature swaps." Such ventures would also help to resuscitate the global economies and, in so doing, reinforce political mechanisms of integration that would contribute to regional cooperation in the Third World.[34]

The most carefully conceived environmental policies will founder, however, if a majority of the world is functioning at a subsistence level. As the flow of refugees and asylees illustrates, the social, economic, and military costs of ignoring the world's poor are unmistakably mounting, and they will have to be paid in one way or another. Government outlays for developmental assistance amounted to a niggardly 0.33 percent of GDP for the OECD states in 1992 and even less in 1993 and 1994, or half the target set by the United Nations. At the World Summit for Social Development, which convened in Copenhagen in March 1995, the advanced, industrialized states pledged to earmark 0.7 percent of GDP for foreign aid. Although only Sweden, Denmark, Norway, and Holland currently meet this target, self-interest is likely to prod other rich states to accelerate the flow of aid in the future. During the Cold War, the ideological competition for the mantle of progress determined the flow of aid to the Third World. Aid, like foreign policy, was defined in zero-sum terms. In the future, the necessity of social cooperation in an interdependent world order will be the ideological basis for the dispensation of aid, which is more likely to be viewed as an investment in a common undertaking rather than as an eleemosynary gesture.[35]

The corrosive effects of excluding two-thirds of the world from the benefits of modernity are self-evident. In an interdependent world, not even the rich will be able to escape the political, economic, and military consequences of the despairing rage that is the product of alienation. Ideally, priorities would be assigned to programs that address the root causes of international instability and that promote the immediate interests of the community as a whole. In addition to its developmental assistance to poor countries, the world's rich would accordingly also need to share the costs of the immunization of infants, family planning, and the prevention of AIDS.

CULTURAL CONSONANCE

Social and economic integration will not succeed, however, without the requisite understanding of different cultures. Immemorial customs that relate social utility to procreation, for example, or that discriminate against women even in the dissemination of medical care pose a formidable challenge to family planning. Cultural mores are similarly likely to inhibit the success of AIDS prevention in macho societies or ecological awareness among peoples who have traditionally relied on the magical properties of nature to feed, clothe, and shelter them. In the same way, the survival of hatreds and injustices from some murky past weigh against the evolution of peace among peoples in Northern Ireland, former Yugoslavia, the Middle East, and Africa.

Nevertheless, in spite of the tumult of change that presently envelops the world, there are coruscations of hope that even the most adamantine cultural impediments to cooperation may lose their rigidity. In the first instance, the movement of peoples, ideas, and techniques is contributing to the intermixing of different cultures.[36] Societies are becoming cultural microcosms of the world. Just as East Europeans gradually acculturate themselves to democracy and other Western institutions, they are simultaneously adding to the cultural diversification of the West. The cross-border transfer of peoples and commerce are similarly reducing cultural barriers between Asia and the West. European fashions and cuisine are as conspicuous in Japan as in the United States, and they are becoming more evident in other Asian societies. By the same token, Asian cultures—from popular interest in the martial arts to interior design and business technique—is influencing Western attitudes.

In parts of the Islamic world, Asia, and Latin America, westernization is reflected, *inter alia*, in the greater independence women are exercising in defiance of societal customs and religious taboos. At the same time, the global migration of peoples from the Middle East and Africa is altering the cultural landscape in Europe, the United States, and Latin America, as the proliferation of mosques, Near Eastern grocery stores and restaurants, and Arab-language television programming attest. In an integrated international economy, it is becoming difficult to define the nationality of a corporation headquartered in one country with the majority of its employees, research and development, and manufacturing elsewhere. In the evolving peripatetic character of the global culture, it will become no less difficult to answer the question, who is us?[37]

Many receiving societies, of course, have found the mass transfer of strange peoples and customs to be culturally uncongenial. Rather than embracing newcomers, host societies, not for the first time, are erecting barriers against the outside world to stave off the perceived threat to their cultural integrity. In many cases, this has taken the form of immigration restrictions. In others, more subtle protective measures have been taken. In the Middle East and North Africa, as Bernard Lewis has pointed out, Islamic fundamentalism is largely a defensive reaction against the cultural seduction of the West. For the majority of the Puerto Rican public that opposed American statehood, the ballot was the means to resist the feared loss of cultural identity. In an interdependent world, however, societies will not be able to resist the penetration of foreign cultures indefinitely. But the recognition that the costs of retreating from the world will exceed the benefits will only become meaningful if societies acknowledge that their creative potential is inseparable from that of the international community as a whole.[38]

Cultural syncretism requires the tolerance of diversity. Toleration of the beliefs and values of other peoples implies a renunciation of the cultural imperialism exercised by Europe, pre–World War II Japan, and, more recently, the United States in the name of civilization, moral duty, or human rights. It also abjures the cultural marginalization of subject peoples such as we are experiencing in India, Africa, and in Russia's transparent efforts to reimpose its cultural dominance over the agglomeration of states in the Commonwealth of Independent States. Host societies that persist in marginalizing linguistic and religious outsiders are likely to do so at the cost of their social and political cohesion. Deprived of their proportionate share of influence, wealth, and power, and lacking the legal, political, or military protection from arbitrary actions on the part of dominant groups or states, outsiders will eventually demand their own political legitimacy, whatever the cost. The formation of multicultural societies, like the emergence of regional associations from NAFTA to the CIS, can only be sustained if they allow for a more equitable distribution of influence, wealth, and power among their constituent parts and if the dominant groups or states are subject to collective rules and obligations that preclude them from acting arbitrarily.[39]

Cultural tolerance also rejects the imperialism of ideas. The force-feeding of American values, frequently as a condition of economic assistance, may be viewed in the United States as a moral obligation to spread democracy's word to the multitudes. No matter that the overthrow of Chilean president Salvador Allende, the extralegal efforts to oust the Sandinistas in Nicaragua, or the indulgence of political violence in pre-Khomeini Iran or present-day Egypt have tarnished the incorruptibility of American virtue, the public face of the United States is invariably that of democracy's defender. This is as much for America's image of itself as it is for the world's image of America. Elsewhere, however, such policies as the Reagan–Bush refusal to provide family planning assistance to the Third World or the Clinton administration's threat to hold trade relations with China hostage to human rights are judged as arrogant intrusions on the cultural space of other peoples.[40]

The American preoccupation with its moral exceptionalism aside—which seems to be intensifying at the same time the global political dominance of the United States is receding—it is dubious that the entire world is destined to embrace liberal-democracy. Whatever new political forms economic reform is creating in East Asia, liberal-democracy Western-style is not likely to figure prominently among them. By and large, East Asian societies are far more likely to conflate market economics with Confucian authoritarianism. In the future, China, for example, will probably look like Singapore. In the Middle East, democracy will be circumscribed by the laws of sharia and the power of oligarchies and autocrats. In Africa, the collectivist, consensual rule of village elders rather than adversarial forms of government stands the best chance of replacing monoparties and military strong men. In Latin America, too, where Peru's Alberto Fujimori, Venezuela's Rafael Caldera, and Argentina's Carlos Menem have altered the election rules so they could succeed themselves, democracy will probably be a hybrid of liberalism and statism.[41]

Besides, for many states, the United States is no longer a model society, "no longer an island of the blessed—neither in political nor economic terms," as a *Die Zeit* editorial bluntly put it. Growing economic stratification, social decay, and rampant crime have clouded the American dream. Middle-class Americans, sociologist Daniel Bell has pointed out, now face the disheartening prospect that they cannot promise their children a better life, as they and generations before them had come to expect as their birth right. Worse yet, the integrity of the legal system has been increasingly circumvented by Wall Street, elected officials (including presidents), and the public at large, which, in the highly publicized trial of the young thugs accused of beating senseless an innocent truck driver during the Los Angeles riots of 1992, abdicated their respect for the law and their allegiance to standards of fairness and justice.[42]

Perhaps the most insidious form of cultural imperialism, however, is that imposed by the owners of information. Thanks to satellite feeds and computerized data banks, the electronic media, largely but not totally controlled by the United States, manufacture and disseminate information in every nook and cranny of the world. Technology threatens to homogenize culturally distinct societies. So-called rap music now blares in Japan and Costa Rica as deafeningly as it does in the United States. Worse still, some observers worry that "the threat to independence in the late twentieth century from the new electronics could be greater than was colonialism itself." Paradoxically, however, the information technocracy is also subtly dispensing reality to people in ways that reinforce cultural stereotypes and social divisions. The televised coverage of the fighting in Bosnia, for example, has unquestionably inflamed anti-Western sentiment in the Islamic world, and it could contribute to social turmoil in countries such as Egypt that retain close ties with Washington and European Western capitals. The accumulation of knowledge could create new centers of power. Indeed, knowledge is likely to be the major stake in future international competition. Some predict that states, influenced by corporations and other subnational actors, may even go to war over its acquisition.[43]

Nonetheless, given the growing political assertiveness in the world, one may question whether the imperialism of ideas will be any more likely to ensure control over dependent peoples than state imperialism was. "History," Said reminds us, "also teaches us that domination breeds resistance." This is the moral lesson of the democratic revolutions of 1989–90 and the collapse of the Soviet imperium. In the end, cultural imperialism, like the exaltation of the state, is likely to sow the seeds of its own destruction. Suppressed peoples eventually see the self-serving explanations that justify cultural imperialism for the fictions they are; and they set out on their own paths to the future. Because of education, travel, and the access to information that have politicized publics around the world, such assertions of cultural autonomy, whether expressed peacefully or violently, are likely to occur more frequently in the future than they have in the past. One can only hope that the spread of political anarchy in the world will have a sobering effect on industrially advanced, technocratic societies, and that it may encourage greater toleration of other peoples and their traditions and eventually the discovery of the rich and variegated cultural tableau of which we are all a part.[44]

For cultural tolerance to take root and support the development of regional social and economic integration, the international community will have to find ways to contain the spread of political anarchy. In the frothy days of hope and harmony that followed the fall of communism, world opinion had almost uniformly rallied around the United Nations as the guardian of international stability and order. After more than four decades of Cold War slumber, an aroused and energized United Nations had undeniably advanced the cause of peace in Angola, Namibia, El Salvador, the Western Sahara, and it provided the legitimizing framework for the expulsion of Iraqi forces from Kuwait. Since then, however, the UN has been less successful in resolving the fratricidal conflicts in former Yugoslavia, Somalia, Rwanda, and Tajikistan that have become the order of the day. This is attributable in part to the lack of resources and manpower at its disposal—including from key donor nations such as the United States—to respond effectively to the mounting post–Cold War crises the world faces (15 peacekeeping missions were in train at the beginning of 1995) and the spiraling cost of refugee assistance, which more than doubled between 1990 and 1993. But there are also structural impediments that in the future will almost assuredly circumscribe the ability of the UN or any other universal actor to serve as a peacemaking rather than purely peacekeeping organization.[45]

In the first instance, as the increasing demand for diminishing resources makes all too clear, the sheer number of civil and international conflicts are bound to exceed the size of the UN's intervention forces. Were the problem of ensuring world security reducible to increased forces and contributions, the situation might be rectifiable. But it is complicated by the lack of shared perceptions of danger, which, in turn, begs the question of national interests. It is fanciful to believe, for example, that states in Asia or Latin America will be importuned to intervene in Bosnia, when those nations closest to the conflict and thus most likely to be affected by it have, until recently, been reluctant to do so. Not only does the absence of shared interests inhibit member states from supplying the necessary resources to perform peacekeeping missions, it also precludes shared objectives. The alternative, as we have witnessed in Somalia, is to conceal conflicts of interest in ill-defined aims that only serve to undermine the idea of collective or consensual security. Despite the paladin-like appeals for a global security organization, the reality is that states will continue to follow the dictates of national interest. In contrast to the past, however, the national interest may be defined more broadly in the future to encompass shared regional goals and aspirations.[46]

No doubt, the sovereignty-enhancing propensity to retain control over one's national security and the incipient sovereignty-diminishing trend toward international interdependence will be problematic. The transition from exclusivist state-based authority structures to the transnationalism of the postmodern epoch of mutualism will be just as unstable as was the transformation from the cosmopolitan-feudal authority of antiquity to the territoriality of the modern epoch. For the foreseeable future, the combination of national rediscovery and the asymmetries in the distribution of power and wealth are bound to foment challenges to world order. Just how conflictual the passage from progress to mutualism will be is likely to be a function of three concurrent conditions: the capability of revisionist states to wage war; the tolerance, generosity, and security vigilance of rich states and influential institutions; and the predisposition of poor states to evaluate their interests in inclusivist rather than exclusivist terms.

As long as the world's wealth, power, and status are disproportionately distributed, warfare will be an ineradicable part of the human condition. Nevertheless, the lethality, if not the frequency, of violence can be contained. As stated above, so long as the possibility that nuclear weapons will never be used is greater than zero, every effort must be made to ensure that undeclared as well as acknowledged nuclear states reduce their arsenals. Prohibitions on the production of plutonium and other fissile materials and on nuclear testing and adherence to the various nonproliferation regimes would further limit the diffusion of weapons of mass destruction or the technologies that permit states to develop such weapons.

Although it will be harder to constrain the flows of conventional weaponry, much of which can be justified on grounds of self-defense, intra- and interregional controls need to be established that will proscribe the introduction of sophisticated and inherently destabilizing weapons into areas of conflict. Happily, the global transfer of conventional arms has dramatically declined since the end of the U.S.–Soviet rivalry. Assuming that this trend continues and that poor as well as rich states recognize that their interests are best served by cooperative inclusion rather than competitive exclusion, the international regulation of conventional as well as nuclear arms may not be a hopeless dream.[47]

It is unimaginable that Third World states would accede to restrictions on their freedom of action without some compensation from the industrialized world. Rich states would not only face the prospect of a dwindling arms market and restrictions on their participation in it, they would also somehow have to redress the disparities of wealth that result from structural inequities in the international economic system. At the very least, this would probably entail opening their markets to Third World goods. All the market-reforming efforts of developing countries will be forever in vain unless they can generate export earnings to pay down debt, sustain social services, and create jobs.

International lending institutions, including regional development banks, would also have to be more tolerant of deviations from economic austerity on the part of governments wrestling with the social effects of market reform and more hesitant to mete out penalties such as the withholding of credits or financial aid that sap the spirit of reform. The increased incidence of rescheduling of interest payments, debt-equity (or debt-nature or debt-arms proliferation) swaps, and debt forgiveness on the part of donor institutions and countries would further contribute to economic modernization.

The gradual integration of developing countries in the world trading system also redounds to the benefit of the industrialized world. Third World job creation is bound to increase the demand for imports. Over time, the short-term costs incurred by the advanced states would in all likelihood be offset by the creation of value-added jobs and the economic benefits of environmental conservation. Furthermore, the developing world would be obliged to share the burden of modernization. Poor states would have to overcome or, at least, sublimate, the tendency toward retributive violence unleashed by the liberating sense of autonomy and self-determination.

Third World publics will not be able to overcome their rage, however, unless they first understand the unforgiving consequences of refusing to participate in the social and economic processes of the international community. In the increasingly competitive international economic order that lies ahead, poor states that want to survive will have little alternative but to pursue policies that promote economic growth and market-extending cooperation. In this eventuality, resources that might otherwise be invested in military competition would be channeled in economic, educational, and ecological endeavors designed to make poorer regions of the world more attractive to foreign investment.

This is the rationale underlying the economic linkages of Mercosur or AFTA, both of which have been inspired by the developed world's efforts toward integration. Indeed, just as the West previously served as the developing world's model for the formation of the nation-state, it is now becoming the exemplar of regional integration. In the future, similar associations may evolve in southern Africa, where small states such as Lesotho, Botswana, and Namibia are bound to intensify their already strong ties to the Republic of South Africa. The burgeoning Mexican economy is likely to be the polestar of economic integration in Central America, as are China in Taiwan, Hong Kong, and parts of Southeast Asia and Russia in the Caucasus and Central Asia.

As the stakes of regional social and economic integration rise, the protection of common interests will assume increasing importance. Disputes between states or, worse, actions that threaten to undermine cooperation are likely to engage the political interests of the whole community. Assuming that the fiction of a global policeman is allowed to fade, and that NATO's post–Cold War immobility, of which former Yugoslavia is a casualty, finally induces Western Europe and the United States to overcome their *dialogue des sourds* and acknowledge that it is European stability, not NATO, that needs to be preserved, attention may begin to focus on the creation of regional and subregional security associations.[48]

The model for such associations is not the gossamer Partnership for Peace (PFP) initiative NATO has floated before the impressionable East European states, but rather the moribund Visegrad declaration of economic, political, and, implicitly, security integration signed by Hungary the (then) Czech and Slovak Federal Republic, and Poland in the spring of 1991.[49] The consultative approach of the Visegrad states laid the basis for a more extensive arrangement in the future that would affirm the inviolability of borders, institutionalize military arrangements, and set force sizing and other conditions for mutual security. Similar groupings could be formed in the transalpine area (Hungary, Austria, Slovenia and, once the internecine struggle in former Yugoslavia ends, Croatia), the Baltic region, and, in the distant future, conceivably even the Balkans. In time, Ukraine, Belarus, Moldova, and Russia too might become affiliated with one or more association that could establish linkages with the Western European Union.

Unlike the pre–World War II alliances in Eastern Europe that France and Britain encouraged to contain Germany, these localized associations would be seen as spokes in an expanding wheel, the integration of which would be steadied in its formative stages by NATO, or, more accurately, the United States. Each association would accordingly be joined by at least one member of the Western European Union or EU. Germany, for example, would be a natural partner in the East Central European and, along with the Scandinavian states, the Baltic associations. Italy would be a logical addition to a transalpine association and, joined by France, to a Balkan grouping that might also include Greece and Turkey.

The inclusion of rich West European states would also provide political direction and, even more important, instill hope in the democratizing states to the East that their economic sacrifice and political restraint would eventually lead to their integration in the EU. In due course, regional security responsibility would devolve from NATO to a European Security Union. To allay the anxiety of abandonment that its diminished presence would probably arouse, the United States might find it judicious to leave prepositioned equipment in Europe, maintain adequate air- and sea-lift capability, and participate in the discussions of the North Atlantic Council–equivalent of the European Security Union.

Thus far, the same fear of American military withdrawal has confined the security dialogue in the Asia–Pacific region to little more than a *beau geste* designed to shore up the string of bilateral alliances with the United States. But here, too, in the absence of a single power that threatened to dominate the region or the outbreak of warfare on the Korean peninsula or the Indian subcontinent that invited the possible use of nuclear weapons, Asians may also be forced to police local disruptions of the peace and thus to prepare for the asianization of security arrangements. Although geography and the absence of a preexisting security structure such as NATO will complicate the process, the formation of loose regional associations in both Northeast and Southeast Asia could be formed while the comforting presence of the United States is still visible and before other states act to fill the perceived vacuum.[50]

In Northeast Asia, persisting tensions between North and South Korea, the unresolved relationship between China and Taiwan, and other issues continue to hamper security coordination. Nonetheless, there are glimmers of cooperation. Anxiety about the possibility of conflict on the Korean peninsula has contributed to closer political coordination between Seoul and Tokyo. Japan and South Korea are sharing the cost of providing North Korea new civilian reactors as part of the agreement to defuse nuclear tensions on the peninsula. In addition, bilateral military talks that could become the basis of an integrated network of discussions on force levels, arms proliferation, and other issues have been initiated by Japan and China and China and Russia. Assuming that North Korea does not renege on its agreement with the United States to terminate the production of plutonium, the passing of Kim il-Sung could be the prelude to the eventual reunification of the Korean peninsula.

Political discussions within ASEAN are already producing buds of security cooperation in Southeast Asia. Intelligence is being shared, and joint military exercises are now taking place. Moreover, the ASEAN Post-Ministerial Conference (PMC)—an annual gathering of foreign ministers from Europe as well as from the Asia–Pacific area—appears to be taking the first steps toward security cooperation. In July 1994 representatives of this group, joined by Russia and Vietnam, among other countries, agreed to form the ASEAN Regional Forum (ARF) at their annual meeting in Bangkok. Although the new multilateral body has yet to define an agenda, its signatories anticipate that it will increase the prospects of cooperation on the exchange of military information and arms transfers and on the prevention of regional conflicts. In this or in some other security structure, working groups could also be set up to defuse tensions over potentially troublesome territorial issues such as sovereignty over the Spratly Islands, a subject that was addressed in Bangkok, as well as to strengthen cooperation on joint military exercises, arms procurement, and the harmonization of political, economic, and security ties between Southeast and Northeast Asia.[51]

In due course, one might anticipate the creation of joint fora on Northeast and Southeast Asian defense matters, perhaps in the form of security wings in APEC and ASEAN, that could become the chrysalis of a more formalized security association. Such security associations would further attract investment capital from rich states within and without the area that would reinforce the flow of financial resources and technology to joint economic, ecological, and social projects in underdeveloped areas such as North Korea, China, Vietnam, and the Russian Far East. As in Europe, the United States could help to guide and reinforce the process of security integration. America's strategic deterrent and conventional capability to project power in the region would be necessary for at least the foreseeable future to ensure the Asian and Pacific states of its continuing commitment to their security as they establish new mechanisms of cooperation.[52]

In other regions of the world, a congeries of economic, political, ethnic, and religious obstacles still impede the development of regional peace, leave aside a security dialogue. At the same time, NAFTA, the renewed Arab–Israeli talks, and the end of apartheid are suggestive of the possibilities for regional cooperation and, in time, political-security collaboration as well.

NAFTA promises to be a politically stabilizing force for change in two respects. First, it offers a powerful stimulus for other states in the region to adopt peaceful, inclusivist approaches to social and economic reform, as Mercosur and other subregional structures demonstrate. In addition, regional cooperation will further mitigate against political polarization between classes within nation-states and between states within the region, which will reinforce political and economic integration. In addition to reducing military tensions, Brazil's and Argentina's decisions to scrap their nuclear arms programs have also permitted more productive use of financial and human resources, accelerated the pace of modernization, and buttressed the efforts to integrate the economies of the Southern Cone. Assuming the development of localized political, economic, and security associations in the Andean area, Central America, and in the Caribbean, the Organization of American States might some day emerge as the regional peacekeeping institution that its architects envisioned.[53]

It is doubtful that the Organization of Arab States, which, by definition, excludes Israel, Iran, and Turkey, could play such a role in the Middle East. Arab unity has been more conspicuous by its absence. Some cooperative frameworks do exist, however. Although it faces more than a few obstacles, the Gulf Cooperation Council that nominally underwrites the security of the Gulf States could become the basis of a broader peacekeeping structure. To be sure, its chances would be much improved if Iraq and Iran were to direct their energies toward economic cooperation rather than political and military confrontation and if Egypt and Saudi Arabia could temper their competition for leadership.

Recently signed Middle East peace accords and the promising prospect of a land-for-peace deal between Israel and Syria could also act as a catalyst for mutual cooperation in the Levant and elsewhere in the region, much as NAFTA is likely to do in Latin America. Doubtless prompted by the landmark agreement in 1993 between Israel and the PLO that sanctioned Palestinian self-rule in parts of the West Bank and the Gaza Strip, Jordan ended its state of belligerency with Israel in July 1994. Two months later, Morocco established diplomatic relations with the Jewish state. Shortly thereafter Israel and its Arab neighbors met at a summit in Casablanca to discuss economic cooperation on a range of issues from trade and water resources to the creation of a regional development bank. Although Israel and the PLO have not yet reached agreement on Palestinian self-rule and substantively little has resulted from the Casablanca summit, the willingness to address contentious political and economic issues is nonetheless a hopeful sign that countries in the region might find it in their common economic interest to convert mutual antagonism into mutual cooperation.[54]

At some point, one could further envision an interlocking set of social, economic, and environmental arrangements between Egypt and Saudi Arabia and the other Gulf States and between the Fertile Crescent and Turkey. Of course, none of these linkages would automatically dispel historic prejudices and enmities; Syria, the crumbling Arab boycott against Israel aside, remains opposed to regional economic arrangements. But war-weariness and the exigencies of economic competition will probably loosen even these bonds of mistrust and, in time, facilitate the deflection of longstanding differences in informal security agreements that reinforce mutually beneficial enterprise.[55]

Given their low levels of economic development, the states of Africa, the Organization of African Unity notwithstanding, are even less likely to develop a regional security structure in the foreseeable future. Until now the intranational rather than international nature of conflict in Africa has provided little incentive for a multilateral security dialogue. Given the growing cross-border movement of peoples, however, tribal warfare may spill across national boundaries—as could soon happen in Rwanda, Burundi, Tanzania, and Zaire, or in Uganda, which has become entangled in Sudan's civil war—and galvanize such a dialogue, just as cross-border incursions from South Africa and Angola into Namibia ultimately led to a multinational security framework.[56]

There are also pressing economic considerations. Tribal violence has been kindled by the parlous economic conditions that afflict most Africans; these, in turn, have been exacerbated by the end of the Cold War and the liquidation of foreign aid from the United States and the former Soviet Union. In the same way that desperate economic realities have planted the seed of regional cooperation in other parts of the developing world, however, it is not unimaginable that they will also compel the formation of localized associations in Africa, including the establishment of some form of security cooperation to safeguard common interests. The best bets are localized security associations revolving around large, resource-endowed states such as Kenya, Nigeria, Zaire, and South Africa, which would emulate the hub-and-scope concept in Europe and Asia.

THE LAGGARD AND THE LAWLESS

Not all states, of course, will be satisfied with their share of international wealth and influence. Economically declining nations might opt for a military reversal of their fading fortunes. Even prospering countries might conceivably quarrel over territorial or economic interests or sur-render to some irrational impulse to aggrandize themselves, the com-plaisant belief that democracies do not make war notwithstanding. As studies show, however, industrialized and newly industrializing states tend to resist belligerent actions, not because they are inherently peace-ful, but because they reckon such behavior will jeopardize their national interests.[57] In short, the ideology of mutualism will only be meaningful if it leads to material improvements in people's lives. Stated differently, the diminution of national sovereignty must be recouped in the enhanced wealth and status that derive from shared interests.

For those developing countries on the international periphery of wealth and power whose expectations of eventual social and economic inclusion are rising, the temptation to lash out against the international system may be suppressed. For others, the expectation and reality of so-cial inclusion will be dangerously incompatible. Despite the aid of the advanced economies and international lending institutions, some devel-oping states will, for varying reasons, fail to modernize as quickly as others. For all the assistance it has received from the United States, Eu-rope, and the oil-rich Arab states, Egypt, for example, has not achieved a sufficient level of productivity to sustain its nearly 60 million people, one third of whom earn less than $25 per month.[58]

Other poor states less generously subsidized by international bene-factors face a still bleaker future. Non-oil- producing states such as Yemen and Jordan, large parts of Central America and the Caribbean and South Asia, and most of sub-Saharan Africa are rapidly forming an internationally alienated underclass analogous to the indigent that crowd the inner cities of the United States. Nation-states are falling prey to the same hopelessness and violence that afflicts the urban poor, and for many of the same reasons: unchecked population growth, for one, which perpetuates the cycle of poverty and despair; and the constant bar-rage of information spewed out by the communications media, for an-other, which heightens the awareness of social and economic inequality and thus magnifies the resentment of poor states toward the interna-tional community.

For the most part, the socially alienated will vent their rage on those around them, including ethnic or tribal interlopers who offer convenient scapegoats for their plight. In some instances, international outsiders may mobilize their aggression and direct it against other states that they, justifiably or unjustifiably, hold accountable for their condition. Iraq's invasion of Kuwait in the summer of 1990, for example, did not result solely from Saddam Hussein's exploitation of disputed territorial claims. It also reflected the tensions within the Arab world between the rich Gulf sheikdoms and, its rich natural endowments aside, poorer states like Iraq, whose decade-long war against Iran, in Saddam's view, protected rich oligarchies from the expansion of Shiite radicalism.

In some parts of the world—in Latin America, Europe, Asia—existing, evolving, or emerging security structures offer the prospect of containing and, if necessary, militarily neutralizing threats to their mutual well-being. Elsewhere, however, regional security organizations may be incapable of responding to military challenges without help from the larger international community. One only needs to remember the Gulf Cooperation Council's flaccid response to Iraqi expansionism, which not only threatened the community's vital interests but Kuwait's survival.

In an interdependent world order, uncontained instability in one region will inevitably affect the economic, political, and social well-being of states in other regions, particularly if its prolongation poses serious harm to their vital interests, as was the case with Iraq's potential domination of world oil supplies. As envisioned in the concept of mutualism, such transgressions against the interests of the international community would prompt multinational reactions of the type, if not the character, of the coalition against Iraq. To be sure, the universalistic, quasi-religious nature of that international crusade to exorcise the perceived defiler of post–Cold War peace and harmony is not likely to be replicated. Although the United Nations will continue to play a useful role in peacekeeping, the responsibility for peacemaking is likely to devolve to a de facto international security directorate composed of representatives from the five major regions of the world.

Such a directorate might number as many as ten countries. The United States, along with one Latin American country serving on an alternating basis, could represent the Americas. The rotating president of the EU or European Security Union and Russia could do the same for Europe. Japan, China, and probably India could be Asia's proxies. The directorate's members from the Middle East and Africa might include Israel and a rotating Muslim state and, say, Nigeria and South Africa. Whatever the composition at any time, the security directorate would necessarily require participation from every region. Each region would assume the responsibility for maintaining its own security, that is, for balancing local power relationships. If that proves impossible, it would likewise be incumbent on regional actors to initiate the formation of international coalitions, possibly including countries from outside the region whose interests may be directly affected by rogue state behavior.

Not all deviant behavior will threaten the integrity of regional stability. As is the case today in Bosnia, Somalia, and Haiti, most future conflicts are likely to stem from civil strife. They will occur with greatest frequency in the poorest areas of the world. One can accordingly expect the incidence of civil disorder to be higher in Africa, South Asia, Central America and the Caribbean, and in the Fertile Crescent of the Middle East. Moreover, as the unrest in Somalia, Rwanda, and, until the United States militarily intervened at the nominal behest of the world community, Haiti makes all too clear, efforts of the United Nations and other international agencies to help the parties to the conflict resolve their differences may be of little avail in those cases where peoples are incapable of governing themselves.

At the same time, in an age of electronic communication that instantly internationalizes human suffering, national governments can no longer treat civil wars and other internecine quarrels in remote corners of the world with the benign neglect that was commonplace in the epoch of progress. For one thing, televised images of human carnage appeal to a sense of compassion that forbids indifference. For another, the political and economic costs of allowing such chaos to continue—as reflected in the rising population of refugees and the possible spread of civil warfare beyond national borders—are rapidly becoming intolerable to the international community.

In the interests of human decency as well as international stability, the day is consequently drawing near when the international community will be forced to establish some form of political trusteeship over states that cannot peacefully manage their own affairs. De facto, such intervention will be a form of recolonization, whatever other euphemistic lubricant one chooses to soothe its application. In contrast to the exploitative nature of nineteenth-century imperialism, however, which shackled peoples to dubious virtue, the envisioned trusteeships need not be inhumane—certainly no less humane than the custodial care exercised by municipalities that remove from society those people who violate its norms. Moreover, they need not be either elitist or permanent. Regional states, including those from the Third World, could be called upon to administer trusteeships, and only until such time that indigenous peoples can manage their own affairs.

Facing the Future

The advent of mutualism in international affairs is objectively discernible in the trends of historical change. Whether mutualism defines the way the human community interacts, however, also depends on the subjective judgments societies make about the future. The future is neither historically determined nor deducible from rationalistic models. It is neither the accumulated pasts that illuminate the present nor the incandescent present that obscures the past. The future is the fusion of past and present in the context of our expectations and aspirations. There is no unequivocally right way to make sense of the world, no preordained path out of the confusing thicket of the present. The future is what we choose it to be, not directly, in the clairvoyant realization of what lies ahead, but indirectly, in the paths we take into the unknown.

CHANGE AND CHOICE

To be sure, for many in the developing world who live at subsistence levels or worse, the options are few. The abjectly poor, like the vast stretches of humanity before the epoch of progress, will invest their energies in sheer survival. This, of course, they can do cooperatively or competitively. Modernizing societies like those that have emerged from the former Soviet empire are approaching the future cautiously, lest some misstep destroy their fragile networks of social security. Even the rich and powerful are resisting the effects of change. This is apparent in Japan, where farmers, businessmen, and bureaucrats seek to protect their institutional fiefdoms against the encroachments of political reformers and the broad public is loathe to accept a larger political-security role in the world. Judging from their opposition to the denationalizing implications of economic union and their pusillanimous dependence on the American military presence—all the while they question the future of NATO—Europeans, whatever they say to the contrary, are no less reluctant to make choices that disrupt ingrained institutional arrangements and practices.

For its part, the United States has responded contradictorily to international change, denying or defying reality, as it were. It spouts new world rhetoric, but it clings to old thinking about the world and its stewardship of it. Having judged the end of the Cold War as the validation of its historic mission, it sees little need to reevaluate its actions, much less question beliefs that others are only too eager to emulate. The democratizing/marketizing victory of that ideological struggle is the apotheosis of change. It is the universalization of progress embodied in the American experience. It is, in Arthur Schlesinger Jr.'s view, the realization that the ideals which impelled America's global intervention in World War II and beyond "[lie] at last within humanity's grasp." [1]

Given the violent upheaval in the world, however, it may be premature to take flight from the world on the wings of History's liberalizing spirit. Muddling through the perturbations of change may not be wiser, especially for those who have the most to lose. The savagery the world has witnessed in Bosnia and Rwanda are not isolated (or altogether unrelated) developments. They could be repeated, say, in Albania or Nigeria. In theory, states can remain aloof from conflicts that do not impinge directly on their interests. In practice, however, crises in one part of the world unavoidably affect the international community as a whole because of the human and economic dislocations they create.

As a result of the rapid dissemination of information, intra- and interstate tensions between rich and poor, or between insiders and outsiders, are more likely to spill across borders, as the spread of the Iranian revolution demonstrated. The proliferation of military technology increases the chances that local conflicts will expand into international crises in the future. Geographic and sociological factors have insulated the international community from the conflicts in Somalia and Haiti. The world may not be as lucky if nuclear-armed India or North Korea were to socially implode or if the festering hatreds in the Central Asian republics of the former Soviet Union were to foment hostilities between Turkey and Iran.

PERCEPTION AND REALITY

It is not only who we are, or who we think we are, that influences how we respond to change. It is also what we see. It is human nature to construe reality from appearances. The more vivid the image the clearer the presumed level of understanding. Modern telecommunications facilitates the process of appearance making. The repetition of the same imagery becomes the focal point of reality. It concentrates the mind to apprehend only what is in the glare of publicly acknowledged and accepted view. But focal clarity unavoidably obscures whatever is not unmistakably recognizable. It ignores the subtle shades of meaning that are not visible under its laser light. In the despondency of American decline, few perceived the approaching transformation of Japan Inc. Similarly, in the euphoria of communism's collapse, the socially disintegrative aspects of change were concealed from the mind's eye, until the slaughter in Bosnia, revived authoritarianism in Russia, and the nuclear scare in North Korea redirected the focus of attention.

Such events, and the horrors that await, are bound to influence the way we see the unfolding future, as the punditry of the new apocalypse illustrates.[2] The completion of the protracted Uruguay Round of the GATT talks has only temporarily cooled protectionist fever. Regional economic aggregations such as the European Union and NAFTA may create trading blocs that incite economic warfare. Influenced by the growing gap between haves and have nots, ethnic, tribal, religious, and racial hatreds can be expected to consume still more of humanity and nature in obeisance to some primordial duty.

Nor have we seen the end of the struggle for power in Russia, where governability is becoming hostage to ethnic warfare, economic decay, and political incoherence, or in China, where the transition from the revolutionary rule of the Old Guard to the generation of technocrats born after the "Long March" is just beginning. Economically desperate states in Central Asia and the Caucasus are slowly returning to the Commonwealth of Independent States and to the perceived security of Russian markets. Meanwhile, the political polarization of reformers and reactionaries and the recentralization of Russian authority over the territories in the "near abroad" are trampling the promise of liberalization. The specter of civil war looms. In China, political change has not kept pace with economic modernization. The devolution of economic decision making from Beijing to the provinces and the growing demand for political autonomy may likewise plunge China into civil war after Deng's death or lead to the reimposition of central control under some legitimizing Confucian–Leninist ideology. Efforts on the part of former finance minister Liu Zhongli to increase the flow of tax revenue from the periphery to the center have met considerable opposition from the poor provinces, which remain dependent on state-run enterprises, as well as the rich areas. The poor are pouring into cities, displacing urban workers and contributing to labor unrest in factories. In the countryside, banditry and violence are rising.[3]

Even more ominous, the prospect that nuclear arms will end up in the hands of international terrorists or psychotic Third World leaders with megalomaniacal ambitions will remain a disquieting uncertainty to humankind in the future. Despite signs of growing domestic dissatisfaction with Saddam Hussein and the religious oligarchy in Teheran, Iraq and Iran continue to pose threats to international peace and stability. Now that Pyongyang has agreed to cease the production of plutonium and to allow the International Atomic Energy Agency to inspect its reactor sites, the situation may be somewhat less worrisome in North Korea. But doubts persist; the combination of an erratic, if not irrational, leadership and the socially explosive effects of economic collapse could revive nuclear tensions.[4]

Not all is bleak, however. Outside the immediate and direct focus of social awareness are a host of other factors of which we are indirectly and implicitly cognizant but cannot yet articulate that provide a synthetic and intuitive composite of the reality we confront. Translucent in the shadows of the present is the future that we are unforeseeably creating. NAFTA, the European Union, and the incipient concertation of trade and investment policies in Asia is the future for increasing numbers of industrially and culturally diverse states that are building frameworks to consolidate markets, research and development planning, and communications networks. Economic integration, in turn, is contributing to the creation of a regional and subregional identification that will facilitate the formulation of common policies on technology-sharing, arms proliferation, and military security.

Even if the difficulties of achieving global trade liberalization hamper the success of the World Trade Organization, interregional economic interdependence would seem to preclude the possibility that the world would relapse into the autarkic behavior that led to the collapse of the international trading system in the 1930s. Indeed, the signs point in the opposite direction. The European Union is eager to improve trade with Asia, which already exceeds its transatlantic trade. China has expanded its trade with Mexico, Argentina, and other flourishing economies in Latin America. For their part, Latin American countries, especially the Southern Cone states that are economically integrating in imitation of the trend in North America and Europe, are eager to penetrate lucrative foreign markets, particularly those in East Asia. What is more likely to occur is a shift in the political gravity of trade liberalization from the center to the periphery, that is, from the global framework of negotiations to intra- and interregional trade agreements.[5]

To be sure, economic growth requires a peaceful international climate. Here, too, the subregional economic compacts that are springing up in Latin America and Southeast Asia are giving rise to a consumer-oriented middle class that, as it entrenches, will become less tolerant of authoritarianism. Communication, travel, and commerce are increasing cultural contact among peoples and, in the process, encouraging them to define sovereignty in broader regional rather than narrowly nationalistic terms. As a consequence of the breakdown of cultural stereotypes, "steps toward full [regional] integration now come much more naturally," Peruvian writer Hernando de Soto has observed. "All of a sudden, it's not that big a problem, gringos and Latinos getting together. Nor is it a problem to ignore Washington, as the Latin American countries are doing by establishing closer business relations with Cuba in defiance of the American trade embargo."[6]

Meanwhile, in South Africa, continued outbursts of violence between followers of the ANC, Inkatha, the Pan African Congress, and others and rising crime have not halted the efforts of President Nelson Mandela to establish a new framework of political cooperation between blacks and whites. Elsewhere in Africa, states like Ghana eagerly solicit the technical and economic assistance of newly industrialized Asian countries. And although there will be frequent slips between the lip and the cup, the "framework for peace" issued in December 1993 by Britain and Ireland and the subsequent cease-fire announced by the Irish Republican Army offer real hope that a quarter-century of violence has finally proven to be intolerably costly to Protestants and Catholics. There are glimmers of hope in the Middle East as well. Only the cynical would discount the continuing dialogue between Israelis and Palestinians. Interestingly, some Arabs seem to have concluded in the aftermath of the Gulf War that old rivalries and artificial amities will be insufficient to sustain social and economic cohesion in a world in which the United States and the former Soviet Union no longer define the rules of the game.[7]

Not surprisingly, given the embryonic condition of regional integration, states have yet to concert their efforts in the solution of planet-threatening issues such as nuclear proliferation. Economic cooperation could provide some incentive for denuclearization, as it did in Argentina and Brazil. In addition, the diminution of historic antagonisms between Israel and its Arab neighbors might make it possible eventually to dismantle nuclear arsenals in the Middle East, although the probable emergence of Iraq, Iran, and possibly still North Korea as nuclear states will greatly complicate the task. In some instances, defense guarantees on the part of the United States may be required, say, to cap the nuclear arms race between India and Pakistan. Without an initiative on the part of the acknowledged nuclear powers to bring massive international political and economic pressure on recalcitrant would-be proliferators, however, the issue is likely to remain moot.[8]

The prognosis for an improvement in other planet-threatening conditions is more encouraging, however. At the United Nations conference held in Cairo in September 1994, 180 countries approved a resolution to stabilize world population in 2050. Partly as a result of population pressures on family resources, partly because of the spread of education, developing countries have begun to take the initiative for family planning. On the basis of studies conducted in 44 countries throughout the developing world over the past two decades, the average number of children per woman has dropped dramatically from 6 in the mid-1960s-to-1970s—the high point of Western efforts to promote industrialization and family planning—to about 4 today. In Colombia, for example, the average number of children per woman has declined from 4.7 to 2.8 during this period; in Morocco from 5.8 to 4; and in Bangladesh from 6.1 to 5.5. This is a long way from the replacement level of 2.1 children per couple, but it is nonetheless ground for hope that the swelling world population, and its implications for migration, social instability, and thus international conflict, may slowly be coming under control.[9]

There is also a growing sensitivity to ecological issues in the international community. As is the case with family planning, countries that have until recently scoffed at the West's appeal for the conservation of nature as a subtle form of lingering imperialism have begun to reconsider the message. In some cases, the image of the rapacious West has helped to spur environmentalism. The movement in Latin America to save the rain forests, for instance, has been motivated in part by the desire to preserve the region's natural patrimony from the ravages of Western commercial exploitation.

In the industrializing countries of Asia, the environmental movement, like so much else, has followed the lead of Japan, whose impressive efforts to curb pollution may become the model for others in the region. Although Asia remains far less ecologically conscious than Europe or the United States, its fledgling green movement has begun to challenge the conventional wisdom that environmental degradation is worth the price of economic growth. Given the disparities of wealth between the world's advanced and developing societies, it would be foolhardy to expect a convergence of views on environmental policy in the near future. Still, the increasing global awareness of the interdependence between society and nature improves the prospect of devising collective responses in the future that virtually all states will find in their interest to support.[10]

NARCISSISM AND AFFILIATION

That seventeenth-century scrivener of moral maxims, the Duc de la Rochefoucauld once said, loosely paraphrased, that things were never quite as good or as bad as we imagined them to be. But they can be made better or worse, depending on the way in which we tend to our own garden. The changing world may not be a matter of our choosing, but what we do about it is. Today, to a degree far greater than any other time in history, humanity is in a position to chart its own future. The primacy of knowledge over matter has expanded our vistas of the world. Conformity to inveterate social traditions and deference to hierarchical political structures have atrophied in the process. In contrast to Rochefoucauld's time, we are now all part of the willing society. Witness the almost ubiquitous political turbulence that is transforming old patterns of behavior and the amoeba-like proliferation of new states and autonomous regions that represent the entelechies of peoples who have emerged from some prehistoric hibernation.

What the international landscape will look like after this revolutionary torrent of human will subsides will depend in large part on the interplay between self-interest and social attachment. The pathological excesses of the willing society are the ethnic state, beggar-thy-neighbor economic policies, and warlordism. We may witness the return of avenging angels of freedom in Russia or Romania, in Pakistan or Peru. They may reappear in Japan, where reformers battle an obstructionist bureaucracy, or in politically fractious Europe. The absence of community is the anomie, cynicism, and amorality that despoil the physical and social environment, the self-indulgence and narcissism.[11]

But we are no more condemned to consume ourselves in our depravity than we are to bask in our virtue. Just as progress freed knowledge from religious dogma, mutualism may yet liberate life from knowledge. One reason why we may not descend into anarchy and egoism is the recognition that such behavior will in the end be inimical to our interests. As already discussed, no state is sufficiently powerful to go its own way any longer, at least not for long, to pursue unilateral policies that ignore the well-being of the larger international community of which it is a part.

It is becoming increasingly clear that the political and economic costs of unilateralism, much less hegemony, are prohibitive even for the richest states. Besides, as a result of the spread of technology and knowledge, power has become increasingly diffuse. No less important, the consumption of unreplenishable natural resources, coupled with the socioeconomic pressures of population growth and massive migration—even if fertility rates continue to decline—and the proliferation of weapons of mass destruction are forcing the world to come to terms with human finitude. As the movement toward regional economic and political cooperation suggests, self-interest and mutual well-being are becoming synonymous concepts. Save for its nostalgic value to the myth-makers, rugged individualism, like the marketplace of perfect competition, is already an historical anachronism.

Some evolutionists suggest as much. Recent interdisciplinary research on the part of biologists, anthropologists, and psychologists suggests that it is naive to believe that people are single-mindedly interested in feathering their own nests. Like our animal ancestors farther down the phylogenetic scale, we are also capable of what biologists call "reciprocal altruism." Indeed, selfishness and selflessness may be complementary rather than contradictory aspects of human nature. In a resource-limited interdependent world, ruthless opportunism is more likely to undermine rather than sustain international comity, hence, individual self-interest. Paradoxically, however, the more cooperative we are, the more likely we are to advance our own interests.[12]

The egoistic excesses of autonomy are also likely to be contained by social needs, in particular, the need for affiliation. The desire for community attachment is, needless to say, not new. Without it there would be no human history. The need for belongingness, as this interpretive excursion has tried to show, was just as essential to the foundation of the empires and religious communities of antiquity as it was to the modern formation of nation-states and business enterprises. Furthermore, the post–Cold War aggregation of peoples along religious, national, ethnic, or tribal lines bears striking resemblance to past forms of sociocultural identification. Comparisons between past and present forms of affiliation may be more apparent than real, however, for it is becoming increasingly difficult to define communities in exclusivist terms, no matter how hard we try. In an increasingly interdependent world, we are becoming socially and psychologically less and less differentiated.

Technology, the relentless cross-border movement of peoples, and the regionalization of economic and political relationships have created polymorphous communities of such ethnic, religious, and cultural diversity that we will be forced to establish new definitions of affiliation. Although nation-states will not disappear, nationhood will become a component of a broader, more inclusivist identity. Nationalism and the cultural parochialism that it breeds are paradoxically likely to intensify feelings of social alienation, which can only be overcome by participating in the cultural diversity of change. Nor will cultural distinctions be effaced. Quite the contrary, as peoples come to understand that their own well-being, indeed, survival, depends on the well-being of their neighbors, regardless of racial or ethnic or religious differences, they are likely to be enriched in the process of lived-experience.

CREATIVE RENEWAL

For all the material and cultural differences that divide the world into its discrete parts, peoples everywhere face a common existential challenge of learning how to get along in order to go along. Given the interdependence of the world's peoples and the finiteness of its resources, it is hard to ignore the reality that our fate, for good or ill, lies as much in the hands of others as it does in ourselves. Human achievements accordingly need to be fashioned to human needs in new ways. Assuming that our commitment to life is greater than our fantasies of immortality, we may be on the verge of creating a postmaterialistic order in which the excesses of economic inequality, technological insensibility, and ecological ignorance are providing the creative stimulus to rewrite history's evolving story. Slowly, reluctantly, intuitively, we may be erecting the foundations of a new international system, albeit an imperfect system.

It is not that humanity is undergoing some religious conversion. We have not suddenly become angels. The demonic side of our nature has not been miraculously expunged. We simply have no better alternative. Others have drawn the same conclusion. Despite the continuing turbulence in Algeria and the failed efforts of Maghrebian unity, some form of cooperation will eventually occur, as a North African diplomat put it, because "the world has become very small, and that means the necessity of links between nations." Even in war-stricken former Yugoslavia, the late dissident Milovan Djilas observed that Serbs and Croats and the other peoples that inhabit the space of the former kingdom of the South Slavs "will be condemned to collaborate with each other—perhaps even closer than ever," for no other reason than economic necessity.[13]

Mutualism, however, must not be confused with utopia. We are not engaged in some evolutionary free fall to global tranquillity. The hopes of Djilas and others aside, some peoples will refuse to go along. Some will fail to make the sacrifice required. Others will need to be contained, if not managed, in the interests of the well-being of the larger community. Most, however, will in their own selfish interests eventually overcome their practice of self-denial and, in accepting their limitations, liberate themselves form their fantasies of unlimited progress. "Self-limitation is the fundamental and wisest step of a man who has obtained his freedom," Alexsandr Solzhenitsyn has mused. "It is also the surest path toward its attainment. We must not wait for external events to press harshly upon us or even topple us. Through prudent self-restraint we must learn to accept the inevitable course of events."[14]

The inevitability that we face is not the end of ideology or history, but the onset of the approaching future. We can resist the future or we can break free of our illusions and find meaning in new ways of living. The nascent frameworks of international social, economic, and political cooperation that are being constructed suggest that the human community has already intuited that the path toward a more productive and peaceful future lies in the direction of mutualism. Like Columbus's confirmation of the belief that the earth was round, we simply need the courage to sail into the creative void of our imagination and verify what we tacitly know.

Adjusting to the collective undertakings and commitments of mutualism will be no easy chore for any society. Disparities in the distribution of income, growing urban violence, the breakdown of the family, and the debilitating effects of consumerism on cultural innovation afflict most societies to some extent, especially those in the West.[15] For none, however, will the task be as difficult as it will for the United States. In accepting such obligations, the United States will be inextricably entangled in the world, an element in the undulating sea of history, a moment in the pulse of time. The inherent moral egalitarianism of mutualism precludes the belief in one's chosenness, its worldliness the paradisaical mission that continues to inspirit the American identity.

Thus far, however, Americans have tried to distance themselves from the implications of social and cultural change. It is apparent in the psychological alternation between the utopian dream of global amity captured in the vacuous new world order slogan and in the political unilateralism to which the breakdown of that fantasized order has given rise. Both reflect a detachment from a messy world. Better to believe that Kuwait, in whose defense the Gulf War was nominally fought, is an emerging democracy, or that Russia and other "deideologized" states are or should be engaged in a kind of mimetic Jeffersonianism that is at once their baptism and our confirmation in a universal church of shared liberal-democratic values. Detachment is also America's retreat from an incorrigible world when its peoples have fallen short of our expectations for them.

The American retreat from reality is also apparent in our social, intellectual, and material escapism. It is the zealotry of single-issue crusaders and their intolerance of those who do not share their narrow vision. It is populism run amok: the Contract *with* America's quick-fix political agenda and, far worse, the "government-hating, home-schooling, scripture-quoting" radicalism, which, in its extreme form, is the terrorism of local militias and the rubble of Oklahoma City. It is the learned class of professionals and intellectuals who refine their knowledge into specialized gradations of expertise when a broader understanding of the complexity of the whole is required. It is the larger public that is caught up in the material gratification of its own success: the well-heeled who will not make the social sacrifice to correct inequities that tear the fabric of society and the less fortunate who sanctimoniously excuse themselves from taking responsibility for their own lives.[16]

Detachment is our ignorance of the world and of ourselves and our history, as we insist on being what columnist Bob Herbert called "a nation of nitwits." It is the cultural insensibility of a society in which the arts have steadily lost patronage. Classical music and theater have been forced to commercialize art in a desperate attempt to attract audiences and advertisers from a public that would prefer the emotional unobtrusiveness and happy superficiality of easy listening or made-for-television bathodrama. Worse yet is the decline of literacy. Books that make it to the best-seller list are more often than not the how-to manuals of technical proficiency or voyeuristic incursions into the lives of popular icons. The cumulative costs of such smug parochialism, or, as Daniel Bell says, cultural nihilism, is the ignorance of other peoples and cultures that art, literature, and music provide and, in reversal of the frontier myth, a contraction of our intellectual horizons. No matter the approaching future and the historic change it augurs, we slumberously confide our faith in the irrepressible force of progress. For Americans, the way to the future is providentially paved, whether it is the conservative road of government deregulation and trickle-down prosperity or the liberal road of social empowerment and judicial intervention.[17]

It is not that the world is not changing, it is simply not changing for Americans. Elected officials, intellectuals, and pundits may pay lip service to the changing world, but Americans as a whole resist its implications. One policy consequence of this self-image is inertia. Despite the collapse of the Soviet empire, the United States continues to behave as though the world were still bipolar and the former Soviet Union were still the centerpiece of its foreign policy. It intones the virtues of multilateralism while basking in its self-image as the world's only remaining superpower. It hypes the post–Cold War peace dividend yet fields military forces designed to respond to yesterday's threats.

Intellectual inertia is especially evident in the stolid support of NATO on the part of both government officials, who conform to bureaucratic proprieties to preserve their status in the policy-making community, and political analysts on the fringe of the policy-making community, who hope thereby to enter the government. In such an infertile environment, phrase-mongering substitutes for policy, the more obscurantist the better. The new world order shibboleth that had been in vogue has been replaced by the Zen-like policy of "enlargement" and, given the Clinton administration's penchant for the oxymoronic, by the nebulous "assertive multilateralism" and the more mysterious "pragmatic neo-Wilsonianism."[18]

Another consequence of the denial of change is the confusion of tactics with strategy. Policies tend to be formulated in an ad hoc manner rather than as part of a strategic framework that guides statecraft around the shoals of change. The United States, for example, seems disposed to build closer ties in the Asia–Pacific region through the APEC framework, yet it constantly threatens to impose trade sanctions against Japan, which is the pivotal actor in APEC. Although Washington acknowledged the importance of China's role in defusing the nuclear time bomb on the Korean peninsula, it persists in taking Beijing to task over its human rights record at the possible expense of future support in Korea and broader Asian security relations. Worse, some legislators are jangling China's nerves with talk of recognizing Taiwan. Others are irritating Canada and Mexico by threatening to extend America's laws beyond national boundaries. Apparently indifferent to the NAFTA agreement and the integrity of the World Trade Organization, some senators are intent on penalizing countries that do business with Cuba.

For the time being, it may be harmless to behave as though the

United States were impervious to the process of historic change. At some point, however, the future will invade America too. Like the rest of the world, we will then have to accept the reality from which the circumstances of our national origins and the fortuitous accident of our geography have distanced us that we are also being swept up in the movement of historical time. Rather than have the world conform to the United States, the United States will have to conform to the world.

This is no cause for despair. In fact, there is reason to welcome the deluge of historically transforming change. The United States still has an important role to play in contributing to the peaceful transformation of the international system. Indeed, the concept of mutualism is part of the American liberal tradition. It underlies the egalitarian ethos of a nation that, with no small amount of social upheaval along the way, has gradually extended the privileges of freedom to a broader and more diverse political community. It animates the creed of internationalism that has guided the nation's political and economic orientation to the world, its periodic withdrawals from the political rough-and-tumble of global affairs, its frequent lapses into self-serving moralism, and its protectionist proclivities notwithstanding.

As a consequence of the national experience in melding different peoples into a stable polity, the United States can be a model for the emergence of polyethnic societies in other countries. It can similarly adopt concrete measures to preserve the environment and restrict arms sales that will increase the likelihood of inducing compliance on the part of other states. As it has expanded its community of economic interests in the NAFTA agreement, it can enter into accords to multilateralize regional security ties with the objective of building complementary security communities.

For this to occur, of course, the United States will have to recognize that it is part of a larger community in which it will sometimes follow and sometimes lead. It will have to overcome its ignorance of the world, its fear of enduring political commitment, its engineer's penny-wise, pound foolish suspicion of planning. It will further require a sense of service to others—especially in government but in business as well—and an intellectual willingness to take risks that we have progressively abandoned in the materialistic complacency of the twentieth century.

In accepting the necessity of shared interests and shared responsibilities, of course, the United States will no longer be above the fray, a *super*power that is in but not of the world. In rejoining time, however, the United States will be able to liberate itself from its self-defeating mythology of perfectionism. In doing so, it may find it easier to accept itself in its moments of failure as well as in its moments of success. The dawning epoch of mutualism does not signal the end of the American story. Rather, it is a new beginning with the world America never left.

Unless the human community chooses to consume itself in world-weary self-indulgence and destructive self-loathing, it is also likely to be a new beginning for others who are willing to participate in their own creative renewal. As has been true in other historic divides, however, humanity is bound to resist the process of change—irrationally, violently, even barbarically—until it is forced to fashion a future from the vestiges of the past. This is the existential space contemporary societies inhabit as they make their way through this long, painful, and uncertain transition to the future that is shaping them and simultaneously being shaped by them. There is no assurance that tomorrow will be better than today or yesterday. Nevertheless, humanity presses on in the hope that things will work out for the best, fortified by its faith in life in its infinite varieties and in its endless recurrence.

Chapter One

1. Ezra F. Vogel, *Japan as Number One: Lessons for America* (Cambridge, Mass.: Harvard, 1979).

2. Bill Emmott, *The Sun Also Rises: The Limits to Japan's Economic Power* (New York: Touchstone, 1989), pp. 3–5, 238–44. Precisely who invoked the Pacific Century theme is a mystery. Its provenance probably lies in an off-the-cuff quip by Lawrence S. Eagleburger, then Under Secretary of State for Political Affairs, who told a group of visiting college students in January 1984 that the center of international gravity had shifted from the Atlantic to the Pacific. Two months later, Eagleburger repackaged his off-hand remark in an address before the National Newspaper Association, in which he left little doubt in this formal statement that increased trade with Japan and the dynamic economies of South Korea, Taiwan, and the Association of South East Asian Nations (ASEAN), would inevitably lead to closer institutional links with the Pacific Basin. Eagleburger's address of March 7, 1984 is reprinted in *The Department of State Bulletin,* April 1984, pp. 39–42. See also Dan Oberdorfer, "Asia Watch: At the Dawn of the Pacific Century," *Washington Post,* July 31, 1988, pp. C1, C4; Alvin Toffler, *Power Shift* (New York: Bantam Books, 1991), pp. 422–24; Peter Drucker, "Japan's Not-so-Secret Weapon," *Wall Street Journal,* January 9, 1990, p. A14; and Lester Thurow, *Head to Head* (New York: William Morrow, 1992), chap. 4.

3. See, as examples, Joseph Burstein, *Yen! Japan's New Financial Empire and Its Threat to America* (New York: Simon & Schuster, 1988); Michael Montgomery, *Imperial Japan: The Yen to Dominate* (New York: St. Martin's Press, 1988); Clyde V. Prestowitz, *Trading Places: How We Allowed Japan to Take the Lead* (New York: Basic Books, 1988); and the hysterical fictional or semifictional accounts by Michael Crichton, *Rising Sun* (New York: Random House, 1991), and George Friedman and Meredith LeBard, *The Coming War with Japan* (New York: St. Martin's, 1991). See also Shintaro Ishihara and Akio Morita, *The Japan That Can Say No* (Kobunsha: Kappa-Holmes, 1989), p. 17. Americans were particularly disturbed that Sony Chairman Akio Morita coauthored such a polemic. See also Nancy Yoshihara, "Japanese Firms' Toughest Sell: a Better Image," *Los Angeles Times,* February 18, 1990, pp. D1, D4; Shintaro Ishihara, "FSX—Japan's Last Bad Deal," *New York Times,* January 14, 1990, p. F13; and

Fred Hiatt, "A New Aristocracy in the Land of the Rising Sun," *Washington Post,* April 10, 1988, pp. A21, 24. Reputable economists also reminded American audiences of Japanese barriers to investment as well as trade. As late as 1990, Thurow noted (pp. 132–33), there were only 132 majority-owned foreign firms in Japan with sales in excess of $5 million per year. Meanwhile, Japanese investment beyond its shores had skyrocketed. In a *Fortune* poll conducted early in 1990, 44 percent of Americans believed that Japan was their least trustworthy ally, as opposed to 29 percent who listed Germany.

4. Stephen W. Bosworth, "The United States and Asia," *Foreign Affairs, America and the World* (1991/1992): 114–21; Steven Greenhouse, "The Calls for an Industrial Policy Grow Louder," *New York Times,* July 19, 1992, p. F5; also see Prestowitz and Thurow for a good overview of recent trade policy; Merit E. Janow, "Trading with an Ally: Progress and Discontent in U.S.-Japan Trade Relations," in Gerald L. Curtis, ed., *The United States, Japan, and Asia: Challenges for U.S. Policy* (New York: W. W. Norton, 1994), pp. 53–95. In the same volume, Curtis addresses some policy alternatives in "Meeting the Challenge of Japan in Asia," pp. 216–51.

5. Zbigniew Brzezinski, "America's New Geostrategy," *Foreign Affairs* (Spring 1988): 680–99.

6. Paul Kennedy, *The Rise and Fall of the Great Powers: Economic Change and Military Conflict from 1500 to 2000* (New York: Random House, 1987).

7. Robert Hormats, "The Roots of American Power," *Foreign Affairs* (Summer 1991): 144–45; Jonathan Peterson, "How Are We Doing?" *Los Angeles Times,* February 18, 1990, pp. D1, 6.

8. During the 1980s Japanese investment in the United States rose from $3.5 to $66.1 billion, versus an increase from $6.2 to $17 billion for U.S. investment in Japan. Greater still was Britain's stake in America, which grew from $9.8 billion to $122.8 billion during the decade, compared with an increase from $23.7 billion to $58.8 billion for U.S. holdings in Britain. See Peter Riddell, "Foreign Investment in US Rises by $61.3bn to Record $390.1bn," *Financial Times,* March 15, 1990, p. 6. Also see Peter Schmeisser, "Is America in Decline?" *New York Times Magazine,* April 17, 1988, pp. 24–27, 66–68, 96.

9. Kirkpatrick, cited in George Will, "Role of the Body Politic is to Choose a Nation's Destiny, Not Adjust to One," *Los Angeles Times,* March 7, 1988, II, p. 7; Charles Krauthammer, "America in Decline? What Nation Are These People Looking At?" *Los Angeles Times,* March 11, 1990, p. M5; *The Economist,* February 24, 1990, pp. 11–12 Robert L. Bartley, "Time to Shake Our Hypochondria," *Wall Street Journal,* January 2, 1990, p. 16.

10. Francis Fukuyama, "The End of History," *The National Interest* (Summer 1989): 3–18.

11. Richard Bernstein, "Judging 'Post-History,' The Theory to End All Theories," *New York Times,* August 27, 1989, p. E5; Henry Allen, "The End. Or Is It?" *Washington Post,* September 27, 1989, pp. 1, 13.

12. Ian Davidson, "News of the End of History Fails to Reach Europe," *Financial Times,* October 19, 1989, p. 8; Jonathan Peterson, "U.S.-Style Capitalism May Not Be Model for East Bloc," *Los Angeles Times,* February 18, 1990, p. D6; also see the editorial in the *Atlanta Constitution,* August 30, 1989, p. 8; and "Responses to Fukuyama," *The National Interest* (Summer 1989): 19–35.

13. Richard Bernstein, "The End of History, Explained for the Second Time," *New York Times,* December 10, 1989, p. E6; Fukuyama, "Beyond the End of History," *Washington Post,* December 10, 1989, pp. C1, 4.

14. Roosevelt quoted in George H. Blakeslee, ed., *China and the Far East* (New York: Thomas Y. Crowell, 1910), p. xi; for the nineteenth-century fascination with Asia, see Richard Hofstadter, *The Paranoid Style in American Politics* (New York: Vintage Books, 1964), pp. 145–87; Thomas J. McCormick, *China Market: America's Quest for Informal Empire, 1893–1901* (Chicago: Quadrangle Books, 1967); Julius W. Pratt, *Expansionists of 1898* (Baltimore: Johns Hopkins University Press, 1936); and for a microcosmic view, Hugh De Santis, "George Bowen and the American Dream," *Chicago History* (Fall 1977): 143–54.

15. Speech by Vice President Dan Quayle to Council on Foreign Relations, New York, April 27, 1992, p. 3; Andrew Pollack, "Japanese Trade Surplus Leaps to a Record," *New York Times,* January 22, 1993, p. 37. I have also relied on the *Japan Economic Survey,* a monthly review of U.S.–Japanese relations published by the Japan Economic Institute, for current statistics. Measured in yen, Japan's surplus is actually smaller in 1994 than it was a year earlier. Moreover, the rising yen—itself the result of Japan's continuing massive surplus with the world—is likely to retard future economic growth, which would, in turn, stabilize the exchange rate of the yen against other currencies. See "The Struggle to Slim Japan's Surplus," *The Economist,* July 30, 1994, pp. 29–30; and Robert J. Samuelson, "The Yen: Japan's Reality Check," *Washington Post,* July 20, 1994, p. A19; and the overview of Japan in *Asia 1994 Yearbook* (Far East Economic Review/National Fair: Hong Kong, 1994), pp. 145–47.

16. See T. R. Ross, "Japan-Basking: New Pacific Era?" *Washington Post,* June 16, 1991, B1, B4; Hobart Rowen, "Dispelling Some Myths about Foreign Investment," *Washington Post,* March 18, 1990, H1, H18; Jacob M. Schlesinger, "Japanese Act in Bid to Trim Trade Surplus," *Wall Street Journal,* March 19, 1990, p. A3; and James Sterngold, "Japan's Trade Surplus Hits New High," *New York Times,* October 15, 1992, pp. D1, D9.

17. Paul Blustein, "Japan's 'Bubble' Bursts amid Tumble in Land, Stock Values," *Washington Post,* April 20, 1992, pp. A1, A12; "Overburdened," "Into the Red?" and "The Good News from Japan," *The Economist,* July 25, 1992, pp. 77–78; September 12, 1992, pp. 84, 89; and January 29, 1994, pp. 35–36, respectively; Andrew Pollack, "Japan Inc.'s Struggle to Refill the Pipeline" and "Japan Says Its Economy Was Stagnant in First Quarter of Year," *New York Times,* December 30, 1992, p. D5, and June 21, 1995, p. D5; "Psst! Wanna Buy

a Used Steel Plant?" and "That Sinking Feeling in Japan," *Business Week,* August 22, 1994, pp. 48–49, and May 8, 1995, pp. 52–54; and Michael Williams, "Japanese Growth Rate May See Slowdown, Some Economists Say," *Wall Street Journal,* March 6, 1995, p. A11.

18. "When Do the Parachutes Open?" *Business Week,* April 17, 1995, pp. 56–57.

19. "Into the Red," "Withdrawal Symptoms," "Safe as Post Offices," "Death of a Role Model," "Riding for Another Fall," "The Big One," and "Japanese Finance: Grim," *The Economist,* September 12, 1994, pp. 84, 89; December 19, 1992, p. 75; December 26, 1992/January 8, 1993, p. 104; July 9, 1994, pp. 13–15; December 17, 1994, pp. 75–76; April 1, 1995, pp. 60–61; and June 17, 1995, pp. 76–77. Also see Craig Forman, "Takemura Says Economy Is Recovering, Calls a Further Rise in Yen Unjustified," *Wall Street Journal,* September 29, 1994, p. A9; James Sterngold, "Banks Rescued in Japan in Sign of Deeper Woes," *New York Times,* October 13, 1994, p. D2; and "No Floors Under Japan's Banks?" and "Bank Alarms Are Blaring," *Business Week,* April 3, 1995, pp. 110–11, and June 26, 1995, pp. 52–53.

20. Andrew Pollack, "Software—Japan's Little Nightmare in the Making," "A Lower Gear for Japan's Auto Makers," and "Japan Buys More U.S. Auto Parts," *New York Times,* October 11, 1992, p. F5; August 30, 1992, pp. F1, F6; and July 14, 1994, p. D5, respectively; Valerie Reitman, "In Japan's Car Market, Big Three Face Rivals Who Go Door-to-Door," *Wall Street Journal,* September 28, 1994, pp. A1, A13; and "Japan's Auto Shock," *Business Week,* May 29, 1995, pp. 44–47.

21. Andrew Pollack, "Japan's Taste for the Luxurious Gives Way to Utility and Frugality," and Miki Tanikawa, "In Japan, Some Shun Lifetime Jobs to Chase Dreams," *New York Times,* January 3, 1993, pp. 1, 12, and June 25, 1995, p. F11; "Death of a Role Model" and "One in Ten?" *The Economist,* July 9, 1994, pp. 10–12, and July 1, 1995, pp. 26–27.

22. Emmott, pp. 75–87; James Sterngold, "Japan's Health Care: Cradle, Grave, and No Frills," *New York Times,* December 28, 1992, pp. 1, A8; and "Borrowing Time," *The Economist,* July 9, 1994, pp. 34–35.

23. "Hacking Back," and "Wielding a Sword," *The Economist,* July 11, 1992, p. 76, and September 5, 1992, p. 70, respectively; James Sterngold, "For Tokyo Brokers, Time of Pain"; Steven R. Weisman, "More Japanese Workers Demanding Shorter Hours and Less Hectic Work"; and Yoshi Noguchi, "Dropping Out of Tokyo's Rat Race," *New York Times,* October 7, 1992, pp. D1, D14; March 1, 1992, p. F11, March 3, 1992, p. A8; Urban C. Lehner, "Japanese May Be Rich, But Are They Satisfied with Quality of Life?" *Wall Street Journal,* January 9, 1990, pp. A1, A10; "The Boomers Take Over in Japan," *Business Week,* October 25, 1993, pp. 128–33.

24. Thurow, pp. 75–85. See Paul Krugman, *Geography and Trade* (Cambridge, Mass.: MIT Press, 1991), pp. 4–34; and John H. Dunning, *Explaining*

International Production (London: Unwin Hyman, 1988), pp. 11–12, passim. According to the Congressional Research Service of the Library of Congress, Japan now imports nearly as much from Asia as it does from North America. See Dick K. Nanto, *Japan and an East Asian Trading Bloc* (Washington, D.C.: Library of Congress, February 6, 1992), p. 12. The EU figures take into account the accession of Sweden, Austria, and Finland. Statistics are from the Office of Public Information, Delegation of the Commission of the European Union in Washington.

25. Emmott, pp. 192–94; "China Goes for Broke," "Deng's Last Show," and "China Feels the Heat," *The Economist*, July 25, 1992, pp. 33–34; October 10, 1992, pp. 13–14; and January 23, 1993, pp. 31–32; also see in the same publication "Japan and Asia: A Question of Balance," April 22, 1995, pp. 21–23. Also see "China: Is Prosperity Creating a Freer Society?" "Japan's New Identity," and "Korea," *Business Week*, June 6, 1994, pp. 94–107; April 10, 1995, pp. 108–14; and July 31, 1995, pp. 56–63; and Dan Biers, "Asia's Four Tigers Spring into the First World," *Wall Street Journal*, February 28, 1995, p. A17.

26. "Japan and Asia: A Question of Balance," *The Economist*, April 22, 1995, p. 22; David E. Sanger, "Poll Finds Japanese Less Sure of Future," *New York Times*, December 30, 1994, p. A8; and, on the influence of the offshore Chinese, Andrew Tanzer, "The Bamboo Network," *Forbes*, July 18, 1994, pp. 138–45.

27. "How Japan Will Survive Its Fall," *The Economist*, July 11, 1992, pp. 65–66; Emmott, p. 254; Thurow, pp. 213–14. Bill Javetski, "The Ice Cracks in Japan and Europe," "Japan's New Identity," and "The Japanese Have a New Thirst for Imports," *Business Week*, April 4, 1994, pp. 48–49, April 10, 1995, pp. 110–11, and June 5, 1995, pp. 52–54; Andrew Pollack, "Japan's Jobless Rate at Highest Level Ever," *New York Times*, May 31, 1995, p. D6.

28. Christopher A. Bartlett, "Japan's Achilles Heel," *Los Angeles Times*, November 12, 1989, p. D3; "The Sun also Sweats," *The Economist*, September 10, 1994, pp. 33–34; "Rougher Trade," *Business Week*, July 17, 1995, pp. 30–32.

29. Paul Blustein, "Japan Gets a Hard Look from Within," *Washington Post*, October 18, 1992, pp. H1, H8.

30. Clyde Haberman, "The Presumed Uniqueness of Japan," *New York Times Magazine*, August 28, 1988, pp. 39–43, 53, 74; Yoichi Funabashi, "Japan and the New World Order," *Foreign Affairs* (Winter 1991–92): 58–74. Japan already assumes about three-fourths of the nonsalary costs of the 50,000 American servicemen stationed there. Also see "The New Nationalists," *The Economist*, January 14, 1995, pp. 19–21.

31. Kennedy, pp. 521–35.

32. Mismanagement during Philip's reign led to bankruptcies in 1575 and 1596. Kennedy, pp. 52–54. See also Peter Gay and R. K. Webb, *Modern Europe*, 2 vols. (New York: Harper & Row, 1973), vol. 1 *(Modern Europe to 1815)*, pp. 187–98; Fernand Braudel, *The Mediterranean and the Mediterranean World*

in the Age of Philip II, vol. 2, trans. Siân Reynolds (New York: Harper & Row, 1973), pp. 911–24, 1195–96; Immanuel Wallerstein, *The Modern World-System,* vol. 1: *Capitalist Agriculture and the Origins of the European World-Economy in the Sixteenth Century* (New York: Academic Press, 1974), pp. 191–93; Wallerstein, *The Modern World-System,* vol. 2: *Mercantilism and the Consolidation of the European World-Economy, 1600–1750* (New York: Academic Press, 1980), pp. 182–85.

33. Kennedy, pp. 86–88, 100–106; Gay and Webb, vol. 1, pp. 189–96, 302–16; Wallerstein, vol. 1, pp. 185–213; vol. 2, pp. 37–46, 51–57, 70–80, 92–93, 121–25, and idem., *The Modern World-System,* vol. 3: *The Second Era of Great Expansion of the Capitalist World-Economy, 1730–1840s* (San Diego: Academic Press, 1989), pp. 246–50, 268–89. The stadholder (formerly Spain's representative in each of the Dutch provinces) attempted to establish a centralizing authority, but control remained with the merchant oligarchs in the provinces.

34. Wallerstein, vol. 3, pp. 83–85, 194–200. Kennedy, pp. 151–58, 228, 367–72; see also Peter Gay and R. K. Webb (see above, n. 32), vol. 2, pp. 918–22, 995–98, 1043–44, 1088–89, 1098–1100.

35. Peter Passell, "America's Position in the Economic Race: What the Numbers Show and Conceal," *New York Times,* March 4, 1990, p. E4; Leonard Silk, "Some Things Are More Vital than Money When It Comes to Creating the World Anew," *New York Times,* September 22, 1991, p. E2; Aaron Bernstein, "Inequality," *Business Week,* August 15, 1994, pp. 78–83; David P. Calleo, *Beyond American Hegemony* (New York: Basic Books, 1987); Walter Russell Mead, *Mortal Splendor: The American Empire in Transition* (Boston: Houghton-Mifflin, 1987).

36. Sylvia Nasar, "U.S. Rate of Output Called Best," *New York Times,* October 13, 1992, pp. D1, 19; Robert D. Hormats, "The Roots of American Power," *Foreign Affairs* (Summer 1991): 137, 146. Joseph S. Nye Jr., *Bound to Lead: The Changing Nature of American Power* (New York: Basic Books, 1990), pp. 6–7, 73, 77. Also see *Historical Tables, Budget of the U.S. Government* (Washington, D.C.: Office of Management and Budget, FY1994), pp. 230–31. The Progressive Policy Institute provided the deficit statistics. Corporate restructurings have led to improved operating efficiency. According to a study by the McKinsey Global Institute, a branch of McKinsey & Co., the management consulting firm, in 1990 American workers produced $49,600 in goods and services per year versus $44,200 and $38,200 for their respective German and Japanese counterparts.

37. Terry Eagleton discusses the application of Gramsci's concept of hegemony in nineteenth-century Britain in *Ideology* (London: Verso, 1991), p. 123. For a fuller discussion, see Quintin Hoare and G. Nowell Smith, eds., Antonio Gramsci, *Selections from the Prison Notebooks* (New York: International Publishers, 1971). See also Gay and Webb, vol. 1, p. 214.

38. Susan Strange, "Toward a Theory of Transnational Empire," in Ernst-Otto Czempiel and James N. Rosenau, eds., *Global Changes and Theoretical Challenges* (Lexington, Mass.: D. C. Heath, 1989), pp. 161–76; Susan Strange, "Protectionism and World Politics," *International Organizations* (Spring 1985): 256. See Arnold Toynbee, *A Study of History* (New York: Dell, 1965), vol. 1, pp. 271–82; Nye, pp. 190–95.

39. Paul Kennedy, "A Guide to Misinterpreters," *New York Times,* April 17, 1988, p. E27.

40. Francis Fukuyama, *The End of History and the Last Man* (New York: Free Press, 1992), Introduction and chap. 1. See G. W. F. Hegel, *Introduction to the Philosophy of History* [from *Lectures on the Philosophy of History*], in Monroe C. Beardsley, ed., *The European Philosophers from Descartes to Nietzsche* (New York: Random House, 1960), pp. 537–608.

41. George Gilder, "Four Cheers for Liberal Democracy," *Washington Post Book World,* January 12, 1992, pp. 1, 6. For less orgasmic reviews, see William H. McNeill, "History Over, World Goes On," *New York Times Book Review,* January 26, 1992, pp. 14–15; and Alan Ryan, "Professor Hegel Goes to Washington," *New York Review,* March 26, 1992, pp. 7–13; Fukuyama, pp. 46, 51.

42. Samuel P. Huntington, "Repent! The End Is Not Near," *Washington Post,* September 24, 1989, p. B3; Fukuyama, pp. 46, 123.

43. Geoffrey Barraclough, *Turning Points in World History* (London: Thames & Hudson, 1977), p. 87.

44. Fukuyama, chaps. 17–18, esp. pp. 300–312.

45. Fukuyama, pp. 262–64, 335–36; Michael W. Doyle, "Kant, Liberal Legacies, Foreign Affairs," *Philosophy and Public Affairs* 12, no. 3 (Summer 1983): 205–35.

46. Francis Fukuyama, "Rest Easy. It's Not 1914 Anymore," *New York Times,* February 9, 1992, p. E17; Daniel Bell, *The End of Ideology* (Cambridge, Mass.: Harvard University Press, 1988), p. 279.

47. Fukuyama, pp. 139, 338–39.

Chapter Two

1. Daniel Bell, *The End of Ideology: On the Exhaustion of Political Ideas in the Fifties* (Glencoe, Ill.: Free Press, 1960); Theodore J. Lowi, *The End of Liberalism: Ideology, Policy, and the Crisis of Public Authority* (New York: W. W. Norton, 1969).

2. Quoted in Sacvan Bercovitch, *The American Jeremiad* (Madison: University of Wisconsin Press, 1978), p. 19.

3. See J. G. A. Pocock, *Politics, Language and Time* (New York: Atheneum, 1971), pp. 84–89.

4. Pocock, *The Machiavellian Moment: Florentine Political Thought and the Atlantic Republican Tradition* (Princeton, N.J.: Princeton University Press,

1975), pp. 31–33; Bercovitch, "The American Puritan Imagination: An Introduction," in Bercovitch, ed., *The American Puritan Imagination: Essays in Re-
valuation* (Cambridge: Cambridge University Press, 1974), pp. 1–16. According
to the Zohar, or Hebrew Book of Mysteries, the Fifth Monarchy would come
after the fall of Rome. The apocalyptic fervor of the ancient Hebrew rabbis had
a profound influence on Christians, including the Puritans, after the Reformation. Also see Pocock, *Politics, Language, and Time,* pp. 98–100; Bercovitch,
Jeremiad, p. 74.

5. Bercovitch, *Jeremiad,* pp. 29, 63–64, 166–67.

6. David Minter, "The Puritan Jeremiad as a Literary Form," in Bercovitch,
ed., *Puritan Imagination,* pp. 46–47.

7. Minter, ibid., p. 50.

8. Bercovitch, *Jeremiad,* pp. 8–9.

9. Bercovitch, *Jeremiad,* pp. 131, 141, 174; Reagan quoted in Henry Nash
Smith, "Symbol and Idea in Virgin Land," in Sacvan Bercovitch and Myra Jeh-
len, eds., *Ideology and Classic American Literature* (Cambridge: Cambridge
University Press, 1982), p. 26; Pocock, *Machiavellian Moment,* p. 513.

10. Emerson's *The American Scholar* is in Sculley Bradley, Richard Croom
Beatty, and E. Hudson Long, eds., *The American Tradition in Literature* (New
York: W. W. Norton, 1962), pp. 541–56; Whitman's quotation is from *Demo-
cratic Vistas,* included in the same anthology, pp. 912–20.

11. For the born-free formulation, see Daniel Boorstin, *The Genius of Ameri-
can Politics* (Chicago: University of Chicago Press, 1953); and Louis Hartz, *The
Liberal Tradition in America: An Interpretation of American Political Thought
since the Revolution* (New York: Harcourt Brace & World, 1955). For the re-
publican synthesis, see Bernard Bailyn, *The Ideological Origins of the American
Revolution* (Cambridge, Mass.: Harvard University Press, 1967); and Gordon
Wood, *The Creation of the American Republic* (Chapel Hill: University of North
Carolina Press, 1969). Also see Smith, p. 26.

12. Bercovitch, *Jeremiad,* p. 162. David Noble's *The End of American History* (Minneapolis: University of Minnesota Press, 1985) is an excellent exploration of America's hubristic efforts to escape the profane world by transforming
it. For an insightful analysis of ascriptive inequality and the "multiple traditions"
in American political culture, see Rogers M. Smith, "Beyond Tocqueville, Myr-
dal, and Hartz: The Multiple Traditions in America," *American Political Science
Review* 87, no. 3 (September 1993): 549–66.

13. Alexis de Tocqueville, *Democracy in America,* ed. Phillips Bradley (New
York: Vintage, 1945), vol. 2, p. 137.

14. See Ernest R. May, *Imperial Democracy* (New York: Harper & Row,
1961) for a splendid account of the politics and diplomacy leading to the Spanish-
American War. For the historiography of the period, see Hugh De Santis, "The
Imperialist Impulse and American Innocence, 1865–1900," in Gerald K. Haines
and J. Samuel Walker, eds., *American Foreign Relations: a Historiographical
Review* (Westport, Conn.: Greenwood Press, 1981), pp. 65–90.

15. The phrase belongs to Samuel Flagg Bemis, *A Diplomatic History of the United States* (New York: Henry Holt, 1936), chap. 26, but its meaning became imbedded in American historiography until the "new left" revisionists challenged it during the Vietnam era.

16. Noble discusses the new frontier of industry in his chapters on Charles Beard and Richard Hofstadter. See also Bercovitch, *Jeremiad*, p. 38.

17. Alfred Thayer Mahan, *The Problem of Asia* (Boston: Little, Brown, 1905), pp. 86–87, 91, 93.

18. Julius W. Pratt, *Expansionists of 1898: The Acquisition of Hawaii and the Spanish Islands* (Baltimore: Johns Hopkins University Press, 1936), p. 281.

19. Paul S. Reinsch, *Intellectual and Political Currents in the Far East* (New York: Books for Libraries Press, 1911), pp. 29, 31.

20. Archibald R. Colquhoun, *Greater America* (New York: Harper & Bros., 1904), pp. 83, 286, 381; Mahan, p. 148.

21. See Thomas F. Millard, "The Need of a Distinctive American Policy in China," and Willard Straight, "The Present Situation in Manchuria: Commerce, Trade, and International Politics," in Blakeslee (see chap. 1, n. 14), pp. 83–94 and 133–48, respectively.

22. Dr. Tokichi Takamine, president of the Nippon Club, "Japan and the United States," in Blakeslee, pp. 351–57; Launcelot Lawton, *Empires of the Far East* (London: Grant Richards, 1912), vol. 1, p. 134.

23. Lawton, pp. 351–54, 381, 402–3, 546–53.

24. Pocock, *Machiavelli*, p. 542.

25. John King Fairbank's, *The United States and China,* 3d ed. (Cambridge, Mass.: Harvard University Press, 1972) provides a rich history of Sino-American relations, especially chaps. 13–14.

26. Lawton, pp. 614–18, 662; Donald Lach, *Asia in the Making of Europe* (Chicago: University of Chicago Press, 1965), vol. 1, book 1, pp. 305–9.

27. Reinsch, p. 53.

28. Colquhoun, pp. 381–82. For background, see Akira Iriye, *After Imperialism: The Search for a New Order in the Far East, 1921–1931* (New York: Atheneum, 1969) and *The Cold War in Asia* (Englewood Cliffs, N.J.: Prentice-Hall, 1974). See also William E. Leuchtenberg, *Franklin D. Roosevelt and the New Deal, 1932–1940* (New York: Harper & Row, 1963), p. 215.

29. For background, see Iriye, *Cold War in Asia,* chap. 5; and Geoffrey Barraclough, "The Struggle for the Third World," *New York Review,* November 19, 1978, pp. 47–58.

30. Vogel (see chap. 1, n. 1), p. 120; Aaron Bernstein, "Why the Gap Isn't So Great in Europe and Japan," *Business Week,* August 15, 1994, pp. 82–83; Hobart Rowen, "We've Met the Economic Enemy, and He Is Us," *Washington Post,* September 11, 1994, pp. H1, H5. Keith Bradsher, "America's Opportunity Gap," *New York Times,* June 4, 1995, p. 4E. In the United States, those in the upper 10 percent of all income earners made 5.6 times as much per hour as those in the lowest 10 percent in 1992. In Japan and Germany, the differential between

those in the highest and lowest deciles for the same year was 2.8 and 2.7, respectively. A longitudinal study by Gary Burtless and Timothy Smeeding, excerpted in the *Washington Post*, draws similar conclusions. See "America's Tide Lifting the Yachts, Swamping the Rowboats," June 25, 1995, p. C3.

31. For a critical assessment of the rise of the United States after World War II, see Theodore H. Von Laue's provocative *The World Revolution of Westernization: The Twentieth Century in Global Perspective* (New York: Oxford University Press, 1987), chap. 16, esp. pp. 146–64.

32. Pocock, *Politics, Language, Time*, p. 542.

33. William Pfaff, "Is History Over? Only to Those Who Want a Rationale for Quitting," *Chicago Tribune*, October 2, 1989, p. 15; Dan Balz and Richard Morin, "A Tide of Pessimism and Political Powerlessness Rises," and E. J. Dionne Jr., "Speeches, Statistics, and Some Unsettling Facts about America's Changed Prospects," *Washington Post*, November 3, 1991, pp. A1, A16, and January 26, 1992, pp. C1, C3, respectively; and Steven Greenhouse, "Attention America! Snap Out of It!" *New York Times*, February 9, 1992, pp. 1, 8.

34. Von Laue, pp. 163–64.

35. Brook Thomas, *The New Historicism* (Princeton, N.J.: Princeton University Press, 1991), p. 7. Bernard Giesen refers to the difference between text and context, and between social systems and environment, as core elements of paradigmatic change in "The Temporalization of Social Order: Some Theoretical Remarks on the Change in 'Change,' " Hans Haferkamp and Neil J. Smelser, eds., *Social Change and Modernity* (Berkeley: University of California Press, 1992), p. 315.

Chapter Three

1. Ralf Dahrendorf, "The Europeanization of Europe," in Andrew Pierre, ed., *A Widening Atlantic? Domestic Change and Foreign Policy* (New York: Council on Foreign Relations, 1986), p. 5.

2. Sir Nikolaus Pevsner, "The Architecture of Mannerism," in Harold Spencer, ed., *Readings in Art History*, 2d ed. (New York: Charles Scribner's, 1976), vol. 2, p. 139; see also Gay and Webb (see chap. 1, n. 32), vol. 1, pp. 214–16.

3. See John Golding, *Cubism: A History and Analysis, 1907–1914*, 3d ed. (Cambridge, Mass.: Harvard University Press, 1988); and Robert Rosenblum, *Cubism and Twentieth-Century Art* (New York: Abrams, 1982).

4. For a keen analysis of modern decadence, see Marshall Blonsky, "Madonna's Wilde 'Sex,' " *Washington Post*, October 18, 1992, pp. C1, C4. To be sure, hedonism was rampant during the declining days of the Roman empire.

5. Aleksandr Solzhenitsyn, in "The Relentless Cult of Novelty and How It Wrecked the Century," remarks on receiving the medal of honor from the National Arts Club of New York in January 1993; reprinted in *The New York Times Book Review*, February 7, 1993, pp. 3, 17.

6. A good, brief introduction to postmodernism is Charles Jencks, ed., *Post-Modern Classicism* (London: Garden House Press, 1980).

7. See Arno J. Mayer's *Political Origins of the New Diplomacy, 1917–1918* (New Haven, Conn.: Yale University Press, 1959) and *Politics and Diplomacy of Peacemaking* (New York: Knopf, 1967).

8. The relationship between social spheres and time is discussed in Giesen, "The Temporalization of Social Order," pp. 306–8. See also José Ortega y Gasset, *Man and Crisis,* trans. Mildred Adams (New York: W. W. Norton, 1958). The idea of transformative social change, or, what I refer to as epochal change, can be traced to the nineteenth-century writings of Hegel, Marx, and Schopenhauer, among others. Its intellectual appeal, however, has risen considerably in the twentieth century. See, as examples, Pitirim Aleksandrovich Sorokin, *The Crisis of our Age: The Social and Cultural Outlook* (New York: E. P. Dutton, 1941); Lewis Mumford, *The Transformations of Man* (New York: Harper & Row, 1956); and the flood of books on the same theme that have appeared more recently with such titles as Theodore Roszak's *Person/Planet: The Creative Disintegration of Industrial Society* (Garden City, N.J.: Anchor Press/Doubleday, 1978); Robert L. Heilbroner's *An Inquiry into the Human Prospect* (New York: W. W. Norton, 1978); Alan Wheelis's *The End of the Modern Age* (New York: Harper & Row, 1971); John Lukács's *The Passing of the Modern Age* (New York: Harper & Row, 1970); and, of course, Fukuyama's aforementioned *The End of History and the Last Man* (see chap. 1, n. 40).

9. Fernand Braudel, *On History,* trans. Sarah Matthews (Chicago: University of Chicago Press, 1980), p. 10.

10. Dwight E. Lee and Robert N. Beck, "The Meaning of 'Historicism,' " *American Historical Review* 59, no. 3 (April 1954): 568.

11. By freeing history from theology, both Vico and Herder were precursors to nineteenth-century historicism. Erich Kahler distinguishes between "historism" and "historicism." The former, which, in his view, reflects the belief in the objective meaningfulness of the universe, fused history and the idea of progress it otherwise challenged as an abstract concept and thus removed the distinction between the "is" and the "ought." Historicism, which he roots in the latter half of the nineteenth century, is the corruption of historism. By focusing only on the "is," he maintains, it abandoned the normative importance of history and eventually gave rise to ethical nihilism. See *The Meaning of History* (New York: George Braziller, 1964), pp. 166–70, 200. Also see George Iggers, "Progress Denied," in W. Warren Wagar, ed., *The Idea of Progress since the Renaissance* (New York: John Wiley, 1969), pp. 151–53.

12. John E. Grumley, *History and Totality: Radical Historicism from Hegel to Foucault* (London: Routledge, 1991), pp. 68–74; Richard E. Palmer, *Hermeneutics: Interpretation Theory in Schleiermacher, Dilthey, Heidegger, and Gadamer* (Evanston, Ill.: Northwestern University Press, 1969), pp. 195–97; and Hans-Georg Gadamer, *Philosophical Hermeneutics,* trans. and ed. David E. Linge (Berkeley: University of California Press, 1976), pp. 112–15.

13. Leonard Krieger, *Ranke: The Meaning of History* (Chicago: University of Chicago Press, 1977), pp. 5, 18; Iggers, pp. 153–54. For Ranke, truth emerged a posteriori; it was the irreducible residual of myriad individual actions rather than the dominant a priori ideas that reduced humanity to shadows or symbols or some overarching concept. The scientific inquiry into the past, according to the Rankean paradigm, emphasized objectivity, facticity, the uniqueness of all events, and the centrality of politics, that is, the state as the living agent of human destiny.

14. For background, see J. G. von Herder, *Reflections on the Philosophy of the History of Mankind* (Chicago: University of Chicago Press, 1968); Peter Hanns Reill, *The German Enlightenment and the Rise of Historicism* (Berkeley: University of California Press, 1975); and Hans Kohn, ed., *German Historicism: Some New German Views* (Boston: Beacon, 1948). To be sure, there were elements of romanticism in Ranke's thinking, too, as Krieger shows (pp. 92–100, 130–37). There is an ambiguity in Ranke's scholarship that reflects his attempt to synthesize the formal principles of science with the romantic, the national with the universal, the subjective with the objective.

15. Friedrich Meinecke, *Historicism: The Rise of a New Historical Outlook,* trans. J. E. Anderson (London: Routledge & Kegan Paul, 1972); Iggers, pp. 155–58; Kahler, pp. 175–77.

16. Kahler, p. 175; Barraclough, *History in a Changing World* (Norman, Okla.: University of Oklahoma Press, 1955), p. 222.

17. Kahler, pp. 210–14; Iggers, pp. 153–54.

18. Auguste Comte, *The Positive Philosophy,* trans. and abridged by Harriet Martineau (Chicago: Belford Clarke, 1855). Positivism's origins lie in the anti-metaphysical nominalism of fourteenth-century philosophers such as William of Ockham and in the Enlightenment's idealization of science. Galileo, Descartes, and Leibniz were all precursors to positivism in their stress on the acquisition of knowledge through empirical observation. See Leszek Kolakowski, *The Alienation of Reason,* trans. Norbert Guterman (New York: Doubleday, 1968), pp. 18–29, 57, 68.

19. Kolakowski, pp. 39–40; for background, also see W. M. Simon, *European Positivism in the Nineteenth Century* (Ithaca, N.Y.: Cornell University Press, 1963), pp. 264–68.

20. Kolakowski, pp. 89–101.

21. Kolakowski, pp. 104–6, 125–26.

22. Kolakowski, pp. 160, 174–79. The foregoing subsumes logical positivism and analytical philosophy under the same rubric. Not all aspects of the latter school could be considered positivist, however. For more on the subject, see Bertrand Russell, *Human Knowledge: Its Scope and Limits* (New York: Simon & Schuster, 1948); Ludwig Wittgenstein, *Tractatus logico-philosophicus* (New York: Humanities Press, 1963); and Rudolf Carnap, *The Logical Structure of the World and Pseudoproblems in Philosophy* (Berkeley: University of California Press, 1964).

23. Karl R. Popper, *The Poverty of Historicism* (New York: Harper & Row, 1961), pp. 3, 41–49, 105–19.

24. Kahler, p. 177; Lee and Beck, pp. 575–77.

25. Jean-François Lyotard, *La Condition postmoderne* (Paris: Minuit, 1979), pp. 41–47; see also Richard Harvey Brown, "Positivism, Relativism, and Narrative in the Logic of the Historical Sciences," *American Historical Review* 92 (October 1987): 908–20.

26. Lyotard, pp. 11–14; also see Christopher Chase-Dunn, *Global Formation; Structures of the World-Economy* (Oxford: Basil Blackwell, 1989). Chase-Dunn's comments are in *Processes of the World System,* Terence K. Hopkins and Immanuel Wallerstein, eds. (Beverly Hills, Calif.: Sage, 1980), p. 311.

27. Lyotard, pp. 23–31; Brown.

28. Lyotard, pp. 35–41.

29. Kolakowski, pp. 203–206.

30. Capra, *The Turning Point* (New York: Simon and Schuster, 1982), chap. 3, esp. pp. 70–73.

31. See Benedetto Croce, *History: Its Theory and Practice* (New York: Russell, 1960).

32. Palmer, pp. 130–31. See also Martin Heidegger's seminal *Being and Time,* trans. J. Macquarrie and E. Robinson (New York: Harper, 1962); and Louis O. Mink, *Historical Understanding,* Brian Fay, Eugene O. Golob, and Richard T. Vann, eds. (Ithaca, N.Y.: Cornell University Press, 1987), p. 94.

33. Kahler, pp. 177, 208.

34. Palmer, p. 234; Brook Thomas, *The New Historicism* (Princeton University Press, 1991), pp. 102–6; Gadamer, pp. xxiv–xxvii; Lyotard, pp. vii–xxi; Brown, p. 919.

35. This is a transposition of textual hermeneutics presented by G. B. Madison in *The Hermeneutics of Post-Modernity* (Bloomington: Indiana University Press, 1988), pp. 29–30. See also Robert D'Amico's exposition of rational reconstruction, which borrows from Imre Lakatos's attempts to integrate historiography into a theory of knowledge, in *Historicism and Knowledge* (New York: Routledge, 1989), esp. chap. 4.

36. Mink, pp. 75–83. For another view, see Popper, pp. 97–104, 130–61.

37. See Hugh De Santis and Robert A. Manning, *Gorbachev's Eurasian Strategy: The Dangers of Success and Failure,* P-7592 (Santa Monica, Calif.: RAND Corporation, August 1989), pp. 3–7; also see Michael Polanyi, *Knowing and Being: Essays by Michael Polanyi,* ed. Marjorie Grene (London: Routledge & Kegan Paul, 1969), pp. 119–20.

38. See Gerhard Knauss, "The Concept of the 'Encompassing' in Jaspers' Philosophy," in Paul Arthur Schilpp, ed., *The Philosophy of Karl Jaspers* (New York: Tudor, 1957), pp. 162–71. Jaspers argues that we enter the boundary or limit situations by "becoming the Existenz possible within us." In his discussion of "limit situations," he observes that "out of the helplessness of existence, Being soars upward within me. This is Existenz." See Karl Jaspers, *The Philosophy of*

Existence, trans. Edith Ehrlich, Leonard Ehrlich, and George B. Pepper (Athens, Ohio: Ohio University Press, 1986), p. 97.

39. Polanyi (p. 125) calls this "focal" and "subsidiary" awareness. "The concerted advantage of the two processes arises from the fact that normally every dismemberment of a whole adds more to its understanding than is lost through the concurrent weakening of its comprehensive features, and again each new integration of the particulars adds more to our understanding of them than it damages our understanding by somewhat effacing their identity." See also Gadamer, p. 119.

40. Capra, chap. 3; Kenneth E. Boulding, *The World as a Total System* (Beverly Hills, Calif.: Sage, 1985), p. 155.

41. Polanyi, pp. 105–33; Gadamer, pp. 119–28.

42. Braudel, p. 9; Palmer, pp. 164–66.

43. Palmer, 195–97; Friedrich Nietzsche, *The Use and Abuse of History,* 2d ed., trans. Adrian Collins (Indianapolis: Bobbs-Merrill, 1957), p. 6.

44. Gadamer, xliii.

45. Madison, pp. 73–77, 177–81; Gadamer, xv–xix. See also Anthony Giddens, *Modernity and Self-Identity: Self and Society in the Late Modern Age* (Stanford, Calif.: Stanford University Press, 1991), chap. 3, esp. 90–98.

46. This non-normative description of ideology is close to the meaning imputed to it in the early nineteenth century by the French writer Destutt de Tracy, who defined it in *"Elements d'ideologie* as "the system of purely objective true ideas built up from the clear and distinct elements of perception." Quoted in Henry Nash Smith, "Symbol and Idea in Virgin Land," in Bercovitch and Jehlen, eds. (see chap. 2, n. 9). For a fuller discussion of the evolution of ideology, especially in Marxist literature, see Terry Eagleton, *Ideology* (see chap. 1, n. 37).

47. Braudel, pp. 25–54.

48. Barraclough, *History,* pp. 84–96.

49. See Immanuel Wallerstein, "Patterns of Development of the Modern World-System," in Terence K. Hopkins and Immanuel Wallerstein, eds., *World-Systems Analysis: Theory and Methodology* (Beverly Hills, Calif.: Sage, 1982), vol. 1, pp. 41–82; and Chase-Dunn.

50. Raymond Aron, *L'Histoire et ses interprétations: Entretiens autour de Arnold Toynbee* (Paris: Mouton, 1961), p. 21; Lyotard, pp. 79–82.

Chapter Four

1. See, for example, Jonathan Haas, *The Evolution of the Prehistoric State* (New York: Columbia University Press, 1982); Stanley Diamond, *In Search of the Primitive* (New Brunswick, N.J.: Transaction Books, 1974); Daniel Glyn, *The First Civilizations* (New York: Apollo Editions, 1968); Carleton S. Coon, *The Story of Man* (New York: Knopf, 1954); John Grahame Douglas Clark, *World Prehistory: An Outline* (Cambridge: Cambridge University Press, 1961); Childe V. Gordon, *Man Makes Himself* (New York: New American Li-

brary, 1936). Also see William H. McNeill, *The Rise of the West: A History of the Human Community* (Chicago: University of Chicago Press, 1963); the first three volumes of Arnold Toynbee, *A Study of History,* 7th ed. (New York: Oxford University Press, 1954); and Carlo M. Cipolla, *The Economic History of World Population* (Sussex: The Harvester Press, 1978).

2. McNeill, pp. 32–51; Toynbee, vol. 5; Woodbridge Bingham, Hilary Conroy, and Frank W. Ikle, *A History of Asia,* 2d ed. (Boston: Allyn & Bacon, 1974), vol. 1, pp. 26–32; William W. Hallo and William Kelly Simpson, *The Ancient Near East: A History* (New York: Harcourt Brace Jovanovich, 1971), pp. 71–149. Evidence of the drought in the cities of Akkad was reported in John Noble Wilford, "Collapse of Earliest Known Empire Is Linked to Long, Harsh Drought," *New York Times,* August 24, 1993, pp. C1, C10.

3. McNeill, pp. 69–84; 170–75, 219–25; Bingham et al., vol. 1, pp. 132–33, 288–301; Coon, pp. 321–37; Clark, pp. 206–46.

4. McNeill, pp. 32–34, 72; Clark, pp. 100–118.

5. McNeill, pp. 135–202; Toynbee, vol. 1, pp. 26–50.

6. See Oswyn Murray, *Early Greece,* 2d ed. (Cambridge, Mass.: Harvard University Press, 1993), pp. 5–15, 81–101, 246–61; and Clark, pp. 134–63. Murray contends that Greek culture begins not with the Minoan civilization (2200–1400 B.C.) but with the Myceneans, who, though closely linked to Egypt and Mesopotamia, were ethnically and geographically the precursors to the Greeks. These societies were not totally autochthonous. Cultural "borrowings" also occurred, a phenomenon that McNeill, in particular, amply demonstrates.

7. Herschel Baker, *The Image of Man* (New York: Harper Torchbooks, 1967), pp. 112–19 [originally published by Harvard University Press in 1947 as *The Dignity of Man*]; Anthony Snodgrass, *Archaic Greece* (Berkeley: University of California Press, 1981), pp. 163–68, 194–200.

8. McNeill, pp. 211–16, 261–67; Palmer, pp. 164–66; Baker, pp. 3–15. There were exceptions to the rational conception of the universe. Pythagoras, for example, rejected the orderly world of the polis in favor of personal salvation. For the sixth-century Ionian philosophers such as Thales, Anaximander, and Anaximenes, the polis was the model for the world. Following the decline of the polis, however, the larger world increasingly became the model for society.

9. See Fernand Braudel, *On History,* pp. 202–5 (see chap. 3, n. 9); Baker, pp. 16–36.

10. For an erudite, if somewhat tendentious, history of Greek democracy, see A. H. M. Jones, *Athenian Democracy* (Oxford: Basil Blackwell, 1977). The symbol of democracy was the hoplite-farmer, the heavily armored infantryman who was the backbone of Athens' security and the spirit of its social egalitarianism. One must be careful not to idealize the polis, however. Snodgrass points out (pp. 25–47) that the polis existed alongside a different conception of the state, the *ethnos,* which was a large tribal system without urban centers united by customs and religion.

11. Toynbee, vol. 5, pp. 35–58; vol. 9, pp. 260–71, 741–57.

12. Toynbee, vol. 12, pp. 375–92.

13. Toynbee, vol. 12, pp., 380–85.

14. P. A. Brunt, *The Fall of the Roman Republic* (Oxford: Clarendon Press, 1988), pp. 282–97.

15. The standard account, of course, is Edward Gibbon's *Decline and Fall of the Roman Empire* (New York: Modern Library, 1932), vol. 1, chaps. 1–3, and vol. 2, pp. 46–193. The Roman pleb was the peasant-farmer equivalent of the Greek zeugite. At its maximum size, in Hadrian's time, the Roman empire comprised some 60 million people and extended from the Euphrates River to the Atlantic and from North Africa to the Rhine-Danube rivers in Europe, including most of Britain.

16. Michael Doyle provides a useful overview in *Empires* (Ithaca, N.Y.: Cornell University Press, 1986), chap. 4.

17. Brunt, pp. 1–92.

18. Peter Brown, *The World of Late Antiquity,* A.D. *150–750* (New York: Harcourt Brace Jovanovich, 1971), pp. 18–34. See also Aurelio Bernardi, "The Economic Problems of the Roman Empire at the Time of its Decline," in Carlo M. Cipolla, ed., *The Economic Decline of Empires* (London: Methuen, 1970), pp. 16–83.

19. Bingham et al., vol. 1, pp. 288–96; John King Fairbank and Edwin O. Reischauer, *China: Transition and Transformation* (Boston: Houghton-Mifflin, 1978), pp. 21–54; Wolfram Eberhard, *A History of China* (Berkeley: University of California Press, 1969), pp. 22–24; and Jacques Gernet, *A History of Chinese Civilization,* trans. J. R. Foster (Cambridge: Cambridge University Press, 1982), chap. 1.

20. John King Fairbank, *China: A New History* (Cambridge, Mass.: Harvard University Press, 1992), pp. 49–51; Gernet, pp. 87–98; and Charles O. Hucker, *China's Imperial Past* (Stanford: Stanford University Press, 1975), pp. 69–95. I wish to thank Paul Godwin for his clarifying insights on "imperial Confucianism."

21. Fairbank, chap. 2, esp. 49–69; Hucker, pp. 120–33; Bingham et al., vol. 1, pp. 310–26; Fairbank and Reischauer, pp. 55–83; Eberhard, pp. 71–103. At the height of Han power, China's population reached 60 million (Fairbank, p. 89), ironically the same size as that of Rome at the apogee of its power.

22. Lach, vol. 1, book 1, pp. 5–19; see also McNeill, pp. 298–304; and Bingham et al., vol. 1, pp. 148–57.

23. Bingham et al., vol. 1, chap. 18; Fairbank and Reischauer, pp. 96–99; Eberhard, pp. 166–91.

24. S. N. Eisenstadt provides a good sociopolitical analysis of the rise and fall of empires in *The Political Systems of Empires* (New York: Free Press, 1969). For a recent study of the role of religion in early societies, see Norman Cohn *Cosmos, Chaos, and the World to Come: Ancient Roots of Apocalyptic Faith* (New Haven, Conn.: Yale University Press, 1994).

25. Brown, pp. 18, 40–43, 62–68, 118–25; Doyle, pp. 92–103.

26. Bingham et al., vol. 1, pp. 369–74, chap. 18.

27. For further background see Donald Wilber, *Iran Past and Present,* 9th ed. (Princeton, N.J.: Princeton University Press, 1981), pp. 33–36; Stanley Wolpert, *A New History of India,* 3d ed. (New York: Oxford University Press, 1989), pp. 55–87; and Percival Spear, *India: A Modern History* (Ann Arbor: University of Michigan Press, 1972), pp. 3–93.

28. McNeill, pp. 167–88, 363–84; Wolpert, pp. 88–103.

29. See Georges Duby, *The Early Growth of the European Economy; Warriors and Peasants from the Seventh to the Twelfth Century,* trans. Howard B. Clarke (Ithaca, N.Y.: Cornell University Press, 1974), p. 49; Arthur Goldschmidt Jr., *A Concise History of the Middle East,* 4th ed. (Boulder, Colo.: Westview, 1991), p. 91; J. J. Saunders, *The History of the Mongol Conquests* (London: Routledge & Kegan Paul, 1971), pp. 17–43. See also J. J. Saunders, *The Muslim World on the Eve of European Expansionism* (Englewood Cliffs, N.J.: Prentice-Hall, 1966).

30. The tenuousness of life from about 500 B.C. to the twelfth century is described concisely in Douglass C. North and Robert Paul Thomas, *The Rise of the Western World: A New Economic History* (Cambridge: Cambridge University Press, 1973), pp. 19–89, and in great detail in William H. McNeill, *Plagues and Peoples* (Garden City, N.Y.: Anchor Books, 1976), chap. 3; also see Duby, *Early Growth,* pp. 5–30; Henri Pirenne's detailed study of urban and rural life in *Histoire Economique et Sociale du Moyen Age* (Paris: Presses Universitaires de France, 1969) chaps. 2–3; and Marc Bloch, *Feudal Society,* trans. L. A. Manyon, (Chicago: University of Chicago Press, 1961), vol. 1, pp. 60–61, 65–69.

31. Brown, p. 155; McNeill, *Plagues and Peoples,* pp. 71–72, 89–94; 103–20.

32. Eisenstadt, pp. 13–30.

33. McNeill, *Rise of the West,* p. 325; Eisenstadt, pp. 33–49, 94–112. In China, a moderation of the autocratic system of rule took place in the eighth century. During the late T'ang and Sung periods, as part of the Confucian (or neo-Confucian) ideal of egalitarianism, the landowning class broadened and bureaucrats began to rise to social prominence on the basis of talent rather than birth. See Edwin O. Reischauer, John King Fairbank, and Albert M. Craig, *East Asia: The Great Tradition* (Boston: Houghton-Mifflin, 1958), vol. 1, pp. 116–51. Further reforms took place in the eleventh century as a result of gains in agricultural productivity, rising incomes, and the spread of education. Although the governing elite still exploited the poor, the emergence of a rentier class moderated their exploitation. For more, see Fairbank, *China,* pp. 60, 83–87; and Gernet, pp. 305–308, 312–14.

34. Duby, *Early Growth,* pp. 39–40; Fairbank, *China,* chap. 3; Gernet, pp. 149–53.

35. Bingham et al., vol. 1, pp. 142–57, 310–26; Spear, pp. 59–68.

36. For an interesting discussion of social decay and philosophical individualism in ancient Greece; see Baker, pp. 84–119. The Buddhists refer to the Mahayana form of their faith as the "Greater Vehicle," as opposed to the "Lesser Vehicle," or the more ascetic strain. See Wolpert, pp. 49–50; Fairbank, *China*, pp. 53–54, 72–76.

37. Brown, pp. 24–34, 47–68, 118–25, 134–35. See also Friedrich Heer, *The Intellectual History of Europe*, trans. Jonathan Steinberg (Cleveland: World Publishing Co., 1966), pp. 7–15.

38. Brown, pp. 143–48; Heer, pp. 20–24, 37; Sir John Glubb, *The Course of Empire: The Arabs and Their Successors* (Englewood Cliffs, N.J.: Prentice-Hall, 1965), pp. 21–33; also see John Esposito, *Islam: The Straight Path* (New York: Oxford University Press, 1988).

39. Goldschmidt, pp. 27–76; Bingham et al., vol. 1, pp. 86–94.

40. Bingham et al., vol. 1, pp. 278–79; Saunders, *History of Mongol Conquests*, pp. 57–87.

41. Heer, pp. 380–407; North and Thomas, pp. 33–45.

42. J. G. A. Pocock eloquently describes the concepts of time and salvation in European society in *The Machiavellian Moment*, pp. 31–33 (see chap. 2, n. 4).

43. See Heer, pp. 25–42; Geoffrey Barraclough, *The Crucible of Europe: The Ninth and Tenth Centuries in European History* (Berkeley: University of California Press, 1976), pp. 10–13; Barraclough, *History in a Changing World* (see chap. 3, n. 16), pp. 33–37.

44. On the alternatives to Christianity, see, for example, Emmanuel LeRoy Ladurie, *Montaillou: village occitan de 1294 a 1324* (Paris: Gallimard, 1975); Barraclough, *Crucible*, pp. 28–33, 41–50, 58–78; and Duby, *Early Growth*, pp. 57–72.

45. The word feudalism derives from the French or English *fief* or the Old German *fehu-od,* or land held in return for military service. See "Feudalism," in *International Encyclopedia of the Social Sciences*, vol. 12, pp. 393–402; Duby, *Early Growth*, pp. 78–110; Joseph R. Strayer, "Feudalism in Western Europe," in Rushton Coulborn, ed., *Feudalism in History* (Princeton, N.J.: Princeton University Press, 1956), pp. 15–25; Bloch, vol. 1, pp. 145–62, 219–30, 241–79, and vol. 2, pp. 345–56.

46. Georges Duby, *Les Trois Ordres ou l'Imaginaire du Féodalisme* (Paris: Gallimard, 1978), pp. 28–31, 183–205. Also see his *Rural Economy and Country Life in the Medieval West,* trans. Cynthia Postan (Columbia, S.C.: University of South Carolina Press, 1968), pp. 208–39. Duby's findings challenged the chronology of feudal life advanced by Marc Bloch.

47. Barraclough nicely details the evolution of feudal structures in *Crucible*, pp. 84–142; see also Duby, *Early Growth*, chaps. 6–8.

48. Feudal antecedents can be found in the Sassanid empire in Persia and as far back as the Kassite kingdom in Mesopotamia. See "Feudalism" (above, n. 46). Also see Burr C. Brundage, "Feudalism in Ancient Mesopotamia"; and

William F. Edgerton, "The Question of Feudal Institutions in Ancient Egypt," in Coulborn, pp. 93–119 and 120–32, respectively.

49. John Whitney Hall, "The Nature of Traditional Society: Japan," in Robert E. Ward and Dankwart A. Rustow, eds., *Political Modernization in Japan and Turkey* (Princeton, N.J.: Princeton University Press, 1964), pp. 14–19; Bingham et al., vol. 1, chaps. 26–27; Derk Bodde, "Feudalism in China"; and Daniel Thorner, "Feudalism in India," in Coulborn, pp. 26–48 and 133–50, respectively. For an elaboration of feudalism in Japanese culture, see Edwin O. Reischauer and John King Fairbank, *East Asia: The Great Tradition,* vol. 1 (Boston: Houghton-Mifflin, 1958), chaps. 12–13.

50. Hall, in Ward and Rustow, pp. 35–41; Duby, *Trois Ordres,* pp. 77–81.

51. Heer, pp. 61–69; Duby, *Trois Ordres,* pp. 401–22.

52. For a Turkish perspective, see Hilal Inalcik, *The Ottoman Empire: The Classical Age, 1300–1600* (London: George Weidenfeld & Nicolson, 1973), pp. 9–34; and Lord Kinross, *The Ottoman Centuries: The Rise and Fall of the Turkish Empire* (New York: William Morrow, 1977), chaps. 2–3; for the European, see Braudel, *Philip II,* vol. 2, pp. 911–24, 1083–1142, passim.

53. For a more detailed exposition, see J. J. Saunders, *The History of the Mongol Conquests,* esp. pp. 73–90, 119–39; also see Kinross, chap. 4.

54. McNeill, *Rise of the West,* pp. 456–62, 524–31, 633–34; Fairbank and Reischauer, pp. 152–76; Eberhard, pp. 232–41.

55. Duby, *Rural Economy,* pp. 123–25, 146–49; Wallerstein, *The Modern World-System,* vol. 1, pp. 15–21, 189–221 (see chap. 1, n. 32). According to Duby, money began to circulate as early as the ninth century, although the idea of exchange value and the decentralization of commercial activity came much later (see pp. 130–34).

56. Heer, pp. 126, 257–65.

57. Georges Duby, *Early Growth,* pp. 189–94; Wallerstein, *The Modern World-System,* vol. 2, pp. 36–51.

58. Lach, vol. 1, book 1, pp. 81–83; Duby, *Early Growth,* pp. 267–70.

59. Ladurie and J. K. Hyde examine the social conditions, including the role of religion, of the medieval poor in France and Italy, respectively. See Ladurie's *Montaillou.* Also see Hyde's *Society and Politics in Medieval Italy: The Evolution of Civil Life, 1000–1350* (London: Macmillan, 1973). The Gregorian reforms, which were inspired by the conflict between the papacy and Emperor Henry IV over the feudal practice of lay investiture—the award of ecclesiastical jurisdiction by secular rulers—led, in 1122, to the Concordat of Worms, which formalized the beginning of the end of imperial domination of the Church.

60. Heer, pp. 80–82, 94, 120–25; Lach, vol. 1, book 1, pp. 30–33.

61. Heer, pp. 142–44, 153–54; Gay and Webb (see chap. 1, n. 32), vol. 1, pp. 22–45.

62. McNeill, *The Rise of the West,* pp. 512–19. The first Bulgarian Empire was overthrown by Basil II in 1018.

63. Bingham et al., vol. 1, pp. 441–48.

64. Bingham et al., vol. 1, chap. 24; McNeill, *The Rise of the West,* pp. 535–36.

Chapter Five

1. Barbara Tuchman devotes considerable attention to the effects of the plague in *A Distant Mirror: The Calamitous Fourteenth Century* (New York: Random House, 1978), chap. 5. Protection of the Jews declined in part because the nobility, which increasingly turned to the large banking houses that began to emerge in the twelfth and thirteenth centuries, no longer valued their social utility. In this period of great social change, there was also a general decline in religious tolerance. The plague intensified religious hysteria. Perceived enemies of Christendom, Jews lost their property and their lives in countless persecutions. Pope Clement VI issued a bull in 1348 urging the clergy to protect the Jews, but it had little impact on a public that hardly stood in awe of the Church's authority.

2. On the basis of documentary evidence, Duby estimates the onset of the depression at around 1330. See *Rural Economy,* p. 130. Wallerstein notes that the depression lasted until around 1450; see *The Modern World-System,* vol. 1, pp. 36–51. For background, also see Robert-Henri Bautier, *The Economic Development of Medieval Europe,* trans. Heather Karolyi (London: Harcourt, Brace Jovanovich, 1971), chap. 4; Emmanuel LeRoy Ladurie, *The French Peasantry,* trans. Alan Sheridan (Aldershot, England: Scolar Press, 1987), chap. 5; and Douglass C. North and Robert Paul Thomas, *The Rise of the Western World* (see chap. 4, n. 30).

3. McNeill, *Rise of the West,* pp. 583–85 (see chap. 4, n. 1); Gay and Webb (see chap. 1, n. 32), vol. 1, pp. 201–5.

4. John Gerard Ruggie, "Territoriality and Beyond: Problematizing Modernity in International Relations," *International Organization* 47, no. 1 (Winter 1993): 151. The rich, wine-producing land in Guienne and Gascony that passed to Henry in the twelfth century was part of the dowry of Eleanor of Aquitaine.

5. Lach (see chap. 2, n. 26), vol. 1, book 1, p. 64. By the mid-fifteenth century, Portuguese ships regularly visited the neighboring Azores and Madeira Island and the coasts of Africa.

6. Charles Diehl, "The Economic Decay of Byzantium," in Cipolla, ed. (see chap. 4, n. 18), pp. 92–101.

7. Braudel, *Philip II,* vol. 2, pp. 661–78, 1083–1142, 1167–1204; Bingham et al., vol. 2, pp. 116–22.

8. Bernard Lewis, "Some Reflections on the Decline of the Ottoman Empire," in Cipolla, ed., p. 230; McNeill, *Rise of the West,* pp. 490–94.

9. Percival Spear, *India: A Modern History,* pp. 94–101; Stanley Wolpert, *A New History of India,* pp. 104–25. (For both, see chap. 4, n. 27).

10. Spear, pp. 115–45; Wolpert, pp. 149–67; Bingham et al. vol. 1, pp. 280–82; Lach, vol. 1, book 1, p. 382.

11. McNeill, *Rise of the West,* pp. 558–59, 611–16; Wolpert, pp. 173–86; Immanuel Wallerstein, "Patterns of Development of the Modern World-System," in Hopkins and Wallerstein, eds., *World-Systems Analysis* (see chap. 3, n. 49), vol. 1, pp. 49–58; Geoffrey Barraclough, *Turning Points in World History,* pp. 24–27 (see chap. 1, n. 43).

12. Gernet (see chap. 4, n. 19), pp. 326–29.

13. Hucker (see chap. 4, n. 20), chap. 12, esp. pp. 351–56. Bingham et al. also provide a detailed description of Ming history (chap. 23).

14. Lach, vol. 1, book 1, pp. 226–27, 305–9, vol. 1, book 2, 646–52, 822–35. The arrival of the Europeans in China is also discussed in Immanuel C. Y. Hsu, *The Rise of Modern China,* 2d. ed. (New York: Oxford University Press, 1975), pp. 129–50.

15. Lach, vol. 1, book 2, pp. 654, 677, 719–29; Bingham et al., vol. 1, chaps. 26–27; Hall, "The Nature of Traditional Society," in Ward and Rustow (see chap. 4, n. 49), pp. 14–19. Like Europe, Japan had developed a warrior-based feudal society dating from the Kamakura period, or the end of the twelfth century, in which authority was hierarchically centralized in the person of the shogun.

16. For background on the rich history of this period, see Braudel, *Philip II,* vol. 2, pp. 911–54, 1178–85; see also Wallerstein, *The Modern World-System,* vol. 2, pp. 182–92.

17. Braudel, *Philip II,* vol. 2, pp. 725–34, 755–56; Franz Borkenau, *End and Beginning: On the Generations of Cultures and the Origins of the West* (New York: Columbia University Press, 1981), pp. 133–201.

18. Ladurie, *Montaillou,* supra (see chap. 4, n. 44); for the varieties of religious and pseudo-religious experience in other parts of Europe, see Carlo Ginzburg, *The Cheese and the Worms,* trans. John and Anne Tedeschi (London: Routledge & Kegan Paul, 1980), which views society through the eyes of a sixteenth-century miller. The preoccupation with magic in post-Renaissance England is described by Keith Thomas, *Religion and the Decline of Magic* (New York: Scribner's, 1971).

19. Gay and Webb, vol. 2, pp. 123–60; Tuchman, chaps. 5, 19. The theme of death became a prominent part of European popular culture after the Great Plague, as the processional plays of the fourteenth and fifteenth centuries reflect. The sense of personal abdication that attended the death rituals of the time bears similarity to what Franz Borkenau (pp. 89–92) has referred to as the "death-embracing" totalitarian cultures of the post-Christian twentieth century. As for the Lollard movement, which foreshadowed the French Revolution, it began as a revolt of intellectuals. But, as it spread to the poor, it became increasingly radicalized, its passion consummated in the Protestant Revolution.

20. The classic psychological study of Luther is Erik Erikson's *Young Man Luther* (New York: W. W. Norton, 1958). From the dawn of Christianity, the East had been a cauldron of heresy and irrational spiritualism that was aroused by the hatred of an aristocratic, rational, ideologically alien order imposed on a

conquered but hardly defeated barbarian world. See Heer (see chap. 4, n. 37), pp. 218–32.

21. Heer, p. 318.

22. To relegate the Renaissance to the epoch of order, as some intellectual historians have done (Herschel Baker, for example: see chap. 4, n. 7, pp. 203–22), because of the continued influence of religion and Scholasticism is to ignore the material changes in fourteenth- and fifteenth-century European society and the skeptical view of classical certainties repackaged by Thomistic dogmatism. Conversely, Stephen Toulmin argues that modernity began in the Renaissance. See *Cosmopolis: The Hidden Agenda of Modernity* (New York: Free Press, 1990), pp. 17–30. Also see Kahler, p. 132; Robert Nisbet, *The Idea of Progress* (New York: Basic Books, 1980), pp. 101–6, 172; Raymond Duncan Gastil, *Progress: Critical Thinking about Historical Change* (Westport, Conn.: Praeger, 1993), p. 19; and Franco Ferrarotti, *The Myth of Inevitable Progress* (Westport, Conn.: Greenwood Press, 1985), pp. 17–18.

23. In his psychobiography, Erikson makes note of Ockham's influence on Luther, pp. 190–91. Also see Heer, pp. 167–70.

24. Pocock, *Politics, Language and Time,* pp. 84–92 (see chap. 2, n. 3).

25. See Toulmin, pp. 36–44; Heer, pp. 328–29; Pocock, *Politics,* p. 276.

26. Braudel, *Philip II,* vol. 2, pp. 826–29; John Rupert Martin, "The Baroque in Art History," in Spencer (see chap. 3, n. 2), pp. 161–71. From 1600 to 1650 the combination of an agricultural recession, declining population, and the concentration of estates displaced peasants and small farmers everywhere. This dislocation, in turn, led to some refeudalization. See Wallerstein, *The Modern World-System,* vol., 2, pp. 25–26, chap. 4.

27. Martin, pp. 161–171. See also John Rupert Martin, *The Baroque* (London: A. Lane, 1980).

28. Heer, pp. 307–14.

29. Heer, pp. 228–44, 418–19; Toulmin, pp. 30–42, 69–71. See Descartes' *Meditations on First Philosophy* [orig. 1641], esp. part III, in Monroe C. Beardsley, ed., *The European Philosophers from Descartes to Nietzsche* (New York: Modern Library, 1960), pp. 33–40. For the entire text, see the version edited and translated by John Cottingham (Cambridge: Cambridge University Press, 1986). Also see Leibniz's *Theodicy, Essays on the Goodness of God, the Freedom of Men, and the Origin of Evil,* ed. Austin Farrer and trans. E. M. Huggard (London: Routledge & Kegan Paul, 1957).

30. For more on the specialization of learning in history, see Kenneth E. Boulding, *The Meaning of the Twentieth Century* (New York: Harper, 1964), chap. 2.

31. Leibniz's famous dictum can be found in *Monadology,* paragraphs 78–83, in Beardsley; see also Heer, pp. 368–81.

32. See Thomas Hobbes, *Leviathan,* ed. Michael Oakeshott (New York: Collier Books, 1962 [orig. 1651]); Locke's *Two Treatises of Government,* ed. Mau-

rice Cranston (Collier Books, 1965 [orig. 1690]); Jean-Jacques Rousseau, *The Social Contract,* trans. G. D. H. Cole (New York: E. P. Dutton and Company, 1950 [orig. 1761]). Descartes' *Discours,* which develops the a priori belief that individuals are capable of reasoning to their own conceptions of reality, and Leibniz's notion of self-contained monads emphasize the uniqueness of the individual and, a fortiori, anticipate the ideology of progress they were self-consciously helping to create.

33. Michael Polanyi and Harry Prosch, *Meaning* (Chicago: University of Chicago Press, 1975), pp. 7–9. Herr maintains (p. 361) that the English Revolution was the prototype of the French and Russian revolutions. But the heavenly kingdom on earth that the French and Russians aspired to was far less tolerant and inclusivist than the constitutional monarchy that emerged from the events of 1688–89 in England. The extremism of the French and Russian revolutions was closer to the Cromwellian "democracy" of 1640–60.

34. See Heer, pp. 382–90; Gay and Webb, vol. 2, pp. 290–316.

35. See Grumley (see chap. 3, n. 12), pp. 1–7; Heer, 387–407.

36. This formulation reflects the contemporary criticism of realist and neo-realist theories of international relations, which assert that states are inherently driven by the desire for universal domination. See the essays in Robert O. Keohane, ed., *Neorealism and its Critics* (New York: Columbia University Press, 1986).

37. Heer, pp. 423–25; see also Polanyi, *Knowing and Being* (see chap. 3, n. 37), pp. 6–8. Wars over monarchical succession—in Spain, Poland, Austria—were relatively bloodless affairs that provided opportunities to settle old scores and exploit the infirmities of one's neighbors. In the case of the War of the Austrian Succession, for example, the entire cast of European characters participated, including those on the periphery, like England, which joined the fray against Austria, in part to avenge the loss of a naval captain's ear.

38. Wallerstein, *The Modern World-System,* vol. 3, chap. 3 (see chap. 1, n. 33); McNeill, pp. 695–704.

39. Wallerstein, *The Modern World-System,* vol. 3, chap. 3; Kennedy (see chap. 1, n. 6), pp. 115–26.

40. Goldschmidt (see chap. 4, n. 29), chap. 10.

41. Reischauer, Fairbank, and Craig (see chap. 4, n. 33), pp. 254–57, 413–18.

42. Gay and Webb, vol. 2, pp. 563–76, 713–39. Still the best book on the revolutions of 1848 is Louis Namier, *1848: The Revolt of the Intellectuals* (New York: Anchor Books, 1964).

43. It is ironic that Adam Smith's *Wealth of Nations* was published in the same year that the American revolutionaries severed their ties with Britain for its failure to apply precisely such principles of natural law in its relations with its colonies. *An Inquiry into the Nature and Causes of the Wealth of Nations,* ed. Edwin Canaan (New York: Modern Library, 1937) bears the influence of Hume

and the French physiocrats, notably François Quesnay, who coined the term "laissez faire."

44. See Cipolla, *The Economic History of World Population*, pp. 27–34 (see chap. 4, n. 1); see also Karl Polanyi, *The Great Transformation* (New York: Holt, Rinehart & Winston, 1957), chaps. 5 and 7, esp. pp. 72–83. For the introduction of technology in early modern Europe, see Fernand Braudel, *Civilisation et Capitalisme Matérielle (xve–xviiie siècle) (Paris: A. Colin, 1967)*, chaps. 5–6. For the later period, see J. H. Clapham, *Industrial Development in France and Germany, 1815–1914* (Cambridge: Cambridge University Press, 1968); Phyllis Deane, *The First Industrial Revolution, 1750–1850* 2d ed. (Cambridge: Cambridge University Press, 1979), and David S. Landes, *The Unbound Prometheus: Technological Change and Industrial Development in Western Europe from 1750 to the Present*, 4th ed. (London: Cambridge University Press, 1969).

45. For the effects of technology and industrialization on peoples' lives, see Charles Tilly, *Coercion, Capital, and the European States* (Cambridge, Mass.: Harvard University Press, 1990), and the essays on the proletarianization of the working class in Charles Tilly, Louise A. Tilly, and Richard Tilly, eds., *Class Conflict and Collective Action* (Beverly Hills, Calif.: Sage, 1981).

46. Karl Polanyi has persuasively argued that the Reform Act of 1832 and the Poor Law Reform Act of 1834 politically and economically defined the British working class (p. 166). See also Immanuel Wallerstein, *The Modern World-System*, vol. 3, pp. 125–26.

47. Gordon A. Craig, *Europe since 1815* (New York: Holt, Rinehart & Winston, 1961), pp. 260–66, 316–19, 345–50, 371–82; Gay and Webb, vol. 2, pp. 826–39; Clapham, pp. 158–74, 195–200, 265–70, 328–38, 402–7; Cipolla, pp. 30–31. In 1900, 35 percent of Germans and 42 percent of Frenchmen were still employed in agriculture. Sixty percent of Austrians, Hungarians, and Italians, and 77 percent of Poles were still working on farms.

48. Gay and Webb, vol. 2, pp. 612–17.

49. See A. P. Thornton, *The Imperial Idea and its Enemies: A Study in British Power* (New York: Anchor Books, 1959), pp. 1–17; Gay and Webb, vol. 2, p. 851.

50. National glorification and its emphasis on language, folklore, and the flag derived in part from Herbert Spencer's social interpretation of Charles Darwin's *Origin of Species*. Writers such as Charles Dilke, Sir John Seeley, Heinrich von Treitschke, and Charles Maurras, along with an increasingly jingoist European press, trumpeted grandiose, nationalistic themes that provided gullible, ill-informed publics an emotional escape from the turmoil of social change. Not surprisingly, defense spending also grew by leaps and bounds. In the two decades between 1880 and 1900, the combined military and naval personnel of the six European powers grew by more than 40 percent. For more, see Thornton, pp. 24, 58; Craig, pp. 263–64; Heer, pp. 431–33; Gay and Webb, vol. 2, pp. 668–74; Kennedy, p. 203.

51. Thornton, p. 86; Craig, pp. 191–92, 237–41.

52. Romania and Bulgaria gained their independence during the Congress of Berlin. In addition, Bosnia and Herzegovina passed to Austria, and Bessarabia was ceded to Russia. As part of the division of spoils, Britain received Cyprus, and France was given a free hand in Tunisia, which it annexed in 1882. In that year, Britain occupied Egypt, nominally under Ottoman suzerainty, thereby adding another protective link to the chain of possessions that fortified its control of India.

53. H. K. Takahashi, "The Transition from Feudalism to Capitalism," *Science and Society* 16, no. 4 (Fall 1952): 313–45.

54. Daniel Bell, *The End of Ideology* (see chap. 2, n. 1), pp. 394–96, 401–7; Anthony Giddens, *Modernity and Self-Identity: Self and Society in the Late Modern Age* (Stanford, Calif.: Stanford University Press, 1991), chap. 1; Karl Polanyi, chap. 13. See also Karl Mannheim, *Ideology and Utopia,* trans. Louis Wirth and Edward Shils (New York: Harcourt, Brace & World, 1936). Not all Marxists favored revolution. Eduard Bernstein, the German critic of Marxist orthodoxy, for example, advocated a peaceful, democratic approach to social change.

55. Michael Polanyi attributed the nihilistic excess of the twentieth century to eighteenth-century rationalism and the unbridled—indeed, immoral—individualism unleashed by the philosophes. By World War I, however, the sovereignty of the individual had become absorbed by the dictatorship of the elite. See *Knowing and Being,* pp. 4–8.

56. Von Laue (see chap. 2, n. 31) points out (pp. 32–33) that the emergence of pan-Negroism was also attributable to Western influence, specifically, the Pan African Conference that W. E. B. DuBois and other black leaders held in London in 1900.

Chapter Six

1. Tillich, quoted in Michael Polanyi, "The Message of the Hungarian Revolution," in *Knowing and Being* (see chap. 3, n. 37); Sidney Pollard, *The Idea of Progress* (New York: Basic Books, 1968), pp. 6–39; Christopher Lasch, *The True and Only Heaven* (New York: W. W. Norton, 1991). For the view of progress as theodicy, see John Baillie, *The Belief in Progress* (New York: Scribner, 1951); and Karl Lowith, *Meaning in History* (Chicago: University of Chicago Press, 1949).

2. J. B. Bury, *The Idea of Progress* (London: Macmillan, 1932), and Baillie and Robert Nisbet, *History of the Idea of Progress* (New York: Basic Books, 1980), are two of Bury's critics.

3. See W. Warren Wagar, *Good Tidings: Progress from Darwin to Marcuse* (Bloomington: Indiana University Press, 1972) and Carl Becker, *The Heavenly City of the Eighteenth Century Philosophers* (New Haven, Conn.: Yale Univer-

sity Press, 1932). Kahler (see chap. 3, n. 11) (pp. 126–31) traces the rudimentary notion of progress to monastic scholars such as the German bishop Otto of Freising, a Cisterian. By the thirteenth century, he noted, the writings of Azo, a Bolognese jurist, anticipated the later view that human nature incrementally develops through its knowledge of the world. Gay and Webb, vol. 1 (see chap. 1, n. 32), pp. 60–65, also point out the change in human perspective that took place during the Renaissance.

4. Kahler, pp. 135, 173–74.

5. Carl Becker, "Origins and Definitions," in W. Warren Wagar, ed., *The Idea of Progress Since the Renaissance* (New York: John Wiley, 1969), pp. 12–16, and the chapters on Kant and Condorcet in the same volume; Nisbet, pp. 171–85.

6. Pollard, pp. 43–83. According to Nisbet (pp. 176–78), eighteenth-century and early nineteenth-century philosophers shared little of the twentieth-century intellectual's revulsion toward capitalism.

7. Pollard, pp. 99–106, 144–47.

8. Iggers (see chap. 3, n. 11), p. 150; Nisbet, p. 178.

9. Henry Vyverberg, *Historical Pessimism in the French Enlightenment* (Cambridge, Mass.: Harvard University Press, 1958), pp. 75–95, 140–200; Nisbet, pp. 318–21; Iggers, p. 153; Gastil (see chap. 5, n. 22), pp. 17–19; and the chapter on Burckhardt in Wagar, *Progress since the Renaissance,* pp. 119–29.

10. Pollard, chap. 4.

11. Gay and Webb, vol. 2, chap. 22.

12. As examples, see Brooks Adams, *The Law of Civilization and Decay* (London: Macmillan, 1903) and Henry Adams, *The Degradation of the Democratic Dogma* (London: MacMillan, 1919). Also see Pierre Teilhard de Chardin, *The Future of Man,* trans. Norman Denny (New York: Harper & Row, 1964 [1959]); C. P. Snow, *The Two Cultures and the Scientific Revolution* (Cambridge: Cambridge University Press, 1959); and Margaret Mead, *Twentieth Century Faith* (New York: Harper & Row, 1972). Also see the realism of Reinhold Neibuhr, *Faith and History: A Comparison of Christian and Modern Views of History* (New York: Scribner's, 1949); and Franz Boas, *Anthropology and Modern Life* (New York: Norton, 1928).

13. Kenneth A. Boulding, *The Meaning of the Twentieth Century* (see chap. 5, n. 30), pp. 123–25.

14. von Laue (see chap. 2, n. 31), pp. 63–64, passim.

15. Akira Iriye briefly touches on the Japanese self-image in the context of post–World War I policy making in *After Imperialism* (see chap 2, n. 28), pp. 4–13, passim.

16. See Arnold J. Toynbee, *The World and the West* (New York: Oxford University Press, 1953); von Laue, chap. 8.

17. Gadamer's essay, "The Philosophical Foundation of the Twentieth Century" (see chap. 3, n. 12), is a concise statement of the changing intellectual orientation of Western society after World War I (pp. 107–29).

18. For a good overview of the collapse of progress in the twentieth century, see Gastil, chap. 1.

19. See William Barrett, *Irrational Man* (New York: Doubleday, 1958), chaps. 1–2. The nihilistic impulse appears to be representative of what Borkenau (see chap. 5, n. 17) calls "death-embracing" cultures (pp. 71–75). In contrast to other civilizations, however, such as the Aztec or the Indian, nihilism denies individual immortality. On reflection, Borkenau likens totalitarianism to the death-denial of prehistoric, primitive societies that defined death as the consequence of black magic. The witch hunts that followed and the murderous passions they released reflected the breakthroughs into consciousness of "death paranoia." "This modern form of the worship of death, therefore, tends to call forth phenomena analogous to those produced in past ages by the denial of death. Just as the denial of death could only be maintained by 'uncovering' a magic murderer for each case of actual death, so the modern worship of death can only be maintained by seeking to destroy each soul that gives a sign of life. In either case, the result is murder without end . . ." (p. 92). Michael Polanyi argues in *Knowing and Being* (see chap 3, n. 37) that the might makes right idea grew out of Hegel's teaching of immanent reason. "The strength of immanent morality is proved by the violence of manifest immortality (p. 17)."

20. See Capra (see chap. 3, n. 30), pp. 56–71, chap. 3. George Gilder succinctly traces the origins of quantum theory in *Microcosm* (New York: Simon and Schuster, 1989), chap. 1.

21. Robert Gilpin, *American Scientists and Nuclear Weapons* (Princeton, N.J.: Princeton University Press, 1962), pp. 42–43.

22. See Boulding, *Twentieth Century,* pp. 142–43; Herman Kahn, William Brown, and Leon Martel, *The Next 200 Years* (New York: Quill, 1976), pp. 205–26; William J. Broad, "Strange Oases in Sea Depths Offer Map to Riches," *New York Times,* November 16, 1993, pp. C1, C15.

23. Felix Rohatyn, "The New Domestic Order," *New York Review,* November 21, 1991, p. 8.

24. For an insightful sociocultural analysis of religious fundamentalism, see Martin E. Marty and R. Scott Appleby, eds., *Fundamentalisms Observed* (Chicago: University of Chicago Press, 1991), pp. 814–42; also see Richard Morin, "Harmonic Resurgence," and T. R. Reid, "The Doomsday Guru" and "New Cults Flourish in a Changed Japan," *Washington Post,* June 27, 1993, pp. C1, C4, and March 24 and 27, 1995, pp. A25 and A1 and A16, respectively. For L'Ordre du Temple Solaires, see *Newsweek,* "Suicide Cult," October 17, 1994, pp. 10–15.

25. Lasch, p. 49.

26. See Pollard, pp. 194–200; Lasch, pp. 80–81. Lasch's indictment of progress contrasts with Herman Kahn's earlier, more technologically based future in Kahn et al. Writing nearly 20 years ago, Kahn and his colleagues concluded (p. 10) that, except for population, "there is no persuasive evidence that any meaningful limits to growth are in sight." A more recent, upbeat prognostication

of the future is Carl H. Builder, *Patterns in American Intellectual Frontiers,* N-2917-A (Santa Monica, Calif.: RAND Corporation, 1990).

27. Lyotard (see chap. 3, n. 25), pp. 20, 107–8. The term is Michael Polanyi's. See *Meaning,* p. 12.

28. Kahler, p. 206.

29. Lyotard, pp. 60–67. The notion that there is no "objective" meaning in history is a central tenet of existentialism. See Iggers, pp. 156–57.

30. See Pocock, *Machivellian Moment,* supra (see chap. 2, n. 4); and Quentin Skinner, *Machiavelli* (New York: Oxford University Press, 1981). Also see R. B. J. Walker, "The Prince and 'The Pauper': Tradition, Modernity, and Practice in the Theory of International Relations," in James Der Derian and Michael J. Shapiro, eds., *International/Intertextual Relations* (Lexington, Mass.: Lexington Books, 1989), pp. 25–46; Matei Calinescu, *Five Faces of Modernity: Modernism, Avant Garde, Decadence, Kitsch, Post-Modernism* (Durham, N.C.: Duke University Press, 1987); and Frank Ninkovich's deconstructive critique of the views of George Kennan and Charles Beard, "Interests and Discourse in Diplomatic History," *Diplomatic History* 13 (Spring 1989): 135–61.

31. See Richard K. Ashley, "Living on Border Lines: Man, Poststructuralism, and War," in Der Derian and Shapiro, pp. 259–321.

32. Vaclav Havel, "The End of the Modern Era," *New York Times,* March 1, 1992, p. 15; also see Barraclough, *History in a Changing World,* pp. 226–30; and Giddens, *Modernity,* chap. 3.

Chapter Seven

1. For an elaboration of international political change, see James N. Rosenau, *Turbulence in World Politics: A Theory of Change and Continuity* (Princeton, N.J.: Princeton University Press, 1990), pp. 92–96. For more on the emergence of nonstate actors and on regime theory, see Stephen D. Krasner, ed., *International Regimes* (Ithaca, N.Y.: Cornell University Press, 1983). The interaction of state and nongovernmental actors is what Ernst-Otto Czempiel refers to as "internationalizing politics" in "International Politics: Some Questions of Who Does What to Whom," in Czempiel and Rosenau, eds., *Global Change and Theoretical Challenges* (see chap. 1, n. 38), pp. 117–31. See also Keohane, *Neorealism* (see chap. 5, n. 36); and Kenneth Waltz, *Theory of International Politics* (Reading, Mass.: Addison Wesley, 1979).

2. Peter Drucker, *The New Realities* (New York; Harper & Row, 1989), pp. 124–25.

3. Paul Lewis, "Gains Cited at U.N. on Cutting Infant Deaths"; "A Computerized Attack on a Virus"; Jane Brady, "Researchers Discover New Therapies to Avert Repeated Miscarriages"; and Howard W. French, "Scientist Says Test Show New Vaccine May Prevent Malaria," *New York Times,* October 3, 1993, p. 21; August 11, 1991, p. F9; December 15, 1992, p. C3; and September 22,

1994, p. A17, respectively; also see Hugh De Santis, "Commercial Observation Satellites and Their Military Implications: A Speculative Assessment," *Washington Quarterly* (Summer 1989): 185–87.

4. A useful source for the statistics of global arms sales is Richard F. Grimmett, *Conventional Arms Transfers to the Third World, 1986–1993* (Washington, D.C.: Congressional Research Service, Library of Congress, July 1994), pp. 5, 46, 60. The total value of U.S. arms sales in 1993 rose slightly to $14.8 billion from the previous year, but the U.S. share of the value of all arms agreements soared to 72.6 percent versus 55.8 percent in 1992.

5. Although Russia's deliveries of arms have declined dramatically since the end of the Cold War, its impecunious condition has prompted it to sell top-of-the line fighter aircraft, surface-to-air missiles, Kilo-class diesel submarines, and T-72 and T-74 tanks to China, Iran, Syria, and other states. See Grimmett, pp. 6–8. Also see Don Podesta, "Latin Weapons Industries Slip in Post Cold-War Chill"; Thomas W. Lippman, "Ex-Soviet Arms Exports Plunge"; Rick Atkinson, "Prague Says Uranium Found in Czech Auto Could Trigger Bomb"; and Raymond Bonner, "Iran Buying 100 Tanks from Poland," *Washington Post,* June 25, 1993, pp. A27–28; June 13, 1993, p. A28, December 21, 1994, pp. A27, A30; and May 17, 1995, p. A3, respectively; William E. Schmidt, "Neutral Sweden Pursues Arms Sales"; Michael R. Gordon, "Moscow Selling Weapons to China, U.S. Officials Say"; Steven Erlanger, "Moscow Insists It Must Sell the Instruments of War to Pay the Costs of Peace"; Jane Perlez, "Czechs Gear Up to Resume Weapons Exports"; Elaine Sciolino, "Russia Is Halting Arms-Linked Sale"; Douglas Jehl, "Who Armed Iraq? Answers the West Didn't Want to Hear"; and Richard W. Stevenson, "Europe Uniting in Building Arms," *New York Times,* February 17, 1992, p. D1; October 18, 1992, pp. 1, 14; February 3, 1993, p. A6; July 4, 1993, p. F7; July 17, 1993, p. 4; July 18, 1993, p. E5; and August 16, 1994, pp. D1, D14. See also "Pistols at a New Dawn" and "Czech Arms: Buyers, Please," *The Economist,* April 10, 1993, pp. 68, 71, and November 6, 1993, p. 90. On the smuggling of nuclear materials, see Craig R. Whitney, "Germans Seize 3d Atom Sample, Smuggled by Plane from Russia," and Patrick E. Tyler, "As China Upgrades Its Nuclear Arsenal, It Debates Need for Guns versus Butter," *New York Times,* August 14, 1994, pp. 1, 12, and October 26, 1994, p. A10. Some experts believe that the spread of sophisticated weaponry and computerized information presage a military revolution. Unlike the industrial era of attrition warfare, in the future, military forces will engage one another on an electronic battlefield with stand-off weapons. See Thomas E. Ricks, "How Wars Are Fought Will Change Radically, Pentagon Planner Says," *Wall Street Journal,* July 15, 1994, pp. 1, A5.

6. The terms of the extension of the nonproliferation treaty are presented by Stephen W. Young and Daniel T. Plesch in "A Permanent Non-Proliferation Treaty," *Basic Reports,* a newsletter on international security policy published by the British–American Security Information Council, June 1, 1995, pp. 1–8;

also see Thomas W. Lippman, "START I Agreement Takes Effect Monday," *Washington Post,* December 4, 1994, p. A46; Grimmett (1994), pp. 8–9.

7. See Stephanie G. Neuman, "Controlling the Arms Trade: Idealistic Dream or Realpolitik?" *Washington Quarterly* (Summer 1993): 61–67; and Ian Anthony, "Current Trends and Developments in the Arms Trade," in Robert E. Harkavy and Stephanie G. Neuman, eds., *The Arms Trade: Problems and Prospects in the Post–Cold War World, Annals of the American Academy of Political and Social Science* (Thousand Oaks, Calif.: Sage, 1994), pp. 36–42. China has sold fuel and nuclear technology to Algeria and Iran, and it has transferred nuclear research reactors and M-9 as well as M-11 missiles to Pakistan and Syria. India has sold nuclear technology to Iran and Scud missiles to Iran and Syria. See Brad Roberts, "From Nonproliferation to Antiproliferation," *International Security* 18, no. 1 (Summer 1993): 143. For press accounts, see Eric Schmitt, "Arms Makers' Latest Tune: 'Over There, Over There' "; Steven Greenhouse, "Russian and China Pressed Not to Sell A-Plants to Iran"; William J. Broad, "Atom Powers Want to Test Despite Treaty"; and Barbara Crossette, "Gore, at UN, Says Nuclear Powers Are Fair on Weapons Treaty," *New York Times,* October 4, 1992, p. F5; January 25, 1995, p. A6; March 29, 1995, p. A6; and April 20, 1995, p. A14, respectively; Stuart Auerbach and John Mintz, "Cocom Becomes Agency to Promote Technology Transfers"; John Lancaster and Barton Gellman, "Dispute Over Nuclear Weapons Strains Egyptian–Israeli Ties"; Jessica Matthews, "Leadership on the Cheap"; Steven Mufson, "China Holds Nuclear Test: U.S., Japan Join Protests"; R. Jeffrey Smith and Michael Dobbs, "Russia Promised to Sell Centrifugal Plant to Iran"; and R. Jeffrey Smith and David B. Ottoway, "Spy Photos Suggest China Missile Trade" and "Anti-Nuclear Protests Mar Bastille Day," *Washington Post,* November 25, 1992, pp. D1, D3; January 19, 1995, p. A22; February 5, 1995, p. C7; March 16, 1995, p. A13; and April 29, 1995, p. A18; "The Covert Arms Trade: The Second Oldest Profession" and "Between the Bomb and a Hard Place," *The Economist,* February 12, 1994, pp. 21–23, and March 25, 1995, p. 23–25.

8. Stephanie G. Neuman, "Arms Transfers, Military Assistance, and Defense Industries: Socioeconomic Burden or Opportunity?" in Harkavy and Neuman, pp. 101–7; Neuman, "Controlling Arms Trade," p. 65; David B. Ottoway, "South Africa Said to Abandon Pursuit of Nuclear Weapons," Thomas W. Lippman, "Is the World More Violent Or Does It Just Seem That Way?" and R. Jeffrey Smith, "U.S. Waives Objection to Russian Missile Technology Sale to Brazil," *Washington Post,* October 18, 1991, pp. A23, A26; July 1, 1993, pp. A14, A18; and June 8, 1995, p. A23, respectively; Chris Hedges, "Iran May Be Able to Build an Atomic Bomb in 5 Years, U.S. and Israeli Officials Fear," *New York Times,* January 5, 1995, p. A10; "Asia's Arms Race: Gearing Up," "Russia Muscles In," and "Flying High, Shooting Higher," *The Economist,* February 20, 1993, pp. 19–22, July 17, 1993, pp. 33–34, and December 18, 1993, p. 33; Marcus W. Brauchli, "Security Tensions Rise in Southeast Asia," and Jeff Coles and Sarah Lubman, "Weapons Merchants Are Going Great Guns in Post-Cold

War Era," *Wall Street Journal,* March 31, 1993, p. A10, and January 1994, pp. 1, A6.

9. Lyotard (see chap. 3, n. 25), p. 5; "Let the Digital Age Bloom," *The Economist,* February 25, 1995, pp. 13–14.

10. David Ronfeldt, *Three Dark Pieces,* P-7607 (Santa Monica, Calif.: Rand Corporation, 1990); Nicholas D. Kristof, "Satellites Bring Information Revolution to China," *New York Times,* April 11, 1993, pp. 1, 12.

11. Lyotard, pp. 79–82.

12. For a comprehensive view of the ecological devastation in the former Soviet Union, see Murray Feshbach and Alfred Friendly Jr., *Ecocide* (New York: Basic Books, 1992). The effects of naval nuclear waste are discussed in D. J. Bradley, *Radioactive Contamination of the Arctic Region, Baltic Sea, and the Sea of Japan from the Activities in the Former Soviet Union* (Richland, Wash.: Pacific Northwest Laboratory, 1992). See also Walter Sullivan, "Soviet Nuclear Dumps Disclosed," and Malcolm W. Browne, "Lithuania's Dangerous Orphans: 2 Huge Reactors," *New York Times,* November 24, 1992, p. C9; April 7, 1990, p. 5; and November 15, 1992, p. 3, respectively; Michael Dobbs, "In the Former Soviet Union, Paying the Nuclear Price," and Lee Hockstader, "Vast Oil Pipeline Spill Fouls Russia's Arctic," *Washington Post,* September 7, 1993, pp. 1, A12–13, and October 26, 1994, p. A25. Seventy nations signed the London Convention banning highly radioactive waste in November 1972. At the sixteenth consultative conference of the London agreement in 1993, the convention was extended to the dumping of low-level waste. The comprehensive ban was subsequently endorsed by the United States (over the objections of the U.S. Department of Defense) and Russia.

13. Early press accounts of the devastation disclosed after the collapse of communism include, Marlise Simons, "A Green Mayor Takes on the Industrial Filth of Old Cracow" and "Central Europe's Grimy Coal Belt: Progress, Yes, but at What Cost?"; and "Paul Lewis, "Eastern Europeans Vent Anxiety Over Safety of Nuclear Reactors," *New York Times,* March 25, 1990, p. A8; April 1, 1990, pp. 1, 10; and April 7, 1990, p. 5; Mary Battiata, "Eastern Europe Faces Vast Environmental Blight"; John Pomfret, "Clearing the Air in Krakow"; and Marlise Simons, "Eastern Europe Sniffs Freedom's Air, and Gasps," *Washington Post,* March 20, 1990, pp. A1, A23, and August 19, 1994, pp. A1, A14. See also "Eastern Europe's Nuclear Power," *The Economist,* July 24, 1993, pp. 19–21.

14. Rachel Carson's *Silent Spring* (Boston: Houghton Mifflin, 1962) sensitized the American public to environmentalism. Paul Ehrlich's *The Population Bomb* (New York: Ballantine Books, 1968) and the report of the Club of Rome, Donella H. Meadows, Dennis L. Meadows, Jorgen Randers, and William W. Behrens III, *The Limits to Growth* (New York: Signet, 1972) also contributed to environmental awareness. Also see William K. Stevens, "Earth Summit Finds the Years of Optimism Are a Fading Memory," *New York Times,* June 9, 1992, p. C4; and Maura Dolan and Larry B. Stammer, "Planet Worse Off Since First

Earth Day in 1970," *Los Angeles Times,* April 15, 1990, pp. A1, 20–21; William Drozdiak, "French Ecology Parties Seen as Potent Force," *Washington Post,* March 6, 1993, p. A30; "Public Opinion on Environmental Issues in West Europe," U.S. Information Agency Research Memorandum, May 26, 1992, pp. 1–7; "The World This Week" and "Shell on the Rocks," *The Economist,* June 24, 1995, pp. 6 and 57–58, respectively.

15. Lester L. Brown, "A New Era Unfolds," in Lester L. Brown, Christopher Flavin, Sandra Postel, et al., eds., *State of the World 1993: A Worldwatch Institute Report on Progress Toward a Survivable Society* (New York: W. W. Norton, 1993), pp. 6, 7, 10, 13; Keith Schneider, "As Earth Day Turns 25, Life Gets Complicated," and William K. Stevens, "Earth Day at 24: How Has Nature Fared?" *New York Times,* April 16, 1995, p. E6, and April 18, 1995 pp. C1, C5.

16. William Booth, "Hole in Ozone Layer Found at North Pole Too," *Washington Post,* March 16, 1990, p. A 10; Al Gore, *Earth in the Balance* (New York: Plume, 1993), pp. 84–89. The Vienna Convention of 1985 set the tone for the decision to ban ozone-depleting substances, which was reached in London in 1990. According to Worldwatch, world production of CFCs had fallen by nearly 50 percent between 1988 and 1991. See Christopher Flavin and John E. Young, "Shaping the Next Industrial Revolution," in Brown et al., p. 186.

17. Natalie Angier, "Warming? Tree Rings Say Not Yet," and William K. Stevens, "Scientists Confront Renewed Backlash in Global Warming," *New York Times,* December 1, 1992, pp. C1, C4; and September 14, 1993, pp. C1, C6.

18. "Stay Cool," "Global Warming and Cooling Enthusiasm," and "Reading the Patterns," *The Economist,* April 1, 1995, pp. 11–12, 32–33, 65–67, respectively; Jessica Matthews, "Signals from Earth," *Washington Post,* March 19, 1995, p. C7; and Mark Hertsgaard, "Global Warming," *New York Times,* April 8, 1995, p. A23.

19. Craig Whitney, "Scientists Warm of Dangers in a Warming Earth"; Paul Lewis, "Island Nations Fear a Rise in the Sea" and "Air Pollution May Damage Food Supply"; and William K. Stevens, "A Global Warming Resumed in 1994, Climate Data Show," *New York Times,* May 26, 1990, p. A5; February 17, 1992, p. A3; April 3, 1994, p. 15; and January 19, 1995, pp. A1, A3; and Boyce Rensberger, "A Threat to Ozone Layer Diminishes, Scientists Say," *Washington Post,* July 14, 1995, p. A3.

20. Sandra Postel, "Facing Water Scarcity," in Brown et al., pp. 22–41; Shirley Christian, "Ecologists Act to Save Ancient Forest in Chile from Industry"; James Brooke, "Harvesting Exotic Crops to Save Brazil's Forest"; Nathaniel C. Cash, "Bolivia's Rain Forest Falls to Relentless Exploiters"; William K. Stevens, "Loss of Species Is Worse than Thought in Brazil's Amazon"; Alan Cowell, "Hurdle to Peace: Parting the Mideast's Waters"; Chris Hedges, "Industrious Egypt Is Choking Its People to Death"; and Barbara Crosette, "Severe Water

Crisis Ahead for Poorest Nations in Next 2 Decades," *New York Times,* April 22, 1990, pp. 1, 16–17; April 30, 1990, p. C6; June 21, 1993, pp. A1, A8; June 29, 1993, p. C4; October 10, 1993, pp. 1, 10; November 26, 1993, p. A4; and August 10, 1995, p. A13, respectively; Julia Preston, "Brazil's Logging 'Free-for-all' Compounds Threat to Amazon Rain Forest"; and William Branigin, "Phnom Penh Said to Undercut U.N. Effort to Save Forests" and "International Watchdog Agency Sees Rise in Energy Use, Global Warming," *Washington Post,* February 25, 1992, p. A13; February 3, 1993, p. A22; and April 25, 1995, p. A3. See also "Problems over Water in Middle East," Background Brief, British Foreign and Commonwealth Office, London, January 1992.

21. Lester R. Brown, Derek Denniston, Christopher Flavin, et al., *State of the World 1995: A Worldwatch Institute Report on Progress toward a Sustainable Society* (New York: W. W. Norton, 1995), pp. 3, 16–19; Wolfgang Lutz, "The Future of World Population," *Population Bulletin* 49, no. 1 (June 1994): 26. Using United Nations Food and Agriculture Organization projections, among others, Lutz maintains (p. 23) that food supplies could support only a population of between 10 and 15 billion over the next century. According to the World Bank, life expectancy at birth has jumped from 46 to 63 years in the Third World since 1960, and neonatal mortality (age 5 or below) has declined by two-thirds. See *Health Care in the Developing World: World Development Report 1993* (New York: Oxford University Press, 1993). For a stimulating account of the development versus environment debate, see Vaclav Smil, *China's Environmental Crisis: An Inquiry into the Limits of National Development* (Armonk, N.Y.: M. E. Sharpe, 1994).

22. *World Development Report 1992* (New York: Oxford University Press, 1992); Donnella H. Meadows, Dennis L. Meadows, and Jorgen Randers, *Beyond the Limits* (Post Mills, Vt.: Chelsea Green, 1992), pp. 37–41, 48–49. The desperate plight of the world's poor is also statistically described by Paul Kennedy in *Preparing for the Twenty-First Century* (New York: Random House, 1993), chap. 10. Population pressures and the scourge of famine that swept Ethiopia and sub-Saharan Africa in the 1980s have nearly exhausted nature's ability to replenish itself in many places. The demand for firewood already exceeds the regenerative ability of forests in China, South Asia, and parts of Africa. See Brown, in Brown et al. (1993), pp. 5, 16.

23. Susan Okie, "Developing World's Role in Global Warming Grows; "Caryle Murphy, "Middle East Faces Major Water Woes"; and Anne Swardson, "Net Losses: Fishing Decimating Oceans' 'Unlimited' Bounty," *Washington Post,* May 15, 1990, p. A4; March 10, 1990, p. A4; and August 14, 1994, pp. A1, A28, respectively; Brown, in Brown et al. (1995), pp. 6–8, 14–15, and (1995), pp. 5–6; Maura Dolan and Larry B. Stammer, "Planet Worse Off Since First Earth Day in 1970," *Los Angeles Times,* pp. 1, A20; Postel, pp. 24–26; Alan Cowell, "Hurdle to Peace: Parting the Mideast's Waters," *New York Times,* October 10, 1993, pp. 1, 10; "The Tragedy of the Oceans," *The Economist,* March 19, 1994,

pp. 21–24. Also see Peter Weber, "Protecting Oceanic Fisheries and Jobs," in Brown et al. (1995), pp. 21–37.

24. "The Deadly Hitch-Hikers," "One Bite is One Too Many," and "The Hobbled Horseman," *The Economist,* October 31, 1992, pp. 87–89, August 21, 1993, pp. 33–34, and May 20, 1995, p. 79, respectively; William K. Stevens, "Estimates of Warming Gain More Precision and Warn of Disaster"; Malcolm W. Browne, "New Clues to Agent of Life's Worst Extinction"; John Holusha, "Environmentalists Try to Move the Markets"; Peter Passell, "Disputed New Role for the Pols: Putting a Price Tag on Nature"; John F. Burns, "Thousands Flee Indian City in Deadly Plague Outbreaks"; Michael Specter, "Russia Fights a Rising Tide of Infection"; and Howard W. French, "Sure, Ebola Is Bad. Africa Has Worse," *New York Times,* December 15, 1992, pp. C1, C9 and C1, C13; August 22, 1993, p. E5; September 6, 1993, pp. 1, 36; September 24, 1994, pp. 1, 5; October 2, 1994, p. A9, and June 11, 1995, p. E3; Paul R. Epstein and Ross Gelbspan, "Should We Fear a Global Plague?" and Paul Taylor, "AIDS Overwhelming Zimbabwe's Advanced Defenses," *Washington Post,* March 19, 1995, pp. C1, C4, and April 12, 1995, pp. A1, A30; Brown, in Brown et al. (1995), p. 14. Also see John Bullock and Abel Darwish, *Waterways: Coming Conflicts in the Middle East* (London: Gollancz, 1993). Also see Kahn et al. (see chap. 6, n. 22), pp. 49–51, 122–35, chap. 6; Emily Yoffe, "Silence of the Frogs," *New York Times Magazine,* December 13, 1992, pp. 36–38, 64–66, 76; and Richard Horton, "Infection: The Global Threat," *New York Review,* April 6, 1995, pp. 24–28. For an analysis of the potential economic costs of environmental degradation, see William R. Cline, *The Economics of Global Warming* (Washington, D.C.: Institute for International Economics, 1992).

25. Gilder, p. 354; Theodore Roszak, "Green Guilt and Ecological Overload," *New York Times,* June 9, 1992, p. A27.

26. Eugene Robinson, "Worldwide Migration Nears Crisis," *Washington Post,* July 7, 1993, p. A24; Barbara Crossette, "This Is No Place Like Home," *New York Times,* March 5, 1995, p. E3.

27. *Trends in International Migration* (Paris: OECD, 1992), Part II, pp. 14–17, 49–89, and the appendices on pp. 123–56; Paul Lewis, "Stoked by Ethnic Conflict, Refugee Numbers Swell," *New York Times,* November 10, 1993, p. A10. See also *World Refugee Summary 1994* (Washington, D.C.: Immigration and Refugee Services of America, 1994), pp. 2–9.

28. Many Central Europeans and Middle Easterners have temporarily relocated for economic reasons. Thousands of Muslims in Myanmar have crossed the border to Bangladesh to escape war and persecution. Iran alone has more than 4 million refugees, mainly Afghanis and Azeris, some of whom are transients, and Pakistan more than 1.5 million. Cross-border migration is especially evident in Africa, where tribal conflicts and the spoliation of the land have set in motion a dizzying procession of humanity from Ethiopia, Somalia, Sudan, Zaire, Rwanda, Burundi, Angola, and Mozambique to the Congo or Nigeria or

Ivory Coast or Gabon or Tanzania or South Africa or Kenya. For contemporary commentary, see Jane Perlez, "Refugees: Will Malawi Shut Its Door?" and James Brooke, "Caracas Getting Continent's Biggest Mosque" and "Iran Is Encouraging Afghan Refugees to Go," *New York Times,* April 6, 1990, p. A4; January 3, 1993, p. 13; and March 9, 1995, p. A10; Paul Taylor, "War-Ravaged Mozambique: A Case Study of Famine Abroad," *Washington Post,* December 27, 1992, p. A29; Tyler Marshall, "Europe Busy Closing Door to Foreigners," *Los Angeles Times,* May 7, 1989, pp. 1, A13–15; "The World's Shame," *Economist,* November 13, 1993, p. 45. See the country reports in *World Refugee Summary,* pp. 46–170.

29. In a poll taken by the European Community at the end of 1991, majorities in Belgium, Britain, France, Germany, and Italy said there were too many foreigners in their countries. See Alan Riding, "Europe's Growing Debate Over Whom to Let Inside," *New York Times,* December 1, 1991, p. E2.

30. Ferdinand Protzman, "German Attacks Rise as Foreigners Become Scapegoat"; Youssef M. Ibrahim, "France Bans Muslim Scarf in Its Schools"; and John Tagliabue, "Sunny Italy Turns a Scowling Face to Immigrants," *New York Times,* November 2, 1992, pp. A1, A6; September 11, 1994, p. A4; and January 5, 1995, p. A4; William Drozdiak, "Protesters in Paris Assail Racism"; Marc Fisher, "Anti-Immigrant Violence Grows in Germany"; Eugene Robinson, "Anti-Asian Violence Jars London" and "Immigrants Gunned Down, Raising Specter of Racism in Spain"; and Jonathan C. Randal, "Killings Spur French Crackdown on Muslim Activists," *Washington Post,* January 26, 1992, p. A23; September 30, 1991, p. A13; September 16, 1993, p. A26; November 18, 1992, p. A27; and August 12, 1994, p. A36, respectively. Elizabeth Pond, "Don't Doubt Germany's Commitment to Democracy," *Wall Street Journal,* May 8, 1995, p. 8.

31. Alan Cowell, "Attacks on Immigrants Raise Concern in Italy" and "Italy Poll Sees Rising Feeling Against Jews"; Stephen Kinzer, "3 Big Parties Suffer in Volatile Hamburg Elections"; and Craig R. Whitney, "When Its Tires Go Flat, Europe Veers Right," "In Europe, the Right also Rises," and "Far-Right Vote Raises Alarms in France," *New York Times,* February 9, 1992, p. 21; November 15, 1992, p. A15; September 20, 1993, p. A9; October 23, 1994, p. 4; November 14, 1994, p. A8; and June 13, 1995, p. A6, respectively; Rone Tempest, "Le Pen: Dark Side of the French Soul," and William D. Mantalbano, "For Spain, the Shadow of Racism," *Los Angeles Times,* May 29, 1990, pp. H1, H7, and November 14, 1990, pp. A1, A6. Also see William Drozdiak, "Alarmed about Crime, Joblessness, Europeans Turn to Extremist Parties" and "Extreme Right Makes Gains in French Municipal Voting," *Washington Post,* October 11, 1994, p. A14, and June 19, 1995, p. A13; "The Rise of the Outside Right," *The Economist,* October 15, 1994, pp. 68–70; and Stanley Hoffman, "The New France," *New York Review,* July 13, 1995, pp. 50–55.

32. William Drozdiak, "Pulling Up a Worn-Out Welcome Mat"; Marc Fisher,

"Germany Sets End to Asylum Guarantee"; and "Rick Atkinson, "German Law Discourages Asylum-Seeking Migrants," *Washington Post,* July 13, 1993, pp. A1, A11, December 8, 1992, p. A29, and November 15, 1994, pp. A1, A16, respectively; Alan Riding, "New Law in France Allows Random Identity Checks" and "France to Deport More Immigrants"; John Darton, "Western Europe Is Ending Its Welcome to Immigrants"; and Stephen Kinzer, "Germany Closing Migrants' Hostels," *New York Times,* June 12, 1993, p. 2, and January 7, 1994, p. A5; August 19, 1993, p. A8; and September 8, 1993, p. A7; "Zero Option," "The British Way of Life," and "Excessive Use of Force," *The Economist,* June 12, 1993, p. 57, August 21, 1993, p. 47, and June 15, 1995, pp. 39–40.

33. Craig R. Whitney, "East Europe's Frustration Finds Target: Immigrants"; Frank J. Prial, "Survey in Moscow Sees a High Level of Anti-Jewish Feeling"; Celestine Bohlen, "Irate Russians Demonize Traders from Caucasus"; and Serge Schmemann, "Russia May Curb Foreign Religions," *New York Times,* November 13, 1992, pp. A1, A8; March 30, 1990, p. A5; October 20, 1992, p. A3; and July 18, 1993, p. A9, respectively; David Remnick, "Soviets Publish Solzhenitsyn Call for Slavic State," *Washington Post,* September 20, 1990, pp. A1, A17; "The Russians Are Coming"; "Tea Anybody?" and "All at Sea," *The Economist,* October 28, 1989, p. 55, June 12, 1993, pp. 59–60, and January 7, 1995, p. 30; Adam Michnik, "The Two Faces of Europe," *New York Review,* July 19, 1990, p. 7. See also Michael A. Hiltzik, "Ethnic Somalis Chafe Under Official Scrutiny in Kenya," *Los Angeles Times,* April 15, 1990, p. A6; Edward A. Gargan, "Rising Tide of Hindu Hostility is Worrying India's Muslims," *New York Times,* September 17, 1993, pp. A1, A8; "At America's Door," *The Economist,* July 24, 1993, pp. 11–12; and Lou Cannon, "California's Default," *Washington Post,* August 17, 1993, p. A21. Peter Brimelow's *Alien Nation* (New York: Random House, 1995) is a highly charged criticism of America's immigration policy. Also see Stephan Thernstrom's more temperate review and his comments on American Balkanization in "Has the Melting Pot Begun to Boil?" *Washington Post Book World,* April 2, 1995, pp. 1, 10. In 1992, Hindu fanatics destroyed a mosque in Ayodhya, India, that they believed the Mogul conqueror Babar had erected on sacred ground. As British historian Eric Hobsbawm has pointed out, the mobs who destroyed the mosque erroneously believed that it was built on the birthplace of the Hindu god Rama. See "The New Threat to History," *The New York Review,* December 16, 1993, pp. 62–64.

34. Celestine Bohlen, "Hungary Suspends Emigre Flights after Muslim Militants' Threat"; Larry Rohter, "As Hispanic Presence Grows, So Does Black Anger"; and James Brooke, "Argentina's Jews Cry for Their Torn Heart," *New York Times,* March 22, 1990, p. A8; June 20, 1993, pp. 1, 27; and July 21, 1994, p. A10, respectively; Robin Wright, "Hezbollah Seen Setting Up Terror Network in Africa," and "Bombings Underscore World's Vulnerability," *Los Angeles Times,* November 27, 1989, pp. A1, A16, and August 1, 1994, pp. A1, A6;

Caryle Murphy, "19 Killed during Police Raids in Egypt," and Steve Coll and Steve LeVine, "Global Network Provides Many Haven," *Washington Post,* March 11, 1993, p. A20, and August 3, 1993, pp. A1, A12.

35. For current trends on the spread of infectious diseases, see Keith B. Richburg, "Somalis Bring Refugee Crisis to Kenya"; and Don Podesta, "For South America, a Return to a Time of Cholera," *Washington Post,* February 7, 1992, p. A22, and February 28, 1993, p. A25; Marlise Simons, "Mozambique War Creates Refugees"; Jane Perlez, "Cholera Highlights Zambia's Plight"; and Lawrence K. Altman, "Doctors Say a New Cholera Poses a Worldwide Danger," *New York Times,* November 15, 1992, p. A13; April 12, 1990, p. A6; and August 13, 1993, p. A2, respectively. Also see "Never Had It So Good," *The Economist,* August 28, 1993, pp. 46–47; and Robin Marantz Honig, "Flu Pandemic," *New York Times Magazine,* November 29, 1992, pp. 28–31, 55, 64–67. Much of the discussion of AIDS derives from the findings of Jonathan Mann, director of the World Health Organization's Special Program on AIDS, Daniel Tarantola, and Thomas W. Netter, *AIDS in the World 1992* (Cambridge, Mass.: Harvard University Press, 1992). See also Philip J. Hilts, "Poorer Countries Are Hit Hardest by Spread of AIDS, U.N. Reports"; Eric Eckholm, "AIDS, Fatally Steady in the U.S., Accelerates Worldwide"; Lawrence K. Altman, "At AIDS Talks, Science Confronts Daunting Maze"; and Marlise Simon, "The Sex Market: Scourge on the World's Children," *New York Times,* June 13, 1990, p. A6; June 28, 1992, p. E5; June 6, 1993, p. 20; and April 9, 1993, p. A3; Susan Okie, "AIDS Spreads in Eastern Europe, Islamic Nations," and Jane E. Stevens, "Indonesia's Streetwise War on AIDS Has the World Watching," February 22, 1990, p. A17; February 20, 1995, p. A3, *Washington Post.*

36. "Growing and Growing," *The Economist,* October 3, 1992, p. 36; Roger Cohen, "A Tighter Belt for Europe's Welfare States," "Europeans Fear Unemployment Will Only Rise," and "Europe's Recession Prompts New Look at Welfare Costs," *New York Times,* December 27, 1992, p. E1; June 13, 1993, pp. 1, 12; and August 9, 1993, pp. A1, A8. See Paul Krugman, *The Age of Diminished Expectations* (Washington, D.C.: The Washington Post Company, 1990), chap. 2. See also the *Business Week*/Harris poll in *Business Week,* July 13, 1992, p. 119; Mark Landler, "Move Over, Boomers," and Christopher Farrell, "Shut Out Immigrants and Trade May Suffer, *Business Week,* December 14, 1992, pp. 74–82, and July 5, 1993, pp. 82–84; and Nathan Glazer, "The Ethnic Factor," *Encounter,* August 1981, pp. 6–15. As for the probability of increased immigration into the United States, past patterns suggest that as domestic conditions improve living standards, in this case Mexico, rising expectations of prosperity in the early phases of economic growth tend to stimulate migrate to countries where economic opportunities are greater still, in this case the United States.

37. "Plucked Velvet" and "The White Man's Burden," *The Economist,* January 8, 1993, p. 63, and September 25, 1993, pp. 49–50; Werner

Fournos, "Population Politics," *Technology Review,* February–March 1991, pp. 43–51; Wolfgang Lutz, "The Future of World Population," *Population Bulletin* 49, no. 1 (June 1994): 27–29.

38. See "Eastern Europe's Diaspora," and "Steady Does It," *The Economist,* December 26, 1992/January 8, 1993, pp. 73–76, and January 30, 1993, p. 48.

39. Judith Ingram, "Hungary's Tiny Immigrants: The New Foundlings," *New York Times,* May 18, 1993, p. A6. It was the return of the Armenian exiles to the mountainous region of Nagorno-Karabakh that had been their home since the third century that has given impetus to that enclave's war of independence against Turkish-speaking Azerbaijan.

40. Stephen D. Krasner, "Regimes and the Limits of Realism: Regimes as Autonomous Variables"; Robert O. Keohane, "The Demand for International Regimes," and John Gerard Ruggie, "International Regimes, Transactions and Change: Embedded Liberalism in the Postwar Economic Order," *International Organization* 36, no. 2 (Spring 1982): 497–510, 325–56, and 379–415, respectively.

41. Craig R. Whitney, "With Europe in Flux, No More Politics as Usual"; "Scandal is Infecting France, Sparing No Party"; and "Scandal over Paris Luxury Apartments Embarrasses Chirac"; Alan Cowell, "Europe's Worry: A Generation of Leaders Not Up to the Task?" and "Italian Party Feeds on Others' Shame"; Alan Riding, "In a Time of Shared Embrace, the Young Embrace Europe," and John Darnton, "Spain's Modern Quixote Awaits a Final Tilt," *New York Times,* April 4, 1993, p. 3; March 23, 1995, p. A3; July 7, 1995, p. A3; August 11, 1993, p. A6; April 5, 1993, p. A5; August 12, 1993, pp. 1, A12; and April 12, 1995, pp. A1, A17, respectively; William Drozdiak, "Justice Italian-Style Unleashed in Europe," *Washington Post,* July 25, 1994, p. A12; "Voting Green," "A New Great Idea," "Hands Up All Those Hit by Sleaze," "Spain: Success Aborted," and "Belgium: Holding Together," *The Economist,* January 23, 1993, pp. 47–48, May 22, 1993, pp. 13–15, and October 29, 1994, pp. 65–66, March 11, 1995, p. 51, and May 27, 1995, pp. 44–45. Also see "Twilight of the Czar," *Business Week,* April 3, 1995, pp. 68–69.

42. The manifest reason for the Japanese public's change of heart was its revulsion over the unaccounted discovery of $50 million in the safe of LDP kingpin Shin Kanemaru. The Kanemaru episode follows the Lockheed scandal in the 1970s that forced Prime Minister Kakuei Tanaka's resignation and the Recruit affair in the 1980s, which deposed Prime Minister Noboru Takeshita and his then Finance Minister Kiichi Miyazawa. See David E. Sanger, "Attack on Nagasaki Mayor Stirs Fears of Speaking Out"; "Japan's New Scandal: The More Things Change . . . "; and "How Scandal Undercut Japan's Smug Leaders"; James Sterngold and Nicholas Kristof, "TV Stars Defeat Politicians in Tokyo and Osaka Governor Races" and "New Shock for Politics in Japan," *New York Times,* January 21, 1990, p. 6; October 2, 1992, p. A10; June 27, 1993, p. 10; November 27, 1994, p. 4; and April 10, 1995, p. A7. See also Ronald E. Yates,

"Japanese Fear Tactics as Rightists Increase Campaign of Terror," *Dallas Morning News,* February 11, 1990, p. A32; and "Changing Japan: The World Breaks In," "Japan Chooses Between Past and Future," "The First Glint of a New Japan," "Japan's Long March," and "The Next Target in Japan," *The Economist,* June 26, 1993, pp. 21–23; July 17, 1993, pp. 31–32; July 24, 1993, pp. 33–34; October 1, 1994, pp. 42–46; and February 18, 1995, pp. 29–30, respectively. Japanese electoral reforms replace the old multiple constituencies with a combination of single-member districts and proportional representation.

43. For contemporary accounts of change elsewhere in Asia, see George Wehrfritz, "Taiwan Holds Key Vote for Parliament Today"; William Branigin, "Singapore's Party Past Burdens New President"; Lena H. Sun, "Chinese Feel the Strain of a New Society"; Steven Mufson, "Taiwan Elections Raise Questions of Ethnicity and Reunification"; and Keith B. Richburg, "Opposition Party Wins Plurality in Thai Parliamentary Elections," *Washington Post,* December 19, 1992, p. A10; September 2, 1993, p. A21; June 13, 1993, pp. A1, A29; December 3, 1994, p. A21; and July 3, 1995, p. A16, respectively; "The Real Power in Taiwan"; "Cleaning Up the Brass"; "Let Battle Commence," "Taiwan's Passionate Democrats"; and "South Korea's Local Heroes," *The Economist,* August 21, 1993, p. 27; May 8, 1993, pp. 42–43; March 13, 1993, pp. 41–42; December 10, 1994, pp. 31–32; and July 1, 1995, pp. 25–26; Barbara Crosette, "Across Southeast Asia, Awakenings to Democracy," and Philip Shenon, "Freed Burmese Democrat is Conciliatory," *New York Times,* May 24, 1992, p. E3, and July 12, 1995, p. A30. Also see *Far East Economic Review Asia Yearbook 1993* (Hong Kong: National Fair, 1993), pp. 191–92, 198–200, 213–15; and *Asia Yearbook 1994,* pp. 192–94, 214–15.

44. See, for example, Timothy Garten Ash, "Eastern Europe: Apres Le Deluge"; Theodore Draper, "A New History of the Velvet Revolution"; Jeri Leber, "Slouching Toward Democracy"; and Istvan Déak, "Post Post–Cold War Hungary," *New York Review,* April 16, 1990, pp. 51–57; January 14, 1993, pp. 14–19; January 14, 1993, pp. 24–27; and August 11, 1994, pp. 33–38, respectively. For a good overview of the transition from communism to political and economic pluralism, see Karen Dawisha, *Eastern Europe, Gorbachev and Reform* (Cambridge: Cambridge University Press, 1988); Ivo Banac, ed., *Eastern Europe in Revolution* (Ithaca, N.Y.: Cornell University Press, 1992); and Gale Stokes, *The Walls Came Tumbling Down* (New York: Oxford University Press, 1993). A useful history is Joseph Rothschild, *Return to Diversity: A Political History of East Central Europe Since World War II* (New York: Oxford University Press, 1989). Among journalistic accounts, see Jane Perlez, "Visions of the Past Are Competing for Votes in Poland," "Fast and Slow Lanes on the Capitalist Road," "Once-Promising Hungary Struggles with Economic Slump," "Bulgaria's Communists Claim Parliament Election Victory," and "Ex-Communist Picked to Be Polish Premier"; and Ferdinand Protzman, "Czech Republic Doing Well, for Now," and "Estonia's Government Is Ousted in Vote Signalling Slower

Reform," *New York Times,* September 12, 1993, p. E5; June 22, 1994, p. D4; October 7, 1994, pp. A1, A12; October 26, 1994, p. A14; December 19, 1994, p. A5; February 8, 1995, p. A6; and March 7, 1995, p. A10; John Pomfret, "The Big Leap into Capitalism," *Washington Post,* October 25, 1994, pp. A1, A13; "Tea Anybody?" "Ugly Memories," the survey "Souls in a New Machine," and "Getting Nastier," *The Economist,* June 12, 1993, pp. 53–54; September 11, 1993, pp. 59–60; April 16, 1994, pp. 1–22; and February 4, 1995, pp. 47–48.

45. For background to current developments in Russia, David Remnick provides a colorful and insightful journalistic account in *Lenin's Tomb: The Last Days of the Soviet Empire* (New York: Random House, 1993). For contemporary developments, see Serge Schmemann, "Yeltsin Says Foes Wage a Campaign to Stir Hysteria," and "Yeltsin Uses Decrees to Curb Dissenters"; Steven Erlanger, "Russian Economic Turmoil Persists, but Not Chaos," "What Russia Wants: Less Pain, a Strong Hand," and "Yeltsin Suspends the Communist Party and Other Ties"; Peter Reddaway, "Desparation Time for Yeltsin's Clique"; and Alessandra Stanley, "Russia's New Rulers Govern, and Live, in Neo-Soviet Style," *New York Times,* November 15, 1992, pp. 1, 10; October 6, 1993, pp. A1, A14; November 29, 1992, p. 3, April 18, 1993, pp. 1, 5, October 9, 1993, p. 3; January 13, 1995, p. A31; and May 23, 1995, pp. A1, A8, respectively; Margaret Shapiro, "Yeltsin Stresses Urgency of Help from the West," and "New Russia: A Country on the Take"; Margaret Shapiro and Fred Hiatt, "Hard Times in Russia Two Years after the Coup"; and James Rupert, "Nationalist Right Tries to Mobilize Russia's Orthodox," *Washington Post,* March 17, 1993, pp. A25, 30; November 13, 1994, pp. A1, A36; August 20, 1993, pp. H25, H27; and August 25, 1993, p. A18; "Russia on the Line" and "Russia's Internal Politics: One Good Thing," *The Economist,* July 3, 1993, pp. 15–16, and December 10, 1994, p. 49; Peter Reddaway, "Russia on the Brink?" and Tatyana Toltskaya, "Boris the First," *New York Review,* January 28, 1993, pp. 30–35, and June 23, 1994, pp. 3–5. Also see Yuri N. Afanasyev, "Russian Reform is Dead," and Stephen Handelman, "The Russian 'Mafiya,'" *Foreign Affairs* 73, no. 2 (March–April 1994): 21–27 and 83–96.

46. Charles Truehart, "Quebec Separatists Seek Voice in Ottawa" and "Polls Buoy Chretian's Ship of State"; Robert J. Samuelson, "The Nadir or His Presidency"; and Anne Swardson, "Conservative Groundswell Spreading in Canada," *Washington Post,* October 10, 1993, p. A39; January 2, 1995, p. A14; December 21, 1994, p. A25; and June 7, 1995, p. A24, respectively. See the polling data on public attitudes toward elected officials in Washington in Ronald Brownstein, "Dissatisfied Americans May Spell Democrat Losses," *Los Angeles Times,* July 28, 1994, pp. A1, A19; Richard Morin and David S. Broder, "Six Out of 10 Disapprove of Way Hill Does Its Job," *Washington Post,* July 3, 1994, p. A1, A8. Also see "Portrait of an Anxious Public," which reflects the American public's gloomy view of government and its support for Colin Powell, in *Business Week,* March 13, 1995, p. 80.

47. John F. Burns, "In the Streets, Praise and Joy and also More Blood"; Christopher Wren, "Rival Congress Wants No Talks in Pretoria" and "Interior Panel Set"; Bill Keller, "Freedom Frays South Africa's Racial Tapestry"; and Howard W. French, "A Mandela Plan Ignites Zulu Rivals" and "Secret Trials are Reported in Nigeria," *New York Times,* February 3, 1990, p. 1; March 4, 1990, p. A6; September 8, 1993, pp. A1, A6; February 20, 1994, p. E5; July 2, 1995, p 8; and July 13, 1995, p. 9, respectively; Mark Fritz, "11 Die as Nigerian Rioters Protest Military Rule"; Neil Henry, "Africans Testing Waters of Dissent" and "Cameroon's Anglophone Minority Leads Burgeoning Opposition"; and Mark Huband, "Zaire's Opposition Calls for Army to Support It," *Washington Post,* July 7, 1993, pp. A23, A28; May 19, 1991, pp. A1, A22; August 11, 1991, p. A27; and January 2, 1991, p. A10. On the Middle East and the Islamic World, see Youssef M. Ibrahim, "Saudi King Trying to Dilute Islamic Radicalism," and Chris Hedges, "Islam Bent into Ideology: Vengeful Vision of Hope," *New York Times,* October 6, 1994, p. A5, and October 23, 1994, p. E3; "If Islamists Rule Algeria," "The Cracks in the Kingdom," and "What's the Difference Between Algeria and Turkey?" *The Economist,* February 25, 1995, pp. 41–42, and March 18, 1995, pp. 21–23, 49–50. For recent developments in South Asia and Latin America, see Molly Moore, "Former Premier Bhutto Wins Narrow Plurality in Pakistan"; James Clad, "India: A World at War with Itself"; and Tod Robertson, "Mexican Voters Choose Stability, Continuity," *Washington Post,* October 8, 1993, p. A29; March 31, 1991, p. B3; and August 23, 1994, p. A15, respectively; Mark Fineman, "Throngs in Capital Celebrate Nepal's New Democracy" and "Restive Nepalese Are Turning Against Harsh Monarchical Rule," *Los Angeles Times,* April 10, 1990, p. A6, and February 25, 1990, p. A10; "Mexico: Respect Restored," and "Brazil: Modest Man, Immodest Task," *The Economist,* February 13, 1993, pp. 1–22, and October 8, 1994, p. 42; "Mexico," *Business Week,* August 22, 1994, pp. 40–47; Tim Golden, "'Down with Fidel!' Is Heard in Cuba, But There Is No Sign of His Fall" and "Another State in Mexico Challenges Government," *New York Times,* January 13, 1993, p. A10, and January 20, 1995, p. A3; John Barham, "Poll Boosts Menem's Ambition," *Financial Times,* April 21, 1994, p. 4; Jose De Cordoba, "Cuba Is Near Crisis as Opposition Grows," *Wall Street Journal,* August 11, 1994, p. A6.

48. See Donatella Lorch, "Thousands Flee Kenya Ethnic Strife"; James Brooke, "Venezuela Still Edgy: Will There Be Coup No. 3?" and "Peru's Leader Clears Path with Sharp Elbows"; David Binder and Barbara Crosette, "In Baring Old Hatreds, the Cold War's End Imperils the Peace"; Bill Keller, "Africa Allows Its Tragedies to Take Their Own Course"; and John Burns, "Bomb and Gunmen Kill 11 at Pakistan Mosque," *New York Times,* September 7, 1993, p. A3; December 3, 1992, p. 8; February 22, 1993, p. A3; February 7, 1993, pp. 1, 14; August 7, 1994, pp. 1, 6; and March 11, 1995, pp. 1–2; "Mexico's Second-Class Citizens Say Enough Is Enough" and "Asia's Answer to Beirut," *The Economist,*

January 8, 1994, pp. 41–42, and July 1, 1995, p. 30; "Will Argentina Stay the Course?" *Business Week,* October 17, 1994, pp. 172–74.

49. Clyde Farnsworth, "Accords Defeat Heartens Quebec Separatists," and James F. Clarity, "Debate for Peace Intense in Ulster," *New York Times,* October 29, 1992, p. A9, and October 3, 1993, p. A9; Charles Truehart, "Quebecer Aggressive on Separatism," *Washington Post,* January 26, 1994, p. A17; Christopher Chipello, "Quebec Party Moves to Woo Soft Nationalists," *Wall Street Journal,* June 13, 1995, p. A5; "What Gerry Adams Didn't Say" and "Scottish Nationalism: An Expensive Proposition," *The Economist,* February 15, 1994, p. 13, and June 3, 1995, p. 53.

50. Judith Ingram, "Fireworks, Tears and Doubt in Slovakia," and Stephen Engleberg and Judith Ingram, "Now Hungary Adds Its Voice to the Ethnic Tumult," *New York Times,* January 1, 1993, p. A14, and January 25, 1993, p. A3; Charles P. Wallace, "Moldavian Nationalism Runs High," *Los Angeles Times,* February 25, 1990, p. A6; "Russia's Armed Forces," *The Economist,* August 28, 1993, pp. 17–19; see Gyula Horn's remarks in *FBIS-Eastern Europe,* May 19 and 29, 1994, pp. 6 and 4; and Daniel Benjamin, "Hungary's Leaders Mull Reconciliation with Neighbors," *Wall Street Journal,* July 18, 1994, p. A8.

51. Mark Fineman, "Pan-Islamic Movements Collide with Secular Policies in Broad Region of Asia," *Los Angeles Times,* March 7, 1992, pp. A14, A16; "Siberia: Exiled No Longer," "Things Fall Apart," "A Country of Countries," "Russians Abroad: Pawns or Knights?," "Russia's Caucasian Cauldron," "Chechens of the Wild East," and "How Many Other Chechnyas?" *The Economist,* November 21, 1992, p. 64; January 30, 1993, p. 47; March 27, 1993, pp. 21–23; July 10, 1993, pp. 39–41; August 6, 1994, pp. 39–40; September 24, 1994, p. 54; and January 14, 1995, pp. 43–45, respectively; Steven Erlanger, "Tamarlane's Land Trembles: Bloodshed at Gates" and "Heirs of the Golden Horde Reclaim a Tatar Culture"; Robert Pear, "Tehran Is Said to Back 'Islamic Zeal' but Not Separatism in Azerbaijan"; Serge Schmemann, "War Bleeds Ex-Soviet Land in Central Asia's Heart" and "Ukraine Facing the High Costs of Democracy"; Celestine Bohlen, "Shevardnadze's Fight with Rebels Links His Fate to Georgia's Future"; and Raymond Bonner, "In Caucasus, Separatist Struggle Is Pursued as Pogrom," *New York Times,* August 22, 1993, p. E4; February 15, 1993, p. A4; August 13, 1993, p. A3; January 21, 1990, p. A10; February 21, 1993, pp. 1, 12; November 6, 1992, p. A10; October 3, 1993, pp. 1, 18; and February 5, 1995, p. 3; James Rupert, "Central Asia Faces Struggle over Future," and "Pacts Reached by Ukraine and Russia"; Michael Dobbs, "Cossacks Ride Again"; Robert Seeley, "Ukrainian Cabinet Falls after 4-Month Power Struggle"; *Washington Post,* December 19, 1991, p. A41; June 10, 1995, p. A10; March 23, 1992, pp. A1, A12; September 22, 1993, p. A31; respectively; Claudia Rosett, "Tatarstan Dances Around the Bear's Hug," *Wall Street Journal,* January 20, 1995, p. A8.

52. With respect to political tensions within the Middle East and North Africa, see "The Islamic Threat" and "A War without Mercy," *The Economist,* March 13, 1993, pp. 25–26, and pp. 49–50; Steven A. Holmes, "Fundamentalism Alters the Mideast's Power Relationships"; Edward A. Gargan, "Afghanistan Always Riven, Is Breaking into Ethnic Parts"; Chris Hedges, "As Egypt Votes on Mubarak, He Faces Rising Peril," "The Mideast Kingdom Threatened by Peace," and "Islamic Hard-Liners Said to Gain Ground in Iran"; Thomas L. Friedman, "The Brave New Middle East" and "Curiously, a Dictator Forces the Middle East to Ponder Democracy"; John F. Burns, "New Afghan Force Takes Hold, Turning to Peace"; and Youseff M. Ibrahim, "In Algeria, Real Power Hides in the Shadows," *New York Times,* August 22, 1993, p. E1; January 7, 1993, pp. 1, 8; October 4, 1993, p. A8; March 30, 1992, pp. A1, A6; August 3, 1994, p. 3; September 10, 1993, pp. A1, A14; and September 2, 1990, pp. E1, E2; February 16, 1995, p. A3; and June 11, 1995, p. E3, respectively; Kim Murphy, "Islamic Fundamentalism Sweeps over Algeria Like Desert Wind"; *Los Angeles Times,* June 16, 1990, pp. 18–19; Caryle Murphy, "Mubarak Set to Win Third Term as Egypt Faces Difficult Times," and "Kurds in Turkey Seem to Be Nearing Full-Scale Revolt"; and John Lancaster, "Praised Abroad, Egypt's Ruler Faltering at Home," *Washington Post,* October 13, 1993, p. A33; March 23, 1992, pp. A1, A6; and March 13, 1995, pp. A1, A12; "Egypt: Better and Worse" and "Algeria: Talks, Maybe." *The Economist,* April 9, 1994, p. 48, September 10, 1994, pp. 45–46. For developments in Asia, see Havid Housego, "Escaping from the Spectres of the Past," *Financial Times,* September 7, 1989, p. 10; and Barbara Crosette, "India's Peril: Kashmir and Punjab Separatism" and "Kashmiris in Pakistan Press Self-Rule, *New York Times,* April 17, 1990, p. 4, and January 25, 1990, p. 3; "Students Stage Protest in Indonesia," *Washington Post,* November 13, 1994, p. A33; Kathy Chen, "Muslims in China Hate Beijing a Bit Less," *Wall Street Journal,* October 21, 1994, p. A8; *Asia Yearbook 1994,* pp. 134–39. On Africa, see Donatella Lorch, "Where Ghosts Dwell, Free Enterprise Moves In," and Jane Perlez, "Barrier to Somali Unity: Clan Rivalry," *New York Times,* September 17, 1993, p. A4; and August 30, 1992, p. 12, respectively; Cindy Shiner, "Angola's Warring Parties Postpone Treaty Signing"; and Jonathan C. Randal, "Liberia's Chronic Civil War Threatens to Burst Its Borders," November 15, 1994, p. A12; and June 12, 1995, p. A12; "Another Country," "That's Democracy," "Tribalism in Africa," "Uncomfortable Neighbors," "Peace, Maybe," and "The Caravan Passes On," *The Economist,* April 24, 1993, p. 20; June 26, 1993, pp. 43–44; September 10, 1994, pp. 46–48; February 11, 1995, pp. . 38–39; February 18, 1995, pp. 42, 46; and May 6, 1995, pp. 42–43; Michael Wrong, "Ethiopia Buries the African 'Nation State,'" *Financial Times,* May 5, 1995, p. 6.

53. "Privatisation: Selling the State," "Leap-Frogging," and "Latin Europe's Troubled Twins," *The Economist,* August 21, 1993, pp. 18–20, August 13, 1994, p. 70; and October 29, 1994, pp. 79–80; Roger Cohen, "A Sagging Italy

Looks to the Sale of State Companies," and "Europe's State-Industry Ties: Successes and Utter Failures," *New York Times,* June 25, 1992, pp. 1 and 7, and November 8, 1992, pp. 1 and 18; "Argentina Plans Sweeping Sell-Off for Privatization," *Wall Street Journal,* September 1, 1994, p. A6. Of course, many governments are continuing to subsidize state-owned firms in an effort to fatten them for the auction market. Moreover, cross-shareholdings often defeat the purpose of privatization. See "Rivals Are Howling Over French Handouts," *Business Week,* October 24, 1994, pp. 52, 56; and "Hard Nuts to Crack," *The Economist,* July 15, 1995, p. 14.

54. On the origins of liberal interdependence, see, for example, Norman Angell, *The Great Illusion* (New York: Putnam, 1911). Also see Robert Keohane and Joseph Nye, *Power and Interdependence* (Boston: Little, Brown, 1977); George Melloan, "Come to Europe, a Land of Opportunities," *Wall Street Journal,* January 4, 1993, p. A11; Miles Kahler, "The International Political Economy," *Foreign Affairs* 69, no. 4 (Fall 1990): 139–51; Craig R. Whitney, "Seen Against Maastricht: Adam Smith's Invisible Hand"; and William E. Schmidt, "European Community Weighs a Tenth Amendment," *New York Times,* December 15, 1991, p. E3; and October 18, 1992, p. A12; Patrick Oster, "Some EC Nations Resisting Move Toward Single Market"; and William Drozdiak, "Europe's Leap Toward Unity in '93 Falls a Bit Short," *Washington Post,* June 1, 1991, pp. B1–B2; and December 31, 1992, pp. A1, 16; "The European Community: A Rough Year," "The European Community: Altered States," and "Getting Europe Back to Work," *The Economist,* December 19, 1992, pp. 19–21; July 11, 1992, pp. 1–30; and August 28, 1993, pp. 43–44, respectively; "Down and Out in Rome, Bonn, Madrid . . . ," *Business Week,* June 21, 1993, p. 56. See also the poll of business opinion conducted by the Brossard Consultants—IFOP and *Le Nouvel Economiste,* in Marie-Louise Antoni, Phillipe Gallard, and Alain Jamain, "Why the Center of Europe Is in Berlin," *FBIS, Western Europe,* May 15, 1990, pp. 5–10. Robert D. Hormats provides a thoughtful assessment of the future of regionalism in "Making Regionalism Safe," *Foreign Affairs* 73, no. 2 (March–April 1994): 97–108. Robert Gilpin's analysis of the regionalization of the world economy in *The Political Economy of International Relations* (Princeton, N.J.: Princeton University Press, 1987) is similar to my own views.

55. Paul Montgomery, "French Sink East Europe Trade Deal"; William E. Schmidt, "In a Post–Cold War Era, Scandinavia Rethinks Itself"; Richard W. Stevenson, "From Leftovers of Communism, a Czech Goulash' "; and Craig Whitney, "East Europe's Path to New Day" and "Western Europeans Cast a Cautious Line Eastward," *New York Times,* September 7, 1991, pp. D1, 38; February 23, 1992, p. E3; October 17, 1993, p. 3; September 30, 1994, pp. A1, A10–11; and December 14, 1994, p. A9, respectively. As Whitney points out, this is not to suggest that West Europeans do not buy East European goods. Poland, Hungary, the Czech Republic, and Slovakia all experienced a substantial

rise in exports after 1989. However, East European imports rose even faster. See also William Drozdiak, "EC Readies Project Proposals to Boost Economies, Link East," *Washington Post,* November 18, 1992, pp. A25–26; and "EC Aid to the East: Good Intentions, Poor Performance," "Germany, France and the Merry-Go-Round," "Preparing to Join the Club," "ECU-Sounder," "Just Do It," and "Fazed," *The Economist,* April 10, 1993, pp. 21–23; October 2, 1993, pp. 49–50; August 20, 1994, p. 42; April 8, 1995, p. 45; July 15, 1995, pp. 35–36; and June 3, 1995, p. 69.

56. Joel Kotkin, "Europe Won't Work"; William Drozdiak, "Voting Day Across Europe"; and Fred Barbash, "Swedes Break with Past, Choose EU" and "Norway Vote Rejects EU Membership," *Washington Post,* September 15, 1991, pp. C1, C4; June 13, 1994, pp. 1, A16; November 14, 1994, pp. 1, A14; and November 29, 1994, pp. 1, A14, respectively; "The Single Market Itself Is in Question," *Business Week,* November 1, 1993, p. 52; Alan Riding, "Europeans Try to Revive a Faded Dream," *New York Times,* June 20, 1993, p. 6; "Family Frictions: A Survey of the European Union," *The Economist,* October 22, 1994, pp. 1–22.

57. Roger Cohen, "Paying for the Fall of Communism" and "Europe's State-Industry Ties: Successes and Utter Failures"; Craig R. Whitney, "Bundesbank: Sound Money Bastion"; and Nathaniel Nash, "Europe Seeks Latin Free-Trade Ties," *New York Times,* March 27, 1992, pp. 1, 6; November 8, 1992, pp. 1, 18; October 22, 1992, pp. D1, D9; and December 7, 1994, p. D2; William Drozdiak, "Europe Seeks Ties to Japan in New Order," *Washington Post,* June 23, 1995, p A30. See the surveys "Altered States," supra, and "East European Economies: Looking Up," "Poland's Economic Reforms: If it Works, You've Fixed It," "Czechs and Slovaks: Plucked Velvet," "Poland: Not as Bad as It Looked—Maybe," "The Single Market: Not Yet, "Back to the Drawing Board," "Germany: Reinventing a Country," and "Sunshine and Showers," *The Economist,* December 19, 1992, pp. 49–50; January 23, 1993, pp. 21–23; December 26, 1992/January 18, 1993, pp. 63–64; July 3, 1993, pp. 1–20; September 11, 1993, p. 49; and April 29, 1995, pp. 79–80. Speech by Foreign Secretary Douglas Hurd at Cambridge University, February 7, 1992, reprinted by the British Information Services, pp. 1–8.

58. "Gearing Up for a 'No,'" *Business Week,* November 1, 1993, pp. 50–51; "Mexico: Respect Restored," *The Economist,* February 13, 1993, pp. 1–22; Larry Rohter, "Mexico's Recovery: Is It in Peril?"; Keith Bradsher, "U.S., in Trade Pact, to Ask Mexican Legal Change"; and Clyde Farnsworth, "Canada's U.S. Trade Experience Fuels Opposition to the New Pact, *New York Times,* February 3, 1990, Business 1, 21; March 10, 1993, p. D1; and October 3, 1993, pp. 1, 12, respectively; Art Pine and Juanita Darling, "U.S., Mexico Open Talks on Free-Trade Pact," *Los Angeles Times,* March 28, 1990, pp. 1, A7; George Will, "NAFTA: It's About Jobs . . . "; and Rufus Yerxa and Pat Choate, "The Great NAFTA Debate," *Washington Post,* August 19, 1993, p. A29; and

October 3, 1993, p. C3. For a thoughtful account of the transformation of socioeconomic attitudes on the Latin American left, see Jorge G. Castaneda, *Utopia Unarmed: The Latin American Left after the Cold War* (New York: Knopf, 1993).

59. "Waking Up to NAFTA," and "Across the Rio Grande," *The Economist,* September 18, 1993, pp. 27–28, and October 9, 1993, pp. 67–68; Tim Golden, "Salinas Calls NAFTA a Test of U.S. Relations with All Latin America"; and Edwin P. Reubens, "NAFTA: Spread the Aid, Spread the Gain," *New York Times,* October 19, 1993, p. A10; and September 12, 1993, p. F11; "What Has NAFTA Wrought? Plenty of Trade," *Business Week,* November 21, 1994, pp. 48–49.

60. Tod Robberson, "Peso's Drop Mars Mexico's Outlook," and John M. Goshko and Peter Behr, "34 Hemispheric Leaders to Seek Free Pact," *Washington Post,* December 24, 1994, pp. A1, A12, and December 8, 1994, pp. A31, A42; and Tim Carrington, "Ties to Mexico Are Becoming Burden for U.S.," *Wall Street Journal,* March 9, 1995, p. A2.

61. "Is This Tough Love—Or Savage Crackdown?" *Business Week,* May 15, 1995, pp. 62–63; Anthony DePalma, "After the Fall: 2 Faces of Mexico's Economy"; and Clyde Farnsworth, "In Canada, Doubts Fade Quickly about Trade Accord," *New York Times,* July 16, 1995, pp. 1, 11; and February 12, 1995, p. 12.

62. At the same time, smaller trade linkages are incipiently emerging in various parts of the Philippines, Indonesia, and Malaysia. Thailand, Myanmar, Laos, and parts of southern China have also begun discussions on a "golden triangle" of trade and transport. See Norman Kempster, "Pacific Rim Nations Seeking Unity," *Los Angeles Times,* November 6, 1989, p. A6; Chris Sherwell, "Turning Talking to Reality on the Pacific Rim"; and Lim Siong Hoon, "Trade and Aid Fears at ASEAN/EC Meeting," *Financial Times,* November 3, 1989, p. 12, and February 16, 1990, p. 10; Mohammed Ariff, "AFTA: An Outward-Looking Free Trade Agreement," PITO Economic Brief No. 14, Program on International Economics and Politics, Honolulu East–West Center, August 1993, pp. 1–32; Paul Bluestein, "Southeast Asia Joins the Bloc Party," *Washington Post,* October 11, 1991, pp. B1, B11; "Too Clean for Comfort," "The Geometry of Growth," and "Fortress Asia?" *The Economist,* September 11, 1993, pp. 13–17, September 25, 1993, pp. 41–42, and October 24, 1992, pp. 3–4; Lawrence Zuckerman, "Asia's Strong Growth Offsets West's Protectionist's Moves," *The Asian Wall Street Journal,* May 12, 1993, pp. 1, 7; "Good Deal? Yes. Great Deal? No," *Business Week,* July 10, 1995, pp. 32–34.

63. Ariff, pp. 15–18; Andrew Pollack, "After Stall, Korea Sees Need for Economic Reform, Too," "Japan's Companies Moving Production to Sites Overseas," and "Japan Unveils a Third Plan to Stimulate the Economy"; Philip Shenon, "As Indonesia Crushes Its Critics, It Helps Millions Escape Poverty," and "Missing Out on a Glittering Market"; David E. Sanger, "From Asia, Mod-

els for Growing Economies"; and Nicholas D. Kristof, "China Sees Market-Leninism as Way to Future," *New York Times,* December 15, 1992, pp. A1, A18; August 29, 1993, pp. 1, 16; September 17, 1993, p. A11; May 27, 1993, pp. A1, A6; September 12, 1993, pp. 1, 6; October 10, 1993, p. E4; and September 6, 1993, pp. 1, 5, respectively; "Fixing," and "China: The Emerging Powerhouse of the 21st Century," *Business Week,* March 29, 1993, pp. 68–74; and May 17, 1993, pp. 54–68. In the 1990–3 period alone, Japanese direct investment in Asia rose from 12 percent to 19 percent of total foreign investment (versus a U.S. decline from 46 to 40.5 percent and a European drop from 25 to 21 percent). Although foreign direct investment will continue to be a major source of development funds in the Asia-Pacific area, economic growth and the demand for capital is causing countries in the region to rely more on equity investment. See *The Economist*'s survey, "Asian Finance," November 12, 1994, pp. 1–30; also "Who's NICst?" and "Asia's Shadow Play," August 13, 1994, pp. 31–32, and November 19, 1994, p. 15. The macroeconomic effect of the Asianization of the Pacific Rim economies is potentially awesome. If one were to extrapolate from current growth rates, Asia—without Japan—would overtake the economies of North America and Europe by the end of the third decade of the next century, according to some estimates. See Urban C. Lehner, "Economic Power May Cost Region in an Expanded International Role," *Asian Wall Street Journal,* May 12, 1993, pp. 1, 9.

64. Andrew Pollack, "Asia-Pacific Countries Near Agreement on Trade," and James Brooke, "South Korean Strives for a Market in Latin America," *New York Times,* November 15, 1994, pp. A1, A14, and April 6, 1995, p. D8; Paul Bluestein, "Pact a Milestone in March of Capitalism," *Washington Post,* November 16, 1994, pp. A1, A22; Kevin Done, "Daewoo Targets European Market," *Financial Times*, May 5, 1995, p. 4.

65. Keith Bradsher, "As Global Talks Stall, Regional Trade Pacts Multiply," and James Brooke, "In Latin America, a Free Trade Rush," *New York Times,* August 23, 1992, p. F5, and June 13, 1994, pp. D1, D5; Kim Murphy, "South America Banking on a New Market," *Los Angeles Times,* July 17, 1990, p. H4; "After NAFTA, AFTA?" "Dreams of Roads and Railways," and "Latin America Savours the Tequila Aftertaste," *The Economist,* August 13, 1994, pp. 15–16; March 11, 1995, p. 48; and May 20, 1995, pp. 41–42; Martha M. Hamilton, "The Latin Boom, *Washington Post,* December 4, 1994, pp. H1, H6; "Why Wait for NAFTA?" *Business Week,* December 5, 1994, pp. 52–54; and Matt Moffett, "Latin Nations Open Up to Long-Term Foreign Capital," *Wall Street Journal,* June 23, 1995, p. A10.

66. Steven Erlanger, "Ukraine Questions the Price Tag of Independence," *New York Times,* September 8, 1993, p. A8; Kim Murphy, "North Africa Moves Toward Joint Market," and "Dream of Unity Rises Again in Arab World," *Los Angeles Times,* April 30, 1991, p. H4, and March 6, 1990, p. A10; Alistair Lyon, "11 States Form Black Sea Bloc," and "At the Mideast Economic Sum-

mit," *Washington Post,* June 26, 1992, p. A28, and November 1, 1994, p. A22; "Great Russia Revives," "Dead Again?" "Central Asia: Eastern Promise," and "Third World Finance," *The Economist,* September 18, 1993, pp. 51–52, October 2, 1993, pp. 54–55, September 25, 1993, pp. 44–45, and September 25, 1993, p. 16. See also "Baltic Leaders Discuss Common Economic Policy," *FBIS– Soviet Union,* October 9, 1990, p. 84. Paul Krugman discusses the clustering of capital-intensive core states and labor-intensive peripheral states in *Geography and Trade* (Cambridge, Mass.: MIT Press, 1991), pp. 70–84. For information on foreign direct investment see IMF, *World Economic Outlook: October 1993* (Washington, D.C.: International Monetary Fund, 1993), chap. 5.

67. Margaret Shapiro, "Belarus Voters Support Resumed Ties to Russia," and James Rupert, "Ukraine's Lawmakers Vote to Boost President's Power," *Washington Post,* May 16, 1995, p. A14, and May 19, 1995, pp. A27, A29; Stever Erlanger, "Yeltsin Wins Small Success at Meeting of Commonwealth," and Youseff M. Ibrahim," Gulf Nations Balk at Proposal for Mideast Development Bank," *New York Times,* May 27, 1995, p. 8, and February 17, 1995, p. A6; "Common Poverty, Dependent States" and "In the Slav Shadowlands," *The Economist,* February 19, 1995, pp. 51–52, and May 20, 1995, pp. 47–49. For the state of play of the Black Sea accord, discussions with officials in the Ministry of Foreign Affairs in Greece and Turkey, May 4 and 8, 1995.

68. World Bank report quoted in Steven Greenhouse, "Third World Markets Gain Favor," *New York Times,* December 17, 1993, pp. D1–2; also see the survey of the global economy in *The Economist,* October 1, 1994, pp. 20–24.

69. Robert B. Reich, "Who Is Us?" *Harvard Business Review* (January–February 1990): 53–64; Ethan B. Kapstein, "We Are Us: The Myth of the Multinational," *The National Interest* (Winter 1991–92): 55–62; John Tagliabue, "Bahrain Group Wins Battle with Gucci for Full Control," *New York Times,* September 28, 1993, pp. D1–2. Gilpin discusses nontariff barriers and others forms of the "new protectionism," including sectoral protectionism, which is the negotiation of trade-offs across industrial sectors such as those the United States has established with Japan (*Political Economy,* pp. 228–30, 401–6).

70. Krugman, *Geography and Trade,* pp. 84–87; "Third World Finance" and "A Shocking Speculation about the Price of Oil," *The Economist,* September 25, 1993, p. 27, and September 18, 1993, pp. 69–70; William Branigin, "Oil-Hungry Asia Relying More on Middle East," *Washington Post,* April 18, 1993, pp. A33, A36; Youssef M. Ibrahim, "Arab Investment Overseas: A Vast Empire"; and Nathaniel C. Cash, "Chile: Japan's Back Door to the West," *New York Times,* April 30, 1990, pp. C1, C6; and April 15, 1993, pp. D1, D3; Michael R. Sesit, "Global Capital Crunch Is Beginning to Punish Some Weak Economies," *Wall Street Journal,* January 12, 1995, pp. A1, A5; and "Second Thoughts on Going Global," *Business Week,* March 13, 1995, pp. 48–49.

71. John H. Dunning, *Explaining International Production* (London: Unwin Hyman, 1988), pp. 299–302; "Multinationals: Back in Fashion" and "Who

Wants to Be a Giant?" *The Economist,* June 24, 1995, pp. 1–22, pp. 14–17; David E. Sanger, "Daimler-Benz and Mitsubishi Negotiating Cooperative Plan"; and Adam Bryant, "Sega Links with Sony to Make CD Video Games," *New York Times,* March 7, 1990, pp. A1, C5; and May 21, 1992, p. D5; Bernard Wysocki Jr., "Cross-Border Alliances Become Favorite Way to Crack New Markets," and Elyse Tanouye, "McKesson PCS Unit and Glaxo Holding Talks" and "Vietnam Firm Selects Four Finalist for Bids on Gas-Flow Project," *Wall Street Journal,* March 26, 1990, pp. A1, A6; June 26, 1995, p. B6; and May 10, 1994, pp. A3, A9; "What's Wrong? Why the Industrialized Nations Are Stalled," "That Burning Sensation at Glaxo," "An Old-Fashioned Feeding Frenzy," and "Look Out World, Samsung Is Coming," *Business Week,* August 2, 1993, pp. 54–59; October 3, 1994, pp. 76–78; May 1, 1995, pp. 34–36; and July 10, 1995, pp. 52–54.

72. "Borderless Management" and "Ford," *Business Week,* May 23, 1994, pp. 24–26, and April 3, 1995, pp. 94–104; "The Discreet Charm of the Multicultural Multinational" and "The Adventurous Life of the Belgians," *The Economist,* July 30, 1994, pp. 57–58, and June 10, 1995, p. 56; and Richard L. Hudson and JoAnn S. Lublin, "Power at Multinationals Shifts to Home Office," *Wall Street Journal,* September 9, 1994, pp. B1, B6.

73. "A Disquieting New Agenda for Trade," *The Economist,* July 16, 1994, pp. 55–56.

74. Miles Kahler, "The International Political Economy," in Nicholas X. Rizopoulos, ed., *Sea-Changes: American Foreign Policy in a World Transformed* (New York: Council on Foreign Relations, 1990), pp. 94–109; "GATT Needs a Hand," *The Economist,* April 21, 1990, pp. 15–16; Robert J. Samuelson, "Europe, Our Former Ally," *Washington Post,* November 18, 1992, p. A23; Andrew Pollack, "Asian Nations Wary on Free Trade," *New York Times,* November 11, 1994, p. A8.

Chapter Eight

1. The term "identity politics" belongs to Edward Said, *Culture and Imperialism* (New York: Knopf, 1993), p. 314.

2. Nicholas D. Kristof, "As China Looks at World Order, It Detects New Struggles Emerging," and Edward A. Gargan, "Though Sikh Rebellion Is Quelled, India's Punjab State Still Seethes," *New York Times,* April 21, 1992, pp. A1, A10, and October 26, 1993, pp. A1, A8; "Yemen at War," "East Timor's Past Won't Stay Buried," and "Russia's Caucasian Cauldron," *The Economist,* May 14, 1994, pp. 46–47; April 23, 1994, pp. 36, 41; and August 6, 1994, pp. 39–40, respectively; Paul Goble, "Russia and Its Neighbors," *Foreign Policy* (Spring 1993): 79–88.

3. In Burundi and Rwanda, violence pits the majority and diminutive Hutus against the taller Tutsis. In Liberia, tribal warfare involves the Krahns, Mandin-

gos, Gios, and Manos. See Cindy Shiner, "As Accord Brings Peace, Liberians Try to Put turbulent Past Behind Them," and Paul Taylor, "Try, The Beloved Country," *Washington Post,* November 3, 1993, p. A19, and June 27, 1993, pp. C1, C4. On the savage conflict in Rwanda that erupted in April 1994, see "Rwanda's Killing Goes On," and "Who Will Save Rwanda?" *The Economist,* April 23, 1994, p. 44, and June 25, 1994, pp. 13–14; and "Relief Agencies Seek Help as Hutus Flee," *New York Times,* July 15, 1994, pp. A1, A10. Kenneth E. Boulding discusses predation in *The World as a Total* System (Beverly Hills, Calif.: Sage, 1985), pp. 24, 56.

4. As illustrations, see Robert D. Kaplan, "The Coming Anarchy," *Atlantic Monthly,* February 1994, pp. 44–76; and Alain Minc, *Le Nouveau Moyen Age* (Paris: Gallimard, 1994).

5. Samuel P. Huntington, "The Clash of Civilizations?" *Foreign Affairs* (Summer 1993), pp. 22–49. Huntington's West versus Confucian-Islamic competition is the U.S.–Soviet/good-versus-evil duality in new guise. It creates a new devil for those Americans who might otherwise be inclined to disengage politically from the world.

6. Braudel defines civilization as the loci or spaces in which cultures manifest themselves; see *On History* (see chap. 3, n. 9), pp. 202–5; Toynbee, *A Study of History* (see chap. 1, n. 38), pp. 11, 21; Barraclough, pp. 87–89. In *Turning Points,* Barraclough (see chap. 1, n. 43) anticipated the decentralization of civilization. For that matter, Huntington's *Foreign Affairs* essay was prefigured by his "Political Development and Decline of the American System," in Bell et al., *2000,* pp. 315–17.

7. Richard Falk, *The World Order Models Project, A Study of Future Worlds* (New York: Free Press, 1975); Ervin Laszlo, *A Strategy for the Future: The Systems Approach to World Order* (New York: George Braziller, 1974), Rajni Kothari, *Footsteps into the Future: Diagnosis of the Present World and an Alternative Design for the Future* (New York: Free Press, 1974); Johan Galtung, *The True Worlds: a Transnational Perspective* (New York: Free Press, 1982); Richard Smoke with Willis Harmon, *Paths to Peace: Exploring the Feasibility of Sustainable Peace* (Boulder, Colo.: Westview, 1987); and Harry B. Hollins, Averill L. Powers, and Mark Sommer, *The Conquest of War: Alternative Strategies for Global Security* (Boulder, Colo.: Westview, 1989). Also see R. B. J. Walker, Saul N. Mendlovitz, and Richard Fleisher, *Contending Sovereignties: Redefining Political Community* (Boulder, Colo.: L. Rienner, 1990); and Seyom Brown, *International Relations in a Changing Global System: Toward a Theory of the World Polity* (Boulder, Colo.: Westview, 1992).

8. Falk, chap. 4; Galtung, pp. 344–52; Kothari, pp. 1–20.

9. Smoke and Harmon, pp. 31–35, 63–64; Seyom Brown, p. 131; Laszlo, pp. 134, 186, 199; Kothari, p. 120; Saul Mendlovitz, ed., *On the Creation of a Just World Order* (New York: Free Press, 1975), pp. xii, xvii.

10. Rosenau, *Turbulence in World Politics* (see chap. 7, n. 1), pp. 133–35 and passim; Gilpin, *Political Economy* (see chap. 7, n. 54); Paul Kennedy, *Pre-*

paring for the Twenty-First Century (New York: Random House, 1993), pp. 335–43; Kenneth E. Boulding, *Ecodynamics: A New Theory of Societal Evolution* (Beverly Hills, Calif.: Sage, 1978), chaps. 3–5; Brown, pp. 137, 168; R. J. B. Walker, *One World, Many Worlds: Struggles for a Just World Peace* (London: Butterworths, 1987). Also see Johan Galtung, *World Conflict Formation Processes in the 1980s: Prolegomenon III for a GPID World Model* (Tokyo: United Nations University, 1981). The acronym stands for the Project on Goals, Processes, and Indicators of Development under the aegis of the UN's human and social development program.

11. See Kenneth N. Waltz, *Man, the State, and War* (New York: Columbia University Press, 1959); Grace G. Roosevelt, *Reading Rousseau in the Nuclear Age* (Philadelphia: Temple University Press, 1990); and Reinhold Niebuhr, *The Children of Light and the Children of Darkness* (New York: Charles Scribner's Sons, 1944), p. 17.

12. Smoke and Harmon, pp. 63–65; Kothari, p. 45; Laszlo, p. 199.

13. Rosenau, chap. 8. My views have been influenced by neorealism, especially Waltz's *Theory of International Politics* (see chap. 7, n. 1), and by regime theory. See Robert O. Keohane, "Structural Realism and Beyond," in Ada Finifter, ed., *Political Science: The State of the Discipline* (Washington, D.C.: American Political Science Association, 1983); Stephen D. Krasner, "Regimes and the Limits of Realism: Regimes as Autonomous Variables," *International Organization* 36:2 (Spring 1982), pp. 497–510; Robert Gilpin, *War and Change in World Politics* (New York: Cambridge University Press, 1981); Robert W. Tucker, *The Inequality of Nations* (Basic Books, 1977); and the wonderful essays in Keohane, ed., *Neorealism and its Critics* (see chap. 5, n. 36).

14. Kothari, for one, takes exception to Western ethnocentrism (pp. x, 30–31). He favors a unified but more culturally diverse set of values. Niebuhr addresses the attempt to revive the universality of progress in *Children of Light,* p. 132.

15. Richard Falk, *The End of World Order* (New York: Holmes & Meier, 1983; also *The World Order Models Project,* chap. 4. In his advocacy of a "pacific union," Kant ruled out the creation of a world state, which he viewed as potentially tyrannical and unacceptable to national sovereignty. See Michael W. Doyle, "Liberalism and World Politics," *American Political Science Review* 80, no. 4 (December 1986): 1155–61. Indeed, such an imperial conception lay behind Dante's view (*De Monarchia*) of a revived and globally extended Roman Empire.

16. Robert L. Heilbroner, *An Inquiry into the Human Prospect* (New York: W. W. Norton, 1974), p. 141.

17. Hoffman quoted in Brown, p. 114. For a more recent critique of neo-Kantian formulations of international affairs, see Christopher Layne's provocative "Kant or Cant: The Myth of the Democratic Peace," *International Security* 19, no. 2 (Fall 1994): 5–49.

18. Boulding, *Ecodynamics,* pp. 332–34; Heilbroner, p. 136.

19. Some of this draws from "The Future Surveyed," *The Economist,* September 11, 1993. Also see Carol Lancaster, "Economic Reform in Africa: Is it Working?" *Washington Quarterly* 13, no. 1 (Winter 1990): 115–28; and R. Stephen Brent, "Aiding Africa," *Foreign Policy* (Fall 1990): 121–140. Also see Clyde Haberman, "Israel says that Peace Effort Will Continue," and Bill Keller, "Southern Africa's Old Front Line Ponders Its Future in Mainstream," *New York Times,* October 17, 1994, p. A11, and November 20, 1994, pp. 1, 16; and "After Hebron," *The Economist,* March 5, 1994, pp. 41–42.

20. Michael Polanyi dates the beginning of this transformation in Europe from the Hungarian Revolution of 1956, which was followed a year later by the Treaty of Rome and the formation of the European Community. See "The Message of the Hungarian Revolution," in *Knowing and Being,* p. 38 (see chap. 3, n. 37). Fritjof Capra (see chap. 3, n. 30) interestingly compares social change to the transition from classical to quantum mechanics (chap. 3). In modern physics, as in the international system, all events are interrelated by the dynamic force of energy. No property of nature is fundamental, as was the case with the building block theory of classical mechanics.

21. Pocock, *Politics, Language and Time* (see chap. 2, n. 3), p. 290; Heilbroner, pp. 127–36.

22. Stephen Hawking, *A Brief History of Time: From the Big Bang to Black Holes* (New York: Bantam, 1988), pp. 38–46.

23. Keohane discusses interdependence and its effect on the national interest in *After Hegemony* (Princeton, N.J.: Princeton University Press, 1984). See also the volume of essays on progress and international change edited by Emanuel Adler and Beverly Crawford, *Progress in Postwar International Relations* (New York: Columbia University Press, 1991), esp. chap. 12. Nor should this definition be confused with W. Warren Wagar's "counterculturalist" paradigm, which is probably closer to norm-based futurology. See *The Next Three Futures: Paradigms of Things to Come* (Westport, Conn.: Greenwood Press, 1991), pp. 40–44. Wagar contrasts this approach with the technoliberalism of Herman Kahn and the radicalism of Heilbroner, Christopher Lasch, Richard J. Barnet, and the German Green Party (pp. 35–40).

24. See the essay by Emanuel Adler, Beverly Crawford, and Jack Donnelly, "Defining and Conceptualizing Progress in International Relations," in Adler and Crawford, pp. 1–42. Boulding discusses progress in the framework of the physical concepts of entropic and antientropic change. See *Twentieth Century,* pp. 142–46. The foregoing rejects the sociological reductionism of communitarianism, as defined by *The Economist*'s essay, "The Politics of Restoration," December 24, 1994/December 6, 1995, pp. 33–36.

25. See Dunning (see chap. 1, n. 24), chap. 2; John Clegg, *Multinational Enterprise and World Competition* (London: Macmillan, 1987), chap. 2; and, for a more technical analysis, Paul R. Krugman, *Rethinking International Trade* (Cambridge, Mass.: MIT Press, 1990). *The Economist*'s surveys of multi-

nationals also offer useful insights on the aggregation of corporate interests. So does its survey on the global economy, "War of the Worlds," October 1, 1994, pp. 1–38.

26. *The Economist*'s survey of multinationals is especially good on this issue. So is its feature article, "The Discreet Charm of the Multicultural Multinational," which points out some of the difficulties of attempting to transcend national borders without losing one's niche in local markets. Also see Keith L. Alexander and Stephen Baker, "Borderless Management," *Business Week,* May 23, 1994, pp. 24–26. Dunning also elaborates on the pull of regionalization in Europe, chap. 11.

27. Dunning, p. 345; Gilpin, pp. 231–62.

28. Terence Roth, "Europe's Safety Nets Begin to Tear," *Wall Street Journal,* July 1, 1993, p. A10; Robert Pear, "Poverty 1993: Bigger, Deeper, Younger, Getting Worse"; and Richard W. Stevenson, "Europe's Economy Looking Up, But Long-Term Worries Linger," *New York Times,* October 10, 1993, p. E5; and July 31, 1994, pp. 1, 5; "A Wobbly Time for Japan's Workers," *The Economist,* December 18, 1993, p. 31; Aaron Bernstein, "Inequality," *Business Week,* August 15, 1994, p. 78; see also the summary of American wage-earners by professors Greg Duncan and Timothy Smeeding, in Keith Bradsher, "America's Opportunity Gap," *New York Times,* June 4, 1995, p. E4.

29. Discussion with Dr. Flemming Larsen, Assistant Director, Research Department, International Monetary Fund, Washington, D.C., October 28, 1993.

30. See the text of the OECD report on Third World Debt in *FBIS—Western Europe,* December 13, 1994, pp. 1–2; "Help the Poor" and "The Debt Trap and How to Escape It," *The Economist,* May 6, 1995, pp. 16–17, 74, 76; Rasmussen quoted in Barbara Crossette, "Talks in Denmark Redefine 'Foreign' Aid in Post–Cold War Era," *New York Times,* March 10, 1995, p. A5.

31. See "Shut Out Immigrants and Trade May Suffer," *Business Week,* July 5, 1993, pp. 82–83.

32. Lord Zuckerman, "The New Nuclear Menace," *New York Review,* June 24, 1993, pp. 14–19; For background on nuclear proliferation, see Martin van Creveld, *Nuclear Proliferation and the Future of Conflict* (New York: Free Press, 1993). Also see John R. Redick, Julio C. Carasales, and Paulo S. Wrobel, "Nuclear Rapprochement: Argentina, Brazil, and the Nonproliferation Regime," *Washington Quarterly* 18, no. 1 (Winter 1995): 107–122. For many, regional disarmament is probably a pipe dream, which, in any case, is not likely to precede reductions by the acknowledged nuclear powers. See Sandy Gordon, "Capping South Asia's Nuclear Weapons Programs," *Asian Survey* 34, no. 7 (July 1994): 662–73; and Ivo Daadler, "What Vision for the Nuclear Future?" *Washington Quarterly* 18, no. 2 (Spring 1995): 127–42.

33. According to Lutz (p. 29), the average age of the current world population is about 28 years, and one in three people is under 15.

34. Lester R. Brown, "Postmodern Malthus: Are There Too Many of Us to

Survive? *Washington Post,* July 18, 1993, p. C3; Harvey Brooks, "The Technology of Zero Growth," *Daedalus* 102, no. 4(Fall 1973): 139–52; Gene Koretz, "Why Global Warming Spells Rising Global Tensions," and Karen Pennar, "The Global Economy Needs Bridges—Not Walls," *Business Week,* March 8, 1993, p. 18, and August 2, 1993, p. 60.

35. "While the Rich World Talks," *The Economist,* July 10, 1993, pp. 11–12. In its commentary on the growth rates of developing countries, *The Economist*'s 1994 survey of the global economy makes the same point. Figures on the aggregate development aid of OECD countries were not available for 1994. A draft report of country-by-country allocations suggests a slight decline from the previous year, however, because countries became more selective about the recipients of aid and more careful about measuring the effectiveness of its application. See also "World's Apart," *The Economist,* March 11, 1995, pp. 42, 45.

36. Raymond Aron and Edward Shils are among the early expositors of the emerging world culture. See Edward Shils, "Roots—The Sense of Place and Past: The Cultural Gains and Losses of Migration," in William H. McNeill and Ruth S. Adams, eds., *Human Migration: Patterns and Policies* (Chicago: University of Chicago Press, 1978), pp. 404–26.

37. Caryle Murphy, "Lowering the Veil," Boyce Rensberger, "Cairo Forum Addresses Inequities Toward Women, and Molly Moore and Gabriel Escobar, "Paths to Power for Asian, Latin Women," *Washington Post,* February 17, 1993, pp. 1, A24–25; September 11, 1994, p. A31; November 11, 1994, pp. 32, 34; also see James Brooke, "Women in Colombia Move to Job Forefront," and Calvin Sims, "In the Macho World of Peru, Women Muscle In," *New York Times,* July 15, 1994, p. A6; December 7, 1994, p. A4.

38. Bernard Lewis, "The Enemies of God," *New York Review,* March 25, 1993, pp. 30–32; Larry Rohter, "Puerto Rico Votes to Retain Commonwealth Status," *New York Times,* November 15, 1993, pp. A1, B8.

39. See Barraclough, *Turning Points,* p. 87; Robert Seeley, "Battle of Moscow Sets the Stage for Political War in the Provinces," *Washington Post,* October 11, 1993, p. A18; Peter Reddaway, "Dictatorial Drift," *New York Times,* October 10, 1993, p. E15; George Melloan, "Yeltsin Guides a New Russian Empire into Being," *Wall Street Journal,* November 15, 1993, p. A13; "All This Is Ours," *The Economist,* November 26, 1994, p. 60; and Octavio Paz, "The Case for an 'American Community,' " *World Press Review,* April 1990, p. 36.

40. The Clinton administration explicitly states that the defense of democracy in Somalia was undertaken not only for Somalia's sake, but for America's as well. See Madeleine K. Albright, "Yes, There Is a Reason to Be in Somalia," *New York Times,* August 11, 1993, p. 19. Samuel Huntington predicted more than two decades ago that the effects of the decline of America's political dominance of the international system would lead to public demoralization far worse than that which befell France after the Fourth Republic's loss of empire. See his "Political Development and Decline of the American System," in Bell, *2000,* pp. 315–17.

The Clinton administration's attempt to mediate disputes between Russia and its neighbors has similarly irritated Moscow. See Steven Erlanger, "U.S. Peacekeeping Policy Debate Angers Russians," *New York Times,* August 29, 1993, p. 3. In the case of China, Washington's drumbeat of human rights is proving to be counterproductive, and it could seriously strain bilateral relations. Beijing's combative tone is described by Patrick Tyler, "Beijing Says It Could Live Well Even if U.S. Trade Was Cut Off," and "The U.S.-China Slide," *New York Times,* March 21, 1994, pp. A1, A10; and May 23, 1995, p. A10.

41. In Indonesia, for example, the state philosophy of *pancasila* defines the parameters of social behavior, including the limits to dissent and other obstacles to national unity. Also see Nicholas D. Kristof, "China Sees 'Market Leninism' as Way to Future," *New York Times,* September 5, 1993, pp. 1, 5; "Asian Values," and "Why Voting Is Good for You," *The Economist,* May 28, 1994, pp. 13–14, and August 27, 1994, pp. 15–17; Said, p. 300; "Uruguay: Democracy, It's Wonderful," "Still Waiting," and "Venezuela's Unfree Press," *The Economist,* November 26, 1994, pp. 15, 43–44, and April 8, 1995, p. 42, respectively; and, on Africa, "A Lull in the Wind," *The Economist,* September 4, 1993, pp. 42–43; and Bill Keller, "In South African, Laws Still Not Hard and Fast," *New York Times,* January 29, 1995, p. E6. I am grateful to Ambassador Herman J. Cohen, former Assistant Secretary of State for African Affairs in the U.S. State Department, for sharing his views on Africa. Also see Anthony Lake, "The Reach of Democracy," *New York Times,* September 23, 1994, p. A35, on the efforts to promote democracy; and Thomas Carothers, "The Democracy Nostrum," *World Policy Journal,* 2, no. 3 (Fall 1994): 47–53.

42. Dieter Buhl, "Between Weakness and Boasting," *Die Zeit,* January 17, 1992, p. 1 (printed in *FBIS-Western Europe,* January 17, 1992, pp. 10–11); Daniel Bell, "Into the 21st Century, Bleakly," *New York Times,* July 26, 1992, p. E16. See also Kevin Phillips, *The Politics of Rich and Poor* (New York: Random House, 1990), pp. 3–25; and "Will Schools Ever Get Better?" *Business Week,* April 17, 1995.

43. See Anthony Smith, *The Geopolitics of Information* (New York: Oxford University Press, 1980), p. 176; Lyotard, *La Condition postmoderne* (see chap. 3, n. 25), p. 5.

44. Said, p. 288. For a contemporary application of the maxim that domination breeds resistance, see also Timothy Garton Ash, *In Europe's Name: Germany's Eastern Policy, Its Motivations and Its Achievement* (New York: Random House, 1993).

45. Paul Lewis, "No Peace for the U.N.," "U.N.: Busier than Ever Globally, Struggles with Peacekeeping Role," and "U.N. Refugee Official Seeks Pledges from Donors"; Richard Bernstein, "Sniping Is Growing at U.N.'s Weakness as a Peacekeeper"; and Boutros Boutros-Ghali, "Beleaguered Are the Peacekeepers," *New York Times,* November 29, 1992, pp. 1, 14; January 25, 1993, pp. A1, A10; and June 20, 1993, p. A3; June 21, 1993, pp. A1, A6; and October 30,

1994, p. E15, respectively; also see "Trotting to the Rescue" and "Can Peace-keeping Survive?" *The Economist,* June 25, 1994, pp. 19–22; February 11, 1995, pp. 37–38.

46. Brian Urquhart, "For a UN Volunteer Military Force," *New York Review,* June 10, 1993, pp. 3–4; George F. Will, "Surrendering the Stars and Stripes"; and Henry A. Kissinger, "Recipe for Chaos," *Washington Post,* September 2 and 8, 1993, pp. A27 and A19, respectively; "Heart of Gold, Feet of Clay," *The Economist,* June 12, 1993, pp. 21–24. Also see the United Nations Report of the Secretary-General, "Improving the Capacity of the United Nations for Peace-keeping; Current Peace-keeping Management Issues," December 15, 1993; Gareth Evans, "Cooperative Security and Intra-State Conflict," *Foreign Policy* 96 (Fall 1994): 3–20; Thomas G. Weiss, "Intervention: Whither the United Nations?" and "The United Nations and Civil Wars," *Washington Quarterly* 17, no. 1 (Winter 1994): 109–28, and 17, no. 4 (Autumn 1994): 139–59; and the essays in Mary Kaldor and Richard Falk, eds., *Dealignment: A New Foreign Policy Perspective* (New York: United Nations University, 1987), which anticipate the post–Cold War interest in universalizing global security. For a realpolitik view, see Saadia Touval," Why the UN Fails," *Foreign Affairs* 73, no. 5 (September–October 1994): 44–57.

47. The accuracy and destructiveness of conventional arms—fighter aircraft, precision-guided munitions, air-to-air missiles, and the like—aided by more stealthy delivery systems and satellite-based target acquisition, is rapidly approaching the level of weapons of mass destruction. See Neuman (see chap. 7, n. 7), pp. 53–60; Grimmett (see chap. 7, n. 4), pp. 1–4, pp. 12–14 (1993), and pp. 1–3 (1994); and David Silverberg, "Global Trends in Military Production and Conversion," in Harkavy and Neuman (see chap. 7, n. 7), *The Arms Trade,* pp. 122–30.

48. For more detailed expositions, see Hugh De Santis, "The Graying of NATO," *Washington Quarterly* 14, no. 1 (Autumn 1991): 51–65; Jonathan Clarke, "Replacing NATO," *Foreign Policy* 93 (Winter 1993–94): 22–40; and Owen Harries, "The Collapse of the West," *Foreign Affairs* 70, no. 4 (September–October 1993): 41–53. For a half-hearted critical assessment of NATO, see Simon Serfaty, "Half Before Europe, Half Past NATO," *Washington Quarterly* 18, no. 2 (Summer 1995): 49–58. Also see Martin DuBois, "Military Cuts Cause Disquiet on the Western Front," and Daniel Benjamin, "German Decision to Cut Military Leads to Unease at Home, Abroad," *Wall Street Journal,* January 28 and February 17, 1993, pp. A10 and A3, respectively; William Drozdiak, "NATO Is Forced by Events into More Assertive Role," and "Recriminations Intensify Strain in Atlantic Alliance"; Lionel Barber, "EuroTrash: Our Allies Up in Arms," *Washington Post,* March 28, pp. A22–24, October 25, 1993, p. A14, and October 24, 1993, pp. C1, C4; and "Europe's Post–Post–Cold War Defense Wobbles into Action," *The Economist,* December 10, 1994, pp. 45–47.

49. PFP was unveiled in the NATO ministerial meeting in January 1994. It

was intended to accelerate the process of NATO enlargement that had begun three years earlier with the formation of the North Atlantic Consultative Council (NACC). Neither NACC nor PFP, both of which are little more than symbols of the West's interest in the post–Cold War security of Eastern Europe, offers a security guarantee to prospective members. Worse, the vaunted PFP, which Russia perceives as a security threat, is sowing the seeds of a redivided Europe. See Hugh De Santis, "Romancing NATO: Partnership for Peace and East European Stability," *Journal of Strategic Studies* 17, no. 4 (December 1994): 61–81; Michael Mandelbaum, "Preserving the New Peace: The Case against NATO Expansion," *Foreign Affairs* 74, no. 3 (May–June 1995): 9–13; and "Partnership for What?" *The Economist,* September 24, 1994, pp. 49–50. Also see Henry Kissinger, "Expand NATO Now," *Washington Post,* December 19, 1994, p. A27.

50. See David E. Sanger, "Asia's Needs and America's Grow Harder to Synchronize," *New York Times,* February 25, 1990, p. E3; Paul Bluestein, "Japan Nudges Asia to Assume Larger Regional Security Role"; and Henry A. Kissinger, "Why We Can't Withdraw from Asia," *Washington Post,* January 17 and June 15, 1993, pp. A45 and A21, respectively. For a notional alternative security arrangement in Asia, see Hugh De Santis, "Europe and Asia without America," *World Policy Journal* 10, no. 3 (Fall 1993): 33–43. Also see in the same issue Robert A. Manning, "The Asian Paradox: Toward a New Architecture, pp. 55–64. Also see Andrew Mack and Pauline Kerr, "The Evolving Security Discourse in the Asia-Pacific," *Washington Quarterly* 18, no. 1 (Winter 1995): 123–40; and Edward Luck, "Layers of Security: Regional Arrangements, the United Nations, and the Japanese-American Security Treaty," *Asian Survey* 35, no. 3 (March 1995): 237–52.

51. "Here Comes Number Seven," *Asia Week,* August 2, 1994, p. 26; Michael Robinson, "ASEAN Security Forum Takes First Step," *Asia-Pacific Defence Reporter,* November 1994, p. 5.

52. De Santis, "Europe and Asia," pp. 41–42. Sheldon Simon discusses changing security arrangements in Asia and the end of the era of Pax Americana in "Regional Security Structures in Asia: The Question of Relevance," in Sheldon Simon, ed., *East Asia Security in the Post-Cold War Era* (Armonk, N.Y.: M. E. Sharpe, 1993), pp. 11–25. Discussions with Marvin Ott have broadened my understanding of East Asia.

53. Conversation with Alfredo Michelena, a Venezuelan diplomat currently assigned to the mission of the Organization of American States, Washington, D.C., November 28, 1994. See Félix Peña, "New Approaches to European Integration in the Southern Cone," *Washington Quarterly* 18, no. 3 (Summer 1995): 113–22.

54. John M. Goshko, "Israel, Jordan End 46-Year State of War; Caryle Murphy, "Morocco and Israel Agree on Diplomatic Relations"; and John Lancaster, "Middle East Summit Opens," *Washington Post,* July 26, 1994, pp. 1, A13; September 2, 1994, p. A27; and October 30, 1994, p. A15; "Under Deadline," *The*

Economist, June 24, 1995, pp. 42–43. For a pessimistic view, see Amos Perlmutter, "The Israel-PLO Accord Is Dead," *Foreign Affairs* 74, no. 3 (May–June 1995): 59–68.

55. Youssef M. Ibrahim, "War-Weary, Arabs in Consensus on Giving Israeli Peace a Chance," and Douglas Jehl, "Clinton Offers a Mideast Economic Plan," *New York Times,* July 2, 1994, pp. 1, 12, and October 27, 1994, p. A14; "The Peace Dividend for Israel and Jordan," *Business Week,* August 8, 1994, pp. 36–37.

56. See, for example, Jonathan C. Randal, "Backers of Ousted Hutus Abandon French Haven in Rwanda for Zaire," *Washington Post,* July 20, 1994, p. A23; Donatella Lorch, "Now Rwanda's Neighbor Hovers Near the Brink" and "Rebels Without a Cause Terrorize Uganda's Poor," *New York Times,* February 3, 1995, p. A3; and June 21, 1995, p. A3; and, on the emergence of a security dialogue, "Neighborhood Watch in Southern Africa," *The Economist,* December 3, 1994, pp. 51–52.

57. Robert Jervis discusses in some detail the improbability of war among industrialized and industrializing states in "The Future of World Politics," *International Security* 16, no. 3 Winter 1991–92): 46–58; also see John Mueller, *Retreat from Doomsday: The Obsolescence of Major War* (New York: Basic Books, 1989), pp. 220–22, 232–35. This view is challenged by Christopher Layne ("Kant or Cant"), who points out several near misses among democracies such as the U.S.–British war scare over Venezuela in 1895 and the near face-off between France and Britain at Fashoda in Egypt in 1898. Also see the thoughtful essay, "The Politics of Peace," in *The Economist,* April 1, 1995, pp. 17–18.

58. William E. Schmidt, "A Deluge of Foreign Assistance Fails to Revive Egypt's Stricken Economy, *New York Times,* October 17, 1993, p. 10. Kennedy addresses the disposition between rich and poor in *Preparing for the Twenty-First Century,* chaps. 8–13.

Chapter Nine

1. Arthur Schlesinger Jr., "The Atlantic Charter Design for Tomorrow," *New York Times,* August 11, 1991, p. A17.

2. See the references to Kaplan, Minc, and Huntington in chap. 8 (nn. 4–5).

3. Patrick E. Tyler, "Chinese Issuing What May Be Deng's Final Book"; Serge Schmemann, "A Once Proud Force Finds Itself Impoverished and Demoralized"; Raymond Bonner, "Pact with Russian Bedevils Georgians"; and Michael Specter, "Yeltsin Threatens Action on Warring Secessionist Area," *New York Times,* November 4, 1993, p. A3; November 28, 1993, pp. 1, 18; December 9, 1993, p. A11; and November 30, 1994, p. A3, respectively; Kathy Chen, "With Games No Longer at Stake, Beijing Reasserts its Authority," *Wall Street Journal,* October 26, 1993, p. A19; Lena H. Sun, "Center May Reclaim Power in China," *Washington Post,* October 29, 1993, p. A33; "Can the Center Hold?" "De-

mocracy: The Missing Piece," "What Next for China?" "How Many Other Chechnyas?" and the surveys of "China: A Vacancy Awaits" and "Russia's Emerging Market: A Silent Revolution," *The Economist,* November 6, 1993, p. 32, September 3, 1994, pp. 53–54; October 22, 1994, pp. 37–38; January 14, 1995, pp. 43–45; March 18, 1995, pp. 1–22; and April 8, 1995, pp. 1–22; also see "China," *Business Week,* June 6, 1994, pp. 94–99; February 6, 1995, pp. 52–54; and May 15, 1995, pp. 60–61; and Richard Hornik and Gerald Segal, "China's Changing Shape," *Foreign Affairs* 73, no. 3 (May–June 1994): 43–58.

4. Youssef M. Ibrahim, "Iraq Is Near Economic Ruin But Hussein Appears Secure" and "Iraq Reportedly Cracks Down on Clan that Tried a Coup"; and Chris Hedges, "Inflation Fuels Discontent Against Iran's Government," *New York Times,* October 25, 1994, pp. A1, A12; June 20, 1995, p. A6; and November 20, 1994, p. 18.

5. William A. Orme Jr., "NAFTA Is Just One Facet of a Growing Economic Cohesion"; Hobart Rowen, "GATT Accord: A Massive but Maybe Moot Success"; and Martha M. Hamilton, "The Latin Boom," *Washington Post,* November 14, 1993, pp. H1, H8; December 19, 1993, pp,. H1, H5; and December 4, 1994, pp H1, H6, respectively. Also see Roger Cohen, "Like the U.S., Western Europe Steps Up Its Trade with Asia," *New York Times,* November 24, 1993, p. A17; and "Tale of Two Dragons," "For Richer, for Poorer," "Double Trouble," and "The Americas Drift Toward Free Trade," *The Economist,* December 18, 1993, pp. 42–44 and p. 66; June 17, 1995, p. 79; and July 8, 1995, pp. 35–36; Axel Borrman and Georg Koopman, "Regionalisation and Regionalism in World Trade," *Intereconomics* 29, no. 4 (July–August 1994): 163–70.

6. de Soto quoted in Larry Rohter, "Latin America Finds Harmony in Convergence," *New York Times,* November 21, 1993, p. E5; also see James Brook, "Latin America Now Ignores U.S. Lead in Isolating Cuba," *New York Times,* July 8, 1995, pp. 1, 5.

7. Also see John Darnton, "A Call for Peace"; William E. Schmidt, "I.R.A. Declares Cease-Fire, Seeing 'New Opportunity' to Negotiate Irish Peace"; and "Bill Keller, "South Africa's Old Front Line Ponders Its Future in the Mainstream," *New York Times,* December 16, 1993, pp. A1, A8; September 1, 1994, pp. 1, A12; and November 20, 1994, pp. A1, A16; Lynne Duke, "Mandela Bridging White-Black Divide," *Washington Post,* July 21, 1995, p. A23; "South Africa's Elections: The Second Struggle," "Southern Africa's Opportunity," "Untroubled," and "Emotional Release," *The Economist,* April 23, 1994; pp. 21–24, November 12, 1994, pp. 16–17; July 1, 1995, pp. 48–49; and July 8, 1995, p. 55; "The Peace Dividend for Israel and Jordan," *Business Week,* August 8, 1994, pp. 36–37. For the observations on Africa and the Middle East, I have benefited from interviews with Ambassador Herman J. Cohen, Washington, D.C., January 14, 1994; and Col. Bandar al-Saud of Saudi Arabia, Washington, D.C., January 5, 1994.

8. Hugh De Santis and Marvin Ott, "Rating Clinton Policy on Nuclear Terrorism," *Christian Science Monitor,* December 14, 1993, p. 22. For a good overview of the proliferation issue, see Brad Roberts, "From Nonproliferation to Antiproliferation," *International Security* 18, no. 1 (Summer 1993): 139–73.

9. Alan Cowell, "UN Population Meeting Adopts Program of Action"; and William K. Stevens, "Poor Lands' Success in Cutting Birth Rate Upsets Old Theories," *New York Times,* September 14, 1994, p. A2; November 2, 1994, pp. 1, 8; Boyce Rensberger, "Cairo Forum Addresses Inequities Toward Women"; *Washington Post,* September 11, 1994, p. A31. Lecture by Dr. Steven Sinding, Director, Population Services, Rockefeller Foundation, National War College, January 12, 1994. The United Nations Population Fund has prepared a plan to stabilize the world population at about 7.8 billion by 2050. The Fund intends to spend more than $4 billion on family planning in the Third World by 2000.

10. "Pollution in Asia: Pay Now, Save Later," "Pain in Japan," "Chainsaw Massacres," "Where There's Muck . . . ," and "Logging On," *The Economist,* December 11, 1993, pp. 36–38, 77–78; June 25, 1994, p. 39; August 20, 1994, pp. 53–54; and April 8, 1995, pp. 34–35. Ironically, some emerging economies of Southeast Asia—Malaysia, for one—have imposed restrictions on Japanese companies that do business there. According to scientists from Princeton and Georgia Institute of Technology, air pollutants from industrial and automobile emissions could drastically reduce the world's food supplies over the next 30 years. See W. L. Chameides, P. K. Kasibhatla, J. Yienger, and H. Levy II, "Growth of Continental-Scale Metro-Agro-Plexes, Regional Ozone Pollution, and World Food Production," *Science,* vol. 264, April 1, 1994, pp. 74–77. Also see Hilary F. French, "Forging A New Global Partnership," in Brown et al. (1995), pp. 170–89.

11. There are surely signs: for example, Serge Schmemann, "Russia's Elections: A Dose of Invective"; Nathaniel C. Nash, "A New Breed of Strongman in the South"; David E. Sanger, "Japan's Promising Prime Minister Seems to Lose His Touch"; and Richard W. Stevenson, "The Nationalist Road Block in Europe," *New York Times,* December 19, 1993, p. E3; January 16, 1994, p. E4; December 17, 1993, pp. A1, A12; and December 19, 1993, p. F9; and "Caught in the Debt Trap," *The Economist,* April 1, 1995, pp. 59–60.

12. See "Evo-Economics: Biology Meets the Dismal Science," *The Economist,* December 25,1993/January 7, 1994, pp. 93–95. This is not dissimilar to Karl Polanyi's argument in *The Great Transformation.*

13. Kim Murphy, "North Africa Moves Toward Joint Market," *Los Angeles Times,* July 17, 1990, p. H4; Jonathan C. Randal, "Dean of Dissidents Speaks Up," *Washington Post,* February 28, 1993, p. A31.

14. Alexsandr I. Solzhenitsyn, "To Tame Savage Capitalism," *New York Times,* November 28, 1993, p. E11.

15. Disparities in wealth are by no means confined to the developing world.

In addition to the United States, the gap between rich and poor has widened in other industrialized societies as well. See Gordon Green, John Coder, and Paul Ryscavage, "International Comparisons of Earnings Inequality for Men in the 1980s," *Review of Income and Wealth* 38, no. 1 (March 1992): 1–15. Also see Norman Stone, "A Plague on the West," *The* (London) *Sunday Times,* April 17, 1994, pp. 8–10. Nor is the deterioration of the family, as a study by the Population Council shows. See Tamar Lewin, "Family Decay Global, Study Says," *New York Times,* May 30, 1995, p. A5.

16. "Populism: Take the Good, Lose the Ugly," *Business Week,* March 13, 1995, p. 110; "Militias: Armed and Angry," *The Economist,* April 29, 1995, pp. 28–29; Philip Weiss, "Off the Grid," and Sean Wilentz, "Bombs Bursting in Air, Still," *The New York Times Magazine,* January 8, 1995, pp. 24–32, 38, 44, 48–51, and June 25, 1995, pp. 40–41, respectively.

17. See, Bob Herbert, "A Nation of Nitwits"; Alex S. Jones, "Rethinking Newspapers"; Joseph Horowitz, "Immortal Masterpieces to Snooze By"; and James R. Oestreich, "Is It Mahler? Or Is It Happy Talk," *New York Times,* March 1, 1995, p. A19; January 6, 1991, Section 3, pp. 1, 6; June 9, 1991, pp. H1, H25; January 6, 1991, pp. H1, H30. See also Bell, op. cit., and Lasch, pp. 33–39. Steven Schlosstein addresses some of these same issues, but from the narrow cultural perspective of revitalizing a Pax Americana. See *The End of the American Century* (New York: Congdon & Weed, 1989).

18. Ronald Asmus, Richard L. Kugler, and F. Stephen Larrabee, "Building a New NATO," *Foreign Affairs* 72, no. 4 (September–October 1993): 28–40; and "NATO Expansion: The Next Steps," *Survival* 37, no. 1 (Spring 1995): 7–33. On enlargement, see the speech by National Security Advisor W. Anthony Lake at the Johns Hopkins School for Advanced International Studies, September 21, 1993, quoted in Thomas L. Friedman, "U.S. Vision of Foreign Policy Reversed," *New York Times,* p. A13. For references to multilateral assertiveness, see Madeleine K. Albright's speech on the United Nations to the National War College, September 23, 1993. Lake's neo-Wilsonian phrase was offered in a press interview. See the *Baltimore Sun* editorial, "Poor Marks on Foreign Policy," November 3, 1993, p. 18.

Ashoka, 72

Asia: African countries solicit aid from, 217; Americans view as opportunity and threat, 29–34; antiforeign attitudes in, 161; cholera epidemic in, 162; competitors of Japan in, 11; cross-border migration in, 260n.28; cultural barriers to the West falling, 197; democracy adapted for, 199; ecological consciousness in, 218–19, 286n.10; economic regionalization in, 174–75, 192, 272n.62; European imperialism in, 117–18; European trade networks established in, 100; European Union trade with, 216; feudalism in, 83; forced into dependency on Europeans, 119; Japanese foreign aid to, 12; Japanese imports from, 11, 231n.24; moving toward integration, 188; national autonomy developing in, 89; Pacific Century, 2, 6–7, 34, 227n.2; political fragmentation in, 165–66; privatization in, 171; regional security integration, 205–6; social and cultural introspection of, 100; threat of global warming to, 155; trade with Japan, 174, 273n.63; trade with United States, 175; Western influence on, 92. *See also* Central Asia; China; Four Tigers of Asia; Korea; Japan; South Asia; Southeast Asia

Asian Free Trade Area (AFTA), 174, 203
Asianization, 146, 163, 273n.63
Asian–Pacific Economic Conference (APEC), 13, 174, 175, 177, 191, 206, 224
Assyrians, 66
Ataturk, Kemal, 129
atom bomb, 132–33
Augustus, 71
Australia, 159, 161, 163
Austria: agricultural population in 1900, 250n.47; antiforeign attitudes in, 160; desire for war in 1914, 118; Eastern European immigrants in, 159; joining European Union, 172; Ottoman territory ceded to, 116, 251n.52; political fragmentation in, 165; in regional security integration, 204; in suppression of

nineteenth century revolutions, 113; Turkish sieges of Vienna, 97; War of the Austrian Succession, 249n.37
autocracy, 67
Azerbaijan, 18, 151

Babylon, 66
Bacon, Francis, 104, 106, 107
Bailyn, Bernard, 26
balance of power, 110, 126, 184
Bancroft, George, 26
Bandung Conference, 139
Baroque art, 105–6
Barraclough, Geoffrey, 51
Becker, Carl, 123
Belarus, 175, 176, 204
Belgium: antiforeign attitudes in, 160; in the Congo, 116; industrial revolution in, 114; political fragmentation in, 165; revolution of 1830, 113
Bell, Daniel, 19, 22, 199, 223
Bentham, Jeremy, 114, 123
Bercovitch, Sacvan, 25, 26
Berlusconi, Silvio, 182
Bharatiya Janata party (India), 161, 165
Black Death, 48, 76, 93–94, 247n.19
Blanc, Louis, 113
Boer War, 117, 118
Bohemia, 87, 89, 113
Bohr, Niels, 132, 133
Bolshevik revolution, 127
Boorstin, Daniel, 26
Borkenau, Franz, 247n.19, 253n.19
Bosnia, 200, 201, 211, 214, 215
Boulding, Kenneth, 60, 127, 138, 184, 188, 278n.24
boundary situations, 59
bourgeoisie, 95, 99, 108
Boyle, Robert, 107
Braudel, Fernand, 60, 61, 183, 276n.6
Brazil: Eastern European revolution's influence on, 149; in Mercosur, 175; nuclear weapons development scrapped, 151, 195, 207, 217; as source of gold, 112; transition from military rule in, 168
Brezhnev, Leonid, 58
Britain: Anglo-French rivalry in North

America, 111; antiforeign attitudes in, 160, 161; arms reduction, 195; Boer War, 117, 118; Chartist movement, 114; conflict with Russia over Afghanistan, 117; conflict with United States over Venezuela, 27, 284n.57; decline of empire of, 14; empire of, 111–12, 116; enclosure of common land, 113; gains from Congress of Berlin, 251n.52; Glorious Revolution of 1689, 108, 249n.33; Hundred Years' War, 95; immigrants in, 159; in India, 98, 112, 116; industrial revolution, 111, 113–14; investment in United States, 228n.8; Lollards, 103, 247n.19; national identity developing in, 89, 95; Northern Ireland, 169, 197, 217; peasant uprisings, 94; Poor Law Reform Act of 1834, 250n.46; privatization in, 170; Reform Act of 1832, 250n.46; Reform Act of 1867, 114; Royal Society of London, 106–7; Scottish nationalism, 169; social welfare legislation, 115; state participation in the economy, 96; strategic alliances with foreign companies, 177; university development in, 88; workers associations, 114

British East India Company, 112
Brown, Lester, 157
Brown, Richard, 57
Brown, Seyom, 184
Brunt, P. A., 70
Brzezinski, Zbigniew, 2–3
Buchanan, Pat, 182
Buddhism, 78, 99–100
Buffon, Georges Louis Leclerc, 107
Bulgaria, 89, 97, 116, 166, 251n.52
Burckhardt, Jacob, 50, 125
Burke, Edmund, 109
Burma (Myanmar), 5, 166, 260n.28
Burundi, 181, 208, 275n.3
Bury, J. B., 122
Bush, George, 4
Byzantine empire: Carolingian empire and, 81; disintegration of, 89; feudalism in, 83; Muslim expansion into, 79; overthrow of, 97; peasant life in, 77; self-image as Christian island in heathen world, 80; Turkish threat to, 84

Calvin, John, 103
Calvinism, 101, 103–4
Canada: Asian immigration, 159; British expansionism in, 116; and NAFTA, 172–74; Quebec separatism, 167, 169, 181; Tory defeat, 167
capitalism: in creation of modernity, 91; development following Black Death, 94–96; emergence of, 88; environmental consequences of, 154; fascism and, 127; instantaneous transfer of capital, 149; integrating world markets, 101; in Japan, 17, 117; multinational corporations, 149, 191, 279n.26; philosophers on, 252n.6
Capra, Fritjof, 56, 278n.20
Caribbean: Cuba, 47, 224; Haiti, 161, 211, 214; incidence of civil disorder in, 211; Puerto Rico, 168, 198; regional security integration in, 207; underclass forming in, 209; West Indies, 111, 112
Carolingian empire, 81–82, 86
caste system, 74
Castro, Fidel, 47
Catholicism. See Roman Catholicism
Caucasus: Armenians, 181; Azerbaijan, 18, 151; ethnic fighting in, 18, 169, 182; Georgia, 18, 151, 169, 181; Russia as polestar of economic integration in, 176, 204
causality, 132
Central America: civil disorder in, 211; immigrants from, 159; Nicaragua, 34, 199; underclass forming in, 209
Central American Isthmus, Economic Community of the, 175
Central Asia: Afghanistan, 117; economic integration in, 176; ethnic violence in, 18, 182, 214; identity politics in, 181; Islamic revival in, 169–70; modernity resisted in, 139; political autonomy asserted in, 169; Tajikistan, 18, 151, 176; water tables falling in, 157
Chaldeans, 66
Chandragupta Maurya, 72
change: new ideologies as mythologies of, 6; understanding of as phenomenological, 60. See also historical change

Charlemagne, 81
Charles V, Emperor, 97, 101
Chartist movement, 114
Chase-Dunn, Christopher, 55
Chechnya, 18, 169
Cheng-ho, 99
Chiang Kai-shek, 31, 32
Chiapas, 168, 182
Chile, 5, 137, 177, 199
China: American opposition to dismemberment of, 29–30; arms reduction, 195; arms trade, 150, 151, 255n.5, 256n.7; attitude toward westernization, 129; Buddhism in, 78; Chiang Kai-shek, 31, 32; Ch'ing dynasty, 63, 100; Chou empire, 67; class distinction in ancient, 76–77, 243n.33; Clinton policy on, 199, 224; Communist victory in, 32; as competitor of Japan, 11; contact with ancient Middle East, 67; early civilization in, 67; European imperialism in, 117; expansion until fifteenth century, 99; feudalism in, 83; Han dynasty, 72, 74, 242n.21; Hong Kong, 11, 204; imperial order in, 71; Japanese fears of, 11; Japanese invasion of, 117; Kublai Khan, 89; Latin American trade, 216; Legalism, 72; loss of, 31–32; Manchus, 100, 112; Ming dynasty, 89, 97, 98, 99; Mongol invasion of, 85, 89; population growth, 156; in predictions of a Pacific Century, 7; in regional security integration, 204, 205; resistance to Western expansion, 92; satellite dish use, 152; separatist movements in, 170; Shang dynasty, 67, 83; Shih Huang-ti, 72; Singapore as model for, 199; struggle for power in, 215–16; Sui dynasty, 74; Sung dynasty, 80, 89; Sun Yat-sen, 129; T'ang dynasty, 74, 78, 79–80; technological inventiveness in, 87; Tiananmen Square uprising, 5, 148, 164; Taoism, 72, 77, 78; water table falling in, 157. See also Confucianism; Taiwan
Ch'ing dynasty, 63, 100
cholera, 162
Chou empire, 67
Christianity: conversion of Slavs, Hungarians, and Danes, 86; fundamentalism,

140; in Japan, 32, 99, 100; origin of idea of progress in, 122; in the Roman empire, 78–79. See also Protestantism; Roman Catholicism
Cipolla, Carlo, 114
CIS (Commonwealth of Independent States), 47, 175–76, 198, 215
cities, 70, 88
civilizations, first, 66–67; Assyrians, 66; Babylon, 66; Chaldeans, 66; Egypt, 66, 67; Indus Valley civilization, 66, 67, 72; Mesopotamia, 66, 244n.48; Shang China, 67, 83; Sumer and Akkad, 66, 241n.2
civil wars, 139
class distinctions: aristocracy, 77, 86; bourgeoisie, 95, 99, 108; class struggle, 119; in late antiquity, 77; in the United States, 26; working class, 118–19, 127. See also peasantry
classical age, 68–73
class struggle, 119
Clinton, Bill, 12, 155, 199, 224, 280n.40
Cold War: American exceptionalism as casualty of, 136; America's violation of its principles as concomitant of, 137; determining the flow of aid, 196; end of, 4, 16, 36–37, 38; as ideological filter, 137–38; Japanese economic expansion in American strategy for, 33
Colombia, 218
command modernization, 129
common good, 190
Commonwealth of Independent States (CIS), 47, 175–76, 198, 215
communications, 115
communism, 127–28; in China, 32; collapse in Eastern Europe, 36, 37; global competition with liberal-democracy, 36; as response to loss of hope in the future, 133; United States faced with discrediting of, 137
communitarian socialism, 190
competition, 191, 192
computers, 148, 149, 152
Comte, Auguste, 52
Concert of Europe, 118
Condorcet, Marquis de, 123
conflict, cooperation and, 182–89

Confucianism: in Asian democracy, 199; on the ideal society, 71–72; imperial Confucianism, 72; in Ming dynasty, 89, 99; neo-Confucianism, 80, 243n.33; as no guarantee of cooperation, 183

Confucius, 71–72

Congo, the, 116

Congress of Berlin, 116, 251n.52

Contract with America, 223

Conwell, Russell, 27

cooperation, conflict and, 182–89

Cracow, 153

Croatia, 169, 204

Croce, Benedetto, 56

Crusades, 84, 87

Cuba, 47, 224

Cubism, 43–44, 126

cuius regio, eius religio, 101

cultural consonance, 197–200

cultural decadence, 44

cultural imperialism, 198–200

cybernetics, 55, 135

cyberocracies, 152

Czech Republic: arms trade, 150; Bohemia, 87, 89, 113; Havel, 143; Prague's pollution, 153; privatization in, 170; separation from Slovakia, 169, 181; Visegrad declaration, 204

Dahrendorf, Ralf, 41

Darius I, 68

Darwin, Charles, 53, 250n.50

Darwinism, Social, 116, 250n.50

Davidson, Ian, 6

death, 247n.19

death-embracing cultures, 253n.19

debt-nature swaps, 196, 203

decadence, cultural, 44

Declaration of the Rights of Man, 110

declinism, 3–4, 34–36

decolonization, 47

deconstructionism, 142–43

deforestation, 154, 156, 157

democracy: Athenian democracy, 69, 241n.10; democratization and order in nineteenth-century Europe, 113–15; introduced into Japan, 48; nations adapting democracy to their own traditions, 199; suppression of advocates of

in Thailand, 164; Tiananmen Square uprising, 5, 148, 164. *See also* liberal-democracy

demographics of migration, 158–63, 197

Descartes, René, 55, 104, 106, 130, 142, 238n.18, 249n.32

despair, 125, 130, 134, 140–43

Destutt de Tracy, Antoine-Louis-Claude, 240n.46

developmental assistance, 196, 280n.35

Diderot, Denis, 125

diseases, infectious. *See* infectious diseases

diversity, tolerance of, 198

Dostoevsky, Fyodor, 125, 130

Doyle, Michael, 18

Droysen, Johann Gustav, 50

Drucker, Peter, 149

Duby, Georges, 82, 244n.46, 245n.55, 246n.2

Dunning, John, 192

Duns Scotus, 104

Dutch. *See* Holland

Dutch East India Company, 101

Eagleburger, Lawrence S., 227n.2

Eastern Europe: acculturating itself to Western institutions, 197; Belarus, 175, 176, 204; broadcasting revolutions in, 148–49; collapse of communism in, 36, 37; Bulgaria, 89, 97, 116, 166, 251n.52; de-Ottomanization and de-Magyarization in, 18; emigration from, 159; environmental catastrophes, 153–54; future membership in European Union, 192, 205; Moldova, 18, 169, 182, 204; Partnership for Peace initiative, 204, 282n.49; political parties in, 166–67; privatization in, 170; redrawing of national boundaries, 169; regional security integration, 204; Romania, 161, 166, 169, 251n.52; scarce funds for social welfare, 162; transition from state socialism to pluralism, 42; Ukraine, 150, 151, 169, 175, 176, 204; Visegrad declaration, 204. *See also* Czech Republic; Hungary; Poland; Russia; Slovakia; Yugoslavia

ecological erosion, 153–58, 195–96, 218–19, 286n.10

Economic Community of the Central American Isthmus, 175
economic interdependence, 190–94, 216
economic regionalization, 170–79, 191–92, 215
Egypt: ancient, 66, 67; modern, 170, 209
Einstein, Albert, 132
Eldredge, Niles, 158
electronic transmission of information, 146, 148–49, 211
Emerson, Ralph Waldo, 25
empires, rise and fall of, 3–4, 13–15
empiriocriticism, 53
endism: in American culture, 22–23; American self-image and, 21–39; as offering solace, 42; theories of conflict of civilizations as, 183. *See also* end-of-history thesis
end-of-history thesis: as consummation of America, 36–38; in Hegel and Marx, 16–17; irrational forces ignored by, 18–19; in Fukuyama, 5–6, 16, 18–19, 36–38
England. *See* Britain
environment, 153–58, 195–96, 218–19, 286n.10
Ephthalite Huns, 75
epochal change, 48–49, 61–63, 141, 145, 237n.8
Eritrea, 170, 181
ethnicity, 18, 181–82, 194
Europe: acid rain in, 154; arms trade, 150; the Black Death, 48, 76, 93–94, 247n.19; Concert of Europe, 118; Congress of Berlin, 116, 251n.52; Crusades, 84, 87; cultural barriers to Asia falling, 197; economic regionalization in, 171–73; ecopolitics in, 155; European world in early modernity, 93–96; feudalism in, 82–83; financial integration in, 192; ideology of progress dying in, 121; imperialism, 115–20; industrial revolution, 111, 113–14; ingrained institutional arrangements and practices, 214; migration to, 159, 197; military and cultural supremacy of, 92; Napoleonic wars, 16, 48; national identities developing in, 89; political fragmentation in,

165; power shifting from Mediterranean northward, 100–101; privatization in, 170; religious pluralism in, 101; revolutions of 1830 and 1848, 113; signs of disquietude in, 45–46; state system of after 1648, 110–11; technological advance in, 87; Thirty Years' War, 100; threat of global warming to, 155; trade networks established in Asia, 100; westernization of the world, 96–102, 112–13, 119–20; World War I's effect on, 47, 126–27, 134–35. *See also* Austria; Belgium; Britain; Eastern Europe; European Union; France; Germany; Greece, ancient; Greece, modern; Holland; Italy; Portugal; Renaissance; Spain
European Union (European Community; EU), 171–73; antiforeign attitudes in, 261n.29; Asian trade, 216; as competitor of Japan, 10–11; future Eastern European membership, 192, 205; Japanese protection opposed by, 12; Maastricht Treaty, 6, 10, 171, 188; Monnet's supranationalism, 145; moving toward integration, 188; potential to incite economic warfare, 215
evolutionary change, 46–48, 61
exceptionalism: America accepting primus inter pares status and, 36; in American ideology, 25; as casualty of Cold War, 136; challenges to in twentieth century, 38; declinism as antithesis of, 34; end-of-history thesis as restoring, 37; globalization of foreign policy not affecting, 41; Great Depression and New Deal as not eroding, 46; historians instilling, 26; intensifying as American dominance recedes, 199; Iran–Contra scandal and Nicaragua war as in defense of, 35
existentialism, 130
expressionism, 126

Fairbank, John King, 72
Falk, Richard, 183, 184, 186
family planning, 197, 199, 218
famine, 75–76, 115, 157, 259n.22
fascism, 127–28, 133

feudalism, 80–85; antecedents of, 244n.48; in Asia, 83; in Byzantine empire, 83; capitalist erosion of, 94–95; etymology of, 244n.45; in Europe, 82–83; in Japan, 83–84, 100, 247n.15

Fillmore, Millard, 6

firewood, 259n.22

first civilizations, 66–67

First World War, 47, 53, 118, 121, 126–27, 134–35

fisheries, 157

Flanders, 86, 94

Florence, 86, 93

food supplies, 157, 195, 259n.21

Foucault, Michel, 143

Four Tigers of Asia, 11; Hong Kong, 11, 204. *See also* Singapore; South Korea; Taiwan

France: agricultural population in 1900, 250n.47; Algerian conquest, 116; Anglo-French rivalry in North America, 111; antiforeign attitudes in, 160; arms reduction, 195; conflict with Spain for European dominance, 101; empire of, 116; feudalism in, 82; French revolution, 109–10, 249n.33; Hundred Years' War, 95; immigrants in, 159; industrial revolution, 114; the Jacquerie, 94; Le Pen's National Front, 160, 165, 182; Louis XIV, 108; manufacturing emerging in, 86; Napoleon, 110, 113; Napoleonic wars, 16, 48; national identity developing in, 89, 95; North African interests of, 171; Paris during Black Death, 93; philosophes, 109, 251n.55; physiocrats, 123; political fragmentation in, 165; privatization in, 170; revolutions of 1830 and 1848, 113; Second Republic, 113; state participation in the economy, 96; university development in, 88

Franciscans, 88

Frederick Barbarossa, 63

Frederick the Great, 111, 128

Freeman, Austin, 126

French and Indian War, 111

French Revolution, 109–10, 249n.33

Freud, Sigmund, 130

Fukuyama, Francis: as disembodying history, 19; end-of-history thesis, 5–6, 16, 18–19, 36–38, 183; on liberal-democracy's triumph, 5–6, 16–19, 36

fundamentalism, religious, 140

Gadamer, Hans-Georg, 60

Galileo, 106, 130, 238n.18

Galtung, Johan, 183, 184

Gandhi, Mohandas, 129, 145

GATT (General Agreement on Trade and Tariffs), 10, 178, 185, 215

Genghis Khan, 75, 85

George, Henry, 125

Georgia, 18, 151, 169, 181

Germany: agricultural population in 1900, 250n.47; antiforeign attitudes in, 160–61; cost of reunification, 139; dispute with United States over Samoa, 27; feudalism in, 82; Frederick Barbarossa, 63; Frederick the Great, 111, 128; gap between rich and poor, 35, 235n.30; Green Party, 44; Hanseatic League, 94, 96; Hitler, 128; immigrants in, 159; industrial revolution, 114; political fragmentation in, 165; post–World War I uprisings in, 127; productivity in, 232n.36; in regional security integration, 204; revolutions of 1830 and 1848, 113; social welfare legislation, 115; strategic alliances with foreign companies, 177; university development in, 88

Giddens, Anthony, 119

Giesen, Bernard, 236n.35

Gilded Age, 27, 31

Gilder, George, 16, 158

Gilpin, Robert, 184

global warming, 155–56

Glorious Revolution of 1689, 108, 249n.33

Goethe, Johann Wolfgang von, 50

Gorbachev, Mikhail, 58

Gramsci, Antonio, 15, 118

Graves, Michael, 45

Great Britain. *See* Britain

Great Depression, 46, 129, 135

Great Migration of 1630, 23–25

Greece, ancient, 68–69; Alexander's empire, 69; Athenian democracy, 69, 241n.10; class distinction in, 76–77; hoplites, 69, 241n.10; Mycenean empire, 67, 241n.6; mysticism in, 77–78; order in, 68–69; origin of idea of progress in, 122; and Persia, 68, 69; religion, 68

Greece, modern: Albanians expelled from, 160; in Black Sea region integration, 176; and European Union expansion, 171; new political parties, 165; in potential Balkan regional grouping, 205

greenhouse gases, 155, 156

Green Party (Germany), 44

Gregory VII, Pope, 87, 245n.59

Guicciardini, Francesco, 105

Gulf Cooperation Council, 207, 210

Gupta dynasty, 74–75

Gutenberg, Johann, 104, 148

Haidar, Jorg, 182

Haiti, 161, 211, 214

Half-Way Covenant, 24

Hammurabi, 66

Han dynasty, 72, 74, 242n.21

Hanseatic League, 94, 96

Harappa, 66

Harmon, Willis, 185

Hartz, Louis, 23

Havel, Vaclav, 143

Hawking, Stephen, 189

Hay, John, 29

Hearst, William Randolph, 27, 31

Heer, Friedrich, 88, 103

Hegel, Georg Wilhelm Friedrich, 6, 16, 50, 52, 54, 124, 253n.19

Heidegger, Martin, 56

Heilbroner, Robert, 187, 188

Heisenberg, Werner, 132

Herbert, Bob, 223

Herder, Johann Gottfried von, 49, 50, 237n.11

Herzen, Aleksandr, 50

Hinduism, 74, 78, 79, 80, 85, 140, 165

Hispanicization, 146

historical change, 41–64; art and, 42–46; ascribing meaning to, 142–43; choice

and, 213–14; as dialectical, 61; dynamics of, 147–79; epochal change, 48–49, 61–63, 141, 145, 237n.8; evolutionary change, 46–48, 61; as fraught with anxiety, 60; ideology legitimating, 61; the lived experience of, 56–61; mutualism discernible in, 213; and national identity, 38–39; as nonlinear, 63; as objective and subjective, 57; order and, 190; patterns of, 61–64; after World War II, 145

historicism, 49–52; assuming that history is linear, 51, 122; defined, 49; departing from humanistic values, 50; emergence of, 49; empiriocriticism compared with, 53; Hegel rejected by, 50; historism distinguished from, 237n.11; national character and cultural uniqueness emphasized by, 141; Popper's criticism of, 54; positivism compared with, 53–54; as retrospective, 52; as time bound, 51; Vico and Herder as precursors of, 237n.11

historism, 237n.11

history: America emerging outside of, 23; as continuous and discontinuous, 57; Croce on all history as contemporary, 56; direction in, 56–57; as freed from theology, 237n.11; Hegel on process of, 16; historians instilling America's mission, 26; liberal-democracy as meaning of, 16; as many stories, 49; as not predictive, 7, 19; as relative and contingent, 19; as textual, 39. *See also* historical change; historicism

Hitler, Adolf, 128

Hobbes, Thomas, 108

Hoffman, Stanley, 187

Holland (the Dutch; Netherlands): colonial empire of, 111; decline of empire of, 14; developmental assistance by, 196; Dutch East India Company, 101; in India, 98; threat of global warming to, 155

Hollins, Harry, 183

Holy Roman Empire, 63, 88–89, 105

Hong Kong, 11, 204

hoplites, 69, 241n.10

humanism, 104–5

human rights, 108–10
Hume, David, 53, 107, 130, 249n.43
Hundred Years' War, 95
Hungary: agricultural population in 1900, 250n.47; antiforeign attitudes in, 160; becoming an independent state, 89; Hungarian minorities in neighboring countries, 163, 169; political parties in, 166–67; post–World War I uprisings in, 127; privatization in, 170; Visegrad declaration, 204
Huns, 73, 75
Huntington, Samuel P., 17, 183, 276n.5, 280n.40
Hus, Jan, 103
Hyde, J. K., 245n.59

identity politics, 181
ideology, 42, 61, 133, 240n.46
Iggers, George, 50
immigration, 158–63, 197
immunization, 149–50, 197
imperialism, 115–20; cultural imperialism, 198–200
inclusivity, social, 194–97
income redistribution, 193
India: antiforeign attitudes in, 161; arms and technology sales, 256n.7; arms reduction, 195; Ashoka, 72; attitude toward westernization, 129; Bharatiya Janata party, 161, 165; British in, 98, 112, 116; Buddhism, 78; caste system, 74; cholera epidemic in, 162; Dutch in, 98; Gandhi, 129, 145; Gupta dynasty, 74–75; Hinduism, 74, 78, 79, 80, 85, 140, 165; Indus Valley civilization, 66, 67, 72; marginalization of subject peoples in, 198; Mauryan empire, 72–73, 83; Mogul dynasty, 98–99, 112; Mongol intruders in, 85; nuclear arms race with Pakistan, 218; political transition in, 168; Portuguese in, 98; satellite dish use, 152; separatist movements in, 170; water table falling in, 157
individualism, 102, 108, 118, 131
industrial policy, 2
industrial revolution, 111, 113–14
Indus Valley, 66, 67, 72

infectious diseases: AIDS, 115, 162, 188, 197; Black Death, 48, 76, 93–94, 247n.19; carried by immigrants, 162; cholera, 162; immunization against, 149–150, 197; in late antiquity, 76; new pandemic possible, 188; as possible result of population growth, 157–58; regional agreements on, 195
information, 146, 148–49, 152, 164, 200, 210
interests, national, 201–2
international trade: agreements, 178; GATT, 10, 178, 185, 215; NAFTA, 172–74, 191, 206, 215, 225; regionalization of, 170–79, 191–92, 215; World Trade Organization, 171, 178, 185, 216
Iran: arms purchases, 151, 255n.5, 256n.7; Iraq war, 210; Mossadeq, 137; overthrow of the Shah, 139; potential for war with Turkey, 170, 214; refugees in, 260n.28; as threat to international peace, 216. See also Persia
Iran–Contra scandal, 34
Iraq, 164, 195, 201, 209–10, 216
iron, 86–87
iron law of wages, 114
Ishihara, Shintaro, 2, 13
Islam: as catalyst of social order, 79; Central Asian revival, 169–70; the Crusades against, 84; expansion of, 79–80; Islamic fundamentalism, 6, 140, 198; Islamicization, 146; in Mogul empire, 98; Muslim terrorism, 161–62; in Ottoman empire, 97; possible spreading of, 17; Shi'a Islam, 17, 80, 97, 210; Sunni Islam, 17, 80
Israel, 151, 188, 195, 207, 217
Italy: agricultural population in 1900, 250n.47; antiforeign attitudes in, 160; Berlusconi, 182; decline of city-states of, 15, 96, 100–101; economic expansion in, 86; feudalism in, 82, 83; Florence, 86, 93; immigrants in, 159; Mazzini, 113; Mussolini, 128; political crisis in, 149; political fragmentation in, 165; privatization in, 170; revolutions of 1830 and 1848, 113; university development in, 88; Venice, 89, 93, 97

Lazlo, Ervin, 183, 184
League of Nations, 134, 135, 136
Legalism, 72
Leibniz, Gottfried Wilhelm, 106, 107, 123, 238n.18, 249n.32
Lenin, 119, 128
Lepanto, battle of, 97
Le Pen, Jean-Marie, 160, 165, 182
Lewis, Bernard, 98, 198
liberal-democracy: American violations of international law in struggle for, 137; apotheosis of fostering complacency, 19; apparent conversion to as revalidating American experience, 36; exported by the United States, 22; Fukuyama on triumph of, 5–6, 16–19, 36; as history's meaning, 16; the printing press facilitating rise of, 152; as unsuitable in some countries, 17, 199; war and, 18
Liberal Democratic Party (Japan), 149, 165–66, 264n.42
liberalism: attempting to institutionalize in Russia, 47; communism and fascism and, 128, 133; emerging in the Renaissance, 105; Lowi's critique of, 22–23; Manchester liberalism, 171; mutualism as part of liberal tradition, 225. See also liberal-democracy
Liberia, 182, 275n.3
Libya, 195
Linnaeus, Carolus, 107
literacy, 223
Locke, John, 37, 108, 123, 130
logical positivism, 53, 238n.22
Lollards, 103, 247n.19
London Convention on radioactive waste, 257n.12
Louis XIV, 108
Lowi, Theodore J., 22–23
Luther, Martin, 103
Lyotard, Jean-François, 54, 55, 64, 152

Maastricht Treaty, 6, 10, 171, 188
Machiavelli, Niccolò, 105, 110, 142
magic, 81, 102
Mahan, Alfred Thayer, 29, 30
Malaysia, 17, 175, 286n.10
Malpighi, Marcello, 107
Manchester liberalism, 171

Manchus, 100, 112
mannerism, 43
Mannheim, Karl, 130
Marsiglio of Padua, 104
Marx, Karl, 17, 51, 52, 54, 63, 114, 124
Marxism, 22, 119
Mather, Cotton, 24
Mauryan empire, 72–73, 83
Mazzini, Giuseppe, 113
McLuhan, Marshall, 145
meaning, 142–43
Meiji Restoration, 30, 117
Meinecke, Friedrich, 50
mercantilism, 96
Mercosur, 175, 203, 207
Mesopotamia, 66, 244n.48
Mexico: Chiapas, 168, 182; Chinese trade with, 216; emigration to United States, 159, 263n.36; influence of Eastern European revolutions, 149; NAFTA, 172–74; peso's collapse, 173; in regional security integration, 204
Michelson, Albert, 131–32
microscope, 107
Middle East: ancient hatreds in, 197; Arabs, 75, 79, 159, 207; Chinese contact with ancient, 67; democracy adapted for, 199; emigrants from, 197; forced into dependency on the West, 92, 119; Gulf Cooperation Council, 207, 210; hope for peace in, 217; immigrants in, 159, 260n.28; incidence of civil disorder in, 211; Iraq, 164, 195, 201, 209–10, 216; Islamicization in, 146; Israel, 151, 188, 195, 207, 217; Jordan, 207, 209; Kuwait, 201, 209–10; Mongol invasion of, 84; as nuclear flash point, 151, 218; Organization of Arab States, 207; Palestine Liberation Organization, 151, 207; privatization in, 171; public discontent in poor societies of, 139; regional economic cooperation in, 176; regional security integration, 207; satellite dish use in, 152; Syria, 207, 208; Turkey, 129, 164, 170, 176, 205; water table falling in, 157. See also Egypt; Iran migration, 158–63, 197
Mill, John Stuart, 50, 53, 114, 123, 124, 125

nuclear weapons: atom bomb development, 132–33; in hands of terrorists or Third World leaders, 216; North Korean program, 215, 216; reduction of, 150–51, 194–95, 202, 217–18; warfare debased by, 185

Nye, Joseph S., 15

order, 65–90; autocratic order in early civilizations, 67; in Carolingian empire, 81–82; change and, 190; in classical Greece, 68–69; democratization and, 113–15; era of order giving way to age of progress, 62, 63; in feudalism, 83–84; in Gupta India, 74; imperial order in China, 71; Legalist approach to, 72; religion and, 65, 79–80; medieval challenge to, 85–90; in the Renaissance, 248n.22; replaced by progress in modern ethos, 92; Roman law and, 70; Roman order imposed on teutonic tribes, 70; security in mutualist epoch, 201–8

Organization of African Unity, 208
Organization of American States, 207
Organization of Arab States, 207
Ottoman Turks, 89, 97–98, 112, 116, 118
Otto of Freising, 252n.3
ozone layer, 155, 258n.16

Pacific Century, 2, 6–7, 34, 227n.2
Pacific islands, 117
Pakistan, 151, 168, 195, 218
Palestine Liberation Organization (PLO), 151, 207
Palmer, Richard E., 57
Pan African Congress (1900), 251n.56
paradigm shifts, 57
Pareto, Vilfredo, 130
Paris, 93
Parsons, Talcott, 55
Partnership for Peace (PFP), 204, 282n.49
peace studies, 183
peasantry: in ancient societies, 77; conditions in late nineteenth century, 115; excluded from modernity, 92; forced off the land, 113, 114; following the frontier in the middle ages, 86, 87; socioeconomic gap between landowners and, 112–13; uprisings, 84, 94

perfectability, 25, 62, 121, 134, 226
Perot, H. Ross, 167, 182
Persia: Achaemenids, 66; and Greece, 68, 69; Safavids, 97, 98; Sassanids, 73, 74, 75, 79, 80, 244n.48. *See also* Iran
Peter the Great, 128
Pevsner, Nikolaus, 43
Philippines, 99, 100, 166
philosophes, 109, 251n.55
physiocrats, 123
Planck, Max, 132
PLO (Palestine Liberation Organization), 151, 207
Pocock, J. G. A., 25, 31, 105, 142
pogroms, 93
Poland: agricultural population in 1900, 250n.47; antiforeign attitudes in, 161; arms trade, 150; becoming independent state, 89; competing with the Hanse, 96; Cracow's environmental degradation, 153; first partition of, 111; political parties in, 166; privatization in, 170; revolutions of 1830 and 1848, 113; Visegrad declaration, 204
Polanyi, Michael, 59, 240n.39, 251n.55, 253n.19, 278n.20
politics: identity politics, 181; of middle-class protest, 182; relocation of political legitimacy, 163–70; trivialization of, 44
Polo, Marco, 97, 99
Poor Law Reform Act of 1834, 250n.46
Popper, Karl, 54
popular culture, 43, 44
population growth, 156–57, 195, 218
population movement, 158–63, 197
Portugal: in East Africa, 111; in European Union, 171; in India, 98; state participation in economy, 96
positivism: American application to daily life, 135; logical positivism, 53, 238n.22; and science, 52–56, 238n.18; as system preserving, 141
postmodernism, 44–45, 57, 146, 164, 190
Powell, Colin, 167
power: balance of, 110, 126; decentralization of, 146–47; diffusion of, 220
Prague, 153
Priestly, Joseph, 123
printing press, 104–5, 148, 152

privacy, 102

privatization, 170–71, 269n.53

progress: Americans viewing in apocalyptic not dialectical terms, 37; despair and, 140–43; dethronement of, 125–27; ecological consequences of technological, 153–58; economic growth and, 123–24; the end of, 121–43; enthronement of, 121–25; in epoch of mutualism, 190; era of order giving way to age of, 62, 63; in ethos of modernity, 92, 121; giving way to epoch of mutualism, 62; ideology of in communism and fascism, 128; illusion of, 133–38; imperialism and, 115–20; Kahn's critique of, 253n.26; liberal democracy's triumph, 15–19; in Marx and Spencer, 51; origins of concept of, 122; perversion of, 127–33; in Reformation and Renaissance ideology, 105, 122–23; revolt against, 138–40; revolution and, 108–10; science and, 106–8; search for general theory of, 53; as secularized version of Providence, 140; society and, 113–15; the state and, 110–13, 115; United States as exemplar of, 135; United States attempts to revitalize, 133–38

Progressivism, 22, 28, 31

property, 26

prostitution, 162

Protestantism: in Britain, 108; Calvinism, 101, 103–4; in France, 108; Luther, 103; the Reformation, 103–4, 105; Pat Robertson, 140; Wyclif, 103

Proudhon, Pierre Joseph, 114

psychoanalysis, 130

Puerto Rico, 168, 198

Pulitzer, Joseph, 27

Puritans, 23–25, 234n.4

Pythagoras, 241n.8

quantum theory, 59, 132

Quebec, 167, 169, 181

Quesnay, François, 250n.43

racism, 160, 161

rain forests, 218

Ranke, Leopold von, 49, 50, 238nn. 13, 14

rap music, 200

Rasmussen, Poul Nyrup, 194

rationalism, 78, 91–92, 130, 241n.8

Reagan, Ronald, 1, 3, 25, 38, 138

realism, 125–26

reciprocal altruism, 220

redistribution of income, 193

Reform Act of 1832, 250n.46

Reform Act of 1867, 114

Reformation, 103–4, 105

regionalization of economics, 170–79, 191–92, 215

Reich, Robert, 176

Reinsch, Paul R., 30

relativity theory, 132

religion: Buddhism, 78, 99–100; in classical Greece, 68; for dealing with historical change, 42; fundamentalism, 140; Hinduism, 74, 78, 79, 80, 85, 140, 165; Jews, 93, 94, 161, 246n.2; in late antiquity, 77–80; magic and witchcraft, 81, 102; order and, 65, 79–80; philosophes on, 109; reconnecting humanity with its past, 81; religious pluralism in Europe, 101; science as the religion of modernity, 123; for solace from life's misfortunes, 73; supernaturalism, 140; Taoism, 72, 77, 78. *See also* Christianity; Confucianism; Islam

Renaissance: art, 43, 102, 104; humanism of, 104–5; modernity beginning in, 104; order and, 248n.22; progress in ideology of, 105, 122–23

revolution: Cuban revolution, 47; French revolution, 109–10, 249n.33; Glorious Revolution of 1689, 108, 249n.33; progress and, 108–10; revolutions of 1830 and 1848, 113; Russian revolution, 127, 249n.33

Rhodes, Cecil, 116

Ricardo, David, 114

rights of man, 108–10

robber barons, 27

Robertson, Pat, 140

Rochefoucauld, François, Duc de la, 219

Roman Catholicism: in the Carolingian empire, 81; discontent with during Black Death, 93; Franciscans, 88; Galileo condemned by, 106; Gregory VII's reforms,

87, 245n.59; Jesuits, 99–100; late medieval challenges to, 87–88; prohibition of usury, 94; Protestant opposition to, 102–3

Roman empire, 69–71; Augustus, 71; Christianity in, 78–79; class distinctions in, 76–77; fall of, 73–74; law, 70; maximum size of, 242n.15

Romania, 161, 166, 169, 251n.52

Roman law, 70

Ronfeldt, David, 152

Roosevelt, Franklin D., 46, 133, 135, 136

Roosevelt, Theodore, 7, 30

Rosenau, James, 146, 184, 185

Rousseau, Jean-Jacques, 108, 124

Royal Society of London, 106–7

Ruggie, John Gerard, 95

Russia: antiforeign attitudes in, 160; arms reduction, 195; arms trade, 150–51, 255n.5; attempts to institutionalize liberalism in, 47; Chechnya, 18, 169; commercial dominions of, 111; conflict with Britain over Afghanistan, 117; in economic regionalization, 175–76; environmental catastrophes, 153; feudalism in, 83; gains from Congress of Berlin, 251n.52; Hanseatic trade with, 94; Lenin, 119, 128; marginalization of subject peoples in, 198; Mongol conquest of, 85; Ottoman territory ceded to, 116; Peter the Great, 128; political disillusionment in, 167; in regional security integration, 204; Russian revolution, 127, 249n.33; Russo-Japanese War, 30, 117–18; separatist movements in, 169, 182; Stalin, 128; state forming around Moscow, 89; struggle for power in, 215; in suppression of nineteenth century revolutions, 113; Yeltsin, 167; Zhirinovsky. 167. *See also* Soviet Union

Russian revolution, 127, 249n.33

Rwanda, 151, 158, 181, 182, 201, 208, 211, 275n.3

Safavids, 97, 98

Said, Edward, 200

Saint Pierre, Abbé de, 123

Saint-Simon, Henri de, 52, 124

Sandanistas, 34, 199

Sassanid dynasty, 73, 74, 75, 79, 80, 244n.48

Savanarola, Giralamo, 103

Schlesinger, Arthur, Jr., 214

scholarly specialization, 51, 55

Schopenhauer, Arthur, 125

Schweitzer, Albert, 126

science: American application to daily life, 135; atom bomb development, 132–33; Boyle, 107; Buffon, 107; Darwin, 53, 250n.50; on fate of the universe, 189; Galileo, 106, 130, 238n.18; on global warming, 155–56; Linnaeus, 107; Newton, 59, 106, 107, 131–32; positivism and, 52–56; progress and, 106–8; quantum theory, 59, 132; relativity theory, 132; as the religion of modernity, 62, 123; in the Renaissance, 104; Royal Society of London, 106–7; uncertainty principle, 132; undermining society's ability to shape its future, 131–33

scientism, 50, 51, 53, 57

Scotland, 169

Second World War, 135–36

security, 201–8

Sekimoto, Tadahiro, 12

self-interest, 190, 220

Seljuk Turks, 84

Serbia, 97, 169

Seward, William H., 6

Shang dynasty, 67, 83

Shi'a Islam, 17, 80, 97, 210

Shih Huang-ti, 72

shinjinrui, 10

Singapore, 11, 17, 159, 187, 199

Sitvatorok, treaty of, 97

slavery, 26, 70, 76, 86, 112

Slovakia, 150, 163, 169, 181, 204

Smith, Adam, 123, 249n.43

Smith, Henry Nash, 26, 27

Smoke, Richard, 183, 184, 185

social contract theory, 108

Social Darwinism, 116, 250n.50

social inclusivity, 194–97

socialism, 114, 119, 137, 190

social organization, 76

social welfare, 115, 162–63, 192–93

society: progress and, 113–15; the willing society, 219

Solzhenitsyn, Aleksandr, 45, 222
Somalia, 151, 181, 201, 211, 214,
280n.40
Soto, Hernando de, 217
South Africa: Boer War, 117, 118; cessation of nuclear arms program, 151, 195;
dismantling of apartheid, 47; Eastern
European revolutions and, 149; political
transition in, 168; prospects for social
integration in, 188, 217; regional security integration, 204, 208; tribal fault
lines in, 170
South America: Chile, 5, 137, 177, 199;
Colombia, 218; democracy adapted for,
199; economic regionalization, 175;
Mercosur, 175, 203, 207. *See also* Argentina; Brazil
South Asia: Nepal, 164, 168; Pakistan,
151, 168, 195, 218. *See also* India
Southeast Asia: ASEAN, 205–6; Buddhism in, 99–100; Burma, 5, 166,
260n.28; economic growth in, 217; Islam in, 79; Malaysia, 17, 175, 286n.10;
Philippines, 99, 100, 166; separatist
pressures in, 170; Thailand, 17, 164,
166; trade with Japan, 174. *See also*
Singapore
South Korea: as competitor of Japan, 11;
and costs of using force, 164–65; democratization in, 5; opening markets in,
174; political reform in, 166; regional
security integration, 205; strategic alliances with foreign companies, 177; tensions with North Korea, 205
Soviet Union: America's demonization of,
136; Andropov, 58; Brezhnev's speech
on decline in, 58; collapse of empire and
end of Cold War, 5, 36–37; Commonwealth of Independent States, 47, 175–
76, 198, 215; and costs of using force,
164–65; democratization in, 5; emigration from, 159; environmental catastrophes, 153; Gorbachev, 58; Lenin, 119,
128; similarity of American and Soviet
means, 137; Stalin, 128. *See also* Russia
Spain: antiforeign attitudes in, 160; conflict with France for European dominance, 101; decline of empire of, 13–14;

immigrants in, 159; national identity developing in, 89, 95; separatist movements in, 169; Spanish–American War,
27, 117–18; state participation in the
economy, 96; Turks defeated by, 97
Spanish–American War, 27, 117–18
specialization, scholarly, 51, 55
Spencer, Herbert, 51, 53, 123, 124,
250n.50
Spengler, Oswald, 13, 51, 63, 126, 130
Stalin, 128
state, the: competition from subnational
and supranational actors, 146–47,
185; nationhood becoming more inclu-
sive than, 221; and progress, 110–13,
115; relocation of political legitimacy,
163–70; supranational state called for,
184; technological diffusion of ideas
challenging, 149; welfare-nationalist
forms of government, 17; welfare state,
115
Staten Island, 167
Stoughton, William, 24
Strange, Susan, 15
Structural Impediments Initiative, 4, 8
structural unemployment, 193
subsidiarity, 171
substitutionism, 128
Sui dynasty, 74
Suleiman the Great, 97
Sumer, 66, 67
Sung dynasty, 80, 89
Sunni Islam, 17, 80
Sun Yat-sen, 129
supernaturalism, 140
supranationalism, 145
Syria, 207, 208

Taiwan, 11, 166, 204, 205, 224
Tajikistan, 18, 151, 176
Takeshita, Noboru, 264n.42
Tanaii, Akio, 8
Tanaka, Kakuei, 264n.42
T'ang dynasty, 74, 78, 79–80
Taoism, 72, 77, 78
technological diffusion, 148–52
terrorism, 139, 146, 161–62, 216, 223
Thailand, 17, 164, 166

xenophobia, 160, 161

Yeltsin, Boris, 167
Yugoslavia: ancient hatreds in, 197; Bosnia, 200, 201, 211, 214, 215; civil war in, 18, 151; Croatia, 169, 204; hope for peace in, 221–22; NATO failure in, 204; redrawing national boundaries in, 169; Serbia, 97, 169; United Nations in, 201

Zhirinovsky, Vladimir, 167